THE ENCYCLOPEDIA OF
WRITING AND ILLUSTRATING CHILDREN'S BOOKS

THE ENCYCLOPEDIA OF
WRITING AND
ILLUSTRATING
CHILDREN'S BOOKS

DESDEMONA McCANNON
SUE THORNTON
AND
YADZIA WILLIAMS

RUNNING PRESS
PHILADELPHIA • LONDON

A QUARTO BOOK

Copyright © 2008 Quarto Inc.

First published in the United States in 2008 by
Running Press Book Publishers

9 8 7 6 5 4 3 2 1
Digit on the right indicates the number of
this printing

Library of Congress Control Number: 2008930842

ISBN: 978-0-7624-3148-9

Conceived, designed, and produced by
Quarto Publishing plc
The Old Brewery
6 Blundell Street
London N7 9BH

Editor: Liz Dalby
Art director: Caroline Guest
Art editor: Emma Clayton
Designers: Joelle Wheelwright,
Karin Skånberg, Tania Field,
Jessica Wilson
Picture researcher: Sarah Bell
Editorial assistant: Amy Kopecky
Photographer: Martin Norris
Creative director: Moira Clinch
Publisher: Paul Carslake

Running Press
2300 Chestnut Street
Philadelphia, PA 19103-4371

Visit us on the web!
www.runningpress.com

CONTENTS

INTRODUCTION

Picture books invite children into imaginary worlds, introducing them to the idea of written language and its relationship to the real world. At their best they engage and entertain, instilling children with a love of books and an inquisitive mode of reading that will last their whole lives.

CRASH COURSE

The Children's Writers' and Artists' Yearbook
A&C Black

Published annually, this almanac provides you with vital information about how to protect your copyright, how to send out your work, and lists up-to-date contacts and addresses.

METHODS OF ENGAGEMENT

Children love to be read to, but they also like the independence and flexibility of reading a book for themselves. Both experiences are valuable. If read to they can listen to the narrative and look at the pictures simultaneously. If reading alone they can actively engage their imagination and construct the story for themselves.

FIT FOR PURPOSE

Picture books give adults and children common ground—to start a conversation about something in the book, to clarify words that the child does not understand, or to share a joke contained in the text or pictures. Most importantly, a book creates a "safe zone" of nurture and understanding between the reader, the child audience, and the imaginative world they are both sharing. The best books leave a positive lasting impression and evoke a safe atmosphere for the child's development. But be advised that not all children's books are beneficial. If a book is unsatisfying, cynical, or plays upon clichéd scenarios, the chances are the author only cared about his next sell.

Arthur Burdett Frost
Arthur Burdett Frost was born in Philadelphia in 1851. He was famous for his illustrations of animals and people, notably Brer Rabbit.

Charles Henry Bennett
Charles Henry Bennett was an untrained comic illustrator who illustrated several books, including *The Fables of Aesop*.

The world of children's book publishing is driven by many factors—a good story, beautiful illustrations, and educational benefit all play a part in the decision to develop a book. The overriding concern of publishers, however, is that the book should succeed in the marketplace.

WHO BUYS CHILDREN'S BOOKS?

Adults buy books for children for a variety of reasons. Educators and librarians have specific remits and requirements; they will be guided by a curriculum to teach and the budget they have to spend. Aunties and grandparents looking for a birthday present often want to buy a special book that will be cherished in years to come. Harassed parents in the supermarket may simply want something that will distract and entertain. A parent and child may take a special trip to the bookstore to pick out a story for bedtime reading, and this can be a treat for both the adult and child.

Publishers of children's books are aware of the different markets that they sell books into and have marketing departments devoted to monitoring and evaluating the financial success of their books. It will probably help you to have an understanding of these commercial demands when you are pitching your picture book idea. Knowing your audience, and also knowing where your idea "fits into" the market, will help give you a stronger case for the publication of your book.

CRASH COURSE

The Uses of Enchantment by Bruno Bettelheim
Knopf, 1976

This is a key text in understanding how fairy stories aid a child's psychological development.

Spells of Enchantment: The Wondrous Fairy Tales of Western Culture by Jack Zipes
Penguin, 1992

A collection of literary fairy tales, showing how the story concerns and structures have changed over time.

Collections of fairy tales:

- The Brothers Grimm
- Hans Christian Andersen
- Mother Goose

Fairy tales never get stale. Read some of the stories above and try writing a fairy tale of your own.

A GLOBAL INDUSTRY

The children's picture-book industry is a global concern. Publishers are usually keen to create co-editions with international publishers to maximize profits and lower the cost of producing each individual book. Each year publishers gather at the Bologna Children's Book Fair in Italy to do business with each other and keep up-to-date with global trends in children's books. If you are interested in becoming a children's book author it would be worth trying to attend an international event like this. Visit the bookfair's website at www.bookfair.bolognafiere.it

Bologna Children's Book Fair
The Bologna Children's Book Fair is a huge international event attended by book publishers and others involved in the industry. It can be a rich source of ideas and information on what's "hot" in the children's book world.

THINK OF YOUR MARKET
A cute little character, highly appealing for a
"picture book" readership (see page 12).

Chapter one

CREATING CHILDREN'S BOOKS

An introduction to the subject of children's books—from the importance of understanding your target market to a general look at possible subjects and themes—this section will help you develop a methodology for brainstorming and researching ideas.

1 THE IDEA OF A PICTURE BOOK

A picture book provides an opportunity for a child and an adult to enjoy sharing something together. It is an event as well as an artifact. The "idea of the book" resides in the people who experience it, and the experience of the book is not as straightforward as you may imagine.

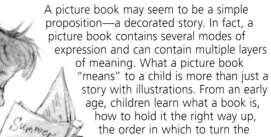

A picture book may seem to be a simple proposition—a decorated story. In fact, a picture book contains several modes of expression and can contain multiple layers of meaning. What a picture book "means" to a child is more than just a story with illustrations. From an early age, children learn what a book is, how to hold it the right way up, the order in which to turn the pages, and how to read—first the images and then later the words. The imagery may be "realistic" or entirely graphic. Imagery and colors may form patterns throughout the book, accruing meaning as motif; white space may imply content and demand that the child mentally "fill in the gaps"; and the illustrations may expand on and extend the information in the text. Sometimes, the illustrations may even tell a different story. This tension between what is said and what is shown makes picture books a unique and exciting form of graphic expression.

Struwwelpeter

Writer and illustrator Maurice Sendak rates *Struwwelpeter* by Heinrich Hoffmann as one of the most beautiful picture books ever made. It is interesting to see such early examples of the picture book form (*Struwwelpeter* was first published in 1845) and compare them with what we think of as innovative design today. The use of white space, typography, and borders to create the landscape of each morality tale is very "modern" in the way it creates an imaginary world and draws attention to the surface of the book.

TRY THIS

It is worth looking carefully at how picture books work before you embark on one of your own. Take an example that you like and analyze how the images and text work together. Study the visual language of the book. Make sketches of the layouts and ask yourself why they are successful. Is the typography graphically expressive? Does it help the child to understand the book, or could it interfere with the legibility? (Does this matter?) Is the book appropriate for its audience? What makes you assume this?

An interesting exercise is to create a story about a child with an imaginary friend that only they can see. Consider how the illustrations will convey the disparity between the child's perception of reality and what is actually there. *Not a Box* by Antoinette Portis (HarperCollins, 2006) is a great example of this.

BEYOND WORDS AND PICTURES

Illustrations may "interrogate" the text by adding to or saying less than the words next to them, but equally important to the deeper message of the book is its format, the stock it is printed on, and even the smell of the ink. Consider books from your own childhood—the tactile qualities of them probably remain as part of the memory. When you plan a picture book in a holistic way, remember that the message of your book—its atmosphere—will not reside in the words and pictures alone, but in the complete experience of the book.

COMMUNICATING THE IDEA

When you start to develop an idea for a picture book, bear in mind that the book is a combination of words and pictures, and both are equally important in communicating the overall message and atmosphere. If you are not confident as a writer, or do not think you can draw well enough to illustrate your own story, you may consider collaborating with someone else. However, it is worth developing the book holistically, sketching out ideas alongside drafting the text, and making small dummy books (see page 138) to test whether the pacing of the story works. In some ways developing a picture book is analogous to working out a film sequence—there are similar concerns of angles of view, composition, and cutting to significant keyframes. You could think of a picture book as a condensed, effectively edited storyboard.

Tactile imagery
Books can be interactive and convey information in many different ways.

Illustrating key moments
Illustrations should show the action of the story at key moments, and add to the drama and surprise of the narrative.

CRASH COURSE

Words about Pictures: The Narrative Art of Children's Picture Books
by Perry Nodelman
University of Georgia Press, 1988)

This book remains a key text in describing and unpacking the ways in which a picture book communicates with a child audience.

Alice's Adventures Underground
by Lewis Carroll

The first draft of the famous children's book *Alice in Wonderland* was heavily annotated with sketches for the illustrator Tenniel to work from. Charles Dodgson (Lewis Carroll) had very clear ideas about how the images should relate to the text.

2 TARGET MARKETS

Relating to your target audience—children—means learning to communicate using words and images that are recognizable and understandable to them. Children have a variety of different attention spans, anxieties, and interests. It is difficult to generalize, although picture books do tend to be put into age-related categories (see below).

In a bid to create characters and stories with unique characteristics but universal appeal, the writer and illustrator will often rely on cliché and stereotypes. This can reflect more about the attitudes of those creating the books than the experiences of their readership. For example, the archetypal kindly grandma with gray hair, slippers, and cardigan, clutching her knitting hardly reflects the dynamic and glamorous woman a child may know as his or her own grandmother.

Whether you choose to reinforce or challenge the prevalent attitudes toward age, gender, race, or disability is up to you. Just remember that what you may find a convenient visual shorthand, someone else could interpret as offensive. Try to always keep in mind that the world of storybook norms is a fiercely strong influence on how a child will grow up thinking about themselves and those around them.

CHILDREN'S TASTES

Every child is unique, although television, books, peer pressure, and the attitudes of adults will all have an effect on their tastes. Although the publishing industry is dominated by a "pink is for girls, pirates are for boys" attitude, it is possible to create characters that appeal to both sexes.

CHILDREN'S AGES AND CORRESPONDING BOOKS

- **0 to 3 years:** board books, novelty books
- **3 to 5 years:** picture books, ABC books
- **5 to 7 years:** picture books, reading primers, color storybooks
- **7 to 9 years:** black and white stories, novels, comics
- **9 to 11 years:** short stories, poetry, novels, graphic novels
- **11 years+:** "young adult" fiction

Some books challenge the preconceptions of age-related categories—for example, so-called "reluctant reader" books are written in simple language but are illustrated to appeal to an older age group.

Subvert stereotypes
Maybe older ladies do wear tweed... but if they do, consider that maybe their pets do too.

Gender programming
Do you agree that girls love ballet and boys want to play cowboys? It is good to be aware of the values inherent in these stereotypes, and decide whether you would like to support or challenge them in your work.

FIRST EXPERIENCES

Consider your own childhood "firsts"—going to the dentist, school, or hospital for the first time, dealing with bullying, coping with the death of a pet or a relative, learning where babies come from, and so on—and recollect any other significant childhood experiences. Many such events are serious issues for a child, and reading a story that enables them to talk about it or hear the perspective from someone else can be a great support and comfort.

OLDER CHILDREN

If you have the ability to draw older children, include black and white examples of illustrations of them in your portfolio; you may receive commissions for storybooks and nonfiction. There is also a market for the illustration of children's books for reluctant readers, with older characters but not text-heavy, in which comic-style storyboarding plays a more significant role.

Depicting roles
What do you think this woman's role in life might be: wife, mother, daughter, worker—or all of the above?

Tweed or sneakers?
In this illustration from *Vegetable Glue* by Susan Chandler and Elena Odriozola (Meadowside Children's Books, 2008), the frail grandmother stereotype is challenged by the depiction of a dynamic, healthy older woman who shows the value of eating your vegetables!

TRY THIS

Happy families

- Many picture books are conceived around the staple routines of family life, but do remember that the stereotypical four-person family often displayed in picture books is not the only sort of family that exists.

- Create a set of cards showing a family group. There should be at least one parent, a child and an older person in each set. They do not have to be "realistic" but should have a shared "culture," be it ethnic or metaphorical. For example they could be West Indian, superheroes, or both!

- On the back of each card write a profile of the character, what his or her interests are, their personality, and so on.

- Use this project to reflect on the way we depict different ages, genders, and cultural groups, and our perception of roles within the family.

READ THIS

Girls, Boys, Books, Toys: Gender in Children's Literature and Culture by Beverly Lyon Clark and Margaret R. Higonnet

John Hopkins University Press, 2000

This book provides an introduction from a feminist viewpoint to the issues and terminologies surrounding children's culture.

3 THEMES

Children's stories can be categorized into general themes. These often address experiences that are difficult for a child to understand in adult terms, such as the conflicting feelings aroused by the arrival of a new baby, the death of a family member, or moving house.

ARCHETYPES AND RULES

A story can be based upon any aspect of experience—a daunting prospect for the aspiring writer, as the scope for content is infinite. Much has been written about the grammar of storytelling, and there are plenty of books that offer formulas and structural advice on how a story should progress. Jungian and archetypal literary criticism sees stories in terms of phases such as "the call to adventure," "the refusal of the call," "the threshold test," and so on. This can be helpful in analyzing what you have written, but do not feel bound by a set of rules. They can all be reduced to one maxim: "a story should have a beginning, a middle, and an end." Do not be distracted from telling a story by overly didactic rules. If your idea has heart and the story has an authentic emotional core it will be more affecting and effective than formulaic rhetoric.

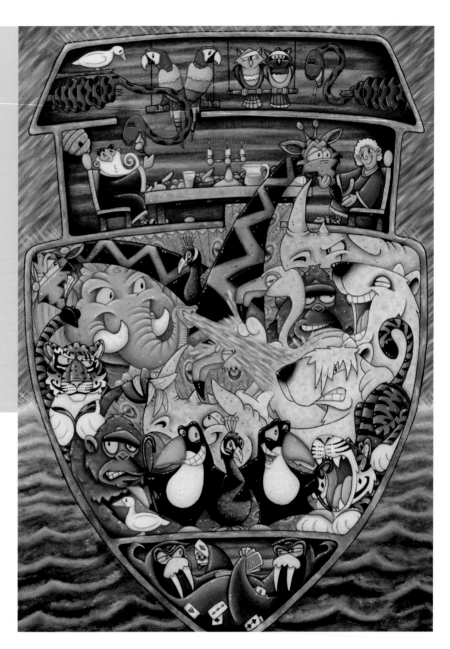

Cultural themes

Stories are passed down through generations and become part of our shared cultural identity. It is interesting to see how similar many of these stories are. How many different flood stories can you find, for example?

THE OLDEST STORIES

Some of the oldest stories, myths, and legends emerged from the desire to explain internal psychological conflict in concrete terms. The names of characters, monsters, and gods have become absorbed into our language and are now used to describe archetypal situations—for example "Oedipus complex," "Cupid and Pysche," or "Echo and Narcissus." Try reading some Greek myths and think about the themes and ideas within them that still resonate today.

Myths

Myths are the received wisdom of a culture expressed in symbolic and allegorical form. Often involving supernatural characters, they express archetypal human situations.

Metaphor

When a story is described as being "disguised," the use of metaphor is generally what is being referred to—understanding things in terms of other things. Aesop, whose fables are some of the oldest surviving stories, uses the characteristics of animals to express aspects of human behavior and common moral dilemmas.

The Fox and the Stork

The story of *The Fox and the Stork* represents human behavior metaphorically by substituting animals and presenting a dilemma in terms of a specific encounter. The fox cannot eat from a tall vase; the stork cannot lick from a plate. The story is about difference and pragmatic relationships, and is also quite entertaining!

TRY THIS

The Fables of Aesop

Find a collection of Aesop's fables (you can find them online) and list the clear moral themes suggested by each. You may decide that some have more than one. This is what makes storytelling fascinating—a complex or multifaceted problem can be presented effectively in a very simple way.

CLASSIC CHILDREN'S STORY THEMES

- **Courage:** adventure; overcoming fears; a hero who finds strength in himself where he thought he had none. *Hiccup: the Viking Who was Seasick* by Cressida Cowell (Hodder Children's Books, 2001) is a good example of this.

- **Friendship:** sharing and helping each other; resolving conflict; good times. *Best Friends for Frances* by Russell Hoban (Red Fox, 2002) is an example of this theme.

- **Loss:** this common theme reflects a central anxiety among children. It can be something huge like the loss of a grandparent or something as everyday as the loss of a toy, but the underlying anxiety is the same. It can make for a simple pivotal plot too, when the thing that is lost is found at the end. A slightly offbeat example is *The Lost Thing* by Shaun Tan (Lothian Children's Books, 2000).

- **Growing up:** accepting change; not always getting what you want or having to wait for things; changing attitudes toward the opposite sex. This theme is about learning a lesson from life that enables you to mature. *The Giving Tree* by Shel Silverstein (HarperCollins, 1964) is a book that encourages empathy.

- **Belonging:** children are conformists and enjoy stories about belonging to a group—however, this needs to be shown sensitively. The related theme of "difference" also addresses anxiety about not fitting in and can be a helpful way of promoting tolerance and understanding. Rosemary Wells' *Yoko* books (Hyperion Books for Children, 2001) are good examples.

- **Anger:** An important theme, offering reassurance to children that they are not alone in their feelings, and ways of visualizing beyond the lack of control. Children have an acute sense of unfairness and are often aware of their lack of power in situations. *Angry Arthur* by Hiawyn Oram (Red Fox, 1993) and *Where the Wild Things Are* by Maurice Sendak (Harper & Row, 1963) are both good examples.

- **Jealousy:** related to the theme of anger, but more specific. There are many books that address the feelings aroused by the arrival of a new baby. *Ginger* by Charlotte Voake (Walker Books, 1998) is an example of this theme being handled creatively.

- **Love:** perhaps the biggest theme of all in children's books. Affirming your love for someone and being loved in return is the lynchpin of a happy childhood, and picture books offer both the occasion (being read to) and the means by which to share this. *Guess How Much I Love You* by Sam McBratney (Candlewick, 1996) is a good example.

As you can see, this list centers around a nexus of anxieties and desires that a child experiences. There are many different ways that these can be disguised and acted out, but essentially all stories address a problem and offer strategies for its solution, however surreal and fantastical the protagonists and settings may be.

Resolving jealousy

In *Ginger,* by Charlotte Voake, Ginger the cat is upset by the arrival of a new kitten, but eventually accepts and befriends it. The theme is jealousy, and the problem is resolved with quiet humor by the interplay between the illustrations and the text.

again,

A kitten!

"He'll be a nice new friend for you, Ginger," said the little girl

TESTING YOUR IDEAS

Running workshops with children is fantastically rewarding, and the feedback you get can be hugely valuable to the development of a book idea. This can involve either going out into schools or bringing a group of schoolchildren into your learning environment to create imagery together and talk about what makes a book a success.

Case study 1

Students on the Illustration for Children's Publishing course at North East Wales Institute (NEWI) in the UK ran a workshop with pupils at a local school. The students' aim was to test the children's "visual literacy" in drawing concepts and information as characters, which the children then used as a basis for creating narratives. This research enabled the students to draw conclusions about how well children could decode conceptual information from imagery without any text. Children's visual literacy is highly developed but often underused in the school curriculum. This pilot project provided material that went on to form the basis of several more research projects and the students also found that it had implications for the way information could be presented to children.

Case study 2

A group of NEWI students also collaborated with children to create a "circus in a day," providing materials and sharing what they knew about circuses in order to create a short animation. The children then created a program for their own "super silly circus" and gave all the characters names. The benefits of collaborating with children in this way are enormous. You can use their spontaneous responses to gauge whether they are enthusiastic about a particular theme or idea that you introduce.

Case study 3

Some students ran workshops in schools in which they presented their work in progress on a story idea in development to a group of children. The children gave the students feedback on their artwork and story ideas. It is always useful to listen to the opinions of children, although in the end you must keep in mind that a few are not representative of all children. Their opinions may conflict with your own understanding of a book—consider carefully whether or not to act on them.

Activities for children
Harnessing the creativity of children through workshop activities can be a great way of finding out what they like and what they don't.

Practical advice

- You must ensure that you have had a criminal record check to reassure a host school or organization that the children will be safe with you.

- Make sure you carry out a "risk assessment" if you are setting up a workshop of your own.

- If you do arrange to visit a school, try to arrange to work alongside experienced teachers if you have no experience of working with children.

4 COMING UP WITH AN IDEA

A blank sheet of paper can be a terrifying prospect and, although you may feel you have latent talent as a creator of children's picture books, it can be hard to start. The following practical suggestions may help.

Character ideas
Working through character ideas in a sketchbook is a good place to start. Imagine the characters engaged in different activities.

you develop the "antennae" to gauge whether your own creations will appeal to a child.

WRITE FOR A PARTICULAR CHILD

It is impossible to write for the generic idea of "children," and if you have children of your own or regularly encounter them you will know that this is true. That is the reason why so many successful children's books have been written for a particular child. For example, Charles Dodgson (Lewis Carroll) wrote *Alice Underground* (the precursor to *Alice in Wonderland*) for his young friend Alice Liddell, and Kathleen Hale wrote the *Orlando* books for her own children.

THINK ABOUT YOUR OWN CHILDHOOD

List memories from your childhood, including your favorite foods, sweets, clothes, board games, toys, journeys, adults, holidays, or particular incidents. This is a useful exercise because it reinforces the sense that all children are different in the way they respond to the world. Try to access the sensations of your particular childhood. There may be material for a story there, or it may help you create imagery with a unique atmosphere. Tapping into these memories will help

BASE A CHARACTER ON A CHILD YOU KNOW

Base a character on a child that you know well and put them in a new situation. For example, *Little Lord Fauntleroy* was based on Frances Hodgson Burnett's own son. Even if the character you create takes another, nonhuman form, the child it is based upon will give it authenticity. Russell Hoban's badger character, Frances, is so acutely portrayed with her songs and sayings that it is hard to believe she is not based on a real little girl.

START WITH OBSERVATIONAL DRAWING

Visit your local zoo and spend time observing and drawing the animals, concentrating on one or two of them to really get a sense of their personality. Drawing from life, even if you feel that your observational drawing skills are not strong, will help focus your attention; you will notice much more detail, and it will be easier to recall back in the studio. This is also true of drawing in art galleries and museums, or drawing landscapes, architecture, and people in cafés and on trains. Take any opportunity that you can to draw.

START WITH A CHARACTER

Try creating a set of "Happy Families" cards (above), with information about each character written on the back. Base them on families you know, animals, robots, amoebas, superheroes, vegetables, or whatever—use your imagination. It is helpful to choose a theme or culture, because then you can conduct research for more ideas.

See where your pen takes you
The artist Paul Klee likened drawing to "taking a line for a walk." Doodling could be seen as letting your pen take your mind for a walk.

START WITH AN INCIDENT

Something may have happened to you today, yesterday, or when you were little that you think is funny, poignant, or just plain strange. Keep a note of events like these to base ideas upon.

START WITH A FACT

Be it a startling piece of information, or just common knowledge, using something "real" from a news item or even a biology textbook can provide a starting point for a character or story.

START WITH A DOODLE

Doodling—drawing when your mind is occupied with other thoughts—is an immensely creative activity. Covering a page with random scribbles, strange creatures that grow of their own volition, patterns, lettering, objects, and shapes will often contain the seed of an idea that can be nurtured and developed in a more "conscious" way later on. Doodle when you are on the phone, in meetings, or while watching the television… the trick is not to be too aware of what you are doing. Look at the drawings afresh the next day to see what can be taken forward.

Get to know your subject
Repeated studies of the same subject (in this case a rabbit, right) will lead you to notice things you might not otherwise have seen.

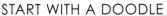

5 RESEARCH

Any intial idea that you have will need researching to enable you to develop it xfurther into a picture book concept.

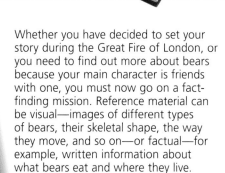

Whether you have decided to set your story during the Great Fire of London, or you need to find out more about bears because your main character is friends with one, you must now go on a fact-finding mission. Reference material can be visual—images of different types of bears, their skeletal shape, the way they move, and so on—or factual—for example, written information about what bears eat and where they live.

Collected material
Gather your research material in a scrapbook or sketchbook. It doesn't have to be neat!

Starting points

"Research" does not mean typing a keyword into a search engine and waiting for 15,000 hits to come up. There are so many places that you can glean information from; don't limit yourself by relying on one method.

- **Libraries:** a good library will provide you will a wealth of different information sources from books to magazines and the internet.

- **Bookshops:** try digging around in secondhand bookstores where the selection is likely to be more eclectic.

- **Magazines and newspapers:** specialist magazines can offer a deeper or more up-to-date insight into a subject than reference books and are often highly illustrated.

- **Interviewing people:** you can find out a lot from talking to people and asking them to share their memories and knowledge.

TRY THIS

Inviting inspiration

Visit your local museum and forage until you find an artifact or room that inspires you. Document what you can while you are at the museum then, when you return home, find out as much as you can from other sources. Use your research to create a story containing the information, but told from an unusual perspective. For example, you could write about Egyptian mummification from a scarab beetle's point of view.

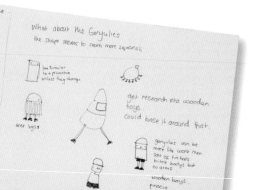

DEVELOPING A FEELING

Before you start the research, you might simply have a "feel" for a book idea, such as a mountainous setting or animal characters. Whatever you have to work with, finding out more about it will help you to develop the characters and storyline. You should know as much as possible about the characters, locations, clothes, and historical period in general.

Even if the story is set in surroundings as familiar as your own kitchen, fill a sketchbook with drawings and photographs of the room and its contents. You may not need to use all the reference but your confidence and grasp of the subject will help you include the most relevant details to tell the story effectively.

VISUAL RESEARCH

Aesthetic considerations will also evolve around the visual research you undertake and the artists, colors, and techniques that you feel drawn to. A lot of the research process is instinctive and intuitive—you are simply analyzing what you like and why. Gathering information together helps you see patterns and similarities in what you are drawn to. Remember that you are in charge of creating an entire world!

Reference material
Reference material can take the form of books, photographs, your own sketches (above and below right)—anything that will spark ideas and trigger memories relevant to your concept.

WEBSITES

Visual research

Sources of information are increasingly visual. There is an abundance of visual archives available online that can be incredibly inspiring and informative:

- **bibliodyssey.blogspot.com**
  This blog is updated constantly and gives access to the finest and strangest visual archives from libraries and museum collections around the world.

- **www.flickr.com**
  A searchable database of photographs (with varying permissions of use). Creative commons licenses allow limited appropriation of imagery; if an image is marked with a copyright symbol you can look but don't steal the idea— respect the owner's right to the image. Flickr is a great reference resource, and there are swathes of images from illustration groups and vintage children's books to look at.

Storing your research

The best practical advice when it comes to research is to store your material in a way that you can access easily. Paper files, digital folders, or even a blog can be excellent repositories for your findings. Classifying the information will help you understand it better too, and will help you to identify patterns and themes in your preoccupations. Annotating your research—why you like a particular thing or what you would like to use it for— will also enhance the process.

Blogging

Many sites now offer free space for a blog (try eblogger. com or wordpress.org). The sign-up process is simple and uploading imagery and posting entries is not difficult. A blog is a robust way of storing and sharing research. It will enable you to categorize information and archive it by date. Over time you can build up a body of information.

MAKE IT MOVE

Pose, viewpoint, body language, and even the media can all contribute
to a feeling of movement in an artwork (see page 40).

Chapter two

DEVELOPING AN IDEA

Essential reading for children's book illustrators, this section describes the key approaches to creating unique and memorable artwork that will stand out in a crowded marketplace: this is as much about developing your own style as it is about creating characters that appeal to particular age groups.

6 SKETCHBOOKS

Sketchbooks can have many different functions. They can be places for observation, doodles, notes, and ideas; they provide a means for gathering visual information from the world in which you live.

TRY THIS

Make sketching part of your routine

Get into the habit of drawing something in your sketchbook daily. It doesn't matter what you draw; more that you draw something every single day. It could be from observation, such as a self-portrait, family pet, kitchen worktop, the view out of a window, while traveling on a bus or train—in fact anything and everything around you is a potential subject.

Adopting this practice will help you to become comfortable with the habit of using sketchbooks; only then can it become a natural and instinctive process.

Drawing is fundamental to an illustrator and to create convincing images for your stories, you need to understand what you are drawing. Therefore gathering visual information and recording ideas, inspired by what you see and experience daily, helps to develop your drawing skills and creates the knowledge you need for further experimentation.

YOUR PERSONAL TOOLKIT

Sketchbooks are personal records that you will create for your own personal needs and interests in a way that suits you. The tools you choose to draw with will also depend on personal preference. The ideal sketching tools are easily portable and can be used instantly with no preparation, such as pencils, ballpoint pens, fountain pens, and magic markers. (See pages 114 to 137 for more about media.) There are no rules dictating how to draw in your sketchbook; this will develop naturally the more you do it.

Pocket sketchbook
A small sketchbook is easy to carry around in your pocket or keep by the bed. A hard cover on your book will protect your work and give you something to lean on when writing.

Sketchbooks are diverse in their shape, size, type of binding, and quality of paper. Your choice will depend on your needs. A small, pocket-size sketchbook is good to keep by you at all times, to record everyday observations while on the move and develop creative thoughts and doodles. A larger sketchbook is useful for more leisurely observational studies and for use in developing your ideas and working through the design process.

CRASH COURSE

Shirley Hughes uses smooth, thin drawing paper to pencil out her images, then fiber tip pen to fill them in, before proceeding to final artwork. Hughes feels that this loose, experimental stage allows her to observe unselfconsciously.

Sara Midda asserts that you can get ideas from anything, be it going to the shops or sitting in the garden. Her minute illustrations are crammed full of detail, a testament to the many aspects of the world her illustrator's mind absorbs.

Paper matters

Rough paper is textured and absorbent, great for washes of color. Hot-pressed paper is smooth and non-absorbent, while cold-pressed paper (known as "not") has a texture that is smooth enough for detail. For drawing and painting, a versatile paper would be 140 lb (300 gsm) not.

7 OBSERVING CHILDREN

Some of the most successful authors and illustrators of children's books have a strong affinity with their audience. Contact with young children can be inspirational, and for some may be the most enjoyable part of the job.

You don't need to have a family of your own, but the observation of children can help enhance your illustration and writing. Subtle details taken from watching children give an honesty and sensitivity to your content—resulting in an altogether more convincing result. You may like to think that you remember what it is like to be a child, but it is only by watching how children eat, play, and stand, for example, that you will truly be able to capture the realism of these actions.

Look at me
The sketch on the right reveals many details of this boy's character. His chest is thrust out and he wears his hat at a rakish angle, oozing confidence. He looks directly at his observer and, with his bare chest and feet, seems comfortable in his own skin. This illustration could only have been drawn from observation.

Drawing from life
Drawing family or children of friends is the easiest way to observe children. If they are asleep or watching television, you will have the opportunity to draw them when they are most likely to stay still for a time; however, this may not be the most interesting or quirky visually.

TRY THIS

Observe group behavior
Try to observe children in a formal situation, such as a school play, ballet class, or assembly. How do the children sit, stand, and interact while they are supervised as a group, and supposedly on their best behavior? What idiosyncrasies and personalities emerge? What do they do as their boredom levels (and potential for fidgeting) increase? Are any of them nose-picking or misbehaving? Such observations will prove useful for future reference. Make written notes if visual notes are difficult to achieve.

The relevance of observation and drawing children from life is strongly advocated in this book. However, this can be a particularly sensitive subject if the children are not your own. It may be necessary to have a criminal record check carried out, if you wish to approach or spend time with children in schools or playgroups for instance, particularly if the children are to be left unattended. Different institutions will have different policies. Take time to find out about these; you must observe them if you are to protect yourself from any anxieties or misinterpretation by guardians.

PHOTOGRAPHIC REFERENCES

There are reference books available that contain images of children in different poses. Such books provide useful reference material without the complication of copyright or criminal record check issues.

TIP

A criminal record check is not always transferable between different schools and institutions, so be aware of this if you wish to work with children in a range of environments.

CRASH COURSE

Any books illustrated by Shirley Hughes offer a wealth of reasons for why observing children can be worthwhile. An illustrator who has always recorded children in sketchbooks, she beautifully transfers her observations to creative, lively characterization. The sense of truth that comes through the drawings engages the reader in the reality of the everyday lives of the children.

Try the following:

The Big Alfie and Annie Rose Story Book
(Red Fox, 1990)

Dogger
(Trumpet Club, 1991)

Lost in play
Children can be most charming when caught in the moment—either playing on their own (above) or helping mom bake a cake (left).

Pencil and gouache
Like Shirley Hughes, this illustrator starts with a pencil drawing to create character and atmosphere. Then gouache is used, which has the softness of watercolor but a better density of color.

8 MEDIA AND DRAWING STYLES

The range of techniques available to an artist is considerable. In response, there are many books available, from step-by-step techniques to analysis of contemporary professional examples. However, your own experimentation is the key to finding a comfortable and original method of working.
The scale of the work will alter according to the technique; this is often difficult to appreciate when artwork is reduced and reproduced in a book.

TRY THIS

Compile a research file

Put together a research file of examples of artwork in categories of media, and shortlists of book prizes, competitions, and so on. This can become unwieldy, so select only what is inspirational to you, or illustrates approaches you have never considered before.

Experiment

- Take a favorite image from your sketchbook and experiment with a wide range of materials, papers, and technology to see how the image responds. Remember to change the scale according to the technique; larger scales will be necessary for broader tools, such as chalks or palette knives.
- Emphasize the line quality in some images, the shapes and mass in others.
- Keep to monochromatic colors so you can focus on the mark-making qualities and tone alone.

Brush, pen, and colored ink
The scale of the artwork is larger than some of the others due to the drawing tools used. Inks are more intense in color than watercolor, so they can be used to create a much brighter result, or watered down to a tint.

Dip pen (and watercolor)
The quality of line varies in thickness as the pressure on the pen is altered. The scale is not large and this is one of the most popular forms of media for book illustration. Simple washes quickly turn drawings into color artwork, so the drawing is of paramount importance.

Charcoal and watercolor
Charcoal smudges easily, so to combine it with watercolor the washes were applied first, and the black charcoal line was drawn on later to pull the form together.

Many artists without previous art-school experience feel nervous moving away from a drawing tool they have become familiar with, and may be disappointed if the results of new tools and media do not yield the same immediate success. The same applies to practicing or professional illustrators who need to rethink or freshen up their portfolio. But what if the same amount of practice given to your regular tool had been given to a different tool? Would it still seem so inept or cumbersome?

FINDING YOUR OWN STYLE

Developing a commercial style takes some research into what standards are already set by professional published artwork. What media is popular? What is the range of drawing styles and color palettes used? What is deemed successful or trendy, and why? A critical eye is a useful requirement if you are to evaluate the success of your own work, and time is also needed to experiment with professional materials, color, and black-and-white media.

CHOOSING YOUR MEDIUM

There is a wide range of media for the illustrator to choose from. If your drawing has an unusual or interesting quality to the line, or you particularly like to work in pen and ink, you may like to try working with transparent media, such as watercolor or dyes. Gutsy mark-making and confidence with color may steer you to work with pastels, oil pastels, acrylics, and mixed media, whereas graphic styles may be more suited to photography, collage, and computerized manipulation in applications such as Photoshop. The list and combination of approaches, materials, and surfaces to work with is endless. Have fun experimenting to find those that appeal the most.

CHECK THIS

- **Bologna Children's Book Competition winning entries**

The Bologna Children's Book Fair in Italy takes place every spring and is an essential event on the children's book publishing calendar.

- **Caldecott Medal winning entries, US**

A prize awarded annually to the artist of the most distinguished American picture book for children.

- **Nestlé Children's Book Prize (formerly known as the Smarties Prize) winning entries, UK**

A prestigious and long-running prize with several categories open to authors and illustrators of children's books.

Acylic
Generally used opaque, the paint has been built up here as washes on acrylic paper, giving a slightly textured appearance. Backgrounds should be painted first so the layers overlap to give a sense of depth to the finished piece.

Colored pencil crayon
Colored pencil crayons can be used with strong, expressive marks, but also with precision and control, as shown here. A watercolor wash has been applied to provide a base to enhance the strength of the color application over the top.

Pastel
Pastels generally need to be used on a fairly large scale. These soft pastels have been blended with a torchon and applied on watercolor paper tinted with a wash (although there are many pastel papers available to provide colored grounds).

DEVELOPING YOUR OWN STYLE

Certain illustrators may inspire you to consider children's publishing as a career, but it is important first to develop a style that is original and instinctive. It is unlikely that publishers will tell you what they are looking for; they will just know it when they see it, so before trying to impress, look at your own abilities to find out what you enjoy and where your strengths lie.

CRASH COURSE

Quentin Blake has a spontaneous, scratchy style using pen and ink. His characters seep personalities that are eccentric and highly original, and his illustrations are immediately recognizable.

Victor Ambrus uses a combination of pencil and color illustration—sometimes in the same piece of artwork—to fire people's imaginations about various historical eras.

ANALYZE YOUR STUDIES

If you are uncertain what you do best, take a good look at your sketchbooks. It is here that you are most likely to observe your natural visual response to ideas and imagery—when you are relaxed, spontaneous, experimental, and uninhibited.

DON'T TRY TOO HARD

Try to avoid preconceived ideas of what drawing is; it is simply a method of recording information and does not need to be labor intensive. Don't view final artwork as something separate from what you do when you sketch or doodle. Many unpublished illustrators try too hard to produce "finished" artwork and images become overworked and static. All they need is to develop a personal style that feels as natural as handwriting.

Spontaneous doodles
Quick-fire sketches can reveal your strengths and weaknesses as an illustrator—and unlock the child within. Don't be afraid to sketch anything that pops into your mind; you may be on the path to your first illustrated story.

Fluid motion

A trip to the zoo initiated these beautiful, fluid pencil drawings that capture an extremely acute realism of the animals observed. Though conditioned to turn finished artwork into something labored and static, the artist took time and care to retain the instinctive quality in her drawings.

TRY THIS

Working on location

Take a range of materials and drawing tools to the zoo or a farm. It is important to draw at the location, and not just to take photographs as reference to work from. Do not be deterred by unfinished studies; these will still increase your confidence and improve your level of observation—providing excellent first-hand reference for anthropomorphism (see page 48). Such studies will also give you a true reflection of your strengths.

Bold and simple

This artist developed her drawing style from successful studies she had made at a zoo, while experimenting with different drawing implements (above). Color is secondary in her work; it is the strength of the calligraphic line and the convincing personalities of her characters that are her strengths.

The big picture

The lively, humorous characterization of these humans and animals (below) is mirrored by the artist's use of color. Dry color such as pastels and oil pastels showcased her talent, but initially required large surface areas to achieve the level of detail she sought to produce. However, she deliberately and successfully found a way to manage the size and scale of her work, maintaining the richness of color and ensuring little was lost in reproduction.

CRASH COURSE

Drawing for the Artistically Undiscovered by Quentin Blake and John Cassidy
(Klutz Press, 1999)

Encyclopedia of Drawing Techniques by Hazel Harrison
(Running Press, 1999)

Drawing with Color by Judy Martin
(North Light Books, 1989)

These titles may help you reconsider the way you think about drawing, and also the tools that can be used for different approaches.

Can you hear all kinds of dogs strolling along the promenade, smelling the fresh autumn air, enjoying the beautiful day? Listen, what else can you hear?

10 DEVELOPING CHARACTERS

To draw a character in a variety of situations as it moves through a narrative demands skill if the character is to remain believable, consistent, and attractive. The illustrator must be familiar with the character and really believe in it if they are to convince the reader.

ENGAGING THE READER

A successful character needs to charm and intrigue readers if they are to engage with it. A character doesn't necessarily have to be "cute" but it does have to be attractive or visually appealing in some way, because publishers generally put the it on the front cover and expect it to sell the book. Plus, merchandising, television rights, and animation productions are always looking for interesting characters to use, so your subjects could become a lucrative opportunity. The more alluring the character, the more money there is to be made.

Characters may be thrust on you from an existing text and come with an author's background and setting. However, the character is often the starting point from which an author or illustrator finds inspiration to generate a story or, even better, a series.

The poor duck was sleepy and weepy and tired.

Animal characters
Helen Oxenbury shows deft characterizations in *Farmer Duck* (written by Martin Waddell). Every animal is uniquely represented through her drawing skills.

READ THIS

How to Write and Illustrate Children's Books and Get Them Published by Treld Pelkey Bicknell and Felicity Trotman (North Light Books, 1988)

Illustrating Children's Books: Creating Pictures for Publication by Martin Salisbury (Barron's, 2004)

Then the cow and the sheep and the hens came back.

"Quack?" asked the duck.

"Moo!" said the cow.

"Baa!" said the sheep.

"Cluck!" said the hens.

Which told the duck the whole story.

Personality pointers

A handshake, a grin, a nervous glance; all of these reveal personality.

A FROG HE WOULD A-WOOING, GO   "HE SET OFF WITH HIS OPERA HAT, AND ON THE WAY HE MET A RAT."   The Rat

"scruffier" rat.   "smaller ears"   longer coat

TRY THIS

Build a character profile

When you start learning about proportion, movement, and anthropomorphism, you will see that there are many points to consider if you are to develop a character the reader is to recognize again and again.

Write a profile or produce a mind map of a character who is about to go to school. Is it a girl or a boy? Are they extroverted or shy? Build up a sense of their home life, friends, likes, and dislikes. What would they wear, for instance?

Developing a character profile will really help you get to know your character.

FINDING INSPIRATION

Inspiration for characters may come from people you already know, or from observing children from life or reference. What is the "profile," or personality, of your character? Does he or she have hobbies, family, and friends? Not all of this information may be relevant to your story but will help to create an individual. Clothes, shoes, props, and hairstyles all contribute to the identity. Nothing can be overlooked.

Mapping it out

Mind maps allow your thoughts to roam free and make their own connections. Using this tool you can create a character full of quirks.

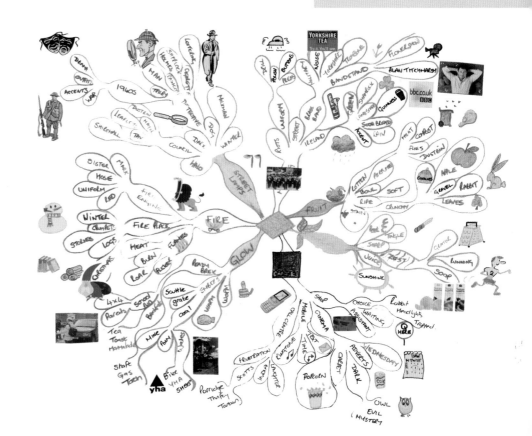

PRESENTING YOUR WORK

Even when an artist finds a character they like and develops it through artwork in their portfolio, it may be a sketch among the development work in a sketchbook that takes the interest of an art director, rather than a more resolved outcome.

Most publishers would only commission an illustrator they believe to have potential to produce character sheets, before giving them a book to complete. This enables the publisher to assess the character's appeal and the consistency of the artist, and the process may continue for some time. This work is usually paid, but offers no guarantee of a complete project.

The eyes have it
Seven sketches, one difference—the eyes. These sketches reveal how telling one single detail can be in the characterization of an animal.

NOW THAT I HAVE FULLY DESIGNED ALL ASPECTS OF THE HORNBILLS BODY AND CHARACTER, I CAN SET ABOUT DOING THE FINAL COLOUR SCHEME FOR THE BIRD......

Face value
Which of these faces is the most appealing? It is only by experimenting that you will find a character and a look to satisfy publishers and readers.

Moving pictures
Practice drawing your character in action, as well as in static poses. The character below is full of personality—not least because of the humorous interaction with her pet.

Most appealing children's characters:

- *Charlie and Lola*, Lauren Child
  (Candlewick, first book published 1999)

  Charlie and Lola feature in a series of books by Lauren Child. Big brother Charlie has his hands full with his energetic sister, Lola, as she copes with different situations such as going to bed, a wobbly tooth, and food she doesn't like.

- *The Snowman*, Raymond Briggs
  (Random House, 1985)

  Raymond Briggs' beautiful illustrations create a character that children and adults immediately fall in love with. There are no words in this story.

- *Mr. Men* and *Little Miss*, Roger Hargreaves
  (Price Stern Sloan: *Mr. Men* first published 1971; *Little Miss* first published 1981)

  With simple, humorous drawings covering over 90 characters, Hargreaves manages to create a set of characters that make adults and children smile.

- *The Cat in the Hat*, Dr. Seuss
  (Random House, 1957)

  If you're looking for a chaotic but likeable main character, then this is the cat for you. The manic Cat in the Hat arrives, disrupts, tidies up, and leaves again. What more could a child ask for in a friend?

- *The BFG*, Roald Dahl
  (Puffin, 1982)

  The ink lines and watercolors of Quentin Blake's illustrations create a giant who is huge and scary, but also kind and friendly. Like Sophie in the story of the BFG, readers can discover that friends come in the most unexpected sizes and shapes.

Character: the sidekick

Age: in the first book, 11. Ages a year per book

Appearance: blond hair, green eyes, chip in front tooth, freckles in summer

Characteristics: quiet, observing, gently guides the main character toward the right decision

Family: divorced parents, lives with mother and sister

Catchphrase: Look out!

Animated animals
Howling, sniffing, rolling, bristling; animal actions speak volumes. But if you can't get these right on the page, your story will fall down. Practice and observation will bring your animal characters to life.

Character checklists
When you need to keep track of your characters over several books, it is essential to keep checklists of all their traits. This will save you time and errors—and keep your favorite characters alive in your imagination.

Character: the girl spy

Age: 12. Stays the same age in each book

Appearance: coal-black hair, tall for her age, wears glasses

Characteristics: inquisitive, clever, sometimes clumsy, nose for a mystery, overenthusiastic

Family: lives alone with her parents

Catchphrase: Cover me, I'm going in!

11

PROPORTION

The age of a character is very difficult to get right. Your story may include a range of different ages, which must remain consistent and believable throughout the book. Correct proportion is key to portraying characters of particular ages.

CHECKING PROPORTIONS

For accurate representations, checking proportions of the body against the face and head is the most common measuring tool, although posture will also make a difference. Character studies that investigate possible poses and viewpoints may use a framework composed of shapes (see opposite). This will help you to calculate how perspective and action poses will alter the proportions. Reference to these shapes, or even the proportions of a stick-like figure, can help a character remain consistent.

SCALE

The scale of children both next to objects and within differing environments can only be improved if you familiarize yourself with everyday situations using your sketchbook. For more realistic illustrations, photographs can be used as a reference.

Head height
This diagram shows how the proportion of a human body in relation to the head changes over time. The number of heads that make up a standing figure differ with age.

0 to 2 years	4 to 6 years	6 to 8 years	12 to 14 years	18 to 20 years (Male)	18 to 20 (Female)
4 heads	5.75 heads	6.25 heads	7.25 heads	7.5 heads	7.5 heads

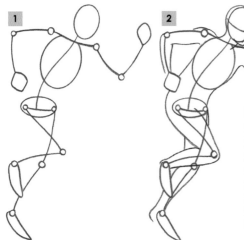

FRAMEWORK OF SHAPES

Using a framework of shapes to position a figure in a pose helps you to consider balance, movement, and poise before committing to a more time-consuming rendition of a character. "Opening up" the space between arms and legs when trying to capture motion creates more interesting silhouettes and negative spaces.

BABIES

Babies are notoriously difficult to draw. It is important to remember that the mask of a baby's face is only a very small proportion of the overall sphere of the head.

1. On the move
The slight exaggeration of a pose makes it more expressive. Tilting the shoulders or the position of the body forward generates movement. Giving the upper body something to do makes a pose less static.

2. Fleshing out
Once you have established the pose and are happy with the effect, you can start to apply the outlines of the body around the basic framework of shapes.

TRY THIS

Fleshing out the framework
Draw with soft, versatile media such as charcoal or graphite sticks to build up drawings of children from photographic reference, viewing them as mannequins and imagining limbs and ribcages where they are covered by clothing. Re-dress this framework with different clothes, shoes, and hair, maintaining the child's original posture and shape.

Now try the same exercise with an older child, and finally an adult. Note the differences.

Drawing practice

- Two- to five-minute poses in life classes will help to build up confidence in your ability to observe quickly and accurately. This also gives you the chance to experiment with drawing tools and media that produce fluid, precise, and descriptive lines. Practice recording the human form in different ways, concentrating on mass and contours. This will help to finely tune your ability to observe information.

- Try drawing figures of all ages from the television, making a note of their approximate age. This should give you access to a wide source of ages and builds, helping you to depict human form accurately. Remember to use drawing tools that enable the line to flow quickly and freely.

READ THIS

The Complete Drawing and Sketching Course by Stan Smith
(Reader's Digest, 2002)

Figures and Faces: A Sketcher's Handbook by Hugh Laidman
(Penguin, 1979)

Find your flair!
In this illustration from *We're Going on a Bear Hunt*, Helen Oxenbury's simple and attractive style appears in her drawings of wide-limbed and rounded-feature children. What's your style?

12 EXPRESSION

The slightest change of expression on the face tells the reader a lot about the way a character is feeling. Using the characters' features to show emotions will enhance and strengthen your narrative.

CHANGING MOODS

Changing the expressions of characters within a story—even subtly—helps to depict the facets of their personalities and their changes of mood from page to page. However, altering the proportions of a face to show expression while keeping the face consistent can be difficult. Most illustrators would expect to explore emotional characterization as a range of studies before embarking on a book. Being able to draw the face in profile and from other angles is important too; remember that a face should not always look out of the page if you want its owner to engage with other characters.

Body gestures

Don't just think about the face—everything about the body language of a character helps to convey a sense of its unique personality.

Get the eyes right

Using pupils and eyelids enables an artist to take complete control of the expression of the eyes. It becomes possible to open the eyes to show shock, or close them to squint. Eyebrows also contribute significantly.

Smug

Disgusted

Warm

Content

Dazed

Scope for expression

Whether the eyes and mouth are open or closed, small or large, or even if the position of the head is altered, even the simplest of faces can show a range of expressions.

TRY THIS

Think of a nursery rhyme with an incident that requires you to consider a strong emotion for the character concerned, for example Little Bo Peep or Little Miss Muffet. Illustrate the essence of the situation, trying to focus on and capture what the character is going through and how they might feel—surprised, frightened, happy, or sad. Don't be satisfied with the first image that comes into your head! Rework the drawings next to each other on a large sheet of paper so you can compare the drawings and see which you think are most successful. Play around with the poem too—if you enjoy writing—twisting the scenario to create alternative situations and possibly emotions.

Exploring character

Exploring the facial expressions of your characters (below left) is a good way to get to know them and consider their personalities. Faces change as the brow, jaw, and muscles in the cheeks around the mouth are altered by expressions.

Dots for eyes

"Dots for eyes" is currently a very popular solution, but can limit the amount of expression you can generate in a face without careful consideration. Large, googly, cartoon eyes are often unpopular with publishers, despite the success of manga and Disney, but keep watching the market trends as this can change.

Restricting expression to the face limits its impact; body language naturally supports it. Don't forget the hands as they add to the impression. They need to fit proportionately with the size and style of the figure and not be deliberately hidden away, even if they are difficult to draw.

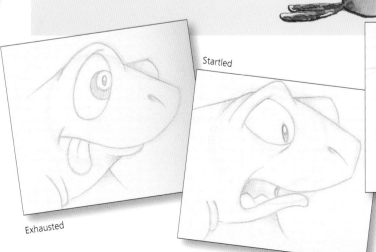

Exhausted

Startled

Sheepish

Disheartened

13 MOVEMENT

In an illustration, movement must be captured in a single, static pose. Considering the options throughout an action, stage-by-stage, like an animator line-testing, can help you to deliver the most effective moment "frozen in time."

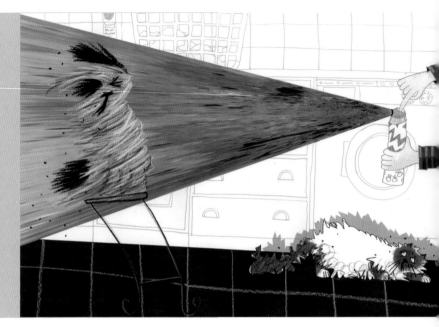

IMPRESSIONS OF MOVEMENT

Selecting the pose, viewpoint, body language, expression, and even the media or technique all contribute to the effect of movement. Media with fluid lines, such as dip pens or brushes, make expressive marks that are ideal for suggesting movement in the drawing.

The overall compositional design may include props and objects that help to strengthen the association with movement, such as trees swaying, cloth billowing, hair lifted, or scarves blowing—but take care to make sure they all move in the same direction!

Lines of movement
Here, the sense of movement portrayed through the positioning of limbs and features is accentuated by lines of movement around the relevant parts.

Speed
The hair streaming out behind this character creates a strong sense of movement at speed.

Up Down

Choose a pose that not only tells the story, but also makes interesting shapes that will add to your design. Imagine the figure silhouetted. Could the shape look more interesting if a limb were extended away from the body or the angle of view changed slightly? Shadows on the ground suggest something up in the air. Movement lines around comic styles can sometimes work, but don't overdo them.

Economy
Use everything about an image to demonstrate its state of movement—shape, color, and line. Make all the elements work together to convey the message.

Inflate Burst

Props
Here, the rug beneath the characters adds to the sense of movement in the image without directly contributing to the movement in a physical way.

TRY THIS

Using a child character you have developed, imagine what would happen if they were playing with an inflated balloon. Try to think of how they would chase it, hit it, catch it, jump with it, and so on as a series of figure studies on a large sheet of paper. Eventually start to format the drawings to consider composition and how angles and cropping can affect the relationship between the child and the balloon, giving a sense of space and action.

The importance of reference

Creating an unintentionally static image is often the result of relying solely on secondhand reference. If you observe figures or animals from life, the chances are they will be moving (drawing at the zoo, people walking in the street, or children playing on the beach, for example). The simplified sketched outlines and shapes of the action taking place— even if incomplete—will trigger memories of what you saw. In this way a drawing can act as a reminder of something that has been observed and understood.

14
BABIES AND TODDLERS

One of the most difficult types of character to draw convincingly, and yet still keep attractive, is a baby. The proportions of babies and toddlers are often unfamiliar to draw and you will need to observe and consider them carefully.

READ THIS

Tickle, Tickle by Helen Oxenbury
(Little Simon, 1987)

Helen Oxenbury draws young children and babies in a simple and attractive style with wide limbs and rounded features that are familiar to this age group.

Peepo by Janet and Allan Ahlberg
(Puffin Books, 1983)

How to be a Little Sod by Tony Ross
(Orion, 1999)

KNOWING YOUR SUBJECT

Knowing very young children, or having your own, can be a distinct advantage if you intend to illustrate for this age group—as reference, or as inspiration for stories and characters. Understanding young behavior, and appreciating how quickly babies develop into toddlers, will help you create convincing characters and situations. There are plenty of books that identify stages of development of young children if your access to babies is limited.

There are wonderful clothes, furniture, and other props associated with babies and very young children—pacifiers, beakers, teddies, blankets, bibs, and strollers—and the way the child interacts with these items will affect its body language and behavior. Catalogs or websites from stores selling baby products may provide much visual reference, but it may be worth spending time drawing a real stroller, for example, no matter how simple. The smallest of details can make your drawing believable.

Shining through
A good baby illustration reveals a personality that shines through from the earliest age. One look at this baby's eyes reveals a friendly soul and a glimmer of cheekiness.

TRY THIS

Collect a number of baby catalogs and magazines for reference (below), and books on baby development to inspire ideas for narratives. Develop baby and toddler characters and combine them with a prop in each pose you draw. Consider the narrative in the situations you are portraying. For example, a child can wear colored sunscreen and eat ice cream while sitting in a stroller with the parasol up. Or perhaps he sits on a potty looking at a book.

Best books for babies and toddlers:

- *The Very Hungry Caterpillar* by Eric Carle (Philomel, 1969)

This is the simple story of how a caterpillar eats and eats until he is transformed into a cocoon and then into a butterfly. Children are presented with a character that faces the same challenge they do: growing up. Carle uses beautiful collage artwork and die-cut holes in the pages.

- *Guess How Much I Love You* by Sam McBratney and Anita Jeram (Candlewick Press, 1995)

Little Nut Brown Hare and Big Nut Brown Hare find unusual ways of showing how much they love each other. For anyone who finds it difficult to put emotions into words, this is an innocent look at different ways of expressing how you feel—with a lovely surprise at the end.

- *Don't Put Your Finger In the Jelly, Nelly!* by Nick Sharratt (Scholastic Children's Books, 1993)

Nick Sharratt's thick lines and bright, simple colors are not dissimilar to the way a child might draw. In this picture book the rhymes and wordplay entertain alongside visual jokes. Die-cut holes in the pages cry out for a small hand to put a finger through them.

- *Where the Wild Things Are* by Maurice Sendak (Harper Collins, 1963)

First published in 1963, this is the story of a boy who gets sent to bed without any tea because he's behaved like such a monster. Max's angry imagination transforms his bedroom into a jungle and he goes out to meet other Wild Things. The story allows Max—and young readers—to experience the highs and lows of extreme emotion.

- *Sylvester and the Magic Pebble* by William Steig (Simon and Schuster, 1969)

Beautiful watercolor pictures illustrate a story that follows Sylvester, a little donkey, and his adventures with a magic pebble that makes his wishes come true. The book explores difficult emotions such as loneliness and sadness. The story ends happily, but helps children understand that the world is full of many emotions—not all of them lovely, but all of them important.

What do they have in common?

Something unexpected: unusual ways to say "I love you," made-up words, jungles in bedrooms, and a donkey who makes wishes. With picture-book writing, the only rule is to use your imagination.

BABY AND TODDLER CHARACTERISTICS

Babies and young children typically have round heads and tummies and chubby, short hands. The forehead protrudes slightly and seems very high when there is little hair, while the chin recedes. It's possible to emphasize the eyes—they are the same size as an adult's, but in a smaller skull—but better to understate or even ignore eyebrows. These are generally so fair they can hardly be seen. Noses are small, and upper lips more prominent than lower.

Body language
A simple drawing of a crawling child with her diaper peeking out and her pacifier in the corner of her mouth displays fun and humor.

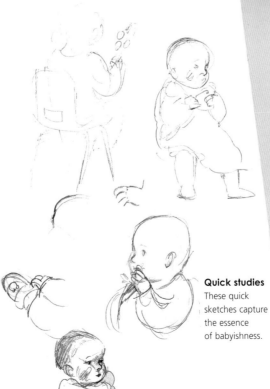

Quick studies
These quick sketches capture the essence of babyishness.

Typical developmental stages

- **3 months:** lifting their heads while lying on their fronts
- **3–5 months:** reaching out for objects
- **5 months:** handling objects
- **6 months:** sitting up without support; starting to crawl; pulling themselves up on furniture
- **10 months+:** starting to walk
- **14 months:** starting to feed themselves
- **18 months:** starting to kick or throw a ball
- **2 years:** learning to ride a bike

15 BOYS AND GIRLS

Finding a method or style for drawing figures is one hurdle; giving them a personality and identity is quite another. But when you take time to consider the trials and tribulations of growing up, it is easier to generate stories and create characters with which the reader can sympathize.

CHARACTER PROFILING

When representing young children it is easy to resort to generalizations: boys get up to mischief, are less focused on schoolwork, and interact more physically; girls are gentler, demonstrate maternal instincts, and throw tantrums. Profiling the children in your illustrations will help you to remain focused on the characters you wish to portray. Love or hate your characters, but never feel indifferent toward them!

Playing with cliché
A checklist like the one below helps you to play with clichés and subvert them. Can you create a child character that challenges the norm?

Character profile checklist:
The little sister who knows more than you do.
The bully who goes home and cries.
The best friend you don't always like.
The naughty boy who's clumsy.
The perfect girl who picks her nose in private.
The other child you say you hate, but secretly like.

Playful outfits
Dressing up as a bee, a fairy, or a Native American—fancy dress allows children to explore different sides to themselves.

REFLECTING DIVERSITY

An illustrator needs to reflect the multicultural society we live in, particularly in nonfiction. Publishers in many countries will demand that this is taken into consideration. Remember though, that characterization of different races is a sensitive issue. You will need good reference to enable you to portray features accurately and in a way that personifies a culture yet without causing offense. Representing religious beliefs other than your own and children with special needs are further considerations.

TRY THIS

Research a particular culture, different from your own, and develop a child character based on it. Study the subtlety of features and skin color. Use catalogs of children's clothes and other sources of reference to gather information about the lifestyle of your chosen character. Dress them in winter and summer outfits, for particular hobbies, or for school according to the unique place where they live.

Child characteristics

As children grow older, they develop more individual features.

The eyebrows and the shape of the nose and mouth become more distinctive. The head is still fairly large in proportion to the body, on a skinny neck and narrow shoulders.

There are interesting hairstyles to consider now, as well as an opportunity for pathos and humor!

Convincing characters
Sketching children at play can help you convince publishers that you have the eye and sensitivity to paint compelling pictures for your audience.

FIRST EXPERIENCES

Consider your own experiences of doing something for the first time, or recollect any other significant childhood experiences. Many such events are serious issues for children, and reading a story that enables them to talk about it or hear the perspective from someone else can be of great support and comfort. Examples include: going to the dentist, school, or hospital for the first time; dealing with bullying; coping with death of a pet or a relative; and understanding where babies come from.

OLDER CHARACTERS

If you have the ability to draw older children, include black and white illustrations of them in your portfolio; you may receive commissions for storybooks and nonfiction. There is also a market for the illustration of children's books for reluctant readers—featuring older characters but not text-heavy—in which comic-style storyboarding plays a more significant role.

All about firsts
An outdoor swim can be a memorable experience for a child. You could feature this type of event in your story.

Child development stages

- **3 years:** Children can catch a large ball, ride a tricycle, and finger-paint. An action-filled illustrated book full of fun activities such as these would engage a young reader.

- **4 years:** What do young children and rabbits have in common? They can both hop! Could you write a story using these two ingredients?

- **5 years:** Children play at make-believe and enjoy dressing up. They can walk on tiptoe. What about a story where a child dresses in costume and tiptoes over to scare his mother?

16 ADULTS

A common trap to fall into when illustrating adult characters is repeating old clichés: a granny with gray hair in a bun and wearing glasses; a family consisting of a mother, father, girl, boy, and dog; the mother staying home while the father goes out to work. Challenge any of these stereotypical portrayals by first asking yourself: is this really the case in today's society?

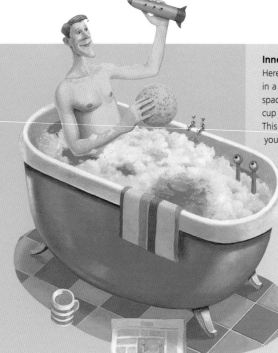

Inner child
Here you can see a grown man in a bubble bath, playing with a space rocket, his newspaper and cup of tea forgotten on the floor. This makes him appealing to young readers and teaches them an important early lesson: inside all of us is a child.

Same difference
The same illustrator, but four very different women. Dressed in tweed or platform sandals, there are no rules for the older generation.

KEEPING IT REAL

Grandparents can be agile and fashionable, and these days they are often involved with raising their grandchildren. Many mothers go out to work and have careers, so childcare plays a much greater role in the life of their child than in previous generations. Equally, fathers often do the vacuumcleaning or prepare the food.

Cultural mixes within families are more common then ever before, as are single parent families. Same-gender relationships are now also entering the equation. The media plays a big part in educating children about the different relationships in society and they tend to accept the changes common to their generation quite naturally. Any preconceptions need to be considered and challenged if books are to reach out to a wider audience. Ambiguity in all aspects of life is possibly more attractive than ever before.

Old and young
Older characters and young readers have much in common—both are outside of the workaday world, free to play and create.

FINDING REFERENCE

Inspiration for characters may come from observing people you already know or from printed or online reference sources. Clothes, shoes, props, and hairstyles all contribute to a unique identity. Take time to research all of this carefully; nothing should be overlooked!

Draw on the familiar
Faces you have seen every day of your life may present unexpected surprises if you take the time to draw them.

Face studies
Sketches reveal the subtle details that age can add to a variety of adult faces.

Engaging adult characters:

- *Father Christmas* by Raymond Briggs (Random House, 1973)

  This version of Father Christmas challenges children's expectations—he's grumpy! Just like some other grown-ups young readers might know…

- *Mr. Large in Charge* by Jill Murphy (Candlewick Press, 2005)

  A series of books in which elephant parents clumsily try to look after their family. Mr. and Mrs. Large show that non-human parents might not always get it right, but they do care.

- *The Adventures of Asterix* by René Goscinny and Albert Uderzo (first published as a series of comic books in 1959)

  Originally the star of a series of French comics, the diminutive Asterix continues to appeal to children of all ages today in many different publishing formats.

17

ANTHROPOMORPHISM

Animal characters imbued with human characteristics have featured in many stories for children.
They crop up in fables, myths, and legends, representing the extremes of human behavior and reinforcing the century-old stereotypical characteristics for certain animals. Crucially, the use of anthropomorphized animals in a story enables the illustrator to depict a situation without any particular reference to age, social standing, gender, or race.

Best anthropomorphic characters:

- *Duck in the Truck* by Jez Alborough (HarperCollins 2000)
  The interaction, expression, and body language between these characters leaves the audience in no doubt as to what is happening.

- *Kipper and Roly* by Mick Inkpen (Red Wagon Books, 2001)
  This mischievous character has huge appeal in his design, humor, and cuddle factor. The characters are simple, sensitive interpretations.

- *Olivia* by Ian Falconer (Scholastic, 2000)
  This very original interpretation of a little pig, with the trademark limited palette, captures the personality of a little girl. The movement and expression translate to human behavior perfectly.

DRAWING FROM LIFE

Attributing human characteristics to an animal is a great deal easier if you have a really good understanding of the animal concerned. Studying an animal from life is by far the best way to develop an original character with a "real" sense of movement, posture, and personality. Any other visual sources will need to show a variety of positions and provide some insight into the animal's behavior. Studying film might be a possible source of reference for understanding an animal's skeletal structure and the way it moves.

PET APPEAL

The close relationship between humans and their pets makes these animals ideal for tackling sensitive issues. The "ahhhh" factor of an especially cute animal will also help to sell your product. Many animals are colorful, or exude personality, and for lots of new illustrators, these can be easier to draw! Children will always love a well designed animal character and the appeal of animals is universal.

Donkey
A four-legged animal stands and skates like a human. Its features are relatively accurate, though the expressions and movement are not.

Four legs to two
The ball-socket and lines drawn to represent the limbs preserve the consistency of the proportions of the character and help you confidently manipulate the pose.

TRY THIS

A 180-degree rotation of a character study—known as a "turnaround"—is part of the initial development process in animation. The lengths of limbs and so on are lined up as the figure turns, usually in a standing pose. Try this yourself as an interesting way of establishing the proportions of an anthropomorphized character, whether the animal is zoologically correct or has a human body with an animal's head.

If you favor a more spontaneous style generated from doodles, test for consistency by repeating your character a number of times next to each other moving from left to right along a horizontal line.

EXPANDING ON THE REFERENCE

When using good photographic reference, it can be helpful to break the animal down into simple shapes or a sticklike figure to learn the essential proportions. View the animal's structure as though it were transparent, using the position of ball joints to help you extend limbs from the torso with accurate lengths in changing positions.

Just as it can help to think of the structure of an animal as a transparent form, the same can be applied to placing the character in situations, such as driving a car or sitting on a chair. Draw the object in perspective first, then draw the character sitting on it or in it. (This is more likely to give a convincing end result than the other way around.)

Badger
Here's a selection of anthropomorphized poses.

The arms and outstretched "hands" exaggerate the wailing.

Tilting the body and lifting the limbs gives an impression of marching forward.

The shadow shows that both feet are off the ground.

Rotation
Drawing the features and limbs as the figure turns helps you familiarize yourself with the character as a three-dimensional object. The repetition also establishes the proportions.

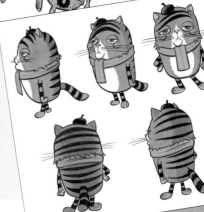

18 FIGURE AND GROUND

When illustrators talk about "figure and ground," they are talking about composition—the relationship between the various characters in the story and their relationship to the situation or environment in the text.

Foreground
In this image, there is only foreground, entirely occupied by the severely cropped character, creating an extreme sense of presence and closeness.

VISUAL INTERPRETATION

Imagine you control the situation like a stage or film set, using the same technical language as would be used in animation and live action. So, you have a foreground, a middleground, and a background in which to move your characters around, trying to achieve the best visual interpretation of a particular scene.

Where you place characters and objects within a given layout on a page, exploiting the depth of field, adds to the impact of the storytelling. There is a variety of ways to help create a three-dimensional illusion for the characters to move through: overlapping, perspective, scale, and placement all heighten the effect and interpretation of the text. Emotionally the child needs to be able to engage with what is seen and what is read. This is affected not only by the placement of characters in the right place within the depth of field, but also through the expression and body language of the characters.

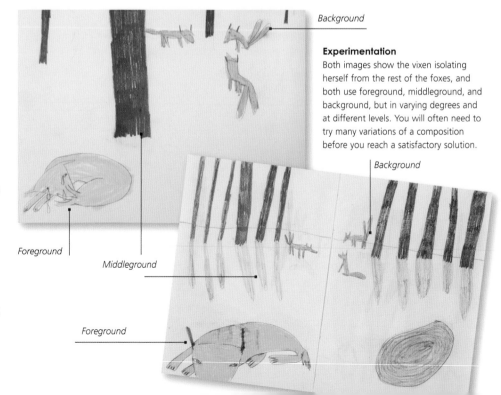

Background

Foreground

Middleground

Experimentation
Both images show the vixen isolating herself from the rest of the foxes, and both use foreground, middleground, and background, but in varying degrees and at different levels. You will often need to try many variations of a composition before you reach a satisfactory solution.

Background

Foreground

Compositional proportions

You are in control of the aesthetic aspects of your composition. A useful guideline is the "Golden Section" in which a line or rectangle is divided into two parts so that the ratio of the smaller to the larger is equal to the ratio of the larger to the whole line. This ratio (approximately 8:3) has been known since antiquity, and was believed to possess inherent aesthetic virtues, bringing art and nature into harmony. You don't need to slavishly follow the principle, and anyway your format may not allow it. But the basic rules are always worth bearing in mind: the picture surface shouldn't be divided symmetrically; figures should not be placed in the center of your paper; a fence should not be positioned so it runs horizontally across your illustration, equally dividing the distance from the bottom edge of your drawing to the horizon line. Of course, there are no rules that can't broken.

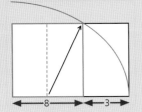

1 Construct a unit square (red outline).
2 Draw a line from the midpoint of one side to an opposite corner.
3 Use that line as the radius to draw an arc that defines the long dimension of the rectangle.
4 You can go on dividing the resulting space into ever smaller proportional units (see above).

In practice
Three examples showing characters or focal points positioned on the golden intersection the last one works from the left and right

Breaking rules
Top, a formal centered composition; above, an anarchic, tightly cropped composition, in keeping with the subject matter.

Viewpoint
Viewpoint is the position that you choose for the reader to view an illustration. Viewpoint can have a dramatic effect on composition and mood. Above, a simple standing-height, eye-level viewpoint. Right, an extreme viewpoint and dizzying perspective give a sense of enclosure and movement from the ground up toward the treetops. The bird occupies the foreground; the owl is flying out of the middleground, and the figure is a tiny presence on the forest floor. This composition creates an illusion of great size and scale. As you look down from one of the towering trees, you feel right at the center of the action.

Sturdy trunks stand short and tall. A trunk supports the body of a tree, like your legs support your body.

19 FRAMES AND BORDERS

Many illustrators use decorative elements and "ornaments" that sit outside the main narrative illustrations to elucidate and elaborate on the story. These can add atmosphere or contain symbolic details from the story.

When you tell a story using images, every element in the story becomes iconic to some degree. In the same way that the relationship between individual words in a poem subtly redefines their meaning in accordance with the overall message and tone of the poem, so too do the images in a picture book work together to create the overall meaning of the book. The representation of objects, animals, clothing, and even colors will accrue meaning as the imagery progresses, and repeated use will draw attention to their significance.

Girl and rabbit
The delicate, detailed line drawing naturally fits within an oval format. The vignette is enhanced by the shape of the border and the subtle colors in the tiny flowers.

CRASH COURSE

Famous examples of frames and borders:

- **Jane Ray**
  Her rich, stylized, and highly decorative illustrations are often associated with her use of gold.

- **Jan Pienkowski**
  Famous for his silhouettes—the intricate outlines enhance the pages alongside full-color work.

- **Nicola Bailey**
  The main illustrations are watercolors, applied with a pointillist technique. Borders balance the design.

Visual integration
Whether your borders add to the story or simply act as a decorative device, they should integrate with the main artwork and are often produced as part of it.

Themed borders
Your borders don't simply have to be decorative; they could add a narrative element as well. Here, festive fairy lights form a whimsical border (below); on another page, a row of stockings are hung up for Christmas Eve (below left).

NAVIGATIONAL CLUES

If you look at very old illuminated manuscripts such as the *Book of Kells*, the distinction between the border and the body text becomes unclear, with marginalia offering interpretations on the text. Historically borders were a way of breaking up the monotony of the printed page, with ornaments used as chapter headings. These also served to give a visual clue to the content of that section of the book and so helped the reader navigate backward and forward in a large text. In picture books today the use of frames and borders in the design often signals a more traditional type of book.

Book of Kells

The beginning of the summary of the Gospel according to Matthew features elaborate decoration of the page, including images and figures within the intense pattern framework. The labored, indulgent use of detail and gold shows the importance of the piece of work.

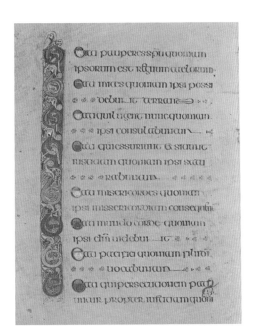

Color plates

The traditional look of a book designed with frames and borders is a result of the way books used to be produced. Before color printing was the norm, illustrated books had color plates that were inserted after the book was printed. The border was printed in black with the rest of the text, and showed where the plate was to go. The borders created visual harmony by connecting the color illustrations with the overall design of the book.

TRY THIS

Commentaries

- Take small details from your story and work up a series of border "commentaries" on the main text.

- Comment, for example, on the mice and pumpkin in Cinderella before they are transformed, or the mirror and apple in *Snow White*, or any detail in your story that you feel is significant—bus tickets, shoes, burned toast, whatever! Look at creating small "spot" type illustrations, and also see if you can work them into a decorative border about 2 in (5 cm) wide. You need only work up two sides of the border, as the rest can be generated digitally from your artwork.

Helen Shoesmith's illustrations for *The Secret Garden*

By highlighting some of the iconic imagery in the story of *The Secret Garden* by Frances Hodgson Burnett, Helen Shoesmith draws attention to the importance of small things in the narrative—a key, a robin, a flower—these are all catalysts for the action and also represent the themes of secrecy, loss, and the regenerative qualities of being among natural things. The stifling, dark, oppressive world of the house is contrasted with the light and airy drawings of the garden, and the frames and borders use imagery to reinforce these concepts.

Chapter three

TELLING THE STORY

This section explores the techniques that writers and illustrators use to tell an engaging story, spur the narrative along, and encourage readers to keep turning the pages.

TIGER, TIGER
Varying the size and crop of visuals on a page can encourage page-turning habits in young readers (see page 82).

20 STORY STRUCTURE

Most fiction stories—from children's picture books to adult novels—have the same basic structure. You will find this structure in everything from ancient Greek myths to the latest Hollywood blockbuster.

Planning for the future

Writing a novel can be isolating and dispiriting, especially if you take the wrong turn in your story and then have to abandon several chapters and thousands of words. The more you plan your story before you write it, the less likely this is to happen. That's not to say you can't deviate from your initial plan. All writers find fresh ideas as their story unfurls. But just writing a story with no clear idea where your characters are going to end up is a recipe for hours of wasted work.

THEME

All fiction invariably has a theme, and it usually involves your main character—the protagonist—overcoming adversity. This can be anything from beating playground bullying to saving the world. Within the theme there is often a moral—such as "working together is better than acting alone," or "doing bad things causes unhappiness to both the perpetrator and others." Although adult fiction writers sometimes write stories with an ambiguous or dubious theme, if you are writing for children you will need to produce a story with a clear and positive moral. It would be an unusual children's publisher who produced a book suggesting that crime does pay, or that bullying is fun and makes you feel good about yourself.

MOTIVATION

Once you've established your setting—where the action takes place—you will need a cause: something that is happening or has happened to make your characters behave as they do. For example: Molly's mother is sick but too poor to pay for medicine; Charlie's best friend Ivan has gone missing… The cause drives the story forward.

ACTION AND ANTAGONISM

How your characters act in response to the motivating "cause" provides the "effect," or action, of the story. So, Molly will try to raise money for her mother; Charlie will search for his friend. In most stories your character's actions will be thwarted by an antagonist—your book's central "baddie," who is trying to stop your hero achieving their aim. Your antagonist could be a person or thing, for example, a classroom rival, the Gestapo, or even the weather. Without an antagonist it will be difficult to create suspense, and your reader will become bored with the story.

BUILDING TO A CLIMAX

All the excitement, suspense, concern, and trepidation in your story has to build to a crescendo. This is the part where all seems lost for your hero—they think their friends are dead and are just about to be murdered themselves by your central antagonist! This should be the part of the story where the reader finds it especially impossible to put the book down. Make sure your crescendo or climax comes close to the end of the book.

THE RIGHT ENDING

The end of the story provides the resolution. It is a brave writer who gives the story an unhappy ending, especially in children's fiction. Your reader will be drawn into your book because they like your main character or characters. They want to feel their struggles have been worthwhile and that all is well in the world when the story ends.

How to write a story plan

- Before you start planning your story, you probably already know what it's going to be about. Try to write two sentences that sum up the story:

"When Sarah and Rosie take a ride on the ghost train, they discover that they don't have to pay money to be scared. The ghost ride takes them down dark tunnels to another world where a terrifying question faces the girls: how will they get home?"

If you find that you're struggling to summarize, you may have a problem with your story.

- From here, sketch out your plan. Make a bulleted list of what you want your story to achieve, and by when.

- Next, write up the story plan. It's a good idea to write this plan in the first tense: *"Sarah and Rosie meet outside the gates..."* This will prevent the plan from morphing into the actual manuscript.

- Avoid inserting dialogue into the story plan. But do think about where and when dialogue will appear.

- Try to have a sense of where chapter breaks will fall. You will need good, strong chapter endings to drive the story on. By this stage, the plan allows you to see any weak spots. Do you have acres of solid dialogue? Does a character spend too much time thinking? Where are the secondary characters? Does the logic of your story make sense? A story plan will highlight these and other issues. Remember, the story plan is the blueprint for your manuscript—rush past this stage at your peril.

The point of view stays with Sarah at all times. You will need to decide what your narrative perspective is going to be.

The story stays in the present tense throughout.

The beginnings of narrative tone are emerging—there are moments of humor. This is a stage at which you can decide the tone your story is going to take.

There are regular references to Sarah's emotions as she moves through the story. Remember your characters' thoughts and feelings as well as actions.

The beginning of a sample story plan

Sarah and Rosie meet outside the gates of the fairground. The lights and noises are exciting and they pool their money—they only have enough for two rides each. They go on the dodgems and have a good time crashing into two older boys in their own dodgem. Sarah feels flushed as she climbs out of the car and she hears the two boys laugh as she and Rosie walk over to the ghost train. Will the boys come on the ride with them? Rosie jokes it might be nice to have the boys hold their hands when they're feeling scared. But when Sarah looks over her shoulder, the boys are wandering over towards the hotdog stand.

Feeling disappointed, she climbs into a waiting car and the ride jerks into action. She feels her smile fade as they plunge into the dark tunnel—she was secretly hoping the boys would join them. Still, the ride soon takes her mind off romantic woes. Strings of fake web get caught in their hair and unimpressive skeletons lunge out of coffins. This ride is a joke—it's not scary at all! But as they turn another corner the ride suddenly plunges and Sarah finds herself screaming with terror. She and Rosie are thrown free of the car into a stinking bog, with mud clinging to their limbs. Where are they? This isn't the fairground anymore!

Sarah pulls herself free of the mud and helps her hysterical friend climb onto dry ground. Two ghouls loom out of the fog and Sarah notices they look familiar—it's the older boys. But now their eyes are nothing more than dark shadows and their emaciated bodies are covered in bruises. They wear torn rags instead of their jeans and hoodies. One of them reaches out a bony hand to take Sarah's. She suddenly doesn't want to hold hands with that boy any more! She and Rosie run away, looking back over their shoulders to see the ghoul-boys

Description is kept to a minimum. This will feature in the first draft.

21 WRITING DIALOGUE

In novels for children, dialogue is probably the single most important element to master. It is where conflicts are dramatized, action takes place, the plot moves forward, and the characters are revealed. Dialogue is also the part of fiction that is closest to what it imitates. If you read it aloud, it takes only a little longer than the same conversation would take in real life. These qualities of realism and drama make dialogue central to fiction for children.

One author's story

The characters in children's author Meredith Sue Willis's novel *The Secret Super Powers of Marco* were based on children she taught in New York City. Outside of school, they cursed like drunken sailors and, in her novel, she included two curse words. One of the first things her editor told her was that the company had a policy against vulgar words in novels for children. Willis reports that her first reaction was to bristle: "That's how those kids talk!" Of course, her second reaction was that she wanted to see her book through to publication. She also noted that in real life, the kids actually cursed more than they did in her book. She had, in other words, already edited reality and was creating an illusion rather than simply transcribing. Also, she had to admit to herself that she didn't really want her eight-year-old son reading children's books full of language like that. In the end, she made her characters taunt each other with silly, invented insults like "Banana Brain!"

CAPTURING REALISM

Generally speaking, in order to capture the realistic quality of dialogue, your best strategy is to draft too much—too many quotidian and phatic exchanges, too many stage directions, even too many bits of description. Once you've captured the real-life quality to your own satisfaction, start cutting out everything but the very strongest parts.

STAGING

Dialogue in fiction is not simply a transcription of people talking. It also has to make crystal clear who is speaking with tags like "he said" when necessary. It must also give stage directions for how people speak using verbs and adverbs, as in "he snarled" or "he said angrily." It has to include some descriptions of gestures and actions. It may also include some narration, description of place or setting, description of the characters, and even a judicious amount of internal monologue.

WHAT TO INCLUDE

The operative word in writing dialogue in children's novels is "necessary." If the exchange is necessary, include it. If the description is necessary, keep it. If it is characteristic of Genevieve or necessary to the plot that she wears a floppy purple hat during the dialogue, by all means describe it. In fact, feel free as you draft your dialogue to describe her jeans and t-shirt as well, but in revising, be sure you get rid of the jeans and t-shirt if they don't help capture her character or advance the plot.

Be especially frugal with description and narration between lines of dialogue. You want as little as possible to slow the flow. "'I don't believe you!' she snarled" is better than "'I don't believe you!' she said, snarling in anger." The first example has fewer words and more momentum. Best of all, if it can be done without confusion, is simply "I don't believe you!"

TRY THIS

Below is a simple exchange of six words. Do anything you want to turn it into an interesting dialogue (combine speeches, add speeches, insert description, make it longer—anything at all).

"Hi."

"Hi."

"Where were you?"

"Nowhere."

Now take the six-word exchange and write another dialogue with it, this time making it a conflict between a teenage boy and an elderly lady. You may add anything you want, but include those six words. Notice in the example below how the teenager says very few words: he is sullen and withholding in this scene. The woman, however, blasts him with a lot of words. Whether people use many or few words is one of the important ways of showing the difference in their personalities.

He ran down the hallway to her doorway and stopped. Her room smelled as bad as usual, sweet and musty.

"Hi," he said.

"Hi?" She shook a skinny finger at him. "Is that all you've got to say, you rude boy? I've been waiting for an hour! Your mother said you'd bring it directly! Where were you?"

"Nowhere," he said glumly, holding out the oily, cold bag.

She snatched it away and started gobbling the sandwiches.

Janie was jumping up and down on the tree-house platform shouting "Hi! Hi! Where were you?" She was jumping so high, Frank was afraid she was going to crash through the boards.

He hurried up the slope with his finger to his lip. "Nowhere special!" he shouted, and then, when he got close enough, he beckoned to her to lean down. He whispered, "Or maybe it was Very Special. Wait 'til you hear what I discovered!"

TRY THIS

Take a notebook to a place where there are a lot of children—a park, playground, or schoolyard. Find an out-of-the-way spot, sit quietly, and transcribe what you hear. You'll quickly notice that you can't write fast enough to get everything down, but that's fine, because it means your brain has already begun to edit. Later, type up only the best of what you transcribed. Then—after you have the actual words spoken—reconstruct the other elements: what the kids looked like, where they were, how they said things. Make up what you aren't able to remember.

To extend the exercise, can you make your dialogue into a story? Might the scene be used in a story you've already started?

Next, take the same six words and use them in a story in which two friends have a mystery to solve. In this sample, the characters are both children, both full of energy, and speaking more or less in the same style. Notice, however, that what is going on in Frank's mind ("Frank was afraid...") gives him the quality of being a thoughtful, caring friend, whereas Janie seems impatient and perhaps reckless, based on the physical action ("She was jumping so high..."). The surrounding material in a dialogue (actions and thoughts) can go a long way toward developing and revealing character, too.

AVOIDING PATRONIZING THE READER

Writing novels for children aged seven to 14 is more like writing for an adult audience than writing picture books. Your story will center around characters who are children, and is probably shorter than a book for adults, but first and foremost it should be a good story about interesting people.

Child's view
Keep in mind that a child's experience of the world is different from that of an adult.

STARTING POINTS

You may begin with a situation or an issue in mind, but the essential rule in writing for children is to start with questions, not answers. If your theme, for example, is bullying, don't start with what you believe to be the best way for a child to deal with bullies. Rather, start off with a real person with a real problem. Approach your material as children approach life: without knowing how things will turn out. Children often don't even realize how things are supposed to come out, or that circumstances can change. The best novels for children are ones in which children simply deal with life and life's challenges. The tone can be funny or serious; the tools the child uses to meet the challenges can be old-fashioned or modern, mundane or magical; but the way to be sure you are writing what children want to read is to write as if you were a child.

A CHILD'S POINT OF VIEW

This may sound obvious, but a writer for children needs to keep in mind that children see a special "slice" of the world. They are physically smaller than adults, and their senses tend to be sharper. They are experiencing many things for the first time, so their observations are especially intense. One way to move in this direction is to recreate some of your own memories as vividly as possible, using your senses in imagination: the odor of a schoolroom, for example, or the flavor of childhood candies and sweets.

There are many ways to tell a story for children, but you may want to experiment with using first person or the close third person as a way of understanding the world as a child understands it. This doesn't mean the story has to be simple. You may put your child characters in any dilemma you please. The child may be pulled in

Physical difference
The fact that a child is smaller than an adult has a subtle effect on their perception of their environment.

The boy I imagine is dark, probably Latino, a small boy with a lot of hair that needs combing. He's all alone in a playground with some broken bottles. He's sitting in a swing. He swings a little, and then seems to decide that's for little kids and gets up and kicks at the broken glass... "I'm sick of being the big brother," he says. "All the time I have to watch my little sister! I'm telling you! She is so little but she's so much trouble! My mom has to work late and it's always me picking up my little sister from the babysitter and I have to make her peanut-butter crackers and she won't eat them if the peanut butter don't go all the way to the edges! I'm telling you. She gets to stay in the babysitter's house and watch television all day, but I have to go to school... school is okay, except for this big ugly boy Tyrone. Tyrone likes to pinch people. And you know what's worst of all? He lives on my block! And he wants to beat me up!"

One author's story

Meredith Sue Willis' first novel for children grew out of a little sketch about a boy who is feeling sorry for himself and starts committing acts of minor vandalism. He breaks off old-fashioned car antennas. In the story, he throws one car antenna into the air, and it turns magically into a star. It was just a scrap of an idea, but when Willis read it to friends, one said casually that she didn't think it worked, but that it might be interesting if told from the little boy's point of view. Willis tried revising it with the little boy telling "legends" about himself. How he got his star was one legend, how his little dog ran away was another, how he got a new friend another. And pretty soon, she had a whole group of linked stories that became her first novel for children.

TRY THIS

Pretending to be a child

Imagine the face of a child. This could be a child you have seen or an invented one, but it works best if it is not someone close to you. Visualize the face first, then where the child is: a specific place and a specific situation—an eight-year-old boy with dark hair that falls into his eyes, for example. He has just moved to a new neighborhood. Now imagine that the boy begins to tell you about his life—he speaks very quietly, close to your ear: his mother is a single mom, his little sister likes to run away, he's worried about making new friends.

Move closer to him in your imagination, so that you slip inside the boy's head and hear his thoughts instead of his voice. He tells you how frightening the school bully is. He tells you a dream. He wants his own dog.

Next write as much of this as you can, not worrying about order or chronology. Just write in the child's voice. This exercise, by the way, is not meant to be an argument for using first person over third person, but rather a way to accumulate material and get to know the child. You might use some of the material in an internal monologue or even in spoken dialogue. It may also give you some ideas for your storyline.

Childhood memories
Think back to your own childhood for inspiration. Don't just consider the physical reality; how did you feel or respond in particular situations?

two (or more) directions. There may be shocks, betrayals; even death. But do keep in mind that the underlying worldview of a child begins with an acute sense of fairness and unfairness, and that children tend to persist in believing in a good outcome to the very end.

This is not to set up rules, but to suggest ways to enter into a child's experience. You may want to begin with your own childhood memories, or you may want to spend time observing children at play. You might also try that most childlike and enjoyable of all techniques: just pretend!

inside the mind of a child
Try putting yourself in his place to get a feel for your story.

23

THE WRITER'S VOICE

Who is telling your story? Is it you, the writer? Or is it the character? In Victorian times it was fashionable for the writer to be a palpable presence on the page, sometimes addressing their "dear reader" directly. Writers in this style would sometimes stop along the way to make their own moral judgments about what was happening in their story.

Dialogue vs. narrative

It is vital in any story to get a good balance between dialogue—the bits of a story where the characters speak to each other—and narrative—the bits where the writer is describing something: the interior of the house, the view over the bay, and so on. Readers are naturally drawn to dialogue. If they see paragraph after paragraph of narrative description they are liable to speed-read or skip them altogether.

VERSION ONE: The band that they made

Dan came up with his Great Idea at lunchtime. It was the start of the fall semester. His friends were on the playing fields sitting among the fallen leaves under the big tree when Dan said, "Hey, who wants to be in a band?"

Dan had a myspace page and a battered Gibson guitar on which he could pick out three chords. Today he was wearing skinny jeans and a faded Ramones tour t-shirt. The t-shirt used to belong to his father, who was once featured on the front cover of *Rolling Stone* magazine under the banner headline, "He ROCKS." That was back in the eighties. Now Dan's dad drove a cab—when he hadn't forgotten to take his medication. Since Dan's mom left, there was no one to count out the little blue pills into the plastic cup.

THE MODERN WAY

Today, most writers would feel the intrusive approach only really works in an autobiography. The job of a fiction writer is to draw their reader into their story. As with film, television drama, and theater, you need to make the reader forget they are reading a book or watching actors on a stage or screen, and become utterly immersed in the story. The way to do this is to make yourself (as the writer) completely invisible.

MAINTAINING INTEREST

If you are writing with your character in the first person you need to adopt a tone of voice that the reader will find palatable or intriguing. No one wants to read 300 pages devoted to the thoughts of a carping middle-aged woman or a whining adolescent boy. Whether your central character is good or bad, the reader needs to be interested enough in them to want to carry on reading about them.

Version one opens with a punch, taking the reader straight to the Great Idea. Details such as Dan's myspace profile and tour t-shirt bring the main character to life. Poignant revelations about family life— his mom's departure, his dad's reliance on pills—are mentioned almost as an aside, making them even more touching.

Show not tell

"Show not tell" is is one of the great rules of writing and one of the most difficult things to train yourself to do.

When you introduce a character don't tell the reader she is rich and beautiful. Say she arrived in a chauffeur-driven limousine and all the boys in the room could not keep their eyes off her. Don't tell your readers someone's mother is bossy or nosy; show her constantly interfering in the lives of her children or habitually asking searching and impertinent questions.

Showing rather than telling will make your characters come alive. They should appear as vivid, three-dimensional people to your reader, rather than cardboard cutouts.

CHARACTER BUILDING

Dialogue is where you are best able to "show" and not "tell" (see above). Is your antagonist unctuous and scheming? Show him flattering your hero and asking leading questions. Is he ill-tempered and prone to violence? Show him complaining about trivialities and threatening those around him with a beating.

Writing convincing dialogue is difficult. You need to ensure your characters are speaking with their own voice rather than yours. Reading your writing out aloud to yourself will help you polish your dialogue.

The version two sample indulges in "tell" rather than "show." The narrator tells the reader that Dan has been wearing the same t-shirt for three days, but it would be more entertaining to learn this by a description of the whiff!

Version two gets bogged down in detail. The reader learns Dan's age, his grade, the school's location, and how old his sister is—all before getting to the meat of the story. Some of the language is detached and adult; this doesn't sound like the story of a young boy. The only piece of dialogue comes right at the end—from a secondary character.

VERSION TWO: The band that they made

Dan was thirteen and in seventh grade at Alderhay Middle School, which was just on the outskirts of a little town in Pittsburgh off Highway 32. It was lunchtime at the start of the fall semester. He'd always wanted to form a band. That morning, in between getting his sister, who was six, ready for school (their mother had left three years earlier) and measuring out his father's medication, Dan had mastered another guitar chord, bringing his repertoire to three. His father was a shambling casualty of the decade of the 1980s and had spent the years in the hugely successful heavy rock band The Parasites. When he received an unusually large gratuity from a satisfied customer the Christmas before, Dan's father had acquired a Gibson guitar from ebay and then impatiently taught Dan to play the chords. "All you need is three chords, son," his father had said. "Just change the order of 'em and you can play anything."

Dan approached his friends (Steve Campbell, Big Phil Sane, Janey "Small Ears" Magoo, Little-Phil-so-as-not-to-confuse-him-with-the-other-Phil, and Lou). They were sitting under the big tree, which is where they always sat, whatever the weather. Dan was wearing tight skinny jeans and a faded Ramones tour souvenir t-shirt two sizes too small for him. He'd been wearing that t-shirt for three days now. "Hey, I've had a Great Idea," he said. "Who wants to form a band?"

24 POINT OF VIEW

Although most stories have the same basic elements there are many ways to tell them. What you need to establish before you start the hard graft of writing is which angle you are going to take, and how this best serves the story.

YOUR CHARACTER'S AGE

If your main character is a 12-year-old boy, do you write "in the moment" or do you write from the point of view of an old man looking back on his life? As an old man you have the benefit of hindsight and wisdom. Perhaps, if your readers are older themselves, they will appreciate this point of view. But for writers of children's fiction, making the hero roughly the same age as your reader is generally far more effective.

Writing as an older character takes away an element of suspense—if your character is relating events that happened in the past, then they obviously survived those events. If you are writing as a 12-year-old caught up in dreadful circumstances, neither your character nor the reader has any idea what will happen next. Will the character survive the battle? Will he get lost in the woods? Will he drown in the shipwreck? Of course the character usually does survive—but the reader will not assume that if the story is written as it is happening.

Choosing the right tense

Some writers use the present tense to impart a sense of excitement. "We walk into the town. There's no-one around. Then I spot the flash of a rifle along a rooftop…" In the right hands this can be effective, but this breathless style can also be exhausting to read and difficult to maintain.

Most books are written in the past tense.

This can still sound immediate, especially if the writer uses terse and simple prose. "We walked into the town. There was no one around. Then I spotted the flash of a rifle along a rooftop…"

Be careful not to make your tenses too ponderous: "When we were walking into the town…" This will make your writing stodgy and slow the story down.

Five boy characters:

- *Stig of the Dump* by Clive King (Puffin, 1963)

  Stig is a caveman who lives at the bottom of a quarry. He's the person all boys would like to be: filthy, with no parents to tell him what to do, and no bedtime.

- *Harry Potter* by JK Rowling (Scholastic, 1997)

  Possibly the best-known hero of recent children's fiction. Seven fantasy novels watch Harry and his friends progress at Hogwarts School. Harry, an orphan, has a lightning-bolt shaped scar on his forehead. He's marked out in more ways than one—and he must learn to conquer the evil Voldemort.

- *James and the Giant Peach* by Roald Dahl (Puffin, 1961)

  Normal-boy James climbs inside a giant peach and, with his creepy-crawly companions, he takes readers on an adventure that defies belief.

- *Alex Rider* by Anthony Horowitz (Penguin, 2001)

  Alex Rider is often described as a young James Bond. This teenage boy is forced into working for MI6 after the death of his guardian. Mature and good-natured, Alex is a teenage spy readers like—and want to be.

- *Horrid Henry* by Francesca Simon and Tony Ross (Orion Books, 1998)

  A series of books featuring a mischievous but likeable boy. Henry hates vegetables and homework—like a lot of other children.

Five girl characters:

- *Anne of Green Gables* by LM Montgomery (Grosset and Dunlap, 1908)

  An orphan character who has charmed generations of readers.

- *What Katy Did* by Susan Coolidge (Dover Publications, 1872)

  A mischievous girl who endears herself to the reader by being less than perfect.

- *The Worst Witch* by Jill Murphy (Candlewick Press, 1974)

  Mildred tries hard at Miss Cackle's Academy, but often gets things wrong.

- Lara from the *His Dark Materials* series by Philip Pullman (Random House, first book of the series published 1995)

  A wild, tomboyish girl who learns to recognize the subtleties of good and evil.

- Cassandra Mortmain from *I Capture the Castle* by Dodie Smith (St. Martins Griffin, 1948)

  A witty heroine, living in a beautiful but crumbling house, faces the challenges of family and romance in the 1930s. Even modern teenage girls about to face adulthood can relate to her.

LOOK WHO'S TALKING

Most children's fiction writers choose to write in either the first person— "I"—or the third person—"he" or "she." In the third person you can still stick to telling your story entirely from one viewpoint, or you can vary your viewpoint by telling it from the point of view of other characters.

Writing in the first person gives your story an unbeatable immediacy. You have a direct connection to the hopes and fears of your main character that can make him or her seem to spring off the page. But, you are limited to telling the story from this one perspective. This can make depictions of epic events—such as a Napoleonic sea battle—quite a challenge. After all, when mighty warships—or even entire fleets—clash, you can only report what your character can see through the nearest gun port. So, seeing your story through the eyes of one character only can be quite restrictive.

A VARIED EYE

Writing in the third person—especially through the eyes of several characters—allows you variety. You can depict the action from whichever perspective will tell the story in the most exciting way. You can also give your reader an insight into the secret thoughts and motivations of other characters. You can tell your story from their point of view as well as that of your main character.

NARRATIVE PERSPECTIVE

First-person narrative: Events can only happen as long as the narrating character is there to see them. The individual's "voice" influences the narrative tone.

I ran up the hill as fast as I could. I had to get away! I could feel my heart beating and the muscles in my legs pumping. When I reached the top, I looked over my shoulder. Oh no! The monster was still following me. I heard him give an almighty roar. There's no way I can outrun him, I thought.

Dan ran up the hill as fast as he could, desperate to get away. His heart was beating and legs pumping. The monster was hot on his heels. When he got to the top, Dan looked over his shoulder and saw that he was being followed. Dan heard the monster give an almighty roar and knew that there was no way he could outrun him.

Third-person narrative: The narrator can see and hear everything that's happening—even things the main character isn't aware of.

25 BEGINNINGS

You have your story mapped out, you're clear where you want to go, and you've settled on your point of view and the age of your character. You're all ready to begin. So how do you draw your reader into the story and make sure they keep on reading?

START WITH A BANG

Do you start your story about Tom the farm-hand by giving an account of his morning visit to the cows, or do you start with "Tom could smell burning..."? Novice writers often make the mistake of opening their story by setting the scene: establishing the main character and the other characters around them, or painstakingly describing the house or village where they live. Even for historical fiction, where such detail is part of the intrinsic appeal of the genre, this is not a recipe for success. You need to grip your reader from the start and the best way to do this is with action and suspense.

PAGE-TURNING APPEAL

Action and excitement are essential ingredients in a story but nothing turns the pages better than mystery and suspense. After Tom has saved the barn from burning down he can come home to a note pinned to the kitchen table with a breadknife, saying "YOUR HOUSE IS NEXT." Then, as the story unfolds, the reader gradually gets to understand why Tom is in such a predicament, and wonders which of the other characters in the village is threatening him.

THE COMPETITION

Children have a bewildering array of distractions and entertainments. When it comes to filling their time, the proactive effort required to read a book faces stiff competition from such easy, passive pleasures as television, the internet, and computer games. Although your entire book should be exciting, the beginning must be unputdownable. After all, if your reader gets bored with it they're not going to make it to chapter two.

This is a poor opening paragraph because:

Rosie's age is stated. Child readers tend to be aspirational—they want to read about characters older than them. If you say Rosie is eight, a nine-year-old reader might put the book down. Leave ages to the reader's imagination.

The reader is given several details about Mark, the younger brother. But who is the main character of the story? These details distract when we should be drawing our first sketch of Rosie—the person whose story we are about to hear.

Eight-year-old Rosie thought about what she'd like to do today. Perhaps she'd go to the park, or perhaps she'd just stay at home. She went to find her brother, whose name was Mark and who liked to dig up worms in the backyard. He was two years younger than her. She was sure Mark would have a good idea about what to do. He always had good ideas. Rosie walked down the stairs and into the kitchen, then out of the back door and into the yard. Where was Mark?

It opens with Rosie thinking about what she'd like to do. Thought is not the most exciting way of opening a story. It's an internal process, and one that only Rosie can have, with no action for the reader to become involved with.

There is too much literal detail about Rosie's actions. The reader doesn't need the minutiae of walking downstairs, through the kitchen, out of the door and into the yard. She can just race outside.

GREAT OPENING LINES

> "There was a boy called Eustace Clarence Scrubb, and he almost deserved it."

C. S. Lewis, *The Voyage of the Dawn Treader* (1952)

> "It was a bright cold day in April, and the clocks were striking thirteen."

George Orwell, *Nineteen-Eighty Four* (1949)

> "It was the day my grandmother exploded."

Iain Banks, *The Crow Road* (1992)

Prologue 1:

Dear Reader

Welcome to a land far away. A young boy lives here—a boy without any parents. He has to find his own path in life, battling evil forces on the way. He will need your loyalty and courage as he encounters great evil. Will you stay by his side?

Prologues

Prologues are introductory paragraphs at the start of a story. They can supply a voice from outside of the story, introducing the world you are about to enter, or they can be a detail from the story you are about to hear, or they can work as notes from the narrator. The prologue works to whet the reader's appetite. It is often set in italic text to make it clear that it is not part of the main story.

The narrator's questions introduce the idea of choices within the story and paths not taken, and lead into the body of the narrative.

Prologue 2:

If I'd known then what I know now—would I have done the same things? Would I have stayed in the school dorms that night, safely tucked up in bed? Or would I have crept out of the latticed window and shimmied down the drainpipe all over again? I'll never know. But one thing I do know. Life throws up the most unexpected surprises—especially when you shimmy down a drainpipe…

This alternative is better because:

The book opens with a bang in the middle of the story—Rosie is already running outside.

It sets up physical details so that readers can imagine the characters: a pigtail bouncing; eyes shining with excitement.

The paragraph ends on a cliffhanger, drawing the reader in to keep on reading. What will Mark decide?

Rosie raced outside, her pigtail bouncing on her back.

"Mark!" she called up the garden. "Where are you?" Her little brother, covered in dirt, ran down the path toward her.

"What is it?" he asked. Rosie could see the excitement in his eyes.

"We're going on an adventure," she told him, holding out his backpack. She looked over her shoulder at the kitchen window, where she could see their mom clearing away the breakfast things. She hadn't noticed them.

"Where?" her brother asked, as Rosie turned back to face him.

She smiled. "You decide."

Instead of telling the reader that Mark likes digging in the backyard, the author shows him covered in dirt. The same detail is conveyed in both versions, but in version two the reader is shown rather than told.

Rather than describing Rosie's thoughts, the writer uses dialogue and action to propel the story: Rosie holds out a backpack to her brother and invites him on an adventure.

26 ENDINGS

A well-structured book will deliver a satisfying ending to make the reader feel all is well in the world and that the effort they have put into reading your book has been rewarded. A poor ending will leave them feeling frustrated and unlikely to want to read any more of your books. It is quite a responsibility to end your story well!

HAPPY ENDINGS?

It's a brave writer who ends his story with a dead main character. This might work in adult books or films (such as *Get Carter*), but it is an ill-advised ploy in children's fiction. Most parents, teachers, and other guardians of your readers' morals will expect wrongs to be righted and good to triumph. This is the only "decent" thing to do. Besides, a reader who has cared enough about your main character to read your book from beginning to end will want and expect them to have a happy ending.

PLOTTING THE END

You need to ensure your story is paced correctly. You don't want the most exciting part of your novel to happen two-thirds of the way in and then slowly unwind to the end.

Here are two common conclusions in children's fiction:

➡ The wind-down: the book climaxes in the penultimate chapter—the hero survives a terrible battle, and the baddie is thwarted and apprehended. The final chapter could then have an elegiac, wistful flavor, where loose ends are tied up and your hero ponders on the lessons he's learned and makes peace with other characters. He looks to the future, full of hope.

➡ The surprise ending: something totally unexpected occurs to tie up the story and explain everything that has preceded it. (Also known as a "twist in the tale.") If you follow this approach successfully, your reader

GREAT CLOSING LINES

The pressure is off if you've brought your readers this far. Unlike opening lines, it's difficult to analyze why closing lines work, being so connected with the text that has gone before. Here are some iconic examples:

> "He loved Big Brother."

George Orwell,
Nineteen-Eighty Four (1949)

> "Thank goodness for that, he said, and handed him the tobacco jar."

J. R. R. Tolkien, *The Hobbit* (1937)

> "He would be in Jem's room all night, and he would be there when Jem waked up in the morning."

Harper Lee, *To Kill a Mockingbird* (1960)

will be gripped to the last, but you must ensure you have left sufficient clues and references in your previous chapters to make the revelation plausible.

BAD ENDINGS

If your reader has persevered with your book it is most likely because they have enjoyed the way you have written it. A bad ending will spoil the good work of the preceding pages.

Here are four pitfalls to avoid:

➡ The ending just tails off and the book ends with a whimper—did you get bored with your own story or find you were well over your word limit?

➡ Loose ends go unexplained—life is often like this, but people feel cheated if you don't explain how some key event earlier in the story came to pass.

➡ Hurried endings with glib explanations—readers want more for their time and money!

➡ Pointless endings—everything is the same as it was at the start and nothing has been resolved. Again, life is often like this, but your reader will expect something more satisfying.

LOOSE ENDS

A good ending should tidy all the loose ends in a story. Who was it that left that note that triggered the whole adventure back in chapter one? Who was the mysterious stranger who rescued your hero in chapter five? Beware though, of tying everything up too neatly, especially if you are thinking of doing a "What happened to them next" summary for your main characters. If your book is a success, your publisher—and your army of eager readers—will be crying out for a sequel. If you have already mapped out the future lives of your characters you will have painted yourself into a corner and have nowhere else to go.

THE OPEN-ENDED ENDING

The end of one book does not necessarily need to mark the end of your character or ideas. In series fiction, there are other ways to conclude a story:

Cliffhanger endings

Cliffhanger endings make it blatantly clear that the story is not complete. A hero who is literally dangling from a cliff, someone being kidnapped, a new romance appearing in the last pages—all of these will encourage the reader to stay with your characters beyond one book.

The subtle clue

The end of a story can leave clues to how another story might lead on. Is there one crucial mystery still to be solved? A missing character or parent your hero or heroine would love to meet? A baddie who has escaped justice? All of these details could lead into a second story.

Character development

In most stories, the reader likes to see the main character mature and learn something about themselves. By the end of one story, your main character may still have a lot to learn. He or she may have learned humility, but still might struggle with impatience. Could that impatience lead into a whole new story?

To be continued...

Three of the most enticing words in language. This old-fashioned but appealing promise to the reader whets any appetite. But make sure you can deliver. If you promise more stories, it is important to map out your series idea carefully.

27

AGE LEVEL

Children change so quickly as they grow up that their books must be carefully crafted to accommodate these changes. As children's understanding of language increases and they grow more confident in their ability to read, there are books to suit every stage of this development.

KNOW YOUR AUDIENCE

To write successfully for a particular age range, use your common sense. Anyone who has children or teaches them will have a head-start on a writer who is unfamiliar with the target reader. If you want to write for children, know your audience.

As your target age-level goes up, you can increase the length of your sentences and the complexity of your vocabulary. As a general rule, the younger the child, the shorter the sentences. Aim for sentences of fewer than 20 words. Avoid too many clauses, like the ones in this sentence, as they can be difficult to read and irritating to the reader.

SIMPLE DOESN'T MEAN DULL

Don't be afraid of invention and sophistication at any level. The successful *Voices in the Park* by Anthony Browne (Corgi Children's, 1999) uses a variety of inventive devices, and yet it's written for the kindergarten and elementary school level. It tells a simple tale—about a visit to the park—from the different perspectives of its four main characters. The artwork is extraordinarily vivid, borrowing from Symbolist and Surrealist painters, and the characters all have flaws and foibles. Yet the text is rarely more complicated than, "I felt really happy," or "I called his name." The end result is a deeply resonant book that *Publishers Weekly* described as a celebration of "the redeeming power of connecting with another human being."

Throw out the rule book
Especially when children share books with siblings and friends, reading ages can become blurred. The age distinctions help parents and teachers choose the right books for the right audience, but they should be used as a guide rather than a set of rules—for readers *and* writers.

TO LABEL OR NOT TO LABEL?

Some children's publishers place a color-coded strip or a suggested age range on the spine or cover of their books. This enables teachers, or other adults buying a book as a gift, to have a clear idea of the level at which the book is pitched. But there is a downside to this practice. A struggling 10-year-old might find a book for six- to eight-year-olds more suited to his ability. But if it is labeled for this age-group, he might feel ashamed to be reading it and also lay himself open to mockery by his classmates.

HOW MANY WORDS?

There are some standard accepted lengths for children's books. Picture books rarely contain more than 500 to 600 words. "Early readers" for seven- to eight-year-olds will have around 1,000 to 6,000 words. Fiction pitched at older children could be anywhere between 30,000 and 60,000 words long. Any writer pitching a book to a publisher should bear these word counts in mind. If you go much beyond them, you will most likely struggle to get published.

MARATHON READS

Novels are invariably broken into chapters. Although you don't need to be consistent with chapter lengths, don't let them run too long. Most children will tire of a really long chapter. Plenty of short chapters will make a book more easily digested, especially for younger or less confident readers.

Broad levels

There are four broad age categories for children. Use the guidelines listed here to help you decide on the proper age range for your book.

AGE LEVELS

Reading ages are split into four broad levels. You will see books organized by these age ranges in bookstores. The word counts and page lengths detailed below are typical, but are not used exclusively; there is always some scope for flexibility:

0 to 3 years

Board books, cloth books, picture books; teaching the alphabet and simple words. These books will have no chapters and will rarely be more than 32 pages long.

4 to 7 years

As a child gets older, they turn to "first chapter books." This is the age at which children will first learn about a story being broken down into chapters, with a list of contents. A typical manuscript for this age-range will be about 4,000 words long. Books are often heavily illustrated and usually no longer than 64 pages.

8 to 12 years

Manuscripts in this age-range will be full-length novels of anywhere between 20,000 and 35,000 words long. A typical book will contain about 160 pages, with incidental illustrations.

13 years+

These books are aimed at the teenage market. Manuscripts can be around 60,000 words long and there is an increasing level of sophistication in terms of subject matter and narrative voice. Some of these books cross over into the adult market.

NOVELS

Children's novels cover the same genres as adult fiction—adventure, fantasy, horror, ghost stories, and gritty social realism. Often it is only the lack of graphic sex and gratuitously sadistic violence that sets them apart.

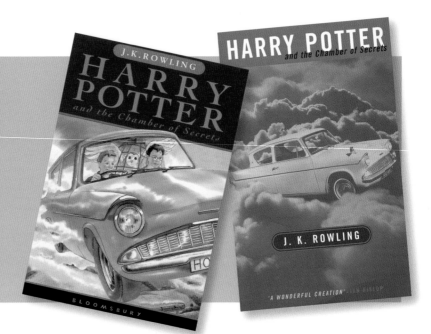

CROSSOVER BOOKS

Twenty-first century children's fiction seems to be going through a golden age—so much so that successful children's authors, such as JK Rowling, are often enjoyed by adult readers, too. This sub-genre of fiction has been described as "crossover." Rowling's UK publishers, Bloomsbury, even produce a separate edition of her Harry Potter series with a different cover, aimed at the adult market.

TWO STRANDS

Although publishers make micro-gradations between ages, pitching books at six- to seven-year-olds or nine- to ten-year-olds for example, children's novels fall into two main categories. First, there are stories for seven- and eight-year-olds often referred to as "first readers" or "primers." Such books are rarely longer than 6,000 words and are often part of a series or reading scheme. Then there are novels for older children. These will be considerably more demanding and run to 30,000 or 60,000 words. Pitching to exact ages here is more difficult. A confident eight-year-old may even enjoy books intended for a teenager or adult.

TABOO SUBJECTS

Some children's novelists, such as Judy Blume and Melvin Burgess, work successfully outside of the standard conventions of what is permissible in children's novels. They write about sex or drug use explicitly, for an early teen readership. While this approach has brought both critical and commercial success, most writers will find that raising these taboo subjects, and introducing swearing to dialogue, will make their books more difficult to sell—especially to schools, the home-school market, and public libraries.

WHAT'S THE DIFFERENCE?

In its own way, children's fiction can be just as demanding and as sophisticated as adult fiction. Mal Peet's novel *Tamar* (Candlewick Press, 2007), for example, gained exceptional reviews. Set in the terrifying netherworld of the Dutch Resistance during the winter of 1944, it is a morally complex tale, unfolding across past and present, in which characters are referred to by several names. Moreover, many of the main characters are adults. The style and complexity of the story makes it an equally suitable read for adults and children.

Mad about the boy

Harry Potter has starred in seven novels that appeal to both child and adult audiences around the world, shown here with their British edition covers.

SOME BASIC RULES

As children's fiction is so varied, and children of all abilities will find their own level, it is difficult to make hard and fast recommendations. But aside from story length, there are a few general conventions that writers seeking to be published should stick to. Children's fiction almost always places children at the heart of the story. Also, the protagonist will usually be at the top of the age range or slightly older than your core readership. So, if you write a book for 10- to 12-year-olds, then your hero should probably be twelve or thirteen. Most children are reluctant to read about central characters who are younger than they are.

ADVENTURE

Stormbreaker by Anthony Horowitz
(Candlewick Press, 2001)

The first in a series of books following teenage spy, Alex Rider.

Artemis Fowl by Eoin Colfer
(Miramax, 2001)

These books may be set in a land of fairies, but they are full of attitude.

All American Girl by Meg Cabot
(HarperTeen, 2002)

This book is full of adventure, humor, and "Top Ten" lists.

Mortal Engines by Philip Reeve
(HarperCollins, 2004)

This futuristic adventure is imaginative, epic, and fast-moving.

Swallows and Amazons by Arthur Ransome
(Red Fox, 1930)

Six children camp on an island in England's Lake District.

FANTASY

Point Fantasy series, various authors
(Scholastic, first book published 1993)

A long-standing series of fantasy stand-alone titles.

The Chronicles of Narnia series by CS Lewis
(HarperCollins, first book published 1950)

Generations of children have had their imagination fueled by this.

Beast Quest series by Adam Blade
(Scholastic, first book published 2007)

This series makes reading exciting for young boys.

Warriors by Erin Hunter
(HarperCollins, first book published 2004)

This series about wildcat clans has a devoted fanbase.

Harry Potter series by JK Rowling
(Scholastic, first book published 1997)

A seven-book series that has changed the face of children's book publishing forever.

HORROR

Point Horror series, various authors
(Scholastic, first book published 1984)

A series of books that has kept children reading after lights out.

The Midnight Library series by Nick Shadow and Damien Graves
(Scholastic, first book published 2005)

Each book is broken down into three stories—ideal for short attention spans.

Horowitz Horror by Anthony Horowitz
(Philomel, 1999)

Creepy short stories with a twist.

GHOST

Goosebumps series by RL Stine
(Scholastic, first book published 1992)

This series satisfies readers who want to come back again and again for another dose of fear.

Roald Dahl's Book of Ghost Stories by Roald Dahl
(Farrar, Straus, and Giroux, 1983)

Dahl did rigorous research before compiling this collection of fourteen stories.

Ghost Chamber by Celia Rees
(Hodder and Stoughton, 1997)

An ancient chamber and the restless ghost of a knight templar.

SOCIAL REALISM

The Illustrated Mum by Jacqueline Wilson
(Corgi Yearling, 1999)

This novel teaches children that no-one is perfect, not even parents.

Angus, Thongs and Full-Frontal Snogging by Louise Rennison
(HarperTeen, 1999)

The first in a series of laugh-out-loud books.

Doing It by Melvin Burgess
(Henry Holt and Co, 2003)

This is a controversial and funny novel for teenagers about sex.

The pitfalls of slang

Writers who choose to portray the real world rather than, say, fantasy or historical fiction, face the difficult task of accurately reflecting how their characters speak. Children love slang, and each generation has its own distinctive argot. Alas, nothing dates like hipspeak, except perhaps for "cool" which seems to have survived unscathed from the 1930s, when it first emerged from the American jazz underworld.

Unless you're writing for naturally transient media such as comics or teenage magazines, current slang should be used sparingly in fiction, if at all. Children today may say "And I'm, like, soooo… whatever!" to indicate indifference, and use "wicked" to mean good, but in 10 years' time these mannerisms will seem as archaic and quaint as the 50s slang spouted by hepcats and chicks in early Elvis movies.

Most people who write fiction from the heart rather than the wallet will want their books to last. The more fashionable slang you use, the more your book will date and it will have less appeal to future readers.

WICKED

GRAPHIC NOVELS

20

Comics, in one form or another, have been popular with children of all ages since the beginning of the 20th century. Hergé's *Tintin* books, for example, have a universal appeal and still sell well even though most were written more than 50 years ago. Although comics can be enjoyed by everyone, their combination of speech and illustration make them the perfect choice for reluctant or struggling readers. Over the last 20 years this form of storytelling has become increasingly more sophisticated, and the term "graphic novel" has been coined to describe comic books with genuine literary merit.

European genius
Created by Hergé (real name George Rémi), Tintin is recognized worldwide. One of the most popular characters from graphic novels, he's also probably the most long-running. The young reporter and his sidekick Snowy the dog first appeared in *Tintin in the Land of the Soviets*, published in 1930. Since then, many more adventures have been published, in more than 80 languages. Over 230 million copies of Tintin books have been sold worldwide.

WRITING GRAPHIC NOVELS

Unless they are without dialogue, such as Raymond Briggs' *The Snowman* or Quentin Blake's *Clown*, graphic novels have to be very tightly scripted. The writer must imagine their story in a series of boxes, like a movie storyboard. Most of the written information will be in the form of dialogue—in speech bubbles—with sparse narrative contained in boxes above or below the action.

SAME RULES, DIFFERENT STYLE

Graphic novels use the same rules of plot and character as any other fiction genre. The stories follow the same basic format of introduction, escalation, and resolution; and characters and dialogue are as important as they would be in a conventional novel. Fans of the genre would argue that giving the story an added visual

Tex Ritter was a western star—one of the best-known "singing cowboys" of the 1930s and 1940s.

element enhances it immensely. Critics would say it takes the fun away from picturing these characters and their dramas in your own imagination. In fact, *The Old Classics Illustrated* series of comic books of 1950s and 1960s were literally books in comic format. Children's classics by Dickens, Jules Verne, H.G. Wells, and many more were simplified and adapted.

Rod Cameron was a film star in the 1940s and 1950s; he starred in westerns among other things and was also immortalized in comic form.

Books in comic format
Here you can see a selection of comic books from the 1950s and 1960s—adapted and simplified from classic stories.

READ THIS!

For a perfect example of the creative use of comic formats in storytelling for younger readers look out for It Was a Dark and Silly Night edited by Art Spiegelman and Françoise Mouly (HarperCollins Children's Books, 2004). Here, famous graphic novelists and illustrators such as Neil Gaiman, William Joyce, and Gahan Wilson take this parody of one of literature's most infamous clichés and use it as a first line to build a story for seven- to nine-year-olds.

Fluffy
Fluffy, by Simone Lia is a fine example of a graphic novel for younger children.

DIFFERENT AUDIENCES

Many of the most popular graphic novels, such as Alan Moore's *Watchmen*, Frank Millar's *Batman: The Dark Knight Returns*, and Art Spiegelman's *Maus*, include levels of explicit sex, violence, and real or imagined horror that make them unsuitable for pre-teen children. But this a broad genre. Comics such as *Flash Gordon* and *Superman* have become iconic figures of popular culture that appeal to both children and adults.

The classics
Many classic novels have made it into graphic format, along with characters from myth and legend, and figures of popular culture such as Superman (left) and Flash Gordon (below).

Renaissance man

British graphic novelist Raymond Briggs, writer and illustrator of classics such as *The Snowman* and *Fungus the Bogeyman*, likens his work to a film. As a writer and illustrator of graphic novels he is also:

- the director placing his characters in the frame;

- the art director designing the sets;

- the costume designer taking care that his actors' clothes are right for them and the period;

- the cameraman, deciding whether to shoot the scene up close, or from a distance.

The Journal of Luke Kirby

The Journal of Luke Kirby first appeared in *2000AD*, scripted by Alan McKenzie and drawn by John Ridgway. Luke is an elementary school pupil who has discovered he has magical powers. Aided by his mentor Zeke, he fights against the evil that tries to infiltrate his hometown. Luke is roughly the same age as his readers— the comic has Disney-like vistas of the countryside that instantly establish a sense of time and place while creating a light-hearted atmosphere for the magical plot-lines.

Establishing time and place
In this early episode of *The Journal of Luke Kirby* the artist provides a wealth of background detail in the opening panel so that the reader has an immediate sense of time and place.

From strip to novel

Walt Kelly's "Pogo" the possum began life as a feature in *Animal Comics* in the late 1940s. When the cartoon became a regular strip in *The New York Star* its popularity soared—eventually, Pogo was signed by a syndicate and featured in four newspapers. Within five years, the possum was in over 400 papers nationwide. Kelly and his creation went from strength to strength—Pogo became the star of over 100 graphic novels, with around 30 million copies being sold worldwide.

Two consecutive dailies from Walt Kelly's Pogo strip. Note how Kelly uses the basic idea of Pogo's relationship to his son to provide several variations on a theme and milks the gag for all it is worth.

30 PAGE DYNAMICS

The design of a book is part of its message. A book with plenty of clean white space looks expensive, while bad typography makes a book look amateurish. This section introduces a few precepts of good book design in the areas of typography, grids, and layouts; it demonstrates how to plan the visual pace and flow of the book; and finally, it offers advice on color design.

TYPOGRAPHY

Fonts "say" something; they are not chosen at random. Although they exist in a different visual plane to the illustrations, we read meaning into the style of the typography as well as what is written. Children, before they can read, are aware of typographic conventions, and can see that typefaces can be expressive too.

FONTS

Fonts are broadly described as being "serif" or "sans serif." Traditional fonts like Times New Roman are serif fonts (defined as having a short decorative "foot" at the end of a stroke on a printed character); more modern fonts such as Arial and Helvetica are sans serif. Sans serif fonts are thought to be more legible for children learning to read. Fabula is quite a new font, developed after extensive research in the typographic department of Reading University in the UK in order to optimize legibility for young children. You can read about this font on their website at www.reading.ac.uk/typography/research/typknowledgetransfer.asp

Three examples of traditional typefaces used in children's books.

New Century Schoolbook — Serif

Georgia

Clarendon — Slab serif

sometimes he used to give me a lift...

Sense of calm
The delicacy of the artwork in pastel blue shades and the choice of font in the same blue sit comfortably together, evoking a sense of calm and mutual friendship.

CONSIDER THE TEXT

Have you left space for the text in your compositions? Many illustrators fall into the trap of overlooking this important factor. Good typographic design is unobtrusive, and works in harmony with the artwork, whereas bad type will draw attention to itself and detract from the smooth telling of the story.

Ask yourself: will a child read this book to themselves or will an adult be reading it aloud? This is an important consideration when deciding on a typeface. Children have less familiarity with different letterforms, so very expressive type will be difficult to decipher for them. If an adult is reading the book to a small child, however, expressive type can be a fun part of the picture—and even onomatopoeic in some cases.

Integrated text and pictures
This example shows how text and images can be skilfully integrated to create exciting visual effects. There is a variety of text used, from designed fonts to hand lettering, which suits the style of drawing and the graphic collage and scanned computer images.

Artworked fonts
In John Lawrence's *This Little Chick* (Candlewick, 2002), the text and images work together, using an engraving print technique. Both image and text are balanced in weight, and the layout of the text reflects the meaning of the words. Most children's books are still designed with a serif or sans serif typeface. This is especially true if there is a lot of text to be read. Good book design relies on the text and images sitting comfortably together. Not all stories or media techniques suit hand-lettered or unusual typefaces.

CRASH COURSE

Stop Stealing Sheep and Find Out How Type Works by Erik Spiekermann and E. M. Ginger (Adobe Press, 1993)

Designage: The Art of the Decorative Sign by Arnold Schwartzman (Chronical Books, 1998)

WEBSITES

Creating your own

Websites such as **www.fontographer.com** are an inexpensive way to create your own font. For a small fee, upload a template to generate your own hand-lettered alphabet, which is then scanned and sent back as a file. Now you can use the keyboard with your own font! Helpful websites include:

- **www.book-by-its-cover.com/**
  A blogger posts interesting book covers.

- **www.itcfonts.com/Ulc/4011/**
  An American typographic magazine.

- **www.eyemagazine.com**
  A graphic design magazine based in London.

TRY THIS

Text grids

Work to a grid when inserting text so that it conforms to a set of boundaries on the page, with controlled line lengths, and won't bunch up or fall into the middle of the page. Your illustrations can work around and through the grid, but the text should be in place before you think about the composition; there needs to be enough space and the artwork should not interfere with its legibility.

HAND-LETTERING AND COVERS

Hand-lettering is often used for cover artwork. The unevenness of the text stands out from the slickness of letterpress fonts and also creates a "cozy" feel suitable for children. Present it as a separate layer from the artwork to allow for foreign co-editions of your book to be created.

Remember that picture books will most likely be displayed with the cover facing outward, but may be stacked with other books. Place the title in the top third of the composition. Avoid using all capital letters; this seems to SHOUT and intimidates a young reader. Book covers can be embossed, foil-blocked, and have fabric and textural inlays.

Child's diary style

This book concept was based on a child's diary about her father needing and eventually having a heart transplant. The use of complementary colors enhances the simplicity.

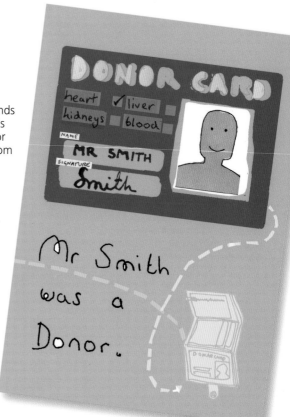

Integrating hand lettering
These three examples demonstrate further how hand lettering can be used to enhance and complement cover design.

Font categories

Decorative

■ *Based on traditional metal type*

Fairgrounds, canal barges, pub signs, and gravestone lettering, are all drawn from the folk art tradition. Illustrators' affinity with hand-lettering and ability to see words as images is part of this tradition.

Collage

■ *Using a mixture of fonts together*

Kurt Schwitters, a 1920s Dadaist artist and graphic designer, created dynamic magazine layouts by using found lettering and defying layout conventions. He has influenced Neville Brody and Sara Fanelli.

Calligraphic

■ *Fluid, "hand-drawn"*

In opposition to the restraints of holding a chisel or a nib pen (which create the serif of old-style fonts), holding a brush demands fluidity and spontaneity from the calligrapher.

Digital

■ *Can incorporate everything*

Interestingly, digital font designers foreground the "drawn" elements of typographic design. No longer tied to a grid, they experiment with legibility and uneven point sizing.

31 PACE AND FLOW—STORYBOARDING

Storyboarding is an essential part of planning a picture book. Since imagery and text are symbiotic, storyboarding helps you work out the relationship between the two in rough form. Picture books are usually 32 pages long: 12 double-page spreads for the story with endpapers, title page, and credits taking the remaining pages. Telling a story in 12 spreads is an art that requires you to tie the elements of pace, composition and color together; storyboarding makes that possible.

CRASH COURSE

Illustrators who use composition in surprising and interesting ways:

Mr. Lunch Borrows a Canoe
by J. Otto Seibold
(Viking Juvenile, 1994)

Biscuit Bear
by Mini Grey
(Red Fox, 2005)

A comprehensive and inspiring book about illustrating children's books:

Writing with Pictures
by Uri Shulevitz
(Watson and Guptill Publications, 1985)

Final composition

The storyboard is quite sketchy and is the perfect place to make notes and annotations about the story arc. However, note that the composition of the final spread artwork is almost unchanged; this is intrinsic to the working of the book as a whole and is fixed early on.

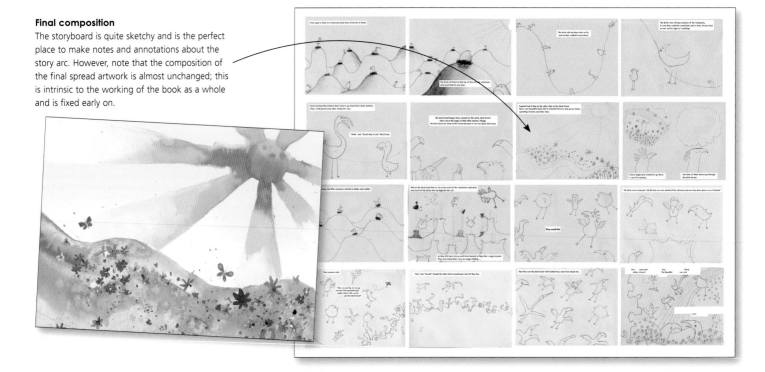

EXAMPLE STORYBOARDS

The varying approaches of these storyboards demonstrate the personal nature of planning a story at this stage. Some illustrators choose to work out the composition as rough geometric shapes; others prefer to block in a dominant color. Some have a very clear idea of the detail in the imagery, even at such a small scale.

This set of work shows how the initial ideas for the book have been clarified and refined through constant reworking and problem-solving. The drawings show a variety of close-up, long-shot, and dynamic compositions that keep the story interesting for a young reader. The color has been thought out too, which is explained in more detail further on in this section.

The book in miniature
Here, the storyboard represents the vision of the finished book in great detail. Nearly every element that will finally appear on the pages is here.

REASONS TO STORYBOARD

- It gives you a "bird's-eye" overview of the narrative.
- It helps you pace the story.
- You can try out different strategies to create visual movement.
- It helps you to check the rhythm of the story and find similarities and anomalies in the page compositions.

Text weights
On a slightly larger scale, you can use the storyboard technique to plan "thumbnails" of spreads, showing where images will be placed and the distribution of text weights. This technique is often used in nonfiction.

TRY THIS

- Draw up a set of 15 spreads on a large sheet of paper, blocking out the first two and the last one. This leaves you with 12 spreads to tell your story. Using layers of layout paper, work out your story quickly in thumbnail form. There is no need for a lot of detail. When you have finished, lay another piece of paper over the first one and work out the story in a little more detail. Now show your work to someone else—can they make sense of the story from your drawings? Is the emphasis of the story in the right place? Have you left room for the text in the compositions? Have you made sure that nothing important is in the gutter? When you come to do the "finished" artwork, you can enlarge these tiny sketches and use them for reference to keep the scale and freshness of your initial ideas.

- Take a picture book with compositions that you admire. Using the same grid as before, thumbnail the compositions in terms of simple geometric shapes and colors. This is a useful way to visually analyze a book's design. You can use the basic layouts and pictorial strategies as a starting point for your own compositions.

T'choupi est en colère contre maman.
Elle ne veut plus lui donner de gâteaux.
– Tu n'es pas gentille, maman !

T'choupi
A thumbnail analysis of an illustration from one of the *T'choupi* books by Thierry Courtin (Nathan).

Nicole Tadgell uses a storyboard to work out the visual pace and flow of a story called *Fatuma's New Cloth* by Leslie Bulion (Moon Mountain Publishing). She plans her storyboards as film directors plan movies, so the first two images are "zoomed out," showing the landscape of Tanzania where the story takes place. Then we gradually "zoom in" and see the two main characters and become involved in their story. The illustrator keeps the action interesting, varying the sizes of the characters from close up to farther away, and even crossing the gutter for more dramatic effect.

Action across the gutter
You need to know the trimmed page size of the book to ensure that no important visual information falls into the gutter.

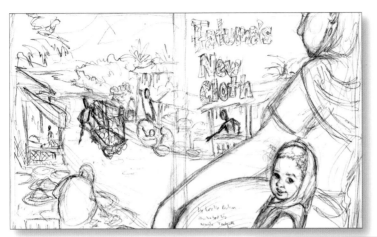

1 Jacket rough

Pencil rough of jacket image with type roughed in, and more final watercolor image. The cover was commissioned to be done first, so the publisher could make catalogs and other promotional materials.

2 Watercolor test

This is a "color test" created on low-quality paper. It's actually a photocopy of the final drawing, painted very loosely and quickly because the illustrator's goal was about making color choices for the whole book. Since both characters were side-by-side on this page, it was good to make sure their kanga cloth colors went well together.

"I am glad to have your help in the market today, Fatuma."

"I like to carry the basket for you, Mama."

3 Final illustration

This is the final jacket illustration. It's watercolor paint on watercolor paper. The composition, surprisingly, did not change at all from the initial sketch (top) to the final image.

VISUAL STORYTELLING

These spreads from *Pudding* by Pippa Goodhart and Caroline Jayne Church (The Chicken House, 2004) show the variety of composition and "film language" employed in telling a story visually.

1 *The characters are shown on different sides of the double page spread, in the same pictorial plane but separated by the gutter.*

2 *The horizon line moves up and pushes the protagonists to the back of the picture plane. In the foreground, other children and other puppies are playing, to underline the message that the girl and the dog should be friends.*

3 *The use of extreme close-up on the dog is a good way to show heightened emotion in a character as it allows you to draw their expression in greater detail. The "long shot" on the girl gives us a sense of her isolation. She is walking away from the dog—this leads the reader into the next page, as we read from left to right. Characters usually move in this direction unless the story is making a point.*

4 *The horizon line of the floor leads the eye up the side of the tablecloth and down the spilt milk to where the dog is hiding.*

5 *The curved diagonal creates a springing dynamic to this composition, adding movement to Pudding's escape.*

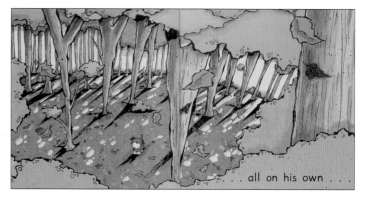

6 *The forest is a mass of vertical lines: the forced perspective gives a bird's eye view of this part of the story. The dog is hard to find, and a sharp-eyed child will see that he is not alone, as the text suggests, but that the little girl is hiding behind a tree nearby.*

7 *The girl reaches over from the right-hand page to stroke the dog on the left hand page. This breaches the visual distance that they had before.*

8 *The two characters find each other but are still separated by the gutter and are on different horizon lines. They have made eye contact.*

9 *Extreme close-up of the two characters together reinforces that this is the emotional core of the book—the point of the story.*

10 *The characters revisit the scene of Pudding's earlier misery and run back down toward his home, away from the woods where they both were lost.*

11 *The characters are together on an adventure, almost moving out of frame at the side of the book.*

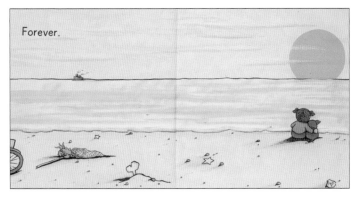

12 *The stable horizon lines emphasize the new-found security of the friends. They are shown with their backs to the reader in a medium long shot as the "camera" disengages from the story.*

32 DUMMY BOOKS

Creating storyboards and rough mock-ups of your book will have allowed you to plan and explore its structure, but to get a real sense of the finished product you need to create a much more accurate "dummy" version. You can use this to convince a publisher that your book is a product worth publishing. The finished dummy should look as similar to the intended end result as possible in terms of format, content, and feel.

ASSESSING YOUR BOOK

This is the point at which you make up pages of the intended size, or format, of the printed book. You may find that what works on a small scale does not work compositionally on a larger scale. Pin your double page spreads sequentially on a wall or lay them out on a table and look at them critically to see if the pace, flow, feel, and structure of the book is exactly as you want. Make changes at this stage if you need to.

Once you are satisfied with all the spreads, make accurate detailed line drawings of the pages, blocking the text as accurately as possible in terms of style, point-size, and the space it occupies on the page, whether it is hand-lettered or a font. Photocopy or scan the double page spreads, and use these copies to make up the dummy book.

You can also produce a more detailed dummy by creating final pieces of artwork for two or three spreads. Use the finished artwork to show your media and technique skills. Photocopy or scan them and integrate these copies with the other detailed line drawing pages. See page 138 for more about making dummy books.

Dummy book example
A dummy book lets the illustrator see how the artwork works dynamically across the spreads, and whether any vital information will be lost in the gutter.

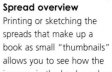

Spread overview
Printing or sketching the spreads that make up a book as small "thumbnails" allows you to see how the imagery in the book works as a whole, and to get a sense of the pacing.

COMPOSITION TIPS

It is often possible to reduce strong page designs into their basic component elements in order to analyze how and why they work to engage the reader and enhance the narrative.

- Contrasting simplicity and lots of white space on some pages with full, complex images on others adds variety and interest.

- Playing with scale can make page layouts more dynamic.

The duckling is standing in a field of simple vertical lines of foliage, looking up at the swans flying in horizontal lines across the top of the page, creating a sense of calm, order, and balance (above and right).

The combination of the hen in the top left corner, the little chick in the middle, and the smaller hen in the bottom right corner creates a sense of movement along this diagonal composition, which is increased by the exaggerated actions of the characters (below and left).

Cropping the elephant to show only one leg and part of the body exaggerates its size and weight. Placing the image within a white space draws attention to the hedgehog straining under the weight of the elephant.

The figure in the foreground is cropped very severely, which forces the reader to engage with the character.

WRAP-AROUND COVER

Many hardback books have a simple, loose, wrap-around cover or dust-jacket. Usually the book binding is plain with the cover design appearing only on the dust-jacket itself. Remember to allow for the width of the cover boards of your book in any measurements you make so that the cover fits exactly. For more on making a dummy book, see page 138.

Prepare the artwork
Prepare the artwork including the necessary extra measurements around the edges. Trim the height of the cover along the registration marks, to fit the height of the cover of the book.

Form the spine
Measure the spine and mark the measurement on the cover illustration. Fold and press the width of the spine on the cover illustration using a bone folder.

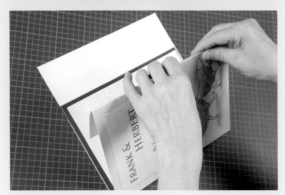

Cover the book
Place the book into the folded space and fold the ends around the edges of the book. Press down firmly with a bone folder. Place the loose cover around the book.

y morning
a prickly
termelon."
special

nt." said

"When I was a boy, I wanted a dog,"
said Grandpap. "You're going to wish
for a dog."
Charlie shook his head.

33 COLOR THEORY

The ever-expanding range of colors available across a wide range of media can be a little overwhelming. It is important to understand how color works and how to mix colors in order to produce a successful and professional-looking piece of final artwork.

LEARNING COLOR CONTROL

Studying the theory behind color combinations will enable you to develop the same level of control over color as you have over the composition of an illustration. Investigate color mixing and color combinations, and explore how you can vary shades and tones to create weight, depth, or atmosphere. Learn by critically assessing how other successful illustrators control their palettes. Take inspiration from nature and all forms of art and crafts. Spending time on basic color exercises may seem laborious, but it is well worth the effort. The color wheel shows some simple but very important color theory principles that you can use to make your work stronger and more characterful. It does not have to be followed slavishly, but understanding a few simple guidelines will benefit you greatly.

THE COLOR WHEEL

When the primary and secondary colors are arranged in a circle they form a "color wheel." The primary colors are red, yellow, and blue. In theory you can mix any color from just these three. Browns and neutrals can be mixed from combinations of the three primary colors. The secondary colors are created by mixing two primaries in equal or varying amounts.

WARM AND COOL COLORS

Cool colors are usually thought to be green, blue, and violet, and warm colors thought to be red, yellow, and orange. In simple terms, they can be used to create the illusion of space and depth; cool colors appear to recede and warm colors seem to come out toward you. Apply cool colors for the backgrounds and warm colors for characters or foreground objects.

Six-section color wheel
A basic color wheel shows the primaries and secondaries. The former can only be bought as manufactured pigments, and the latter can either be bought or mixed from the neighboring primaries.

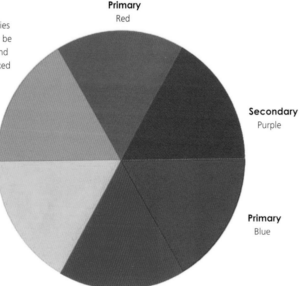

Primary
Red

Secondary
Purple

Primary
Blue

Secondary
Green

Primary
Yellow

Secondary
Orange

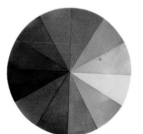

Tertiary color wheel
Mixing the primaries and secondaries on the basic wheel gives six extra mixes, or colors, called "tertiaries."

Two halves
The wheel can be roughly split in half to show warm and cool segments.

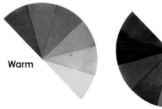
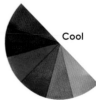

Warm

Cool

Each pigment has its own warm or cool bias. For example, cadmium yellow has a lot of red in it, making it warm, while lemon yellow has a cool blue bias. Keep this principle in mind as you mix clear bright secondaries that aren't dull or muddy. We have seen in the color wheel opposite that red and blue make violet, but which red and which blue? Is it cadmium red or alizarin crimson? And is the blue color cobalt, phthalo, or cerulean?

HARMONIOUS COLORS

This color scheme, also known as "analagous colors," uses hues that lie next to each other on the color wheel; for example, shades of green, turquoise, and blue are harmonious. It is an easy way to be sure that your colors will work well together, although the scheme may lack a central focus or punch.

COMPLEMENTARY COLORS

"Complementary" can be a confusing term when it is used to describe the relationship between colors, because it refers to the colors that lie opposite each other on the color wheel. When put together they seem to dance or vibrate, as in some of Bridget Riley's paintings of the 1960s. This principle can be used to shocking visual effect in your illustrations. For example, if you wanted a lively color scheme, you could use red and green as the main colors. Adding a black outline helps to retain shapes of characters and objects against the background.

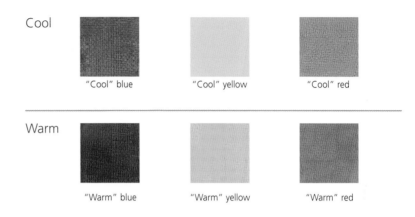

Cool
"Cool" blue   "Cool" yellow   "Cool" red

Warm
"Warm" blue   "Warm" yellow   "Warm" red

Color bias
The color bias of a pigment shows up clearly when it is placed next to a similar hue (right). The choice of primary color determines the resulting secondary mix. Those closest together on the wheel create intense secondaries (below left), while those farthest apart create more muted secondaries (below right).

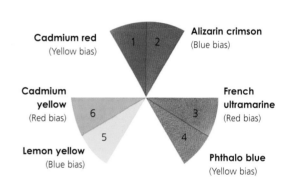

Cadmium red
(Yellow bias)   Alizarin crimson
(Blue bias)

Cadmium yellow
(Red bias)   French ultramarine
(Red bias)

Lemon yellow
(Blue bias)   Phthalo blue
(Yellow bias)

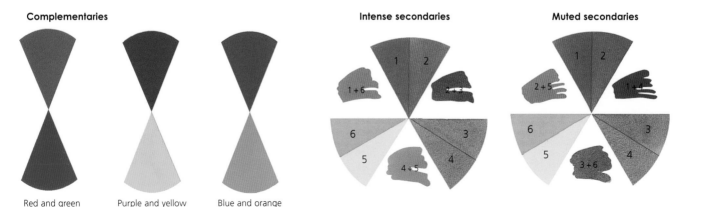

Complementaries

Red and green   Purple and yellow   Blue and orange

Intense secondaries

Muted secondaries

TRY THESE

Art materials can be expensive, so it makes financial and aesthetic sense to try some color exercises so that you know what works best for your illustration.

Use the exercises shown here. If you purchase a new color it is a good idea to test it with your favorite colors to see how the two colors combine. The results just might surprise you.

Flame red   Winsor green

Alizarin crimson   Winsor green

Neutrals test
Mix the complementary colors red and green. See how the blue-biased alizarin crimson adds a more violet tinge to the neutral mix.

White-out test
Test colors in progressively whiter mixes to make lighter tones. Note—it doesn't take as many steps to create the lighter-toned yellow.

Color match test
Paint or shade with pencil your own grayscale in nine or ten graded steps. Then try mixing a color into swatches to match the scale. Here ultramarine has been mixed with black and white to make a shade and a tint respectively. However, it is best to avoid adding black to a color in an illustration as it can make the color dull.

NEUTRALS

Not all your work will require bright colors; sometimes a muted or subtle color scheme is appropriate. Rather than use manufactured grays or neutrals you can mix your own using complementary colors. We have already learned that if they are used as pure pigments set by each other, complementary colors set up a vibrant contrast. When physically mixed, however, they create a neutral gray. The better the visual complement (i.e. the better the position of the two colors opposite each other on the color wheel), the more neutral or unbiased the resulting gray. Experiment with different complementary mixes and see which you prefer.

Mixing gray
The complementaries emerald green and cadmium red mix to make a subtle yet characterful gray neutral.

TONE OF COLORS

This is the degree of lightness or darkness of a color. Each color has its own tone in its pure, unmixed form. The tone of yellow is fundamentally lighter than blue when compared to a grayscale. But you can change this by adding a lot of white to the blue to make it lighter in tone, or by adding ultramarine to yellow to make a rich dark green. So why is this important? Assessing the tones of your work as you go helps you emphasize the elements you want so they have a more dominant tone than the rest of the illustration. Try half-closing your eyes (it simplifies the details so you see the tones more clearly) or looking at your work in a mirror. This way you can assess the range and hierarchy of tones in your visual story.

A blue mixed with white to make a lighter tone— this is known as a tint.

A green mixed with black to make a darker tone—this is known as a shade.

The important secondary

As the main color in nature, green is the most mixed of the secondaries. It can be a difficult color to paint with—many of the most successful greens are mixed from two primary colors (blue and yellow) rather than applied directly from a green pigment. Luckily there is a large range of cool and warm blues and yellows, so the possibilities for creating shades like lime and moss are vast. To begin, acquire a selection of yellows and blues (as well as black) to give you a variety of options for green shades. Not only will your particular shade be more unique, but it's fun to do. You can also modify a bought pigment green to make more varied shades. Then try the deceptively simple exercise as shown here.

Cadmium yellow ⟶   ⟵ Ultramarine blue

Cadmium yellow ⟶   ⟵ Ultramarine blue

Lemon yellow ⟶   ⟵ Cobalt blue

Blue and yellow don't necessarily make green

This is another fun exercise to try. Make a chart by mixing a selection of six or so blues and yellows. Choose colors that will exemplify the full range of possibilities—for example an orangey yellow and a turquoise—so that you discover the subtle brown greens and emeralds that are possible. Keep the chart pinned to your wall for reference, and remember to make notes of the colors. In six months you will have forgotten!

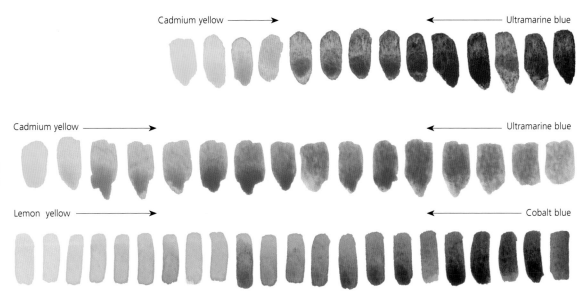

CRASH COURSE

Color Harmony 2: A Guide to Creative Color Combinations by B.M. Whelan (Rockport Publishers Inc., 1995)

The Complete Color Harmony: Expert Color Information for Professional Color Results by T. Sotton and B.M. Whelan (Rockport Publishers Inc., 2004)

Watercolor Mixing Directory by Moira Clinch and David Webb (Walter Foster, 2006)

34 DESIGNING WITH COLOR

Color is an important tool that an artist can use to communicate. In picture books, where the visual impact of illustrations is fundamental, color can have a considerable influence on how a story will be read if it is used carefully.

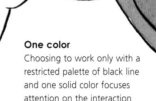

One color

Choosing to work only with a restricted palette of black line and one solid color focuses attention on the interaction between the two characters.

Limited palette

A limited palette of colors, using subtle, dark hues, heightens the mood of the story, in which there are blurred boundaries between dream and reality.

COLOR PSYCHOLOGY

Color enhances the mood and atmosphere of a story. Not only does each color have its own particular associations, but the color in an illustration often communicates the story's tone before words are read. Colors in picture books need not be realistic or true to life. For example, trees may be blue or pink, dogs red, or elephants multicolored (think of Elmer). The important thing is for the child to be able to recognize and identify the images and shapes.

Two colors

The use of flat color as a background focuses attention on the detailed line drawing and creates a contrast between the two. The addition of a small area of a second color directs the eye to the focal point on the page—the sleeping duck.

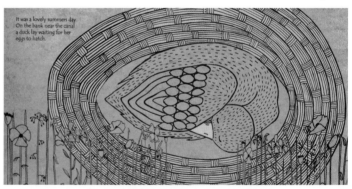

It was a lovely summers day. On the bank near the canal a duck lay waiting for her eggs to hatch.

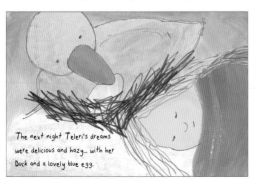

The next night Teleri's dreams were delicious and hazy... with her Duck and a lovely blue egg.

In the morning Teleri woke up and rubbed her sleepy eyes.

She stretched and she yawned as her dreams slipped away from her...

And when she landed back down on the soft dreamy snow, she was surprised to see how like a bird she was.

Your choice of color may be dictated by the story—for example it might be set at night or on a hot, sunny day. Sometimes a limited, or even monochrome, palette is used for reasons of fashion, simplicity, or to emphasize a character in a story where the situation is immaterial. Whatever the reason for your choices, they should be well considered to strengthen the impact and intention of the book.

yellow thing in the garden.

Experiment

Paint a different color option for a central image such as a frog, then try various colors of backgrounds and see how the harmonious colors act as a camouflage while the stong complimentary or tonal contrasts exaggerate the shape or surreal nature of the image.

Pure color

Using primary and secondary colors gives a bright, colorful feel for younger children. Focus on the main character has been achieved by using black for Patch the dog, which creates contrast and makes him stand out from the colorful backgrounds.

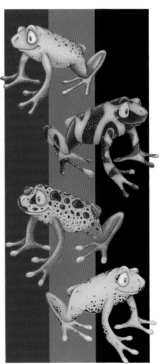

READ THIS

Pumpkin Soup by Helen Cooper (Farrar, Straus and Giroux, 1998)

Moody, atmospheric, and use of limited palette.

Don't let the Pigeon Drive the Bus by Mo Willens (Hyperion Press, 2003)

Contemporary feel to a simple, humorous story.

Princesses oubliées ou inconnues (the Princesses Series) by Rebecca Dautremer (Gautier Languereau, 2004)

A French illustrator uses red and green with sophistication.

Farmer Duck by Helen Oxenbury (Candlewick Press, 1992)

Realistic representation of the weather, time of day, and situation.

CRASH COURSE

Designer's Guide to Color: Bk. 5 by I. Shibukawa and Y. Takahashi (Chronicle Books, 1992)

Looks at combinations of colors to suggest palettes for different psychological needs.

35 PAPER ENGINEERING

Although often classed within novelty books, the tradition of "true" pop-ups (three-dimensional structures formed by creasing paper and activated using kinetic energy) is essentially paper construction based on three simple formulas: the "V" fold, the parallelogram, and the "45" fold.

PAPER ENGINEERING

An artist who creates pop-ups is known as a "paper engineer." Most paper engineers learn their craft by dismantling existing examples, but there is an increasing number of instructional books that explain the basic mechanics. Learning the rules will give you a sound basis and understanding to work from. But once learned, the rules are there to be broken!

The production of a pop-up book is a carefully planned process. During the design process you will need to play with many paper samples to resolve the mechanics. Most often the paper engineer only plans the mechanics and employs an illustrator to create the visual effects.

Pop-ups can be very simple or sophisticated, depending on the target audience they wish to engage, the story or concept, and the budget of the publishing house. The only limitations are those of the imagination of the designer!

Pop-ups for young readers
Paper-engineered books can be great fun for young children. But remember that they will need to be robustly designed and free of sharp corners.

TRY THIS

Making a pop-up

The simplest pop-up construction is the "V" fold. It requires only one folded pop-up piece with gluing tabs and gives you the opportunity to see how size and angles will affect the projection and the composition on the page. It may be simple but it still requires accuracy of folding, cutting, and gluing if the pop-up is to sit comfortably within the double page spread.

Materials you will need:
- Paper or card (149 lb)
- Pencil
- Steel rule
- Craft knife (with a new blade)
- Scissors (with a sharp point)
- Scoring tool—such as a dry ballpoint pen
- Glue—clear, solvent-based (not a glue stick)
- Cutting mat
- Paper knife—to stick down corners and edges and ensure accurate contact

Method:
1 The book is designed by the paper engineer and tested as a rough dummy. Tracings are used for nesting (determining how much paper will be required) and can also be used as a guide for creating the artwork. Minor changes are often made before the die is planned and artwork produced. A working dummy is produced from the first proofs and the operation of the pop-up tested before investment is placed in the mantling of the final die to cut the paper.

Pop-ups are printed and then assembled by hand as a labor-intensive process usually carried out abroad.

2 There are three kinds of folded line in a pop-up mechanism: valley folds: crease goes back from view; mountain folds: crease comes forward toward you; the spine of the book: center of the double page (base to the mechanism). Remember to score all the folds with a ruler and scoring tool to ensure they are straight and crisp.

Arts and crafts
Paper engineering takes beautiful illustrations and artifacts to another level in high-specification books.

Pop-up nonfiction
Pop-ups can be a fabulous way of bringing concepts to life in a very tangible and understandable way for all age levels, making them the perfect medium for highly illustrated nonfiction.

Looking through
Paper engineering can be as simple as an extra fold-out page with a die-cut hole. This provides another layer of possible interaction and interest for the reader.

CRASH COURSE

The Elements of Pop-Up by David A. Carter and James Diaz (Little Simon, 1999)

An excellent range of samples to unpick and put back together.

The Pop-Up Book by Paul Jackson (Henry Holt and Company, 1994)

Simple diagrams, clear explanations, and photographed samples illustrate the professionalism of the craft.

Pop-Up: a Manual of Paper Mechanisms by Duncan Birmingham (Tarquin, 1999)

This book offers clear step-by-step instructions and drawings.

Paper Engineering for Pop-Up Books and Cards by Mark Hiner (Tarquin, 1986)

Read this book to gain a more thorough understanding of pop-up book mechanics.

36

NOVELTY BOOKS

Novelty books are designed to appeal to the curiosity of young children and promote learning through play. Investigation using touch, pull tabs, turning wheels, lifting flaps, and mirrors has inspired and generated a diverse range of published material.

CRASH COURSE

The Very Hungry Caterpillar by Eric Carle
(Philomel, 1981; first published 1969)

This is possibly the most popular novelty book of all time. It is based on a simple storyline, but the overall design of the book is what makes it really special. The use of texture, color, and white space stimulates intrigue and makes it a delightful book for children.

Dear Zoo by Rod Campbell
(Little Simon, 1986; first
published 1982)

Very simple, this book delights children as they uncover the animals from page to page.

Peepo by Alan and Janet Ahlberg
(Puffin Books, 1983)

Slightly more sophisticated, this book is comprised of a series of holes that peep through to the next page. It has lots of interesting elements to reveal!

Pop-out scare
Haunted House by Jan Pieńkowski is a pop-up book full of shocking surprises and creepy scares. As readers enter the rooms page by page, imaginatively designed creatures jump out from hidden corners.

Interactivity
Pirate Pete by Nick Sharratt introduces an element of interactivity by using cut-out "stickers" that can be inserted in slots to complete sentences.

Novelty books can be produced with a wide range of materials. Padded, textured, or cutaway book covers enhance the look of a book, and gimmicks such as plastic squeaky toys are used to attract attention. Microchip technology offers the use of unlimited everyday sounds, play tunes, and nursery rhymes, and it is also popular for books to include small gifts or CDs. The publishing market is competitive and has to respond to the needs of consumers wanting more for their money than just a book!

COMPETITION FOR LEISURE TIME

An increased disposable income of many families, huge technological developments, and changes in the use of leisure time has put tremendous pressure on the traditional pastime of reading. The vast range of entertainment available to the more fortunate and demanding generation of today means that concepts in children's publishing need to be original and eye-catching if they are to compete and survive.

Books or toys?

Increasingly sophisticated production techniques and the resulting lower cost of producing novelty books has led to an explosion of products that blur the line between simple reading material and interactive toys.

TRY THIS

Design some spreads

Using the theme of "Jungle Animals," design five double-page spreads to visually stimulate a young child. Experiment with collage and three-dimensional materials, be imaginative, and remember: if images are produced three-dimensionally, they need to be photographed to indicate how the final artwork would be seen.

Make a board book

Generally, a board book or pop-up book contains six to eight pages, although they can sometimes have 12 to 16. The process of putting together a mock-up board book is the same as a picture book, but uses sheets of stiff card cut accurately to the correct page size, and placed between the photocopied pages.

TIP

Textures and foils can look professional enough in mock-ups—if glued very carefully—but the extra weight will make it more likely to pull apart, so use the appropriate glues. Avoid getting glue on the pages and artwork—mock-ups still need to look clean.

37 BOOK JACKETS

The book's cover, or jacket, not only protects its pages but is a major selling point in the very competitive market of children's books. The marketing of a book relies on the jacket for its success.

MAKING COVERS WORK

Most children's books have illustrated covers, sometimes fully illustrated and sometimes partly illustrated. A good book jacket reflects the style and content of the book in a way that captures the attention of a potential buyer. To ensure that this requirement is met, there is often a close working relationship between the designer and illustrator, editor, and marketing department within the publishing house.

TIPS FOR JACKET DESIGN

Be aware that a picture book will most likely be displayed in bookstores and libraries stacked up with other books. Therefore you should place the title in the top third of the composition, and should design an interesting spine for the book as well. The text font should match the content and style of the story and illustrations. Feel free to have fun with it, but make sure that it reflects the tone of the story and doesn't send mixed messages to the reader.

Remember that the book cover will often be reduced to a thumbnail image for reviews and catalogs; the title should be large and legible.

Since the front cover illustration introduces the characters with a close-up, the back cover illustration can open up into a landscape and create text space.

A book's spine should include the author's name, the book title, the name of the series if there is one, and the name of the publisher.

On this cover the title font matches the polar bear's fluffy fur and the falling snow.

In a picture book, the illustrator is responsible for the images on all 32 pages of the book, including the cover, retaining the same style of drawing and media throughout. Sometimes the image for the book jacket can be an image or a cropped image taken from the pages of the book, but mostly it is an image that has been designed specifically for the cover. In books for older children—especially in paperback form—there are often either no illustrations, or only black-and-white line illustrations. Jacket commissions may come with additional black and white illustrations required, so the whole book is produced by the same artist. However, it is quite common for the cover and the drawings inside a book to be illustrated by different artists, especially if the jacket is for an update of an existing book.

Foreign editions

Sometimes different covers will be produced for different markets—here, the Australian, Italian, and French editions of the same book are shown.

Designing the type

Inside a book you will often be restricted to black type to make it easier for the publisher to sell to foreign markets. But on the cover (which is usually specific to a particular market) you will have the freedom to build colored type into the design.

Illuminating historical facts
Illustrating facts that can't
be represented as photographs
is an important area for
illustrators (see page 108).

Chapter four

NONFICTION

Writing and illustrating children's nonfiction is not simply about creating a shorter version of a book for adults. The whole concept is different and the presentation more direct. There is an art to writing and illustrating nonfiction for a young market, and there should be nothing prosaic about such work.

THE NONFICTION MARKET

It is difficult for an unknown writer to break into publishing, and this is especially so for nonfiction, which is almost a closed shop. Nonetheless, there are still openings, especially for writers with fresh ideas for text-led, rather than design-led, books.

What sells?
Try to get hold of a publisher's catalog to get a feel for the kinds of subjects that sell, year after year.

ORIGINATION OF IDEAS

Most nonfiction book ideas originate with the publisher. They may float an idea—with a makeshift cover and a couple of inside spreads—at the book fairs that are part of the annual publishing calendar. If buyers from the big bookstore chains and supermarkets are enthusiastic, the publisher will then hire a freelance writer to write the book to a specific brief.

WHO WRITES NONFICTION?

Most children's nonfiction publishers consider it such a specialist market that they only employ writers with previous experience of this genre. Some will only employ people who have previously worked with them, regardless of their experience.

The reason publishers like to work with proven authors is fairly simple. Writing information books for children requires specialist knowledge. Unlike fiction, most information books are highly illustrated. Such books are often referred to as "integrated"—where words and pictures work together to provide information. A writer of such books need to understand how best to present information in this way. They often have to work closely with the book's designer, fitting text and captions around illustrations.

Former teachers are considered especially suitable for nonfiction writing. Publishers may also employ people who have some celebrity attached to the subject they are writing about—for example a well-known weatherman who appears on national television may be asked to write a book about weather.

Bright sparks
Today's children are computer-
literate from an early age. Your job
is to spark their imagination and
make sure they keep reading, too.

Stiff competition

Over the last ten years the internet has become a serious rival to nonfiction books. Many children now make Google their first stop when researching homework, rather than the school library. The demand for information books has dropped. Because of this, bookshops have reduced display space. Profit margins have been squeezed and publishers have to contend with lower budgets for writers and illustrations. This is a vicious circle—it makes it more difficult for a book to appear exciting and "cool" compared to the audiovisual possibilities of the internet.

This is a disturbing trend, not least because the quality of information on the internet is unpredictable. Information books are carefully researched and written by a professional writer skilled in communicating with the reader. They will have been checked by an editor and an academic expert. A website, on the other hand, could have been written by an enthusiastic amateur or a blinkered obsessive. It takes a skill and maturity beyond the average school-age child to spot the sites that offer opinion or propaganda rather than even-handed information.

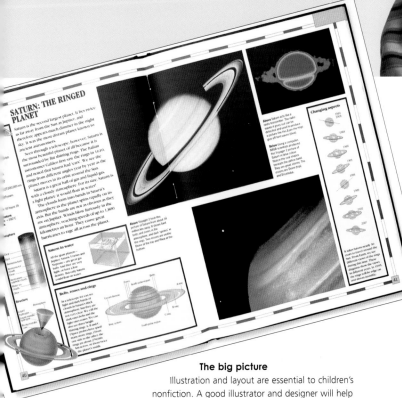

The big picture
Illustration and layout are essential to children's nonfiction. A good illustrator and designer will help you get your message across in an accessible way.

NEW APPROACHES

In the past, nonfiction has been seen as the worthy and dull end of the children's book market. More recently, publishers have had huge success with innovative illustration-led books, such as the *Eyewitness Guides* produced by Dorling Kindersley, and entertaining projects such as Scholastic's *Horrible Histories*.

The world of children's nonfiction is not completely closed to outsiders. If you can think of a new angle to a familiar subject, it is still worth approaching publishers. Find out about publishers who produce books in a similar field to your idea via your library, local bookstore, or a publishing directory, and contact them with a proposal.

STICK TO SCHOOL SUBJECTS

Information books that follow the school curriculum will be more likely to sell than those that do not. Your pet idea about aboriginal peoples in Southeast Asia is less likely to be considered, no matter how interesting, than one about the Civil War or the Industrial Revolution.

ILLUSTRATING NONFICTION

Appealing illustrations are an essential ingredient of children's picture books, and this is also the case with nonfiction books. In making the book a desirable item to purchase, illustrations can have an impact far more immediate than the text. The standard of illustration across all children's publishing is invariably high and illustrators will usually be art-school graduates at the very least.

HOW ILLUSTRATORS WORK

Although artwork in a nonfiction book is central to its appeal, the illustrator will usually be given a much tighter brief than, for example, a picture book artist would. The content will be carefully planned out beforehand by the writer, editor, and designer. The illustrator will then be sent a detailed brief with references, along with a spread worked up by the designer, showing exactly what the illustration needs to look like and how it will fit into the design of the book.

AGENTS

As an illustrator you will have to decide whether to approach publishers directly or employ an agent. Agents know their market, and they know how to match illustrators and publishing clients. They are often approached directly by publishers looking for a particular style of artwork, and they will be able to negotiate a fair rate for a particular piece of work. In return for these services they will charge around 15 per cent of your fee.

ILLUSTRATION STYLES

Nonfiction illustrators work in a variety of ways. Some produce colorful recreations of dramatic moments or everyday lives from history. Such artwork requires a serious knowledge of the period and many thoroughly-researched references. Science and "how things work" books often feature a flatter, more diagrammatic style of artwork. Then there are alphabet and counting books for early learners, where the illustrator's work will be the major selling point of the book. On the edge of the nonfiction illustration genre are puzzle books, such as the hugely successful *Where's Waldo* series by Martin Handford (Candlewick Press, 1987).

Age and subject matter
Nonfiction illustrations can vary in complexity, depending on the age of the reader and the subject matter, as shown in these book spreads.

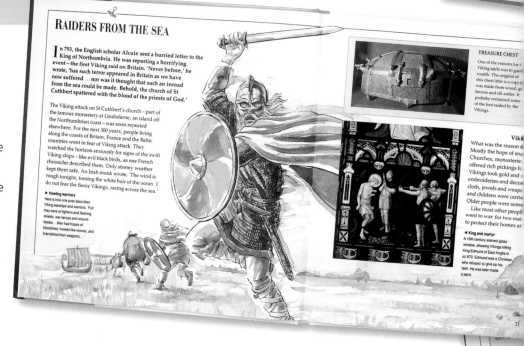

Cartoon care
This nonfiction book illustration relies on simple drawings of a cartoon bear to demonstrate how a young reader should care for their body.

You may prefer not to go through an agent and to approach publishers directly. This can be an uphill struggle for anyone straight out of art college. You will need to identify the kind of publisher who produces books using your style of artwork. Then you need to contact the Art Director or Creative Director there and send photocopied or printed samples of your work. You can find out the name of the person you need to approach by consulting publishing directories such as the *Childrens' Writer's & Illustrator's Market* (Writer's Digest Books). This is published yearly, so be sure to use the latest edition.

GLOBAL MARKETS

Most information books need to have international sales potential. European publishers especially will not make a profit based solely on sales in their own country, so artwork needs to have a universal appeal. Cars, for example, should be shown with reflections on the windshield that do not allow the reader to see the lefthand or righthand position of the driver. Whichever side you draw, one will look wrong in some of the countries where the book will be sold.

Nudity is also a problem—even a rear view that shows only the buttocks. In many European countries a cartoon depiction of a child getting out of a bath or an artwork recreation of seminaked Neolithic people would go unquestioned, but in the United States such illustrations are unacceptable.

Extra elements
Besides an increase in sophistication and detail, illustrations for older readers often include elements like diagrams and maps.

WRITING FOR DIFFERENT AGES

Information books follow all the rules for age-level that apply to picture books and fiction. You need to constantly be aware of your reader's level of understanding and vocabulary. Sentences must be short—aim for under 20 words—without complex clauses, and with an unambiguous clarity.

Ageless appeal
The ancient Egyptians provide an example of a nonfiction subject that continues to fascinate readers of all ages.

ASSUMED KNOWLEDGE

The easiest trap to fall into when writing nonfiction is to assume a knowledge that the reader hasn't got. This is why some nonfiction publishers prefer to use general writers rather than specialists. A lifelong sailor writing about sailing ships, for example, might assume that everyone knows what "port" and "starboard" mean, or what the "mizzenmast" or "yardarms" are. After all, these are terms they may use everyday. But most children will be baffled by these unfamiliar words and quickly lose interest in the book.

Likewise, a historian who spends his professional life writing or lecturing about the Second World War will assume everyone knows who Stalin, Churchill, or Roosevelt are. This is not the case, even for teenage children. Phrases such as "Britain's wartime prime minister Winston Churchill…" or "American president Franklin D. Roosevelt…" will succinctly remind your reader who these people are.

Glossaries

Many nonfiction books have a glossary at the back. This is useful for providing handy definitions of complicated and unfamiliar words, but don't assume a reader will use it. Most children will quickly grow tired of having to look up words at the back of the book—that's assuming they know there's a glossary there in the first place. You need to explain unfamiliar words clearly when you first use them.

PITCH TO AGE

As with other children's genres, nonfiction books fall into categories determined by age range. For preschool children there are broad introductions to the world of history or science, for example. Books for elementary school children will have more specific subjects such as baby animals, how flowers grow, or what happens to our refuse. Information books for older children may consider the Holocaust or systems of government such as democracy or dictatorship. Such books change in complexity and sophistication as the target age grows older.

WHO'S WHO

Younger children have no clear understanding of the chronological framework of history. They often get historical figures mixed up, asking such questions as "Is Hitler the one who had his wives' heads chopped off?"

SCHOOL SUBJECTS

Government and education authorities post information on the internet about which subjects are covered by the school curriculum, and the age children are when they study them. For example, elementary school children often study the ancient cultures of Egypt, Greece, and Rome, so books about these eras are often pitched at the younger end of the nonfiction market. The Second World War may be studied in detail by high school children, so information books about that are pitched at early teens and older.

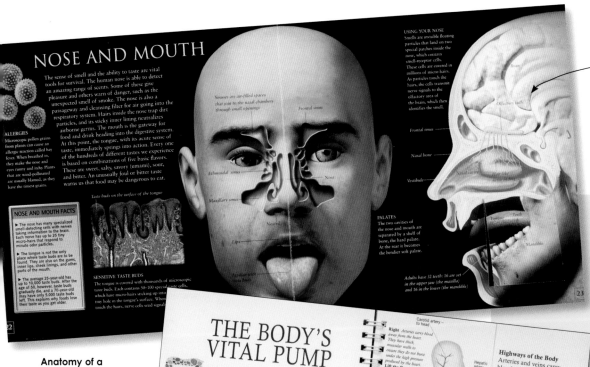

When you generate your text you will need to give suggestions for how it could be illustrated. Every illustration will need a hard-working caption and details of the image may also be annotated with numbered captions or leader lines.

CONTRAST AND COMPARE!

Below are two strikingly different approaches to the subject of sneezing. Both contain the same number of key facts; only one of them is entertaining, and that's the one pitched at children.

Adult non-fiction

A sternutation, commonly known as "a sneeze," is a paroxysmal expulsion of air from the lungs. It is caused by foreign matter irritating the nasal mucus. In the case of the "photic sneeze reflex," sneezing may also be caused by exposure to bright light.

Child's non-fiction

What travels at 100 miles (150 km) per hour? Your snot! Every time you sneeze, mucus is pushed out of your nose at this amazing speed. How come you've never noticed? Because every time you sneeze, you shut your eyes. Go on—try to sneeze and keep your eyes open. It's impossible! Here's another challenge; try saying the word "sternutation." It's a biggie, isn't it? That's the official word for a sneeze. But you're probably still asking: what makes me sneeze? It can be anything from dust to pollen, a cold to sudden light. Make sure you duck next time your friend feels a sneeze coming on. You don't want an unwelcome shower!

Anatomy of a nonfiction book
Nonfiction books (for all ages) follow some fairly standard conventions that you won't find in fiction. You will need to consider these in your writing.

Most nonfiction books are divided into sections, chapters or double-page spreads. Each will need an introductory paragraph or standfirst.

The main thrust of the article is contained in the body text, which is further subdivided under headings. Remember, though, that the reader may never get beyond the captions!

Illustrations are usually commissioned after the text has been written, based on your image suggestions. The editor may ask you to provide reference for the artist.

41 CREATIVE NONFICTION

Creative or "narrative" nonfiction is a way of relating real-life events with the immediacy, emotional involvement, and power of a novel. It is what journalist and novelist Edward Humes brilliantly describes as "the art of being there." As this is very much a text-led (rather than design- or illustration-led) genre, it provides a promising avenue for new writers trying to break into children's nonfiction to explore.

TRICKS FROM TV

Television documentary makers have long used this technique to create "faction" or "docudrama" programs about real events — with actors used to depict scenes based closely on real life. In creative nonfiction, a writer will employ many of the techniques of fiction—lively dialogue, evocative descriptions, glimpses into the secret thoughts and motives of his characters—to weave a story the reader will be drawn into.

WATCH WHAT YOU SAY

In creative nonfiction, in any story set in even the recent past, you need to think dialogue through carefully. Although many children will not understand archaic speech forms and vocabulary, you need to aim to create speech which at least sounds authentic and of its time. In all but the most recent stories you would naturally avoid obvious slang words such as "dude" or "cool." But take care also not to use modern idioms such as "Check out..." (as in "check out those English archers on our flank, your Majesty!").

NONFICTION SUBJECTS WORTH EXPLORING

- History with a twist—entertaining real-life characters and pivotal moments in history would all be good jumping-off points.

- Practical science—children love getting their hands dirty with (safe) experiments to try at home.

- Green issues—this subject is very hot right now and and unlikely to cool off in the near future.

- How to have fun—how can you teach readers without it feeling like a lesson? Turn your book into a big game.

- Anything scatological—children love it!

OVER-PUBLISHED NONFICTION AREAS

- Curriculum subjects are often heavily published. They can guarantee sales, but can you find a new way to approach familiar subjects?

Writing nonfiction
Your nonfiction writing will undoubtedly be influenced by what children are studying in the classroom. Take the time to research what teachers, librarians, and parents are looking for—and then have fun.

What makes for great nonfiction?
Creating a truly great nonfiction book demands an innovative approach—but beyond that, the genre is difficult to categorize, as this list of great examples demonstrates.

USING CHARACTERS

Creative nonfiction offers an attractive freedom to a writer. A story about the Battle of Iwo Jima or the Somme, for example, may start with fresh recruits waiting for a train that will take them away from home. What are they thinking? Are they fearful or excited? Are some keen to escape their dull small-town lives, or are they already missing the wives or sweethearts they have left behind? If the reader cares about the characters in the story they will be engrossed in the struggles and challenges they have to face.

RESEARCH

Writing creative nonfiction properly requires a level of empathy and research similar to that demanded by historical fiction—in fact, the genres are remarkably similar. The main difference is that the creative nonfiction writer must stick rigorously to portraying real people and events, while the fiction writer can be more creative with both their characters and the known facts.

Constantly ask yourself questions like, "How would this feel?" or "What would they be thinking?" As well as reading around the subject, trips to relevant museums and sites of historical importance will be invaluable in helping you gain an understanding of what it was like to be the people you are writing about. Living museums, such as the Plimoth Plantation in Plymouth, Massachusetts will provide any writer with many chapters' worth of material.

BROAD SPECTRUM

Creative nonfiction is particularly well suited to subjects popular with boys: adventure stories of survival, exploration, and heroism; great events in history; and war stories. But recently the genre has been successfully applied to tales of scientific discovery and even advances in mathematics!

FIVE GREAT NON-FICTION BOOKS:

1. _Horrible Histories by Terry Deary_
   (Scholastic, first book published 1993)
   This massively popular paperback series of children's nonfiction uses humor, gore, and cartoon illustration to bring subjects to life.

2. _The Way Things Work by David Macaulay_
   (Houghton Mifflin, 1988)
   Highly-illustrated cross-sections of everything from a car transmission to a body-scanner.

3. _The Grossology series by Sylvia Bransei_
   (Price Stern Sloan, 1995)
   Covering subjects such as animals, the human body, and food these books use the "yuk-factor" to appeal to children.

4. _The Wizardology series by Dugald Steer_
   (Candlewick Press, 2005)
   Full of special features and puzzles, these innovative books get young minds working hard.

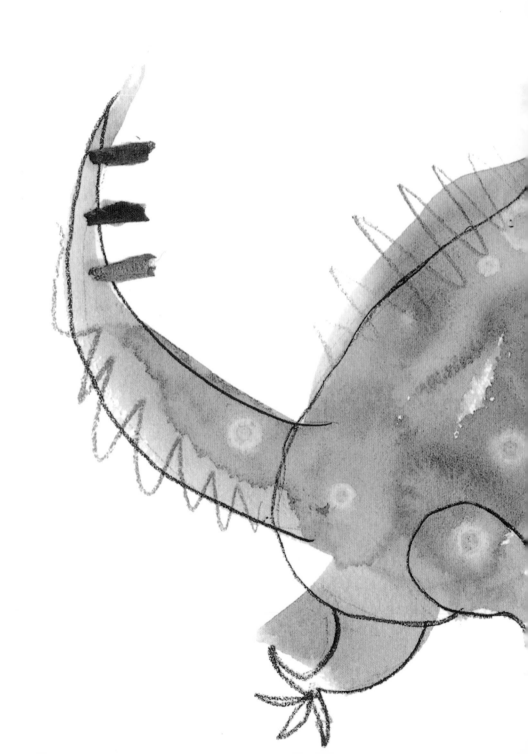

USING WATERCOLOR WASHES
Watercolor is great for creating gentle
color gradations (see page 124).

Chapter five

MEDIA AND TECHNIQUES

A step-by-step refresher course demonstrating some of the most important media characteristics and how to exploit them to create wonderful and compelling artwork.

42 GALLERY OF TECHNIQUES

The gallery of images on these pages provides an overview of the diverse illustration techniques explained in more detail in this chapter.

DRY COLOR

Pastels
Here, colored pencils were used to create a sensitive line drawing, and then soft chalk pastels were blended over the top to create a soft, dusty texture.

TRANSLUCENT

Watercolor
Watercolor is a popular medium. The white of the paper can be used to exploit the transparency of the watercolor over the delicate pencil drawing.

Inks
Simple pen and ink drawings are rendered with vibrant washes of watercolor inks.

BLACK AND WHITE

Crosshatching
Here, the artist used a technical drawing pen and built up tone mechanically with crosshatched lines.

Brush pen
Black watercolor was used to create strong, simple shapes and patterns, washed over in places.

Flat black
A drawing was scanned into the computer and the solid areas were filled in using Photoshop.

MIXED MEDIA

Many media
This artwork is a combination of pen and ink drawing with watercolor, colored pencils, pastels, and gouache layers, creating a textured effect.

DIGITAL

Digitally manipulated
These graphic line drawings were scanned, flat color was dropped into areas using Photoshop, and then printed on colored paper.

43 TRANSLUCENT

Using translucent watercolor media is possibly the most popular illustration technique for children's illustration. It offers fresh, bright color and can be simple or sophisticated in its application. Paint can be used directly in the form of a wash, but generally it is combined with a pencil or ink line.

Brushes
A good starter kit includes: three round brushes (left) for detail and washes; a flat brush (center) for lines; two rigger brushes (right) for fine details; and a pointed mop brush (far right).

WATERCOLOR MEDIA

Watercolor pans provide more concentrated color than tubes. This is because the paint in tubes contains more binding ingredient to keep the pigment soft. Despite the dulling effect, tubes are convenient to use for mixing large amounts of paint for washes.

Watercolor inks are synthetic dyes and have real strength and vibrancy. Even when diluted quite considerably, they still stain the paper and cannot be lifted off with clean water as watercolor paint can.

Both paints and inks make use of the white of the paper to add highlights, and successful application relies on confidence and spontaneity. The translucent effect makes these media more unforgiving than many others. Learning to control flat and gradient washes, and practicing mark-making using items such as rock salt and clingwrap, will help you to appreciate the versatility and control that is possible. There is a great number of books with useful guidelines for using these media, but look at more than one. Many refer to particular styles of working—remember that you are in the process of discovering your own!

Liquid acrylic inks

Liquid watercolor

Liquid acrylic inks and liquid watercolors
Liquid acrylic inks and liquid watercolors are available in a wide range of colors. They can be expensive when used at full strength but provide vibrant, waterproof coverage. The acrylic inks are also lightfast when dry.

TOOLS FOR TRANSLUCENT MEDIA

Brushes: Nylon brushes are adequate, although expensive sable brushes are perfect for watercolor. Use a variety of sizes to carry the watercolor, according to the task—large, flat brushes for backgrounds, and round brushes for "filling in." Take care of your brushes to retain their shape and prolong their life. Keep water clean when mixing and rinsing (use two pots) and don't leave brushes standing in water, as it will damage their tips. Use white tissue to check that a brush is cleaned of pigment before mixing another color.

Paper: Stretch paper if it is lightweight, or if you are going to apply a considerable amount of watercolor, to avoid buckling and the formation of puddles. Using good quality, professional watercolor paper will make a difference to the application of washes and color. Experiment with the range of "hot press," "not," and "rough" papers to see what suits you best.

Masking: Masking fluid helps to protect small areas of paper while you apply washes, and masking film is excellent for larger areas. Wax-resist leaves a soft, broken mark to retain lighter areas, but this is of course permanent. Masking tape works, but does have a tendency to rip the paper.

Traditional watercolor paints in tubes and pans

PAPER TEXTURES

Watercolor paper is made in different weights and textures. Because watercolor techniques rely so much on the texture of paper, it is important to choose the best one for your own style.

Hot-pressed: This paper has a smooth surface, making it ideal for highly detailed work.

Not: This term is short for "not hot-pressed." The paper has a gently textured surface.

Rough: This paper is suitable for broad, expressive work and wet washes.

Watercolor board: As its name suggests, watercolor board is watercolor paper attached to board. It is very useful when you don't want—or have no time—to stretch paper.

Handmade papers: These are produced in all kinds of textures, making them ideal for individual, experimental techniques.

STRETCHING PAPER

Paper has a truly infuriating tendency to buckle when water is applied to the surface, particularly the lighter weights. When you are trying to produce an illustration, this does not enhance its professional appearance. By stretching your paper, you should avoid a wrinkled finished piece.

Tools and materials
- Watercolor paper of your choice
- Wooden drawing board at least 2 in (5 cm) bigger around than the paper
- Large, flat-bottomed washing up bowl (or you can use the bathtub)
- Natural or synthetic sponge
- Gummed paper strips cut to the right lengths a little longer than the edges of the paper
- Scissors

1 Watercolor paper is one-sided, and it is very important that you remember which the right side is— initially the watermark will show you (it will read correctly from the right side). Immerse the paper completely in clean, cold water for a few minutes.

2 Lay the paper, right side up, onto a clean wooden drawing board. Start at one edge and press it down. With a clean sponge, stroke the paper gently in one direction to remove any air bubbles that have formed between the paper and the board.

3 Remove any excess water with a squeezed-out dry sponge and then seal the edges of the paper with gummed tape. Tear a length a little longer than one side of the paper and stroke it with the wet sponge to activate the glue. Take care not to under-or over-soak it.

4 Lay the gummed paper strip so that it covers the edge of the watercolor paper. Repeat for all four sides. You can add small corner pieces to prevent the strip from lifting at the corners. Leave the paper to dry in a warm place—it must be totally dry before it is used. Stretching the paper yourself is a lengthy process; prestretched paper provides a much quicker, though more expensive, option.

MIXING PAINT

When you use watercolors or gouache, the most important consideration is how much pigment to mix with the water. Obviously, this effects how translucent the color will be—the more water, the more transparent the color. Gouache is much thicker, but if mixed with increasing quantities of water it can take on the qualities of watercolor. Meanwhile, some of the chalkier watercolor pigments, such as lemon yellow or cadmium red, can take on an opaque appearance if mixed only sparingly with water. Be careful not to use too much paint though, which will cause your work to look heavy and dull.

Paint consistency
Experiment by mixing in the palette and then painting with varying degrees of water. **Top left and right:** a very thin wash mixed with a lot of water and a little pigment (either watercolor or gouache)—this would probably be too weak for a whole painting, although would work well if used in conjunction with a holding line. **Center left and right:** the classic watercolor strength—there is enough pigment in the mix for the color to become luminescent when the white of the paper shows through. **Bottom left and right:** a thicker mix suitable for dry brushwork or for when you want an opaque effect.

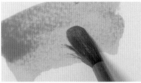

MIXING COLORS

Color mixing can be done either in the palette or on the paper. There are two considerations: first, how much to mix—this will come with experience. If you are painting a large area, mix more than you think you will need if color consistency is important, as you will never manage to match the color if you run out. Second, the tone of the colors will affect how much of each to use.

Mixing in a palette
You can mix paint in a palette (right) and add water, which will allow you to fine-tune the colors. Start with the paler tone (lemon yellow) and add tiny quantities of the darker tone (cobalt blue). Keep adding blue until you have achieved the desired shade of green. If you started with the darker tone and mixed in the paler one it would take far more paint to achieve the same color.

Blending on paper
These colors (sap green and cadmium yellow) were mixed by blending them together on the paper.

Glazing
In a traditional method known as "glazing," layers of transparent color are washed, one over another. This example (right) shows cadmium yellow over cerulean blue. The colors are optically mixed to give a fresh green.

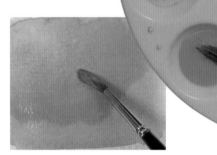

WASHES

The fundametal technique of watercolor is to lay a single-color, flat wash that is useful for backgrounds, skies, or as a basis for a wash containing two or more colors. A wash can be applied in a controlled way as shown in the first example, or in a looser way as in the second example, where a second color is dropped on wet, and allowed to bleed into the first.

Flat wash Load a large wash brush with paint and make a horizontal stroke. Paint will collect at the bottom. Make more strokes, each overlapping the last, until you have covered the desired area.

Gradated wash Similar to the flat wash, thin the paint with more water after every stroke to make a fading wash to white.

Variegated wash Start by making a flat wash. Where you would like to change color, start applying the second color with a clean brush. The two colors will blend with unpredictable results.

WET-ON-DRY

For detailed work, a technique called wet-on-dry is used. The initial wash is left to dry and then the detail is painted on top. Don't press too hard or scrub at the paper to avoid moving the pigment from the first wash; the colors may become muddy, and you will lose any detail you are trying to capture. Using watercolor pigments or inks for the first wash would help as they are less likely to move later.

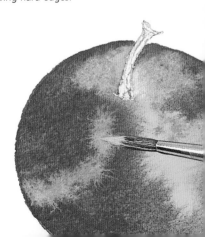

Wet on dry
Very fine wet-on-dry brushwork achieved this level of detail.

1 Draw your image faintly with a pencil, then fill the brush and wet the whole area inside the outline. You need to be accurate to achieve a clean edge.

2 Add color in layers, starting with the palest, and allowing the pigments to mix on the paper. Keep in mind where you want highlights, and work dark areas around them.

TRY THIS

Follow the techniques listed here as you draw and paint simple household objects as reference.

WET-IN-WET

As you will be working with lots of water, there is a risk of the paper buckling. To prevent this, either use a heavy paper—at least 160 lb (340 gsm)—or stretch the paper (see page 119). Rough textures give the best results. Use large brushes to deliver the maximum amount of pigment and water.

1 Draw the outline of the image faintly with a pencil, then fill the brush and wet the whole area inside the outline. You need to be accurate to achieve a clean edge.

2 Add the color in layers, starting with the palest washes and allowing the pigment to mix on the paper. Keep in mind where you wish the highlights to be, and work the dark areas around them.

3 Try to keep the whole area as wet as possible by using very watery washes. This helps the layers of color to mix softly without leaving hard edges.

MASKING

Masking, or preserving, the white of the paper as a highlight is an important technique for illustrators working in transparent media. This is because the white of the paper is always brighter and whiter than white paint would be, so your highlights will sparkle. It also allows you to freely apply washes over the illustration while the masked highlights are protected.

Masks are especially useful if you want to create flat background washes or variegated washes behind characters or objects in the foreground. You will have discovered that if you try to paint around an object, the paint will dry before you finish, which makes it impossible to achieve a flat background. Use film or masking fluid to block out areas: film for larger areas and masking fluid for details or highlights.

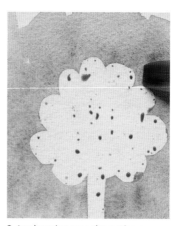

1 To mask an area with film, place transparent sticky-backed film over the drawn image, and use a sharp craft knife or scalpel to cut it out.

2 Apply paint over the entire area with a large brush, working from the center to the left and right. Don't scrub around the film edges.

3 Leave the wash to dry completely before you remove the film. You may need to use a scalpel to help you lift the edge of the film.

1 To mask an area with masking fluid, sketch in the design lightly with a pencil first. Apply the masking fluid with an old brush—it can be difficult to remove from the bristles afterward.

2 Make sure the fluid is completely dry before applying any paint. This technique can be used with any waterbased pigment and, as in this example, is extremely successful with watercolor.

3 Once the paint has dried, remove the fluid with a clean finger or an eraser. Any pencil marks under the fluid will be removed, leaving a clean, white area. Masking fluid can also be used over a dry wash to protect it from the next layer.

EDGE MASKING

Masking tape can be used to achieve crisp edges around your illustration. Take care not to damage the paper when you peel off the tape.

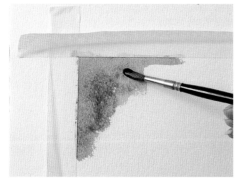

1 Before applying masking tape, measure the dimensions of your illustration and pencil in the area lightly (use a triangle to ensure right angles). Carefully lay down the masking tape, pressing down the inside edge only, and taking particular care at the corners. Make sure there are no air pockets on or near the edge to be painted, or the paint will seep under. Add the wash as usual.

2 Allow paint to dry completely. Carefully peel back the masking tape to reveal the edge. Do not leave the tape in place for too long as it will eventually stain the paper.

SCRATCHING OUT

You may have to work to tight deadlines, so techniques that can speed up your work can be very handy. Keeping small areas for white highlights can be difficult when you are working at speed. "Scratching out" with a blade after the paint has dried is a quick and effective method of reclaiming highlights. (Alternative methods include using opaque white paint such as gouache, or masking fluid.)

This technique is particularly suitable for fine-line highlights. It should only be used on heavier papers—140 lb (300 gsm) or over—as it is possible to make holes in thin ones.

SPONGING

Sponging is a very expressive method that is quick to master and is ideal for experimentation. It can be used on its own to build a complete image, or combined with other watercolor techniques.

1 A small natural sponge is the ideal tool for this technique. It is used quite dry on a rough-surfaced paper to produce a highly textured effect.

Before

After

For straight lines, a little metal ruler is useful to guide your hand. Drag the scalpel lightly at first, repeating the process until you achieve the amount of highlight required.

2 The great value of the sponging technique is that it creates a complete image that is both evocative and decorative in a very short time—always a bonus for a busy illustrator.

READ THESE

An Introduction to Watercolor by Ray Smith
(Dorling Kindersley, 1993)

The Encyclopedia of Watercolor Techniques: A Step-by-Step Visual Directory by Hazel Harrison
(Running Press, 2004)

LINE AND WASH

The line and wash technique allows the creation of a complete image extremely quickly, and has been the preferred medium for many famous illustrators. It combines two traditional techniques: pen and ink and watercolor. Flat wash tints are applied over an ink line drawing.

BASIC EQUIPMENT

It is very important to choose the correct paper for the line and wash technique. It must be strong enough to resist cockling when washed, yet smooth enough to take a pen line. Smooth "not" watercolor papers fulfill these criteria; experiment with different types until you find the one that suits your style.

Traditional watercolor pigments and brushes are used to create the washes, while the drawing is rendered with a dip pen. There is a wide range of nibs available that produce different widths and qualities of lines. You

Inks and pens
For linework, use black or brown waterproof ink and a dip pen (above). Apply washes of color using inks or watercolor (below).

will need to use waterproof ink—it has a tendency to dry quickly, so you will need to clean the nib regularly to keep it from clogging.

GETTING STARTED

There are three approaches to this technique; the most traditional is to start with the ink drawing. When the ink is completely dry, thin color washes are applied. Greater intensity of color can be built up using successive layers, or by working wet-in-wet (see page 123). The second method is to apply the washes first and, when they are dry, add the ink drawing afterward. The third involves working up the two elements together, adding more line and color where necessary.

The key to success with this technique is the integration of the color with the line. Experiment with applying the washes, keeping them wet and loose, and allowing them to break out of the ink lines.

Putty erasers
For erasing the pencil line, putty erasers are superior to traditional erasers as they do not leave rubbings.

TRADITIONAL METHOD

Remember to use waterproof ink, as washes are added over the linework. Use pre-stretched watercolor paper with a smooth surface for this technique.

1 Outline the original drawing lightly in pencil as a guide for the dip-pen line work that will be added over the top. (Once dry, any visible pencil lines can be removed with a putty eraser.)

ALTERNATIVE METHOD

An alternative line and wash method involves laying down the washes first, with the linework added with a dip pen when they have dried. You will discover in time which technique suits you best.

1 Outline the design with a faint pencil line. Apply masking fluid with an old brush to the areas that are to be reserved as white paper. Allow the masking fluid to dry (this may take a few minutes).

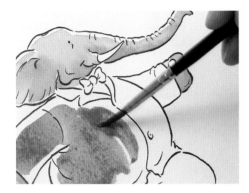

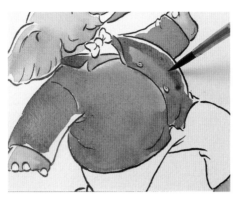

2 Using the pencil lines as a guide, apply the watercolor washes with a sable brush. Two tones of each color are mixed, and the palest is applied first.

3 Before the first wash is completely dry, add the second, darker wash. This darker wash (applied here to the outside edge of the coat), will help to emphasize the elephant's rotund figure. Because the first wash is quite dry, the two tones blend slightly, merging along the soft edge.

4 This technique of two-tone washes is used to complete the whole illustration. It is important not to overwork the color, as you may lose the fresh, spontaneous feel characteristic of this technique.

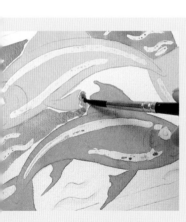

2 Wash over the fish and the background water with a sable brush. At this stage add only the basic wash for each area. Shadow washes can be added later.

3 Once the washes have dried, the masking fluid can be removed with a putty eraser, leaving the highlights on the backs of the fish and in the water. The lines can then be added with dip pen and waterproof ink.

4 A more three-dimensional quality can be added to selected areas of the design once the linework has dried by adding a second, darker wash.

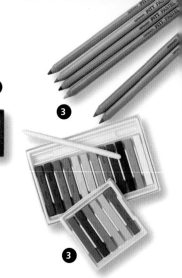

DRY COLOR

Pastels are perfect for producing bold, rich, and expressive illustrations. This is also true of watercolor-based pencils, except that pastels, unlike pencil crayons, are not really suitable for small-scale work.

CRAYONS AND PASTELS

Traditional colored pencils or crayons create a softer quality of image than pastels. They are perfect for sketching and visualizing.

Pastels come in two types—oil and chalk (or soft) pastels—and in a range of qualities from soft (with more pigment) to hard (with more binder). Most pastel work is done on tinted rather than white paper as the process of application is through blending; working light to dark or dark to light. White and light colors can give powerful highlights, and light is often an important element in pastel work.

Oil pastels are more difficult to work with but the density of the color gives a much richer effect. Scale can be a problem for scanning and, as the artwork is necessarily large, details may be lost on reduction. Faces can be difficult to keep attractive and manageable on a small scale. Turpentine can create a wonderful painterly effect, with the opportunity to scratch into the oily surface when applied thickly or to leave it with an impasto effect.

COLOR MIXES AND "WASHES"

With dry media, always lay the light colors first and then build up the image with the colors getting progressively darker. You will need a good range of colors for any dry media, as they cannot be mixed like paint; though you can overlap colors through a blending or crosshatching technique. Only certain media will create a wash effect; use water to bleed watercolor pencils, or turpentine applied with a brush over oil pastels.

PAPER SURFACE

The results that are achievable with dry media vary dramatically depending on the type of paper used. With smooth papers, the pigment within the media covers the whole surface evenly; with rougher papers, it only adheres to the raised areas and therefore less pigment is laid down on the surface.

1 Colored pencils

Although colored pencils are easy to use, they have the potential to produce very rich and vibrant images. Some artists apply a watercolor wash first, to tint the paper. For detailed work, hot pressed paper is best. For looser work, a slightly rougher paper can be used.

2 Oil pastels

Colors can be built up by layering one on top of another, using a series of marks—this is called "feathering." You can blend oil pastels with your fingers or a torchon. Scratch into the surface, using a sharp tool or the end of a brush, to expose layers beneath and create a linear drawing. Blend with a solvent such as turpentine to give a smoother, more painterly effect, using a rag or a brush. Oil pastels will work with most paper surfaces, but specialist pastel papers are available.

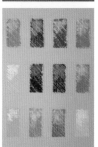

3 Chalk pastels

Colors can be built up by applying the lightest tone first on a slightly tinted paper, then blending it with your finger or a torchon to create a smooth area of color. Darker colors are placed over the top, blended again to create a smooth effect. As you apply more layers of color you will see how each layer enriches the next and how you can create a variety of rich tones. You can also draw lines with pastels.

Colored papers
Even though pastels provide a relatively opaque finish, the color of the background paper still has a startling effect on perception of their colors.

DRY MEDIA STROKES

The strokes or marks made by the two types of pastel and colored pencils are fairly similar. An entire picture may be built up using a network of lines, known as "hatching." Applied evenly and repeatedly these lines can create various gradated tones of color, or may be left as angled strokes. These can then be overlaid with another layer of lines at a different angle—called "crosshatching." At any point a second or third color may be introduced and blended, or hatched, over the base layer. The examples shown here demonstrate some of the possible options.

Hatching and crosshatching: Long, diagonal hatched lines can be used to create form, or as a base layer (above). Two-color crosshatching (above right)—shorter yellow lines over the longer lines of the first layer create a more varied surface texture. Two-color short-line crosshatching (above far right), the red and blue forming small units. Crosshatching using the side of a pastel stick (right) at shallow angles. The variables of color and length and angle of strokes give infinite variety.

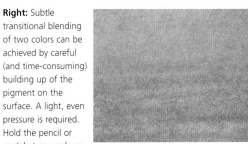

Right: Subtle transitional blending of two colors can be achieved by careful (and time-consuming) building up of the pigment on the surface. A light, even pressure is required. Hold the pencil or pastel at an angle so that the point or edge does not create a visible line. Lay down the faintest layers first so that the pigment is just dusting the surface.

Top: Using the side of a pastel creates swaths of flat color.

Above: Using a mid-toned gray paper adds an extra layer of color.

Above: Feathering the marks gives interesting textures. Here, a red pastel is feathered over a magenta background.

Above right: Lightly blending softens the surface.

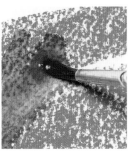

Right: Brushing liquid medium onto oil pastel is another way to vary the surface texture.

Left: A single color may be blended with a finger.

Right: Here, two colors are blended with a finger.

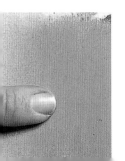

1 The outline of the dog is drawn on smooth paper. The shape of the animal is then roughly modeled.

ERASER TECHNIQUE

Eraser and blade work can enhance the impression of form and texture in a colored pencil illustration. Loose pencil work was applied last of all for a rougher, furry-looking texture.

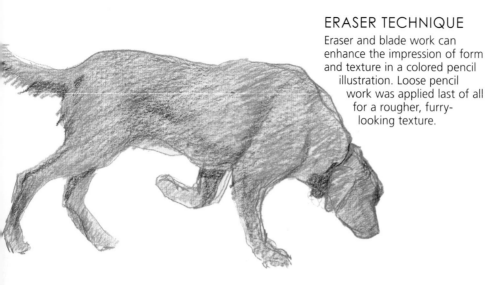

2 To brighten the highlight areas on the flanks and shoulders, the color is scraped back with a scalpel blade.

3 A plastic eraser is used for cleaning up the drawing and burnishing the highlight areas.

BLENDING CHALK PASTEL

Because of the lovely, soft nature of chalk pastel, it is an ideal medium for decorative, impressionistic illustrations created with blending techniques. A wide variety of papers are suitable as backgrounds, including highly textured and colored ones.

1 Over a creamy-yellow textured pastel paper, apply the background yellow with a short length of chalk used horizontally. Blend the pastel surface gently with the pads of your fingers and blow off any excess chalk.

2 Darker colors are then applied over the background. Note how the texture of the paper breaks up the pastel strokes to create optical blending. This time your blending finger both softens the pastel strokes and blends the colors together. Pastel work is messy, but you can blend with a paper stump or torchon if you prefer.

3 When the work is completed it is vital to use a fixative to prevent unwanted smudging. This bonds the pastel to the paper.

OIL PASTEL: BLEND AND REVEAL

As an illustration technique, reveal can be extremely effective. You may find that warming the pastels gently before use will help soften them. This will help you to build up the amount of pigment on the paper necessary for this technique.

1, 2 Build up a thick layer of blended colors. Next, cover the colors with a darker layer of color.

3 With a blunt point such as the end of a paintbrush, the design can then be scratched into the surface, revealing the under-layer. The line thickness depends on the tool you use.

OIL PASTEL: USING SOLVENTS

Although oil pastels have a thick, waxy texture, they can be worked into with a solvent to produce thin, transparent washes. Oil pastels are soluble in turpentine or mineral spirits. A variety of techniques can be used. The paper can be soaked first in turpentine or oil and then drawn on or, as in this example, the pastel drawing can be worked into with the solvent.

1 Starting with pale colors, build up an under-layer of mixed tones. Rough paper is particularly suitable as it helps you to apply a thicker layer of pastel and catches the under-layer in its depressions so that it, and not the paper, is revealed.

2 The turpentine or mineral spirits is applied to a clean tissue or piece of paper towel, which is then used to blend and spread the color over the image with small, circular strokes.

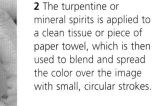

3 Allow the solvent to dry, and then pass more pastel over the top; if the paper remains wet, the overlaid pastel will bleed, making the line fuzzy. You can deliberately exploit this property to produce interesting results.

4 Further blending can be done with a finger and the solvent-soaked paper towel, gradually building up the image. For small, detailed areas, a cotton swab soaked in turpentine may be used.

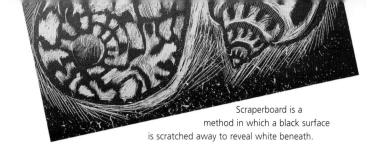

Scraperboard is a method in which a black surface is scratched away to reveal white beneath.

BLACK AND WHITE

Black and white illustrations are usually associated with longer storybooks and novels, in which the illustrations accompany and break up a large body of text. This discipline is still very important in children's illustration but it is often neglected in portfolios. It can be a good way of entering the field and getting your work published.

READ THESE

There are many books that will give you technical advice on the variety of media for drawing. Try the following:

The Manual of Illustration Techniques by Catherine Slade
(A & C Black, 2003)

The Pen and Ink Book by J. A. Smith
(Watson-Guptill Publications, 1999)

TOOLS FOR BLACK AND WHITE

There is a vast range of tools that can be used to create black and white images, including: fiber tip pens, fountain pens, rollerball pens, technical pens, and ballpoint pens. Most of these tools create a line that is even in weight and thickness.

Graphite pencils or sticks, conté pencils, oil pastels, chalk pastels, and charcoal can all be used to create more subtle tonal qualities and monochromatic images, including half-tone.

Scraperboard is a white, chalky material that has been coated with black ink. Various tools are used to scratch into the black surface, exposing the white beneath. Tools can vary from special scraperboard nibs to anything sharp such as a scalpel, a nail, or a pin.

Consistent tone: The side of the point creates consistent tone.

Varied tone: Varied pressure on the point results in altered tone.

Hatching: Hatching and crosshatching build controlled tone.

Blending: Soft graphite can be blended with a finger.

Texture: A single soft pencil is capable of a wide visual vocabulary.

Erasing: An eraser can be used to produce tonal or textural effects.

Coverage: A thick stick of charcoal on its side can cover an area quickly.

Soft marks: Putty erasers can create soft marks for a ghostlike effect.

Hard marks: A hard, vinyl eraser makes sharper, more precise marks.

SILHOUETTE DRAWING

Silhouette drawing has always been a popular style for children's books. Perhaps the most famous practitioner of this style was Arthur Rackham, who used it to create detailed, magical illustrations for books like *Rip Van Winkle*. For a crisp edge to your silhouette, start by creating an outline drawing.

CONTOUR DRAWING

With contour drawing, a subject is described by varying the outline. By making the outline thinner or thicker, rigid or soft, continuous or broken, the difference between materials can be expressed. This is achieved by using the flexibility of the nib of a dip pen. A light amount of pressure with lines at a distance apart creates lighter shading. More pressure and closer lines make darker tones.

1 Use a light pencil to outline the image. Then retrace it with the dip pen. When the ink runs out, re-dip the pen. If there is too much ink in the pen, it will blot, so do a small test on a separate sheet to prevent accidents.

2 When the ink is completely dry, any pencil marks showing can be erased using a putty eraser.

1 The overall design is drawn lightly in pencil. It is then retraced using a dip pen; vary the line, and therefore describe the subject, by applying more or less pressure. Look closely at how the folds in the sleeves are created with a variation in thickness of the line.

2 The whole figure is outlined in this method, allowing the line to tail off gradually by releasing the pressure on the nib. The softness and movement of the fabric can be expressed with a broken line.

3 Use a small brush and the same ink to fill in the outline to create a silhouette. Paint around the eyes of the octopus to give him character. You can speed up the drying time of the ink with a hairdryer. Be careful that it is not too hot or held too close or it may buckle the paper.

3 When the ink is dry, using a thinner nib and working from the top, add in shading by crosshatching. With contour drawing the lines must follow the form of the object it is describing. As the umbrella is reserved, the lines are drawn to follow its contours.

4 Contour drawing is a very similar method to crosshatching, but as can be seen from the example, the quality of this technique is freer and more expressive.

4 The finished silhouette.

MIXED MEDIA AND COLLAGE

Combining different media and materials together has become very popular. It naturally encourages an imaginative and innovative approach to image-making.

TYPES OF MIXED MEDIA

"Mixed media" is traditionally a combination of painting and drawing techniques using a variety of media. This has developed into a more complex combination, with the addition of printmaking, photography, bas-relief, and collage.

COLLAGE POSSIBILITIES

Collage is the gluing together of a variety of materials—though mainly paper—onto a surface to create an image. Perhaps the most well known use of collage in children's book illustration is by Eric Carle in *The Very Hungry Caterpillar*, for instance. This technique can also extend to the combination of many other materials: old photographs, tickets, candy wrappers, magazines, newspapers, brochures, fabrics, and found objects—manufactured and natural. Be aware that if you combine papers and flat materials with three-dimensional objects, they cannot be scanned for reproduction and the artwork will have to be photographed.

Experiment with collage. Collect as many varied paper samples as you can: bought, found, hand-treated; photographs, text and images from magazines; and anything else paper-based you can think of. Experiment with cutting and ripping the samples up. Layer and glue them onto a base of thick paper or card to make your composition.

COPYRIGHT

Most artists working in this way have vast collections of all sorts of miscellaneous materials, although you must remember not to infringe on copyright laws if your work is going to be reproduced. It is therefore safer to use your own original photographic imagery within your illustrations.

Layered media
A variety of media combine here to create a rich and atmospheric, densely layered piece.

Colored pencils

Oil pastels

Gouache paint

Scissors

Tissue paper

READ THIS

The Art of Eric Carle
by Eric Carle
(Philomel Books, 2002)

An autobiography of the artist—an excellent example of paper collage at its best.

Collage Sourcebook
by Jennifer Atkinson
(Apple, 2004)

A good sourcebook for anyone interested in collage techniques. Step-by-step projects and instructions on various techniques.

An Introduction to Mixed Media
by Michael Wright and Ray Smith
(Dorling Kindersley, 1995)

A practical guide to a range of techniques, with gallery pages and step-by-step instructions.

ACRYLIC AND OIL PASTEL

Once you have mastered the basic techniques, there is a whole range of effects that can be achieved by mixing traditional media together. For an illustrator, it is very important to find a distinctive style—similar to a personal signature. A style can be based on drawing technique and special use of media.

1 This example combines acrylic paint used as a background and oil pastel, which is built up over the top. The acrylic is applied with a large flat brush in bold, sketchy strokes. The paint is diluted to allow the paper to show through.

2 When the pastel is laid down and blended, the acrylic wash is still visible underneath. This gives the pastel a textural appearance, very different from a single layer of pastel.

3 The rest of the design is then applied over the acrylic wash, using the same techniques of blending as for traditional oil pastel.

4 The final design is then fixed to prevent any unintended smudging. (Tip: a cheaper alternative to store-bought fixative is hairspray.)

CUT PAPER

This technique is similar to the ancient art of mosaic, which was used in classical Greece and Rome to decorate the floors and walls of villas. It has become a very popular technique for producing decorative illustrations and is often seen on wine labels or food illustrations.

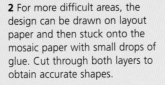

1 The design is drawn out onto the base paper. The other papers are cut to size with a scalpel or scissors and then stuck down.

2 For more difficult areas, the design can be drawn on layout paper and then stuck onto the mosaic paper with small drops of glue. Cut through both layers to obtain accurate shapes.

3 Try to keep the design as simple as possible—cutting tiny details can be very time-consuming and ineffective. The glues most appropriate for this method are the kind that dry clear, so that any residue will not show on the finished work.

TORN PAPER FLOWER COLLAGE

For this collage technique, you may use precolored papers or paint your own. First tear the background shapes, then make the patterns and flower petals. If you are adding a name or greeting, make it at this point and decide where it will fit. Assemble the flower, then glue all of the component parts in place, starting with the background and working up.

The finished flower collage

1 For the main background, paint a gradated wash of red and orange (mixed from yellow and red). Paint more sheets of paper using yellow, cobalt blue, turquoise blue, lime green, and cream.

2 Tear or cut the background rectangles from turquoise, red/orange, and lime green papers. Make sure they will all fit onto your folded card and still leave a slight border area.

3 Tear out approximately thirteen yellow petals for the flower, making each one similar in size.

4 Tear the wavy cobalt blue border shapes, cream dots, and a spiral for the middle of the flower. You can draw the shapes with a pencil first to help make them more accrate, but remember to erase any pencil lines.

5 Glue the end of each flower petal on the back. Assemble the flower by gluing the edge of the petals onto a green central circle. Place each one equidistant from the last.

6 Glue the background rectangles first, followed by the wavy blue borders, white dots, and finally the flower.

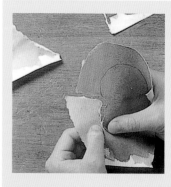

PAINTED PAPER

When white, painted paper is ripped, one edge will show the white paper base, whereas the other will show only the painted, colored edge. Exploit this effect in your collage.

ADDING COLOR TO PHOTOCOPIED SKETCHES

This process also works well with old sheet music and your own sketches. To use your own sketch, take a black and white photocopy. Lightly sand the surface to remove the gloss finish, then apply paint.

1 Using a good-quality black and white photocopy of your own sketch, lightly sand the surface using fine sandpaper.

2 Mix a watery consistency of paint and start to outline the sketch. Cover an area of the background to make it look as if your subject was drawn on a colored background.

3 On the finished image, the unpainted edges of the photocopy have been ripped away.

4 You could try painting strange colors over the photocopy to give the whole image a more surreal effect.

PAINTING A FREESTYLE PATTERN

A simple way to make a repeat pattern is by painting shapes freestyle. Use the finished pattern as it is, or as individual shapes.

1 Decide on a simple motif and consider the size you want it to be in your finished pattern. Paint your shape at intervals on textured paper.

2 When the paint is dry, rip or cut out the individual shapes.

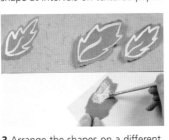

3 Arrange the shapes on a different color or type of paper. Apply glue to the back of each, and stick.

4 The finished sample shows how the scale of each shape can be changed easily. The torn or cutout shapes could be used for a background or border.

DEALING WITH SOURCE MATERIAL

You don't just have to cut out and stick the paper and other materials for your collage. Experiment with other ways of putting things together.

Stitching paper shapes
Carefully stitch shapes together using colored thread and bold, sculptural embroidery stitches. Use this technique to add accents and emphasis.

Chamfered paper edges
Tear the paper insted of cutting it out to exploit the two-tone and textural effects that result.

Weaving paper
Play with the three-dimensional nature of collage by interweaving paper strips.

DIGITAL

Computers have become a very popular tool for illustrators who want to create colorful and sophisticated images that can be manipulated and amended at the touch of a key. Do remember, though, that a computer is only a tool and can only be as creative and effective as the person using it.

Keep a sketchbook to scan from.

A graphics tablet allows you to draw more accurately.

A scanner will scan your linework to allow you to color or manipulate it digitally.

SCANNED DRAWINGS

Many computer-generated illustrations are original scanned line drawings. Software is then used to add color or textures to complete the artwork. A graphics tablet gives you the freedom of a pen and enables you to draw directly onto the screen; many have pressure-sensitive tips for extra control. Software packages offer a wide range of predefined brushes designed to emulate existing media. The range of opportunities within digital illustration can be daunting at first, but after selecting the most appropriate program it is a matter of practice and experimentation. Mistakes are easily rectified with the "undo" command!

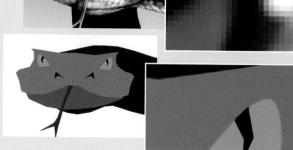

This dragon has been drawn by hand and then scanned into Photoshop. The dragon has been cut out from the white background using the magic wand tool, and the image of the head placed on a separate layer (see page 137) so that any coloring or manipulation is confined to the head and does not affect the white background. By altering the levels in the Hue/Saturation (see page 137) the whole head has been shaded pink. The areas that are a different color were selected using the lasso tool and individually colored.

BITMAP OR VECTOR?

An important thing to take into consideration when approaching digital illustration is the difference between bitmap and vector graphics. Software packages such as Photoshop and Paint are programs that use bitmap graphics, in which each pixel on the screen is a colored block; this creates images which are resolution-dependent and will appear "soft" if they are enlarged too much. Packages such as Illustrator and Flash use vector graphics, in which mathematically calculated curves are used to generate the imagery. These can be enlarged to almost any size.

TRY THIS

The best way to understand and feel confident with the various software is to play with and explore the possibilities, as you would with other media or tools. Take a drawing from your sketchbook and scan it, then have fun manipulating, layering, and coloring; wherever your imagination takes you! Try it in Photoshop initially.

WEBSITES

www.paintermagazine. co.uk

www.pshopcreative.co.uk

www.computerarts.co.uk/ tutorials

www.lynda.com

Working in layers

Illustrator and Photoshop use layers to build up illustrations, manipulate images, and create montages of multiple images. It is very important to master the use and organization of layers. This vector illustration of a teddy has been created in Illustrator; the ability to turn layers on and off shows how you can experiment with the final composition. Layers are useful for collage-type compositions, adding and superimposing images, and switching the order of the layers for different effects.

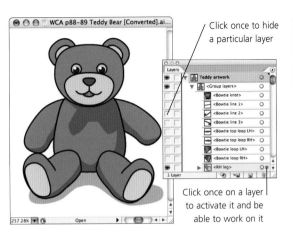

Click once to hide a particular layer

Click once on a layer to activate it and be able to work on it

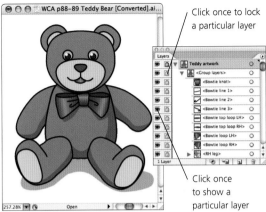

Click once to lock a particular layer

Click once to show a particular layer

Working with effects and filters

Photoshop is used to work creatively with bitmap images. It has a large collection of brushes, filters, and effects with which to create interesting results. This montage has been created using seven separate photographs. The pen tool was used to draw paths in order to cut out parts of the photographs and place them onto the main canvas, on separate layers. The magic wand can also be used for this if the background is a plain contrasting color (such as the fish). Each image can then be manipulated individually before "flattening" the canvas as the final montage.

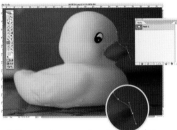

1 The duck was cut out using the pen tool to make a bezier path. Selecting the path, the duck is copied and pasted onto the main canvas. The flying birds, balloon fish, and plane were cut out, copied, and pasted in the same way.

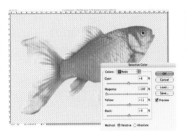

2 The coloring of the fish has been altered—first by using Selective color, then Replace color under the Image/adjustment menu.

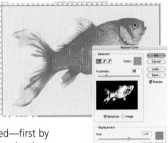

3 A vector mask and the gradient tool created a fade effect to merge the fish into the sea in the final composition. The sea and sky background was merged using the same tools.

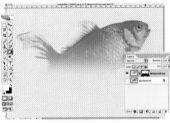

4 The sky layer was altered using the Hue/ Saturation function under the Image/ adjustment menu.

Computer collage

Collage is a particular traditional medium that has benefited from technological developments.

MAKING A DUMMY BOOK

A dummy book is a small, three-dimensional model of your picture book. The first one you make will be for your benefit—you'll be surprised at how your perception of the pace, rhythm, and sequence of the story changes when you hold a tangible version in your hands. The second will be a full-sized model that you'll show to your publisher.

Safety note: work in a well-ventilated room on a protective surface.

PREPARING PAGES FOR A MOCK-UP BOOK

1 Prepare artwork as line drawings, with text for each of the double page spreads, and add registration marks. (These can be original drawn roughs or scanned and printed.)

2 Trim all double pages along registration marks to printed page size.

3 Arrange all the pages in order, from the front endpaper to the back endpaper.

4 Fold each trimmed double page in half.

5 Flatten the folded edge using a bone folder (or similar tool).

6 Stack all the pages together. Check that they are even and level by tapping them on a flat surface at 90 degrees.

MAKING UP THE BOOK

1 Take the first double page, which will be the front endpaper.

2 Place a clean piece of scrap paper in the fold.

3 Spray the back of the page with spray mount.

4 Line up the second double page along the spine. Place it onto the sprayed page and smooth it down to secure it.

5 Repeat this process until all the pages are stuck together.

6 Press down the pages along the spine, to make sure they are all securely glued and even.

7 Place bulldog clips on each end to hold the papers securely.

8 Brush PVA glue along the spine.

9 Attach a strip of thin paper, the width of the spine, along the glued spine.

10 Press down firmly. Leave the book to dry completely for at least a few hours, or preferably overnight.

MAKING THE COVER USING BOOK CLOTH

1 Cut out two pieces of cover board, ⅛–¼ in (2–5 mm) larger on three sides than your glued book, and a strip of board the same width as the spine and the same height as the cover board.

2 Place the two cover boards and the spine onto a piece of book cloth with a ⅛–¼ in (2–5 mm) gap between the spine and covers. Cut the book cloth at least 1 in (25 mm) larger all around. Spray-mount or glue (PVA) the pieces of cover board to the cloth.

3 Turn over and smooth down the book cloth to get rid of any air bubbles, and press along the edges.

6 Trim the book cloth at the corners about ⅛ in (2 mm) away from the crease.

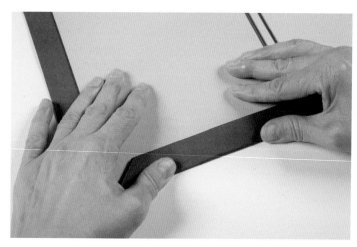

7 Fold each of the edges of the book cloth onto each of the cover board edges and crease firmly.

8 Use a brush to dab small amounts of PVA glue (or a glue stick) onto each length, starting with the top and bottom of the cover.

4 Trim the book cloth evenly around the glued cover boards, no smaller than ⅝ in (20 mm) all around.

5 Fold the book cloth over each corner of the cover and make a crease.

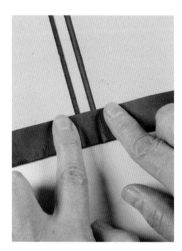

9 Press down well, working from the center out.

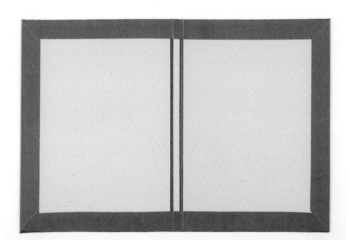

10 When all the edges are glued, they should meet neatly at the corners. Leave the glued cover to dry for a few hours.

11 Fold the cover and start to manipulate the spine with your hands, so that it is flexible and the back and front covers can move freely.

PUTTING THE BOOK AND THE COVER TOGETHER

1 Place a clean piece of scrap paper between the first endpaper and the rest of the book.

2 Spray the back of the page with spray mount. Safety note: work in a well ventilated room on a protective surface.

3 Position the book along the edge of the front cover board.

4 Make sure that the space on each side of the cover is equal.

THE DUST JACKET

1 Prepare artwork in the same way as for covering a book. Trim the height of the scanned or photocopied artwork along the registration marks to fit the height of the cover of the book.

2 Measure the width of the spine.

3 Mark the measurement on the cover illustration.

4 Fold and press down using the bone folder to create the spine width.

5 Bring the glued endpaper down onto the cover and press down firmly.

6 Place a clean piece of scrap paper between the back endpaper and the rest of the book. Make sure that the back cover board is also covered.

7 Spray the back of the endpaper with spray mount. Line the book along the edge of the back cover board and press the glued page down firmly.

8 Close the book. Press and manipulate the spine and cover so it creases the spine and book covers. The process works with both an illustrated piece of paper and plain book cloth for the cover.

5 Place the book into the folded space and fold the ends of the dust jacket around the ends of the book to create back and front flaps.

6 Fold down firmly using the bone folder to complete the book and dust jacket.

TOP TIP

When you design and illustrate the cover, allow for the extra measurements of the cover boards, spine, gaps in between, and the amount that will fold over the edges of the cover board.

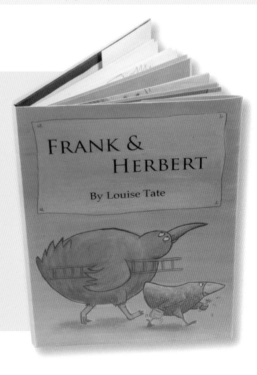

Acting like a professional
Act like a professional and you won't get eaten for breakfast. This chapter gives you some guidelines.

Chapter six

PROFESSIONAL PRACTICE

There are plenty of things first-time authors or illustrators can do to help themselves in their quest for a publisher. This section shows you some approaches to adopt.

50 WORKING LIFE

Being able to commit time and space to your work is an important factor in how successfully you will be able to develop your career.

Having somewhere to work in your home allows you to make the most of your time. A spare room is ideal, but essentially all you need is a designated workspace with room for computer equipment and a telephone. Decide how much space you actually need and be ingenious in creating a place you can leave undisturbed—a workstation under the stairs or in the attic are two obvious examples.

Working in a studio with other artists can be inspiring and fun and allows you to share the running costs. But it can also be disruptive and expensive, with the rent and the commute to a studio a factor in your monthly outgoings. There are advantages to being able to pool resources, share contacts, and publicize yourself as a group. If you take this route, make sure you find like-minded people to share a space with.

Be organized
Have everything close at hand in your workstation. You don't want to have to scramble around looking for a brush or photo reference.

The life of a freelance artist and writer can be immensely rewarding. Being in control of your working day is a major plus. Working on something creative that you love doing and that will hopefully enrich children's lives is also fantastic. However, the life of a freelancer working from home can also be an isolating experience, with much of your contact with others conducted via email and telephone. It can be insecure financially, too. Few writers or illustrators are lucky enough to have a steady stream of work.

Maximize space
If space is at a premium, consider keeping all of your equipment in a portable container, such as an art box, that can be moved around easily.

Work checklist

If you want to become a writer or illustrator, think about the following issues:

- How much time can you commit to the enterprise? Is it going to be a full-time, all-or-nothing endeavor, or is it part of an equation that also includes childcare and part-time work?

- How much space do you need to work? Illustrators traditionally work on quite a small scale, but increasingly this does not have to be the case. You will need space to store artwork as well as a place to generate it from.

- Do you want to work in isolation or would you prefer to share a workspace with others?

- Do you want to engage the services of an agent or are you happier promoting yourself?

- Do you need to engage the services of an accountant or are you confident that you can manage your finances on your own?

Each of these questions needs careful consideration as there is no right or wrong way to approach freelance work—only the way that is best for you.

BUSINESS ESSENTIALS

Invest in some well printed stationery with your own letterhead and logo design to use for correspondence. A business card and compliment slips are also very useful. You will need to generate an invoice template if you have a computer, or use a duplicate book from a stationery store if you don't.

Invoices should include a unique number (devise your own system), your name and contact details, the name and company of the person who commissioned you, a description of the job, and the agreed fee for the work completed. Keep a copy of each invoice you send out and make a note when it has been paid.

It's official! A purchase order from the publisher (below) confirms your commission. You will be expected to sign and return it, along with an invoice (right) for work completed. Don't forget to include your name and address, or they won't know where to send the check.

If you're an illustrator, design your own stationery, use it as an opportunity to shopwindow your skills.

INVOICE

Dean Bassinger
4488 Mandy Way
Hill Valley CA 94941
Tel: 415-384-5368
email: deabs@yahoo.com

To: Patricia Whyte
Art Director
Finest Book Publishing
909 Liondale
Philadelphia
PA 400321

Date: June 20, 2004

Order number: 028-04
Reference code: ICB

To supply: 3 full color illustrations
6 black and white line drawings

(@ 300dpi on disc)

Total: $500

FINEST
Book Publishing

PURCHASE ORDER FOR CREATIVE WORK

THIS PURCHASE ORDER DOES NOT ACT AS AN INVOICE.

PLEASE INVOICE WHEN THE WORK IS COMPLETED

TO: DATE:

PROJECT TITLE: BOOK CODE:

RETURN TO:

DESCRIPTION OF WORK:

DELIVER BY:
(Failure to deliver the work on time or in accordance with the above brief may result in a reduction in or cancellation of the agreed fee).

AGREED FEE:

In consideration of the abovementioned fee paid by Finest Book Publishing to me on delivery and acceptance of the work described above, I hereby grant to Finest Book Publishing ownership of the a non-exclusive license in the said work for the full period of copyright and all renewals and extensions Finest Book Publishing agrees to credit me as the originator of the work. I warrant that the work is original, has not previously been published in any form except as disclosed by me above and is in no way a violation or an infringement of any existing copyright or licence. I hereby indemnify Finest Book Publishing against all actions, suits, proceedings, claims, demands, damages and costs occasioned to Finest Book Publishing in consequence of any breach of this warranty or arising from any claim

SIGNATURE OF CONTRIBUTOR: DATE:

SIGNED FOR AND ON BEHALF OF
FINEST BOOK PUBLISHING BY: DATE:

Please sign and return the green copy of this form to Finest Book Publishing with your invoice. Keep the pink copy as your reference.

FINEST BOOK PUBLISHING   909 LIONDALE   PHILADELPHIA   PA 400321
TEL (215) 770-0670   FAX (215) 770-0671

ACQUIRING AN AGENT

An agent can be extremely useful and will promote your work in an effective and professional manner. He or she will negotiate the appropriate fee for your work, and field requests from clients. Agents take around 15 percent of any money earned through them. Once you work with an agent it is considered bad form to take on work directly.

Agents are interested in seeing new talent, but do not always have the time for a personal appointment. Approach them by sending a letter and samples of your work through the mail. If you have a website, direct them to this, too. All files you send should be compatible with PC and Mac computers. After sending your work, follow up with a phone call to check that it's arrived, but don't bombard agents with calls or correspondence.

READ THIS

The Children's Writers' and Artists' Yearbook
F&W Publications Ltd

An invaluable resource listing contact details of agents and publishers in the

Equipment you will need:

Essential:

- Studio equipment
- A desk and a comfortable chair with back support
- A desk-lamp with a daylight simulation bulb (to ensure your colors stay true even when you're working at night)
- A telephone and answering machine (landline or cell)
- A plan chest for storing your artwork safely
- A filing system for correspondence

For the longer term:

- A computer for graphics software and email
- A scanner for sending roughs
- A color printer for printing samples
- A graphics tablet

51

COPYRIGHT AND LICENSING

As the originator of artwork, you automatically own the copyright to any imagery you produce, whether it is a doodle you did while you were on the phone or a fully realized painting.

WHAT IS COPYRIGHT?

Copyright means the right to copy something, hence the name. You automatically own the copyright to your artwork, but it is possible to sell or gift this right to someone else. Copyright does not necessarily reside in the physical object, but in the right for it to be copied. Someone can own the copyright to your painting without owning the original.

Traditional copyright would give you sole right to approve any copied versions of your artwork, and will not enter the public domain until seventy years after your death. What this means is that it becomes common property, and although you would still be attributed as the creator, the right to copy it is now free to all.

Copyright can be bequeathed, and in some cases extended. For example, the copyright for the story of *Peter Pan* was given to Great Ormond Street Children's Hospital in London, and continues to generate revenue for them.

Don't skim the contract
Always clarify with the publisher what rights you are assigning them—whether they can reproduce your work once or continually, and how you will be compensated for it.

Option clauses
Some contracts include a clause that keeps you from selling the work to other publishers, or states the course of action if the publisher should go out of business or the book goes out of print. If you're uncertain about the terms, seek legal advice.

COPYRIGHT IN CRISIS

Copyright law is currently in crisis due to the ease of duplicating imagery digitally. Organizations such as "Creative Commons" argue the case for a more flexible approach to copyright. However, as a professional artist, it is imperative that you protect your right to be identified and recompensed as the originator of the artwork. The best way to do this is to always insist on retaining copyright of your artwork, but agree to license the work for the specific use intended by your client.

LICENSING

A license allows the client clearly defined rights to use the imagery in a specified format for a specified amount of time and in specified places. Licenses are frequently used for developing a character, as a successful children's book character can generate spin-off merchandise in everything from bedding and toys to food and clothes. It would be very disappointing for you if you realized you had sold your copyright on a creation that became a runaway global success!

Licenses are used to clarify the use of imagery where the following issues may arise:

- **Use:** this is usually clear from the brief, but it may be worth stating that further uses will require a further fee.

- **Area:** the usual categories for this are UK, Europe, USA, and World. The fee should reflect how widely your image is to be distributed.

- **Exclusivity:** the client will want to be clear that they have the exclusive right to use the image. This covers all areas of reproduction for example not only the book but stationery, greetings cards, t-shirts to film and digital rights—in some circumstances you might be able to keep an aspect of this to help boost your fee.

- **Duration:** this is often not clear, and the solution is to give a very long license, even for the duration of copyright.

- **Royalties:** a publisher will offer you a contract that states the terms of the advance and the royalties. The royalties are the percentage of the profits made after the advance is paid back.

CONTRACTS

It is vitally important that you are clear about the use of your artwork, and you should always be aware of what you are being contracted to do. A contract can be a written or verbal agreement, but if it is verbal it is best to follow up the conversation with a letter or email clarifying that both sides understand the terms and conditions of what you are expected to do, and where this obligation ends. Otherwise you may find yourself endlessly tinkering with artwork that should have been approved at an earlier stage.

Protecting your copyright

The simplest way to ensure protection of your copyright is to place a copy of your artwork in a sealed envelope and post it to yourself. Do not open the envelope when it arrives, but keep it safe! This document could be used in a court of law to prove your prior claim to the imagery if any misappropriation of your work occurs.

Who owns what?

One day you may create a character who has licensing potential. You'll want to be sure that you own the rights you thought you owned.

52
SHOWING YOUR WORK

Your "book," or portfolio, is the public face of your work. It should show off your capabilities and ideas in a variety of styles and media while maintaining coherency and consistency. It should also contain a concise resumé detailing your skills. You may consider compiling different portfolios for different markets. Some children's illustrators even work under different names (or pseudonyms) if they have several styles of working.

The ideal children's book illustration portfolio would contain:

- drawings that are full of life and personality;
- character studies showing a character in many moods and poses;
- evidence of good composition and visual storytelling skills;
- black and white work as well as full-color;
- good use of media.

Don't put half-finished work in. Show off your skills! If you don't have ideas for your own stories, it is a good idea to include some illustrations from a well-known fairy tale in your portfolio, as this will give an art director a clear idea of how you approach interpreting a text.

MEETING THE ART DIRECTOR

You have your bright and shiny portfolio with your work displayed coherently and cleanly within. You have printed some business cards to leave as a reminder of you and your work after you have gone. If you are used to working alone at home, you may want to assess your habitual work clothes when setting off to a meeting. This is a rare occasion on which you must look presentable! You are about to meet with someone who is interested in your work.

- Make eye contact, smile, and shake hands. Research has shown that people make up their minds about potential employees within a couple of seconds of meeting them. As so much of children's publishing is based on collaboration, it is important that you come across as friendly and enthusiastic.

- Be confident about your work when talking an art director through your folder—there is no need to point out what you don't like about an image. Highlight your strengths.

- Don't explain everything in enormous detail. The art director is busy and needs to get a quick sense of what your work is like, not a history of every job you have ever done.

TRY THIS

Invest in a professional portfolio with clear sleeves. Think about the size—it doesn't have to be huge, but neither should it be minuscule. Consider what you want to achieve. Do you want to show a lot of double-page spreads from books you are working on? How big are the originals? Have your work copied to a high standard, and include original pieces, too. The portfolio should be clear and clean (no dust, hairs, or footprints!) and should be ordered in a logical way—nobody wants to have to root through piles of paper to get a sense of your work. Around twenty pieces should be ample to give someone a sense of your range and skills. Make sure the work is mounted securely in the sleeves using double-sided tape.

Unfinished work
Avoid the impulse to put unfinished work in your portfolio.

MARKETING YOUR WORK

There are many ways in which you can attract the attention of a commissioning editor or art buyer. Word of mouth through contacts and friends is the most direct and low-key way to start. Or, exhibit your work in local and national galleries and enter competitions. Direct mailshots of your own promotional pack are a good way to show your work around. Another option is to buy space in one of the illustration annuals such as *American Illustration*. These are sent out to thousands of potential clients and—although expensive—can pay for themselves in terms of the amount of work they generate. You need to balance the advantages of targeting people you have researched very specifically against the advantages of the "scattergun" approach. The first is time-consuming; the second expensive. But both can work equally well.

MORE ONLINE OPTIONS

Another option is to sign up to a group website. These have the advantage of being low-maintenance, but they are often vast and the danger is your work will become lost or swamped by the sheer volume of imagery on display. They are also not free, although the cost is small compared to creating and maintaining your own site. The Association of Illustrators has a reputable online portfolio site based around the 'Images' book it publishes every year showcasing the best of British Illustration. (http://www.aoiportfolios.com/)

A "blog" can be an effective way to keep your work in the public eye. They are often free and allow you to upload images and text very easily into a limited set of formats. The content is easily managed and can be updated as often as you like. Many artists choose this form because it allows them to show new work easily, and as it is constantly being updated there is more chance of people returning for a second, third, or even daily look! The blog allows you to index your work into categories and will archive your entries. Blogs may be simpler than a flash-based website, but they are functional, easy, and can be run alongside a more traditional portfolio-based website.

The digital portfolio

Having a website is a definite advantage for an illustrator, as it is an easy way to direct people to look at your work. However, not all art directors like to spend their time sifting through the enormous variety of work online, or waiting for large files to download. You will not automatically get the attention you expect from sending out work in this format. You will still need to use traditional methods to attract some potential commissioners. It is also not enough to build a beautiful website and expect people to find it by chance.

The advantage of having a digital or online portfolio is that it allows you to show time-based work, animated pieces of work, and work with sound files attached. Not all of children's publishing is paper-based, and increasingly children will access content online. This is a tremendously exciting area for illustrators to be aware of, and if you are interested in the possibilities of digital interaction and animation in your ideas for children's publishing, then now is the ideal time for you! Remember, your work does not necessarily have to be generated by a computer to be displayed by one; often traditional work reproduces extraordinarily well on-screen.

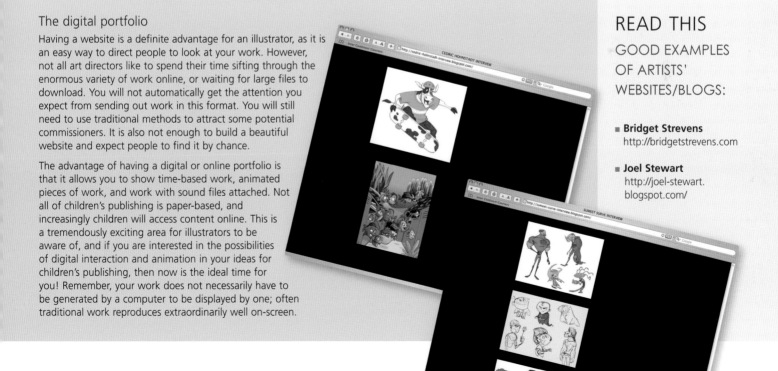

READ THIS

GOOD EXAMPLES OF ARTISTS' WEBSITES/BLOGS:

- **Bridget Strevens**
  http://bridgetstrevens.com

- **Joel Stewart**
  http://joel-stewart.blogspot.com/

53

GETTING A COMMISSION

Congratulations! Your work has made an impression and an art director has asked you to produce some work for them. Do not be afraid of asking straightforward questions if you are not clear about what the task is that you are being asked to do.

Moving forward
From your single piece of artwork, a whole cast of commissioned pieces can develop—to a deadline!

A clear vision
Make sure you know what the brief is before you start writing, illustrating, or even sketching out ideas.

Useful questions

The following questions may help you clarify with the publisher or art director the particular task in front of you:

■ What exactly are you being asked to do? Avoid producing speculative artwork for nothing. However, you can discuss developing ideas and roughs if you are offered a development fee.

■ What is the outcome of the work? Is it to be a book? If so, ask about the format and extent of the book.

■ When is the deadline? Is the deadline realistic? If not, say so. You know better than anyone how long a piece of artwork is going to take you to do.

■ Where is the book being published? A picture book may be translated into many different languages. This may impact the kind of details you can put

into the imagery—for example, yellow cabs and red mailboxes are specific to particular places.

■ How is the work to be presented? Are you expected to send the originals or will a high resolution scan be sufficient?

■ How much are you going to get paid? Although illustrators are notoriously shy of talking about money, it does you no favors to allow yourself to be exploited. Your work has commercial value, and you should appreciate your time.

■ Ask how any advance payments would be structured. Ask about royalties.

Teamwork
You may be an illustrator creating atmospheric pictures, as featured here, or you may be the writer, sparking the artist's imagination. Either way, the two of you are about to embark on a unique experience together. Enjoy!

Negotiation

Tips for negotiating a good deal:

- Be confident when talking about money, without sounding arrogant or demanding. You can be polite and pleased that you have been commissioned without being astonished and overly grateful!

- Be clear about what you can do and what you expect from the publisher. State at the beginning that you expect to retain copyright on your imagery.

- Be mindful of the client's needs as well as your own.

- Be pleasant and cooperative— strive to be polite and professional at all times.

- Be prepared to pass up the job if the terms are not acceptable to you.

ROYALTIES

Royalty agreements usually form the basis of the transaction between the publisher and the author or illustrator. A publisher agrees to invest in the expertise and knowledge of the writer or illustrator by advancing them money to enable them to produce the work. The publisher offers the contributor a percentage of the ongoing profits of their joint enterprise once this initial advance has been repaid. Therefore a large advance means that it takes longer for a book to start earning royalties for you. But if your book is successful, the royalty payments will continue to come in for many years after your initial effort.

Royalties in picture books are usually split 50/50 between the writer and the illustrator. Sometimes this seems unfair, as the text may be minimal yet the illustrations are lavish and detailed. In this case it would be up to you as the illustrator (or your agent) to negotiate a bigger percentage of the royalties.

BOOK PACKAGING

Book packaging differs from publishing in the following important respects. Packagers do not store, distribute, or market the books they produce. They concentrate on creating the book, and then sell it on to a publishing house as an edition or co-edition. Packagers are, in essence, a "freelance" editorial/design/ production unit. They can vary from being very small outfits to larger companies, and in general offer less generous advances than the publishing houses.

Going to print
Remember that the illustrations you supply to a publisher are going out to the world and will be in print for many years to come. This is your moment to shine.

The real deal
A skillful negotiator will get the best deal for the characters they have created.

GLOSSARY

A beginner's guide to print and publishing terminology

BLAD A booklet used in book publishing and usually made up of the intended cover and three to eight printed sample pages. Used to promote new titles at book fairs, sales conferences, and so on.

Bleed (1) Printed matter designed to run off the edge of the paper. Also used by bookbinders to describe over-cut margins. (2) An ink that changes color or mixes with other colors, sometimes caused by lamination.

Blow-up An enlargement from a small original.

Blurb Promotional text on the flap of a book jacket or the outside back cover of a paperback. Often the listed merits on the back of a book are called "bullets."

Body type Text normally used for the main text of a book, not captions or headings. The size range is usually 6 to 16 point. Picture books may have a body type size up to 30 point.

Bulk The thickness of paper—spine widths are calculated from paper bulk and number of pages.

Combination line and halftone work Halftone and line work combined on one set of films, plates, or artwork.

Continuous tone Illustration (photograph, drawing, or painting) consisting of a broad range of tone.

Copy Manuscript, typescript, transparency, or artwork from which a printed image is to be prepared. May also be supplied in electronic form.

Copyright The right of an author or artist to control the use of their original work. Although broadly controlled by international agreement there are substantial differences between countries.

Corner marks These may be on the original artwork, film, or printed sheet and can also serve as register marks during printing or as cut marks for use in the finishing operations.

Cropping Trimming or masking a photograph or artwork so that a detail, its proportions, or size are in line with those required.

Cut marks Marks printed on a sheet to indicate the edge of a page to be trimmed.

Cut-out (1) An illustration from which the background has been removed to provide a silhouette. (2) A display card or book cover with a pattern die-cut in it.

Die-cut Steel cutting rules bent into an image shape and used to cut into board or paper—used in novelty books.

Display type Any type other than body copy designed to catch attention, for examples, heads and titles, often unusual, highly decorative or distorted faces in size 16 to 72 point.

Double-page spread *See spread.*

Dummy A sample for a job made up with the actual materials and to the correct size to show bulk, style of binding, and so on. Also a complete mock-up of a job showing position of type matter and illustrations, margins, and other details.

Endpapers Lining sheets used at each end of a book to fasten the case to the first and last sections of a case binding.

Etching The mordant effect of a chemical on plate or film. In lithography, the solutions are applied to the plate after imaging to make the non-image sections both water-attractive and ink-repellent.

Flat color An area of printed color with no tonal variations.

Flush left or right Type set to line up at the left or right of a column.

Folio (1) A page number and also a page. (2) a large book in which the full-size sheet only needs to be folded once before binding.

Font A set of type of one face or size.

Format The shape and size of a book (and sometimes the binding style and overall layout of the page).

Four-color process Color printing by means of the three primary colors (yellow, magenta, cyan) and black superimposed. Each plate is produced from separations which have been made from the originals on a scanner or process camera.

Grain The direction in which the fibers lie in a piece of paper—some strongly-textured papers can add interesting effects in washes and shadows to watercolor paintings.

Graphics tablet Used in computing by compositors and in electronic-page composition systems for layout or system control.

Gutter The margin down the center of a double-page spread, sometimes equal to to two back margins.

Half up Instruction to prepare artwork 50 percent larger than final size so that it can be reproduced at 66 percent to eliminate any blemishes in the original.

Halftone Printing tone illustrations by breaking them down photographically into dots—used in lithography.

Imposition Plan for placing pages on a printing sheet so that when folded, each page will be in the correct sequence.

In proportion (1) Individual items of artwork that are to be enlarged or reduced by the same amount during reproduction. (2) Instruction that one dimension of an artwork is to be enlarged/reduced in the same proportion as the other.

ISBN International Standard Book Number. A unique ten-figure number that identifies the language of publication of a book, its publisher and its title, plus a check digit. Often also included in a barcode.

Justify Positioning of type lines so they are evenly spaced on left and right.

Laminating Applying transparent or colored plastic films, usually with a high gloss finish, to printed matter to protect or enhance it. Various films are available with different gloss, folding, and strength characteristics.

Line art Artwork entirely in black on white with no intermediary tones.

Layout Any indication for the organization of text and pictures with instructions about sizing and so on for reproduction or printing.

lightbox A box with a translucent glass top lit from below giving a balanced light suitable for color matching on which color transparencies, prints, and proofs can be examined or compared.

Monochrome A single color.

Mordant (1) Adhesive for fixing gold leaf. (2) Fluid used to etch lines on a printing plate.

Offset (1) Lithographic (and sometimes letterpress) method of printing in which the ink is transferred from the printing plate to an offset blanket cylinder, and then to the paper, board, metal, or whatever on which it is required. (2) To reproduce a book in one edition by photographing a previously printed edition.

Prelims Pages at the beginning of a book consisting of half-title, title page, copyright page, contents, and other pre-text materials such as acknowledgments and introduction.

Proof A representation on paper of any type or other image made either from the plates or directly from the film used in their production.

Recto Right-hand page.

Reproduction The entire printing process from the completion of typesetting until litho plates reach the press. This includes the use of process cameras, scanners, retouching, and the imposition and platemaking operation.

Rough An unfinished layout or design.

Rough proof A proof that is not necessarily in position or on the correct paper.

Section Paper folded to form part of a book or booklet. Sections can be made up of sheets folded to 4, 8, 16 but rarely more than 128 pages, perhaps from two 64-page sections.

Spread Printed matter spread across two facing pages.

Vignette Effect applied to halftones that, instead of being squared up or cut out, have the tone etched gently away at the edges.

Verso Left-hand page.

INDEX

CREDITS

Quarto would like to thank the following artists and agencies for kindly supplying images for inclusion in this book:

- **Brian Fijimori**
www.dasgroup.com 6tr

- **Annebicque Bernard** ©/Corbis 74t

- **Dover publications** 10b, 11br

- *Farmer Duck* by Martin Waddell and illustrated by Helen Oxenbury. Reproduced by permission of Walker Books Ltd, London SE11 5HJ. Illustrations © 1991 Helen Oxenbury 32

- *Ginger* by Charlotte Voake. Reproduced by permission of Walker Books Ltd, London SE11 5HJ. Illustrations © 1997 Charlotte Voake 16b

- *Harry Potter* by J K Rowling, children's jacket illustrated by Cliff Wright (tl), adults jacket illustrated by Michael Wildsmith (tr) and published by Bloomsbury 72

- *Marvin Wanted More* by Joseph Theobald and published by Bloomsbury 130tr

- **Nicole Tadgell illustrations** © Nicole Tadgell nic.art@verizon.net 1, 10tr, 26tr, 27t, 45tr, 51ml, 52m, 81m, 84-85, 105

- *Pudding* by Pippa Godhart, illustrated by Caroline Jayne Church. Published by Rachel Ortas 44tr

- **Shutterstock** 15b, 18m&b, 20tr, 21bl, 49tl, 59, 60bl, 61, 62-69, 78, 106bl, 107tr, 110tr

- **Simon Bartram**, from *Man on the Moon – A Day in the Life of Bob* published by Templar Publishing www.templarco.co.uk

- **Stacey Schuett** www.staceyschuett.com 51tl, 51br, 81tl, 91bl, 103tr

- *This Little Chick* by John Lawrence. Produced by permission of Walker Books Ltd, London SE11 5HJ. Illustrations © 2002 John Lawrence 79b

- *Trolls on Hols* by Alan MacDonald, illustrated by Mark Beech and published by Bloomsbury 56

- *We Are Going On A Bear Hunt* by Michael Rosen and illustrated by Helen Oxenbury. Reproduced by permission of Walker Books Ltd, London SE11 5HJ. Illustrations © 1989 Helen Oxenbury 37b

- *Vegetable Glue* by Susan Chandler © 2004, Illustrated by Elena Odriozola © 2004. Published by Meadowside Children's Books in 2004 13bl&r

- **Jess Wilson** www.jesswilson.co.uk 149

About the contributing authors:

- **Desdemona McCannon** is the award leader for the MA Illustration for Children at North Wales School of Art.

- **Sue Thornton** is an illustrator and senior lecturer at the North Wales School of Art and Design. She has worked as an illustrator for children's books, and is the originator and leader of the BA (Hons) Illustration for Children's Publishing program.

- **Yadzia Williams** is a program leader for BA (Hons) Design: Illustration at the North Wales School of Art and Design at the North East Wales Institute.

- **Paul Dowswell** is a freelance writer, specializing in fiction and non-fiction for children.

- **Meredith Sue Willis**'s books for children include a book about writing, *Blazing Pencils*, and the novels *The Secret Super Powers of Marco*, *Marco's Monster*, and *Billie of Fish House Lane*.

- **Karen Ball** has edited children's nonfiction and fiction for 16 years. She is the author of several children's books and short stories and is currently working on a project set in 13th-century Japan.

We would also like to thank the following artists:

Adam Paxman	Heather Allen	Kirsteen Harris-Jones
Amber Lloyd	Helen Bate	Lee Sullivan
Celia Clark	Helen Papworth	Louise Tate
Dai Owen	Helen Shoesmith	Lucy Richards
Daisy Rae	Ian Benfold Haywood	Milena Michalowska
David Bignall	Karina Durrant	Nadia Sarell
Diane Evans	Kate Leake	Olga Solabaurieta
Emilia Robledo	Kathryn Demiss	Phill O'Connor
Gemma Raynor	Katie Cleminson	

Monitoring in Coastal Environments Using Foraminifera and Thecamoebian Indicators

Monitoring in Coastal Environments Using Foraminifera and Thecamoebian Indicators addresses one of the fundamental problems for environmental assessment – how to characterize the state of benthic environments cost effectively in regard to both contemporary and historical times. Foraminifera and thecamoebians facilitate biological characterization of a variety of freshwater and coastal marine environments; they react quickly to environmental stress, either natural or anthropogenic. Because of their small size, they occur in large numbers in small-diameter core samples, and since they have a hard shell, they yield fossil assemblages that can be used as proxies to reconstruct past environmental conditions. This book presents a comprehensive overview of sampling and sample processing methods as well as many examples in which these methods have been applied – from pollution impact studies to earthquake history investigations.

This book is the first of its kind to describe comprehensively specific methodologies for the application of foraminifera and thecamoebians in freshwater and marine environmental assessment. It introduces the topic to nonspecialists with a simple description of these two groups of protozoan organisms and then moves on to detailed descriptions of specific methods and techniques. Case studies are presented to illustrate how these techniques are applied. The appendix includes a glossary of terms and a taxonomic description of all species mentioned in the book.

The main audience for this book will be resource managers and consultants in the public and private sectors who are working on coastal environmental problems. It will also serve as supplementary text for graduate students in many courses that deal with environmental monitoring, micropaleontology, or marine ecology, which are typically found in departments of environmental science, oceanography, marine geology, earth science, marine biology, and geography.

David B. Scott is a Professor at the Centre for Marine Geology, Dalhousie University. Professor Scott has worked with Professor Medioli and Dr. Schafer for over twenty-five years, producing over 100 research papers. Scott and Medioli were the first to show that marsh foraminifera could be used as accurate sea-level indicators, and how they are used around the world by many researchers. They also pioneered the use of fossil testate rhizopods for reconstructing pollution history, storminess, and a myriad of other uses that are detailed in the book.

Franco S. Medioli is Professor Emeritus at the Centre for Marine Geology, Dalhousie University. He is the author and co-author of some ninety scientific papers and book chapters in scientific journals on a variety of microfossils (Ostracoda, Foraminifera, Nannoplankton, Thecamoebians). In the early 1980s, Professors Medioli and Scott developed a micropaleontological procedure for relocating past sea levels using marsh foraminifera, and their method has become more or less standard for most researchers in the field all over the world. They were forerunners in the use of fossil thecamoebians as proxies for reconstructing paleoecological histories of freshwater deposits, and their work in this field spawned a growing number of papers on lacustrine pollution reconstructions.

Charles T. Schafer is an Emeritus Research Scientist at Canada's Bedford Institute of Oceanography in Dartmouth, Nova Scotia. His twenty-seven-year tenure with the Geological Survey of Canada is highlighted by studies on the application of benthic foraminifera as proxy indicators of polluted north temperate coastal environments. Dr. Schafer's research papers on this topic, and on other applications of foraminifera as sentinels of environmental impact, exceed 100 and are often cited in this field of marine research. His detailed survey of benthic foraminifera distribution patterns in Chaleur Bay, a very large and complex east-coast Canadian estuary, stands as a hallmark baseline study. Many of his publications demonstrate the development of unique SCUBA and manned submersible techniques for quantitative sampling and in situ experimental work.

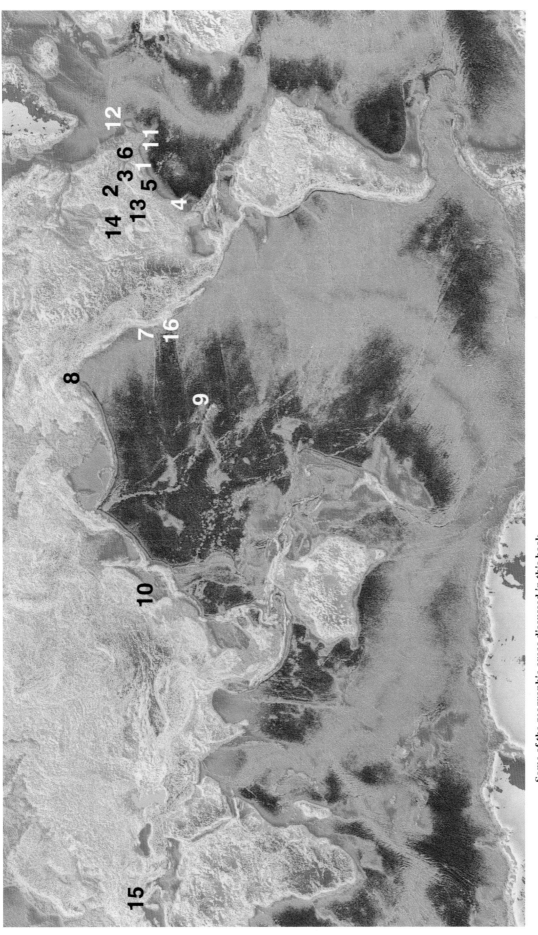

Some of the geographic areas discussed in this book

(1) St. Georges Bay, Chezzetcook Inlet, Halifax Harbour, Bay of Fundy, Journeays Lake, Porter's Lake, Canso Strait, Baie Verte, all in Nova Scotia

(2) Saguenay Fjord, Quebec

(3) Chaleur Bay and Miramichi Bay, New Brunswick

(4) Murrells/Price's Inlets, South Carolina

(5) Bliss Harbor, Southwest New Brunswick

(6) Cardigan Bay, Prince Edward Island

(7) Coastal Oregon and Washington

(8) Girdwood, Alaska

(9) Kahana Harbor, Oahu, Hawaii

(10) Sanya Harbour, China

(11) Emerald Basin, Scotian Shelf

(12) Notre Dame Channel, Newfoundland Shelf

(13) Lake Erie, Ontario

(14) Northern Ontario

(15) Northern Italy

(16) Mission Bay and Tiajuana Slough, Southern California

Monitoring in Coastal Environments Using Foraminifera and Thecamoebian Indicators

DAVID B. SCOTT
Centre for Marine Geology
Dalhousie University

FRANCO S. MEDIOLI
Centre for Marine Geology
Dalhousie University

CHARLES T. SCHAFER
Geological Survey of Canada
Bedford Institute of Oceanography

CAMBRIDGE
UNIVERSITY PRESS

PUBLISHED BY THE PRESS SYNDICATE OF THE UNIVERSITY OF CAMBRIDGE
The Pitt Building, Trumpington Street, Cambridge, United Kingdom

CAMBRIDGE UNIVERSITY PRESS
The Edinburgh Building, Cambridge, CB2 2RU, UK
40 West 20th Street, New York, NY 10011–4211, USA
10 Stamford Road, Oakleigh, Melbourne 3166, Australia
Ruiz de Alarcón 13, 28014 Madrid, Spain
Dock House, The Waterfront, Cape Town 8001, South Africa

http://www.cambridge.org

First published 2001

Printed in the United States of America

Typeface Times New Roman 10/13 pt.   *System* QuarkXPress^R   [GH]

A catalogue record for this book is available from the British Library.

Library of Congress Cataloging in Publication Data
Scott, D. B.
    Monitoring in coastal environments using Foraminifera and Thecamoebian indicators /
David B. Scott, Charles T. Schafer, Franco S. Medioli.
        p.   cm.
    Includes bibliographical references (p.   ).
    ISBN 0-521-56173-6
    1. Environmental monitoring.   2. Coastal ecology.   3. Foraminifera – Ecology.   4.
Testacida – Ecology.   I. Schafer, Charles T.   II. Medioli, F. S.   III. Title.

QH541.15.M64 S36 2001
577.5'1028'7 – dc21   00-058589

ISBN 0 521 56173 6   hardback

Contents

Preface

This book represents a summary of the experience and knowledge amassed by the authors in total of over ninety years of research on foraminifera and thecamoebians. Naturally, it was not possible to include everything that has been written on the subject, and we have drawn heavily on our own work for case studies. It is appropriate here to acknowledge some of the earliest pioneer workers on this subject, particularly Orville Bandy and his former students at the University of Southern California, who were among the first to show how foraminifera could be used as marine pollution indicators. Fred Phleger and his students at the Scripps Institute of Oceanography did pioneering work on modern distributions of coastal foraminifera. One of those students, Jack Bradshaw, introduced David Scott to this field in the early 1970s. At the time when the likes of Bandy and Phleger performed their early work, microfossils were restricted mainly to biostratigraphic applications, and their utility as environmental indicators was almost completely overlooked. We owe them a debt of gratitude for persisting and making this book possible.

This work could never have been completed without the help of countless students, technicians, and colleagues at both Dalhousie University and the Bedford Institute of Oceanography. Anyone who might have participated on surveys or published findings in refereed journals over the past twenty-five years is here collectively thanked. Some of the most interesting work is in the form of undergraduate theses, some of them published, some not; material from a number of these has been utilized for case studies, giving credit where credit was due.

We are indebted to the people who have worked with us over the years. Tony Cole, a paleontological technician at the Bedford Institute of Oceanography, did much of the laboratory work for Charles Schafer over the past twenty-five years and is an author and co-author in her own right. Tom Duffett and Chlöe Younger, technicians at Dalhousie University, have collected and processed countless samples over the past several decades. Eric Collins, Dalhousie University, helped Scott and Medioli in the field and with data-processing problems over the past fifteen years; he has been instrumental in many projects, not the least of which was his own Ph.D. thesis.

Several past Dalhousie students and post-doctoral fellows helped in the preparation of a short-course manual derived from this book: R. T. Patterson (Carleton University), F. M. G. McCarthy (Brock University), E. Reinhardt (McMaster University), S. Asioli (University of Padua), and R. Tobin (Dalhousie University) are all recognized for their contributions. One of the co-authors, Franco Medioli, spent months assembling the artwork. Some of our colleagues from outside the field of micropaleontology were kind enough to review this manuscript in its almost final form and added many comments that will surely help the users of this book. In particular, Jim Latimer of the U.S. Environmental Protection Agency did a lengthy and thorough review that was of great benefit. Some of our colleagues at the Bedford Institute of Oceanography, Dale Buckley and Ray Cranston, also reviewed the manuscript, as well as Chuck Holmes of the U.S. Geological Survey and several students in Scott's 1999 micropaleontology class at Dalhousie. James Kennett, University of California (Santa Barbara), kindly supplied the senior author with an office in 1996–97 where the first cohesive writing of parts of this book took place.

Many agencies helped fund research over the past thirty-five years that is used throughout this book. These are listed in chronological order: The Geological Survey of Canada, Dalhousie University, National Science and Engineering Research Council (Canada), the Bradshaw Foundation (San Diego, California), Sea Grant (California and South Carolina), the National Science Foundation (U.S.A.), Energy, Mines and Resources Research agreements (Canada), Japanese Science Society, and the Environmental Protection Agency (U.S.A.).

Last but not least, we must thank our families, especially Kumiko, Caterina and Dana, and the friends who have so graciously put up with us during the preparation of this book.

Scope of This Book

Literature on coastal benthic foraminifera is spread over hundreds of different journals in many different languages; this makes its perusal extraordinarily challenging and sometimes impossible. However, this is the very situation that underscores the potential of these organisms as proxy indicators of environmental changes that are an inherent feature of many marginal marine settings. The proliferation of scientific reports is due largely to the fact that the most widely known application of microfossils is, in general, in the petroleum industry where they help in the identification of different biostratigraphic horizons, so that potentially productive subsurface reservoirs can be delineated. This aspect of foraminiferal application is covered by many publications that are readily available, and is not treated in this book.

There is an aspect of microfossils that has not been assembled adequately in book form, that of environmental applications. Texts on the application of microfossils as environmental proxies are limited in number and are usually aimed at specialists. This is particularly unfortunate in that the future of applied micropaleontology appears to lie in the broader field of environmental studies, where its applications are almost limitless. This book has been written for the nonspecialist and in nonspecialist terms; it stresses ways to use these organisms and their fossil remains as environmental proxies. Deliberate emphasis is placed on continental margin areas where over 50% of the world's people live, and where most contemporary marine environmental stress problems occur. The authors have attempted to review and highlight some of the key application pathways and to present the relevant information to the nonspecialist in a simple and practical form that deliberately avoids specialized micropaleontological discussions.

Who Should Read This Book

Over the past decade there has been a growth in government policies aimed at meeting the goals of both resource conservation and sustainable development of renewable and nonrenewable coastal-marine resources. This situation has created a demand for cost-effective, baseline assessment and long-term monitoring protocols within the resource-management community. Living benthic foraminifera and thecamoebian indicator species – and their fossil assemblage counterparts – represent a unique set of tools in understanding temporal and spatial variability and, more importantly, the implications of positive and negative anthropogenic impacts. The evolution of these tools and approaches reflects the fact that scientific data on the functional capacity of ecosystems are difficult and relatively expensive to obtain. Conversely, attributes that help to define ecosystems, such as species diversity and distribution patterns, can be evaluated more easily although they fail to explain dynamic processes (e.g., Fairweather, 1999).

As such, this book will be of particular value to resource managers and conservation scientists who must work in a multidisciplinary setting, and under strict budgetary constraints. Strategies described throughout the text should help a generalist supervisor/manager to formulate monitoring and assessment strategies that can be structured into cost-effective proposals and contracts. The subject material outlined in the following chapters is to be augmented in 2001 by a short course for resource supervisors/managers and community conservation organizations that is aimed at facilitating the formulation of monitoring/assessment protocols on a case-by-case basis.

The book is not intended as a review of the literature on the ecology and paleoecology of testate rhizopods. For greater depth and understanding, the reader should consult some key foraminiferal and thecamoebian literature: for foraminifera, Phleger (1960), Loeblich and Tappan (1964), Murray (1973, 1991), Boltovskoy and Wright (1976), Haq and Boersma (1978), Haynes (1981), Lipps (1993), Yassini and Jones (1995), or Sen Gupta (1999); and for thecamoebians, Leidy (1879), Loeblich and Tappan (1964), Ogden and Hedley (1980), and Medioli and Scott (1983).

1

Some Perspective on Testate Rhizopods

TESTATE RHIZOPODS AS RELIABLE, COST-EFFECTIVE INDICATORS

Many types of proxy indices, both physical/chemical and biological, have been used to estimate changes in various environmental parameters that are then related to the problem under consideration. The focus of this book is on environmental proxies derived from two "groups" of testate rhizopods: foraminifera and thecamoebians (Fig. 1.1). These two groups have a great advantage over most other biological indicators because they leave a microfossil record that permits the reconstruction of the environmental history of a site in the absence of original (i.e., real-time) physiochemical baseline data. The utility of foraminifera and thecamoebians as environmental sentinels also derives from a comprehensive field data base that has been compiled for these organisms over a wide range of marine and freshwater settings and not necessarily from an in-depth understanding of their physiological limitations (e.g., Murray, 1991). By their nature, foraminifera and thecamoebians occur in large numbers; this means that small samples (<10 cc) collected with

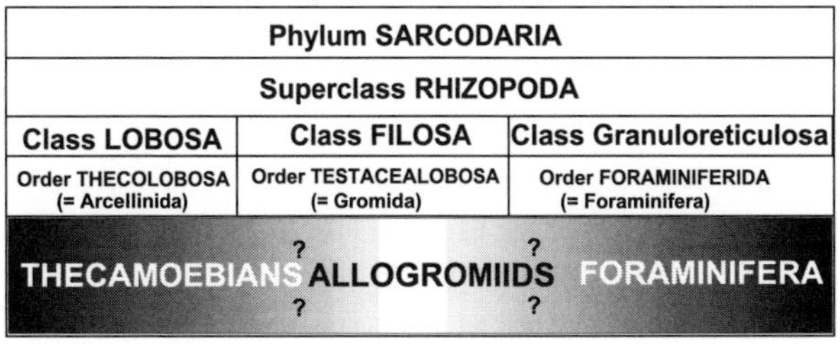

Phylum SARCODARIA		
Superclass RHIZOPODA		
Class LOBOSA	Class FILOSA	Class Granuloreticulosa
Order THECOLOBOSA (= Arcellinida)	Order TESTACEALOBOSA (= Gromida)	Order FORAMINIFERIDA (= Foraminifera)
THECAMOEBIANS	ALLOGROMIIDS	FORAMINIFERA

Figure 1.1. Taxonomic position of foraminifera and thecamoebians. Notice the "fuzzy" distinction between all the groups; most of these differences are based on soft parts, such as pseudopodia, which are typically never observed in the fossil record. (This diagram is a composite from several texts, including Loeblich and Tappan, 1964, and Medioli and Scott, 1983.)

small-diameter coring devices usually contain statistically significant populations. Many biological environmental indicators commonly used in monitoring and impact-assessment studies are organisms that are logistically difficult to collect and expensive to analyze (e.g., molluscs, polychaetes, bacteria, etc.). While these might be more definitive proxies in some situations, they often require large samples (several liters of sediment) or a typically lengthy preparation to retrieve a statistically significant number of specimens/data for an environmental determination. Moreover, the storage of reference samples of these larger organisms can have negative implications for low-budget projects. A critical aspect for the reconstruction of paleoenvironments is that many macro-invertebrates (e.g., polychaetes) leave no easily discernible fossil trace, so that long-term monitoring activities are required to collect a serial baseline data set. Similar information often can be deduced from the fossil foraminiferal assemblages collected in sediment cores. In the case of testate rhizopods, literally hundreds of samples can be collected in a day, and all can be processed within a week. Detailed examination of assemblages and specimen counting takes time, of course, but a skilled micropaleontologist can examine and count as many as ten samples per day. Environmental variation at a particular site is evaluated through examination of the microfossil assemblages contained in successively older core subsamples.

Contrasting these laboratory tasks with those required for macro-invertebrates, other microfossil groups, or even bacteria, shows that foraminifera and thecamoebians can be very attractive from a cost/benefit perspective. Conversely, for quantitative historical studies, macro-invertebrates are usually impractical.

Chemical studies (i.e., isotopes, nutrients, organic matter, trace metals, sulfides, etc.) can sometimes provide chronological and process-related information (e.g., ^{210}Pb; Smith and Schafer, 1987), and can be compared with the microfossil assemblage "signal" to test for environmental impacts (e.g., Schafer et al., 1991). Chemical tracers may not be reliable when used as independent paleoenvironmental proxies because diagenetic processes can change the "fingerprint" of chemical fluxes in subsurface deposits to a much greater degree and more rapidly than would be predicted for the fossil record (e.g., Choi and Bartha, 1994). Many studies have concluded that, whenever practical, chemical and biological parameters should be used together, since they offer greater potential for linking cause-and-effect relationships (e.g., McGee et al., 1995; Latimer et al., 1997).

UTILITY OF TESTATE RHIZOPODS AS ENVIRONMENTAL INDICATORS

Foraminifera and thecamoebians are one-celled animals that are closely related to each other. They form a shell (test) which, when the animal dies, remains in the sediment as a fossil. Foraminifera occupy every marine habitat from the highest high-water level to the some of the deepest parts of the ocean, and they occur in relatively high abundances (often more than 1,000 specimens/10 cc). Thecamoebians have a similar widespread distribution in freshwater environments. The combination of these two groups of similar organisms permits characterization and monitoring of all aquatic environments typically found in marginal marine settings.

There are many reasons that a particular marine organism may be useful as an environmental indicator. Some relate to pressure for worldwide standardization (e.g., the blue mussel, *Mytilus*), while others focus on sensitivity to low levels of certain kinds of anthropogenic contaminants (e.g., bacteria; McGee et al., 1995; Bhupathiraju et al., 1999). Still others have special application because of their ability to tolerate extreme conditions and/or to react quickly to environmental change (e.g., polychaete worms; Pocklington et al., 1994). Because of their comparatively high species diversity and widespread distribution, the testate rhizopods encompass many of these traits. Perhaps more importantly, these organisms are of unique value because of their easily accessible fossil record, which has become a fundamental tool of natural scientists for reconstructing the characteristics and timing of historical environmental variation in a broad spectrum of marine settings.

Foraminifera and thecamoebians are good ecosystem monitors because they are abundant, usually occur as relatively diverse populations, are durable as fossils, and are easy to collect and separate from sediment samples. Although most of them fall into micro- and meio-fauna size ranges (usually between 63 and 500 mm), they can typically be readily observed under a low-power (10–40×) stereomicroscope. No other fossilizable groups of aquatic organisms are so well documented in terms of their environmental preferences for the broad spectrum of locally distinctive environmental conditions found in the coastal zone. Hence, once the characteristics of modern living assemblages have been defined for particular environments, it is usually possible to go back in time using their fossil "signal" to reconstruct paleoenvironments with a high degree of confidence, or to monitor and manage contemporary environmental variation associated with remediation or change of use. Although the model transfer approach may be enhanced by an understanding of the seasonal variation of living populations (e.g., Jorissen and Wittling, 1999; Van der Zwaan et al., 1999), it is not essential since living specimens ultimately accumulate into a total (fossil) population that intergrates small spatial and temporal variations which reflect relatively steady-state conditions (Scott and Medioli, 1980a).

SOME LIFESTYLE ASPECTS OF TESTATE RHIZOPODS

Habitat Preferences

Benthic foraminifera and thecamoebians occupy virtually every benthic aquatic habitat on earth, while planktic foraminifera are usually restricted to open ocean settings. Consequently, in open marine water settings, it is possible to simultaneously study both pelagic and benthic environmental issues. This unique feature of the foraminifera is made possible by the fact that planktic and benthic foraminifera accumulate together as fossils in seafloor sediments in association with living specimens (e.g., Scott et al., 1984). As with most organisms, the diversity of foraminiferal populations usually increases as the environment attains greater stability (i.e., as it becomes more oceanic and warmer). Highest diversities occur in reef environments, which can be considered the marine equivalent of tropical rain forests (Boltovskoy and Wright, 1976; Haynes, 1981; Murray, 1991).

Foraminifera and Thecamoebian Tests

■ Foraminifera

The test – or external skeleton – of foraminifera is composed of several types of material (Loeblich and Tappan, 1964). This characteristic forms the basis for defining the higher taxonomic levels of the group (Fig. 1.2). Subdividing these higher groups can be done using external morphologies, a summary of which is presented in Figure 1.3.

The type of shell material, in general, also determines where various species or their fossil remains can survive. For forms that secrete a $CaCO_3$ test (i.e., "calcareous" forms), this depends on whether or not the environment

is conducive to carbonate preservation (e.g., McCrone and Schafer, 1966; Greiner, 1970). Foraminifera that form their tests by cementing detrital material (i.e., "agglutinated" or "arenaceous" forms) are considered to be the most primitive members of the group. Agglutinated foraminifera, however, can live in sediments where no carbonate is available (i.e., in areas where lowered salinities or colder water make the precipitation of carbonate difficult or impossible). Generally, as salinities and temperatures rise, agglutinated species are replaced by $CaCO_3$ secreting forms (Greiner, 1970), unless the pH is lowered by either low oxygen or high organic matter concentrations (or both in combination). These harsh conditions are often present in polluted coastal environments (e.g., Schafer, 1973; Schafer et al., 1975; Vilks et al., 1975; Sen Gupta et al., 1996; Bernhard et al., 1997) and some, such as high organic matter levels, may influence the bioavailability of contaminants to certain species (e.g., Kautsky, 1998).

■ Thecamoebians

Like foraminifera, thecamoebians can either secrete their test (autogenous test) or build it by agglutinating foreign particles (xenogenous test). A few taxa (Hyalosphenidae) can build either type, depending on circumstances and availability of foreign material. Autogenous tests are either solid and made of silica or complex organic matter, or are built of plates secreted by the organism (idiosomes). Purely autogenous tests are seldom found fossilized. The vast majority of fossilizable thecamoebians possess a xenogenous test built of foreign particles cemented together (xenosomes). The physical nature of xenosomes is exceedingly variable, and their appearance seems to be linked to the nature of local of substrate material (Medioli and Scott, 1983; Medioli et al., 1987). Thecamoebians occupy every niche in freshwater benthic environments, as well as any sufficiently moist niche such as tree bark, wet moss, and so forth. When encysted, they can travel long distances and colonize any available niche, as demonstrated, for example, by their presence in atmospheric dust collected on four continents (Ehrenberg, 1872).

Sensitivity to Environmental Change

The comparatively high species diversity of benthic foraminifera and thecamoebian populations renders local assemblages responsive to a broad range of environmental change. As Scott et al. (1997) and Schafer et al.

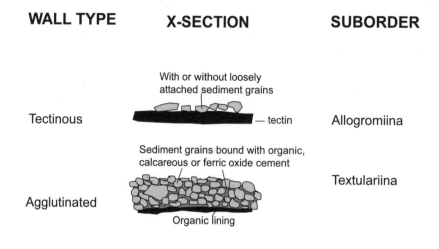

WALL TYPE   **X-SECTION**   **SUBORDER**

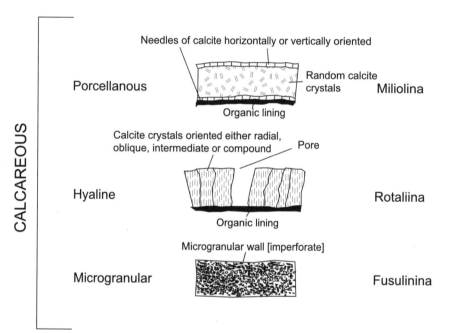

Figure 1.2. Different wall types of the four major groups of foraminifera and thecamoebians (after Culver, 1993).

(1975) illustrated, foraminifera are often among the last organisms to disappear completely at sites that are being heavily impacted by industrial contamination. They can also proliferate in transition zones that do not appear to be utilized efficiently by other kinds of marine organisms (e.g., Schafer, 1973). When observed in a fossil setting, testate rhizopod remains often provide the only proxy information on the spatio-temporal nature of transitional environments (e.g., Scott et al., 1977, 1980). This aspect of the group is most important when studying an impacted site "after the fact," and especially in those circumstances in which original baseline data are not available. In the following chapters we illustrate how foraminifera and thecamoebian populations respond to a variety of environmental changes that may be either natural or anthropogenically induced.

Reproduction Mode in Relation to Environment

■ Foraminifera

There is actually very little known about this topic. Of the 10,000 known living foraminiferal species, only a handful of shallow-water species have actually been observed reproducing in the laboratory (Loeblich and Tappan, 1964), and the life cycle of foraminifera is known for only about fifty species (Lee and Anderson, 1991). It is believed generally that all foraminifera are capable of an alternation of asexual and sexual reproductive modes. In sexual reproduction, millions of swarmers (zygotes) leave the parent cell and mate, producing, presumably, a very large number of

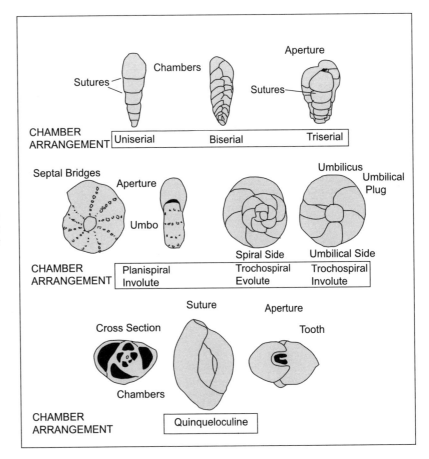

Figure 1.3. Basic patterns of chamber arrangement in foraminifera. Intermediate or mixed arrangements are very common (after Culver, 1993).

new individuals with a small first chamber and large test (microspheric form). Asexual reproduction takes place by multiple fission with the production of, at most, a few hundred new individuals with a large first chamber and small test (megalospheric form). This alternation, however, has been observed directly in only a very small number of species (Loeblich and Tappan, 1964). In most laboratory cultures – the majority of which consisted of small shallow-water forms – only asexual reproduction has been recorded. If the alternation occurred regularly, one would expect that, in an association of empty tests, the microspheric morphotypes should outnumber the megalospheric variety by several orders of magnitude. Careful observations have shown, however, that often the asexual morphotype outnumbers the sexual one in a ratio of between 1:30 and 1:34 (Boltovskoy and Wright, 1976, p. 28). This suggests a very significant dominance of the frequency of the asexual mode in certain environmental settings. Haq and Boersma (1978), in fact, observe that sexuality is very likely a secondary reproductive mechanism, while asexual reproduction is the basic and the more frequent reproductive mode of the majority of foraminiferal species.

There is virtually no solid evidence of why alternation of generations takes place or of how often it occurs. The most rapid reproduction mode is sexual, and it occurs to take advantage of favorable conditions, or it is triggered in response to the development of extremely harsh conditions to help the organism disseminate out of a particular environmental setting (e.g., Boltovskoy and Wright, 1976). In the latter case, the zygotes, being more mobile, can be passively transported out of unfavorable or stressed areas by tidal currents. Both of these ideas are hypothetical since it is virtually impossible to observe this process in a natural setting. Also, the supposedly distinctive features of micro- and megalospheric tests have repeatedly been demonstrated to occur only in some species (Lister, 1895; Schaudinn, 1895; Myers, 1935, 1942; Grell, 1957, 1958a,b; Boltovskoy and Wright, 1976). In summary, very little is known about foraminiferal reproductive strategies in relation to environmental dynamics (e.g., Bradshaw, 1961; Buzas, 1965). However, this situation does not preclude the utilization of distribution data to define environmental change in both a spatial and a temporal context (e.g., Schafer et al., 1975; Vilks et al., 1975). Bradshaw

(1961) showed that the reproductive thresholds, at least for asexual reproduction, are lower than survival limits, so that species will tend to reproduce during the most favorable intervals in otherwise harsh environments and can grow to adult size in less than one month (e.g., Gustafsson and Nordberg, 1999).

■ Thecamoebians

There is even less known about thecamoebian reproduction. In laboratory cultures, binary fission appeared to be the only form of reproduction observed for thecamoebians (Loeblich and Tappan, 1964; Ogden and Hedley, 1980; Medioli et al., 1987). In a virtually forgotten paper by Cattaneo (1878) and in studies by Valkanov (1962a,b, 1966), however, rather convincing cases of sexual reproduction have been documented. Undoubtedly the sexual mode, if it occurs at all, is very rare and seems to have only one function, that of bringing the genotype back to mediocrity.

The Species Identification Problem

Although systematically ignored, the normal biological concept of species, based on the fertile interbreeding of individuals of the same species, does not apply to asexual organisms. Some implications of how this approach has impacted foraminiferal taxonomy are outlined below.

Boltovskoy (1965) discussed a study by Howe (1959) showing that, on average, between 1949 and 1955 two new foraminiferal names were appearing every day. A correspondence between Esteban Boltovskoy and Brooks Ellis revealed that in 1961 the literature contained the names of approximately 28,000 specific and generic taxa. In the specific case of testate rhizopods, the asexually produced individuals of the same "species," as stated by Cushman (1955), are "progressive," while sexually produced populations of the same species are "conservative." In other words, asexually produced populations should be expected to be morphologically highly variable, while sexually produced populations of the same species should be expected to be relatively stable in regard to their test structure. This may explain the presence of well-known, highly variable species of foraminifera and thecamoebians such as *Elphidium excavatum*, and *Ammonia beccarii* (foraminifera), or *Centropyxis* spp., and *Difflugia* spp. (thecamoebians), and so forth, which may not reproduce sexually at all or do so only very rarely. Most highly variable species seem to inhabit relatively dynamic nearshore environments, which is the main area of interest of this book. In these coastal settings they appear to be perfectly adapted to face all of the ecological challenges that the environment continually confronts them with. This creates a problem of species identification that has haunted micropaleontologists for almost a century. Most of the species of testate rhizopods included in this book are characterized by highly variable morphologies. Like human beings who, despite their clearly sexual reproduction, come in many sizes, shapes and colors, testate rhizopods can be grouped together only in the context of a significant sample of a population. In other words, it is almost impossible to reliably identify one single individual in isolation, whereas the identification becomes progressively easier and more accurate as the number of specimens observed increases.

However significant these problems may be, they are an academic matter. This book was written for the non-specialist, and the authors have tried to predigest all of these problems, subjectively circumscribing the "species" discussed in a relatively few manageable and comprehensive units that are deemed to be meaningful for their pragmatic use in monitoring coastal environments.

Trophic Position of Foraminifera and Thecamoebians

Foraminifera are heterotrophic, but they are typically only one step up from primary producers. In addition, many reef forms have symbionts and can function between autotrophic and heterotrophic states (e.g., Hallock, 1981). Some planktic taxa as well as benthic reef-dwelling species have been observed eating copepods and shrimp, forms that are much higher up on the food chain than those generally associated with microorganisms (Rhumbler, 1911; Bé, 1977; Medioli, pers. observ.). For the majority of benthic foraminifera species, however, there is little information on what they really ingest. This situation reflects the fact that the basic biology of these organisms has received relatively little attention compared to investigations on their taxonomy, and on their chronological as well as areal distributions (Lee and Anderson, 1991). In most instances where foraminifera have been cultured successfully, they have been fed with various types of diatoms or ciliates (e.g., Bradshaw, 1957, 1961). It is not known, however, if the cultured species actually feed naturally on diatoms or not. In the case of salt marsh foraminifera, it appears likely that these rather primitive species, like many thecamoebians, may feed on bacteria (e.g., Kota et al., 1999), but as yet there is no hard evidence to support this idea.

There are some research results available on the biology of thecamoebians (Jennings, 1916, 1929; Ogden and

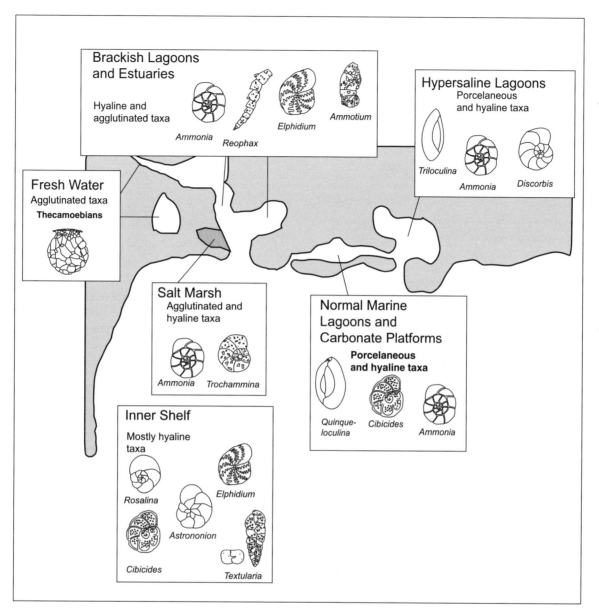

Figure 1.4. A generalized marginal marine nearshore environment showing some typical foraminiferal and thecamoebian species for each environment (after Brasier, 1980).

Hedley, 1980, and others), and several detailed life cycle histories have been worked out for this group. One species has been shown to infest floating algal mats of *Spirogyra* during the summer, forming autogenous tests. From fall to spring, a period during which *Spirogyra* does not float, the species becomes benthic and produces agglutinated tests (Schönborn 1962; Medioli et al., 1987). Thecamoebians are known to have symbionts (zoochorelles), and they are known to eat mostly diatoms and bacteria, although others have been observed to be

cannibalistic (Medioli and Scott, 1983). Only about twenty to twenty-five species of thecamoebians have been reported as fossils (Medioli et al., 1990a,b), some as far back as the Carboniferous (i.e., 400 million years ago, Thibaudeau, 1993; Wightman et al., 1994).

BASIC ECOLOGIC DISTRIBUTIONS

The following is an idealized basic distribution model for marginal marine settings, including continental shelves (foraminifera) and freshwater environments (thecamoebians). Being idealized, it would be expected to change with latitude and water-mass characteristics. The examples shown are meant to be used as a framework for comparing environments from one locality to another (Fig 1.4).

Lakes and Other Freshwater Environments

Forest–lake–bog–upper tidal environments can be differentiated using thecamoebian assemblages. Generally, forms that secrete their own test dominate forest and other environments where sediment supply is low. Forms that use xenogenous material, like silt grains, tend to dominate in lake environments where sediment supply is high; the most common forms in this niche are various species of *Difflugia*. Species diversity decreases markedly with increased marine influence such that close to the upper limit of tidal activity, only *Centropyxis* spp. are found. This relationship permits the delineation of the important and very subtle marine/freshwater transition in intertidal situations.

Marshes

Marshes represent the most extreme of all marine environments, with large variations in temperature, salinity, and pH (see Phleger and Bradshaw, 1966, for a twenty-four-hour record of these variations). Very few species of marine foraminifera thrive in this environment, and their distribution seems to be controlled mainly by physico-chemical phenomena tied to exposure time (i.e., elevation above mean sea level or tidal level). For example, in adjacent intertidal and mud flats environments, oxygen and salinity often explain a significant proportion of the variance observed in macrobenthic community data (e.g., Gonzales-Oreja and Saiz-Salinas, 1998). The same marsh foraminifera species occur worldwide at all latitudes and salinity regimes, especially in the upper part of the marsh. Because of the exposure/time relationship, marsh foraminifera are distributed almost universally in vertical zones that can be used as accurate sea-level indicators, as shown in the applications presented in the following chapters. The species that occupy these high marsh areas are almost exclusively agglutinated, and the few that are not agglutinated do not fossilize in the highly organic and acidic marsh sediments.

Lagoons and Estuaries

Although lagoons and estuaries can be very different environments in terms of foraminiferal content and watermass characteristics, they are grouped together here because they are often perceived as being part of the same set of coastal settings. Lagoons are generally considered to have little or no freshwater input, and typically feature normal marine or hypersaline water. As discussed earlier, higher salinities usually favor calcareous fora-

miniferal species and a higher population diversity. Lagoonal-type environments are most common along warm, arid coasts such as those in the southwestern United States, the Persian Gulf, the Mediterranean, the west coast of South America, and the Australian coastline. In the tropics, special reef-type environments develop that have the highest diversity of foraminiferal faunae (e.g., Javaux, 1999). In contrast, estuaries usually contain a restricted fauna, especially in their upper reaches where salinities are lowest. In this environment, agglutinated species often dominate; calcareous species can tolerate lower salinities in warmer water. Consequently, estuarine foraminiferal associations have a strong latitudinal gradient, with agglutinated forms dominating the assemblages seen in higher latitudes (Schafer and Cole, 1986), and calcareous forms dominating in lower latitudes (e.g., Sen Gupta and Schafer, 1973).

Shelf Areas

Regional differences are perhaps greatest in marine shelf environments. Marine shelf settings span latitudinal gradients with varying degrees of mixing between coastal and oceanic waters (Fig. 1.4). Although shelf areas often are thought of as open marine, many typically "open-ocean" organisms find shelf environments too unstable in terms of temperature and salinity. Nevertheless, shelf species of benthic foraminifera attain high diversities in these environments and can be used to reconstruct the paleo-water mass distribution. As activities on shelf areas, such as petroleum exploration and bottom trawling, are expanded, this environment will come under increasing anthropogenic stress (Auster et al., 1996; Conservation Law Foundation, 1998). As a general rule, a very strong database that is well documented for the modern environments under investigation is required to allow accurate paleodeterminations and reconstructions of former environments. Microfossil assemblages can be used as proxies to reconstruct paleoenvironmental conditions, but if modern faunal information is not available, past conditions cannot be conclusively or confidently defined. Unfortunately, contemporary foraminiferal data are not available in many local areas; they must be collected before fossil assemblage data can be used as a proxy of changing local marine conditions.

SPATIAL VARIABILITY AND PATTERNS

Variability of foraminiferal populations at and between stations has been addressed relatively extensively for most coastal environments (e.g., Schafer, 1968, 1971,

1976; Schafer and Mudie, 1980; Scott and Medioli, 1980a). Much less is known about the synoptic spatial distribution of freshwater thecamoebians. In general, the more stressed an environment becomes, the lower will be the variability within indigenous populations. This characteristic is usually a function of the dominance of several "opportunist" species (e.g., Schafer et al., 1991). As conditions become environmentally stable, biological relationships (i.e., predator–prey, competition, clumping) begin to override physical parameter controls, and local spatial variability of species abundances usually becomes more complex.

Between environments, especially nearshore environments, local variability usually does not exceed the differences between distinct environments (e.g., Scott and Medioli, 1980a). This characteristic is crucial to the utilization of foraminifera for environmental analysis because it facilitates the recognition of distinct zones in both contemporary and ancient sediments that should stand out in relation to spatial distribution "background noise." In a three-year study, Scott and Medioli (1980a) showed that total assemblage (i.e., living+dead specimen counts) differences between high and low marsh zones was always high enough to distinguish those zones regardless of seasonal variations in the living population. Conversely, living populations were often extremely variable compared to total populations, often because of seasonally-modulated variation in reproduction of individual species (e.g., Buzas, 1965; Schafer, 1971) and as a consequence of rapid mixing (bioturbation and turbulent mixing) of the surficial sediment layer. Scott and Medioli (1980a) pointed out that the mixing process is quite fortuitous since total populations are the closest analog to the resultant fossil populations which are what is used in most applications. The density of the total population per unit volume of surficial sediment is essentially a function of bioturbation and sedimentation rate (Loubere, 1989).

One mechanism that contributes substantially to apparent temporal and spatial variability of total population abundance and species diversity is the suite of diagenetic effects that operate on foraminifera and thecamoebian tests following their burial in sediments. The following chapters introduce some of the sampling and analytical strategies that have been used to try and "work around" the difficulties caused by bioturbation and various other diagenetic processes that destroy proxy environmental information imprinted in the marine fossil record.

SUMMARY OF KEY POINTS

- Testate rhizopods occur in large numbers/unit volume and are preserved as fossil assemblages, unlike most other larger invertebrates.
- Compared to other macroinvertebrates, microfossils are cost-effective in both collection and analyzing time, and are the only organisms preserved in statistically significantly numbers in small-diameter cores typically used in nearshore impact studies.
- As with any biological entity, taxonomy (names for species) is a problem, but this book attempts to mitigate this issue by providing detailed morphological information on important indicator species in the text and appendix.
- Distinct species assemblages can serve as proxies to characterize most marginal marine environments. Also, there are abundant data, particularly for benthic foraminifera, that relate environmental parameters to benthic assemblages. Therefore, even though not much is known about the actual biology of these organisms, these data can be used to interpret fossil assemblages.
- Diagenetic processes can have an impact on some fossil assemblages in subsurface environments. These mechanisms may alter fossil content but can often be predicted so that interpretations can be formulated in keeping with a precautionary approach.

Methodological
Considerations

COLLECTION OF SAMPLES

This chapter emphasizes only those techniques that are pertinent to unconsolidated sediments, and essentially applicable to both foraminifera and thecamoebians. The collection and processing of hard-rock samples is rarely necessary for contemporary environmental impact evaluations. For further information on hard-rock processing, readers are referred to papers by Wightman et al. (1994), Thomas and Murney (1981), or any of the many papers dealing with microfossils in shale or sandstone.

Methods of sampling testate rhizopods are greatly facilitated by the small size and abundance of these shelled protozoans. However, because of the need to ensure that the upper several centimeters of sediment remain undisturbed during the collection process, a variety of sampling methods have been developed over the years.

Surface Samples

Most conventional spatial surveys rely on one of several types of grab samplers. Selecting a particular model is influenced by project goals and logistical and sample quality considerations. For nearshore environments that are being accessed using small craft, the 15×15 cm Ekman dredge sampler provides a good-quality small-surface (10×10 cm) sample. The closing mechanism of this device is triggered by a weight that is released at the surface after the sampler has "landed" on the seafloor. The weight slides down the hauling rope and strikes a plate that releases the spring-loaded sampler jaws (Fig. 2.1). Conversely, under exposed continental shelf conditions, where comparatively coarse sandy sediments and water depths in excess of 50 m are the norm, the preferred sampler tends to be heavier but often of a design that causes a greater amount of sample disturbance than is seen in Ekman dredge and box core

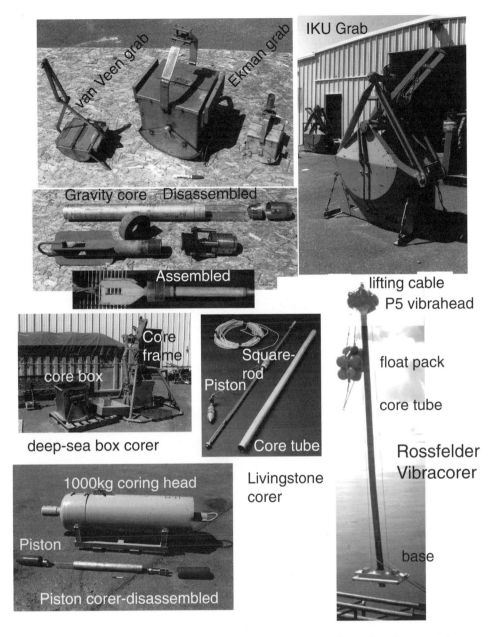

Figure 2.1. Various bottom-sampling devices discussed in the text.

models. The most effective of these robust designs is the Shipek sampler (Fig. 2.2). This tool is a spring-powered device that collects a sediment sample by rotating a cylinder-shaped collector tray through the sediment. Once the collector has rotated 180°, it is effectively isolated from the surrounding environment by the sampler housing. In contrast, various sizes of Van Veen clamshell-type samplers (Fig. 2.1) are used routinely for continental shelf sediment sampling under circumstances in which some disturbance of the sediment surface is not considered critical (e.g., in total population sampling). This sampler design, like the previously mentioned models, is lowered in the "jaws-open" configuration. When the sampler contacts the

seafloor, the load is removed from the hauling line and a retaining link, which holds the jaws apart, releases so that the jaws can be drawn shut as the hauling wire is retracted by the ship's winch. When its jaws are completely closed, the Van Veen sampler also isolates the sample from turbulence generated during the retrieval process (which may take more than ten minutes). The jaws of this device, however, are easily jammed open by pebbles and larger-size clasts. This condition allows disturbance of the sediment sample surface and often results in complete washing out

Ekman dredge being raised full of mud

Diver on the bottom collecting short core

Shipek sampler

Core on deck

Divers placing hand-collected core in scientist's hands

Figure 2.2. Diver-sampling and bottom-sampling hardware discussed in the text.

of the typically loose surficial sediment layer before the sampler reaches the surface. Van Veen samples may be of limited value for living population studies but would be quite adequate for soft-sediment total population investigations where the assemblage reflects essentially a polyseasonal signal that has been generated by local bioturbation processes. In cases where sediment is overconsolidated, and where large bulk samples are needed, an IKU grab can be used (Fig. 2.1).

The solution to obtaining higher-quality undisturbed surficial sediment samples has taken several directions that trade off cost and time considerations. In deep-water shelf settings, the Scripps box corer (Fig. 2.1) and similar designs almost always produce high-quality 50 cm × 50 cm surficial sediment samples. The collection box of this sampler can be fitted with an "ice cube tray" frame, which effectively subdivides the surface of the upper several centimeters of the sediment into nine discrete subsamples during the sediment collection process. The weight of most box core designs usually limits their use to relatively large (>12 m) research vessels. In inner shelf and sheltered coastal settings (e.g., bays, estuaries, lagoons, tidal inlets), sampling using SCUBA divers has proven to be an effective method for collecting undisturbed short cores (Fig. 2.2) (Schafer, 1976; Schafer and Mudie, 1980; Scott et al., 1995a; Schafer et al., 1996). These techniques have been transferred to deeper off-shore environments (up to 50 m depth) using diver lock-out submersibles (e.g., Schafer, 1971). Diver sampling can be relatively expensive and is usually reserved for those cases in which an accurate measure of the quantitative characteristics of a foraminiferal population is needed to refine (i.e., calibrate) empirical models that are needed to interpret mechanical sampler-collected data.

In general, the top 1 cm of sediment in a 10 cm^2 area (total 10 cc) is the sample of choice. This sample size has commonly been used for almost fifty years and reflects a convention that was started at the Scripps Institution of Oceanography by F. B Phleger, one of the pioneers of living foraminiferal distribution studies. In the past several years, a number of investigators have reported foraminifera living within the sediment – that is, up to 10 cm below the surface (e.g., Loubere, 1989; Loubere et al., 1993). This condition poses a concern because it begs the question of just how representative the living foraminifera assemblage of the upper 1 cm layer is with respect to local environmental conditions at any point in time. There are no studies showing that these "at-depth" populations change preexisting total populations significantly. In most cases, the great majority of living specimens occur in the upper 1 cm layer of seafloor sediment. Laboratory studies of foraminiferal burial (Schafer and Young, 1977) have demonstrated that nearshore foraminifera will usually attempt to extricate themselves from redeposited sediment and return to the sediment surface. Conversely, Loubere (1989) points out that the best representation of the total population will likely be found at the base of the bioturbated zone because of infaunal life zonations, bioturbation, and sedimentation considerations. Recent studies indicate that small infaunal species are among the first and most successful colonizers of soft-bottom sediments (see Alve, 1999). As such, a serial sampling methodology applied to a polluted environment could include the evaluation of living specimens over the entire 0–10 cm interval.

Collins (1996) examined three cores from a South Carolina marsh to evaluate the living and total assemblages to a depth of 30 cm in the sediment. He found specimens of some species living to a depth of 20 cm, but in general the great majority lived in the upper few centimeters of the marsh deposit. In this case, the distribution of the living foraminifera with depth in the core did not correspond with the total (fossil) fauna; that is, living population values appeared to have little relation to the total population

numbers at any one level within the core such that the total population was unchanged. This is important when using 1 cm slices of core because it typically means that those 1 cm slices are representative of the environment at that time they accumulated even though they may be infiltrated by younger species of infaunal habit. In marsh sediments, it appears that infaunal living specimens are usually present in such low numbers that they do not affect the overall species proportions of the populations included in deeper (older) layers of sediment. In general, the surface 1 cm should be representative of the contemporary environment at any one time and, depending on local diagenetic processes, 1 cm slices of core below the uppermost 1 cm should reflect older paleoenvironments.

Cores

For waters deeper than 30 m, a range of remotely operated vehicles (ROV) and submersibles have been fitted with articulating hydraulic-powered manipulators that are capable of collecting short, undisturbed sediment "punch" cores. There are, however, a large number of other, less-expensive techniques for collecting sediment core samples in inner shelf settings. These methods usually involve the use of one of several designs of coring devices, either gravity-driven or vibration-powered. These samplers are able to easily penetrate several meters into soft sediment. For deeper penetrations, heavier piston coring or drilling equipment must be used. Fig. 2.1 illustrates some of the commonly used coring devices. In those instances where cost considerations dictate the use of lightweight and relatively small diameter coring devices (typically less than 6 cm in diameter), the value of benthic foraminifera is clearly recognized, because macro-invertebrate fossils are usually not present in statistically meaningful quantities in core samples.

PROCESSING OF SAMPLES

Separation of Fossils from Sediment

For soft-sediment samples, it is relatively easy to wash the sediment through a 63-micron sieve. There has been considerable discussion in the literature on the most effective lower size limit for examination of foraminifera (i.e., >63, 125, 150 or 250 microns). Several researchers have demonstrated (e.g., Schroeder et al., 1987; Sen Gupta et al., 1987) that up to 99% of the fauna is lost even using the >125-micron sieve instead of the 63 micron-size screen. The 63-micron sieve eliminates all the silt and clay size particles, leaving fine sand and larger particles (i.e., the fraction including the size range of most foraminifera). The 63-micron sieve (Fig. 2.3) is generally stacked below coarser ones (500, 850, and 1,000 micron) that retain the larger debris, thereby further concentrating the microfossils in the 63-micron fraction. Thecamoebians, which can be substantially smaller than foraminifera, must be washed using a 44-micron sieve that removes only the clays. Unfortunately, this often results in silty-sand residues, which makes counting

somewhat more difficult. The soaking and washing process is repeated as necessary to completely remove all particles smaller than 44 microns.

Washing of sample material should always be done before the sediment dries out (i.e., before the clay-silt and organic components become semiconsolidated). If the washed residue contains a significant amount of sand, the sample can be dried and a heavy liquid separation technique can be used to "float" the microfossils, which have an overall specific gravity (i.e., envelop density) lower than CCl_4 (now tetrachloroethylene [TCE] since CCl_4 is illegal) or bromoform normally used in a laboratory beaker. This technique allows sand and coarse silt to sink to the bottom of the beaker, while the microfossils float

Figure 2.3. Various sample-handling and sample-splitting devices discussed in the text.

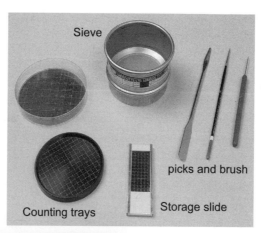

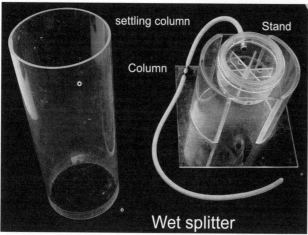

at the surface of the liquid where they can easily be decanted into a paper filter to speed up the identification and counting of specimens under the microscope.

Staining Methods

Since its discovery as a utilitarian technique for identifying living foraminifera, Rose Bengal stain continues to be favored by many foraminiferal specialists throughout the world (Walton, 1952). Some of the difficulties associated with the use of this stain were summarized by Walker et al. (1974) in a paper that described an alternative staining method that employed Sudan Black B. Walker et al. (1974) noted some of the problems with Rose Bengal that had been experienced by various researchers over a twenty-year period following its introduction to the environmental science community. These included (a) staining of symbiotic algae and bacteria associated with both living and nonliving foraminifera (e.g., Bé, 1960), (b) staining of worn and damaged tests of dead specimens (e.g., Green, 1960), (c) failure of the stain to penetrate the test wall of some living specimens (Boltovskoy, 1963), (d) interspecific variation in the amount of stain absorbed (Gregory, 1970), and (e) specimens showing obvious pseudopodial activity but did not stain (Atkinson, 1969). Martin and Steinker (1973) published a review of some of the other shortcomings of the Rose Bengal method. They described many of the observations noted by Walker et al. (1974) and called for a cautious approach. However, the great majority of the problems encountered were a result of samples being dried which limits the transparency of the test and causes the protoplasm to constrict, especially in the case of agglutinated species. When examining Rose Bengal–stained samples, it is suggested that they always be examined in liquid suspension. This technique not only helps in viewing the stained specimens, but also facilitates observing organic inner linings that are lost if the sample is dried. If a sample is dried for heavy liquid separation, it should be resuspended in liquid before analysis for living specimens.

The Sudan Black B method conceived by Walker et al. (1974) was designed specifically to help in distinguishing between foraminiferal protoplasm, the internal organic lining of the test, and detritus adhering to the test. More importantly, the Sudan Black B staining technique was formulated to ensure more reliable penetration of the fixative and stain mixture into at least the last two or three chambers of the test (i.e., the chambers in which the protoplasm usually resides). In the Walker et al. (1974) investigation, staining methods were tried using both heated and unheated stain. Results showed that, when heated to 40° C, the Sudan Black B penetrated relatively deeper into the earlier chambers compared to several other stains that were tested (Rose Bengal, Toluidine Blue, and Asure B). In addition, heated Sudan Black B seemed to have no effect on tests from which the protoplasm had been removed using a low-temperature oxidation (ashing) process. Staining of the test surface of older living specimens (in contrast to freshly collected ones) was reported to be more frequent using Rose Bengal compared to Sudan Black B (50% versus 30%, respectively). Walker et al. (1974) concluded that the Rose Bengal method was not as accurate or reliable as either the heated acetylated or heated saturated Sudan Black B techniques. (In discussions with Scott in 1976, Walker mentioned that most specimens he looked at with Rose Bengal were dry. Since drying the specimens was and still is a standard technique for many laboratories around the world, it is not surprising that many workers obtained poor results with Rose Bengal.) However, both of the Sudan Black B methods lack the inherent simplicity of the Rose Bengal technique, and this difference may account for the continuing popularity of Rose Bengal as the preferred stain. For long-term monitoring projects, an initial intercalibration of the two methods is recommended to help in identifying those species that may be overestimated by the Rose Bengal method. Once the specialist becomes familiar with the strengths and weaknesses of Rose Bengal staining on a species-by-species basis, it should be possible to control the shortcomings of this technique to ensure its reliability with respect to some predefined level of confidence.

HANDLING WASHED RESIDUES

Depending on its nature, washed residue can be stored either dry or kept in liquid. Sandy-silty residue having a minimal organic content can be dried and studied as a powder. Highly organic residue, when dried, often tends to consolidate, or "pancake," a phenomenon that is usually irreversible. Consequently, washed organic-rich residues must be placed in formalin (10%) and water for permanent storage and examination. Alcohol, which lacks the toxic properties of formalin, has also been used for long-term storage. However, it has a tendency to evaporate, so the samples can then be colonized by bacteria that may destroy the foraminiferal tests, especially those with organic inner linings.

For statistical analysis, as opposed to presence/absence data, the number to count is about 300 specimens; it has been demonstrated that larger counts do not significantly improve accuracy (Bandy, 1954; Murray, 1973). When a sample contains many thousands of individuals, it can be split into smaller equivalent subsamples. For dry samples, a small "Otto" microsplitter (Fig. 2.3) can be used (Scott et al., 1980). For many organic-rich samples that cannot be dried, a settling column splitter (Fig. 2.3) can be used (Scott and Hermelin, 1993). Once the microfossil material is concentrated, it is relatively easy to identify and count foraminiferal and thecamoebian specimens with a simple stereomicroscope at magnifications of 20–80×.

Counting can be carried out in two ways. One of these involves spreading the material out in a tray (Fig. 2.3) for dry material, or in a petri dish for wet material, then using a fine watercolor brush (#000) to pick 300 individual specimens out of the washed residue. The specimens are mounted on a special micropaleontological slide that has been coated with a nontoxic, water-soluble glue such as gum tragacanth. Although they are firmly held by the gum tragacanth glue, they can be manipulated or removed easily from the slide with a wet brush. After the specimens are mounted, they can be identified and counted. The slide facilitates the reexamination of the sample at a later time.

The second technique consists of counting the different species without picking the specimens; this requires great familiarity with the species involved but saves an immense amount of time for each sample, especially in the case of wet samples where it is difficult to pick individuals out of the alcohol with a fine #000 brush. For most organic-rich sediments this is the only practical way to be able to process a large number of samples. Usually the first technique is necessary in new areas where the species are still inadequately known; after this initial and time-consuming "calibration" stage, the second method becomes practicable and very effective. There usually are many local references available to help in identifying specimens, especially for Quaternary species (i.e., taxa less than 2 million years old). In the appendix, we supply simplified taxonomic information to assist in the identification of species discussed in this book.

SAMPLING PRECAUTIONS

Following the advent of utilitarian staining methods (Walton, 1952; Walker et al., 1974), comparisons between living and total (i.e., living+dead) foraminifera populations have repeatedly demonstrated the relative heterogeneity of living populations in space and time.

This difference is a function of several environmental and biological factors, and has implications in regard to project objectives and for matching sampling regimens to data treatment styles.

Total populations tend to present a more homogeneous spatial and temporal distribution compared to living ones as a consequence of postmortem lateral and vertical mixing of empty tests by physical (e.g., wave turbulence and tidal currents) and biological (e.g., bioturbation) agents; more importantly, the total population integrates all of the living seasonal variation and spatial clumping into an average "signal" that tends to reduce between-sample variance and is more indicative of steady-state conditions. In contrast, the relatively aggregated or "clumped" spatial pattern of living populations reflects the impact of factors such as seasonality, predation, reproduction mode, sources and distribution pattern of food particles, and species interactions (Schafer, 1968; Buzas, 1968). The dominance of one suite of processes over another, and their degree of interaction, can be expected to change from one environment to another. Alve (1995) cautions about the importance of spatial and temporal variability of foraminifera species in polluted environments. Contaminated areas often occur in marginal marine settings where inherent natural benthic conditions change over small distances, making interpretations difficult at best. Sampling methods should be "fine-tuned" to reduce the collection of redundant living population data and to permit the assignment of confidence limits on single sample results (i.e., sample size considerations). The following section emphasizes the importance of replicate sampling using a series of case examples from various environmental settings, and stresses the need for caution and conservatism in sampling living populations for monitoring or impact assessment purposes.

Nearshore Subtidal Settings

Schafer (1968) reported on the distribution of living foraminifera in a series of coastal environments in which up to four replicate samples (short cores) spaced about 50 cm apart had been collected using SCUBA diving techniques. In New London Bay, Prince Edward Island, living foraminifera collected in water depths of 3.5–4 m ranged from 200 to 750 specimens per standard-size sample in a four-core replicate sample set. The range of between-subsample interval variation also showed considerable temporal change, with clumping increasing considerably between spring and summer seasons (e.g., Schafer, 1968). In an adjacent inner-shelf environment in the southern Gulf of St. Lawrence, the spatial variation of living foraminifera populations collected from an average water depth of 12 m also showed a distinctly "clumped" distribution (Schafer, 1971). The spatial distribution at a 6-m-deep shoreward station showed relatively greater between-sample homogeneity of living population densities compared to those observed at the 12-m-deep location, and included a number of samples in which no living specimens were observed. The three locations are all within a radius of 3 km, but each one is marked by a distinctive set of environmental conditions.

Estuarine Environments

Interseasonal monitoring of total foraminifera population distribution patterns has been done in the lower reaches of the Restigouche Estuary, Gulf of St. Lawrence, using an Ekman grab sampler (Schafer and Cole, 1976). Most of the species observed along several transects showed clumped temporal distribution patterns. The coefficient of variation (V) of a species collected along the same transect on several occasions (where V = standard deviation of species i × 100%/mean abundance of species i) had a range of 40% (relatively homogeneous) to 122% (relatively clumped) depending on the time of sampling (Schafer and Cole, 1976). A water depth-dependence of foraminiferal spatial variation in this setting is suggested. In the shallowest interval of the transect, the range of the coefficient of variation (CV) of interseasonal values for particular species reaches 98%, whereas in the +30-m-depth interval the CV range is only 55%. These data reflect the trend toward increasing benthic environmental heterogeneity with decreasing water depth that is often seen in relatively shallow, nearshore estuarine settings. The importance of these findings for environmental applications is that the inherent living spatial and temporal variation of shallow nearshore populations can obscure signals related to pollution forcing if only living forms are used (e.g., Alve, 1995). In one of the following sections, some data-presentation strategies are outlined that can be used to mitigate the effect of clumped distribution patterns in formulating empirical models for monitoring and impact assessment applications.

Continental Shelf Settings

Living foraminifera inhabiting inner-shelf settings show spatial variability at several scales. In the Gulf of St. Lawrence, the range of variation of living specimens per replicate sample is highest in shallow nearshore environ-

ments. However, it is also significant in some deeper, and presumably lower-energy, habitats (Fig. 2.4). Schafer (1971) concluded that the clumped character of living foraminifera populations is reduced generally in water depths greater than about 24 m and that the distribution pattern of living species at any given time probably reflects the interaction of a suite of complex biological and physical processes (e.g., Van der Zwaan et al., 1999). In the Schafer study, the largest range of variation of living foraminiferal populations found in the 0–1 cm interval of replicate cores, collected by SCUBA divers at the same station (i.e., within a radius of 20 m), was estimated to be 81,700 specimens per square meter. This kind of variability augers against the independent use of living population density data for environmental mapping purposes unless adequate resources for replicate and serial sampling are available.

Throughout the past several decades, many investigators have demonstrated that there are practical limits beyond

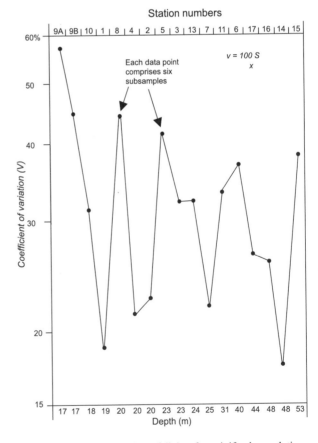

Figure 2.4. Spatial variation of living foraminiferal populations along a transect in the southern Gulf of St. Lawrence. Replicate samples used in this study were collected as short cores by SCUBA divers. Each data point on the graph represents six subsamples (after Schafer, 1971).

which the interpretation of quantitative estimates of living foraminiferal distributions becomes speculative, regardless of the minimum number of specimens that have been counted in any given set of samples (e.g., Lynts, 1966; Boltovskoy and Lena, 1969; Ellison, 1972; Murray, 1973; Scott and Medioli, 1980a). This situation exists because living foraminifera distribution patterns are controlled by both physical and biological processes that continuously interact with each other in complex ways. In some nearshore environments, these interactions can produce living distribution patterns that differ significantly from those that may have existed at the onset of a particular study. These conditions require the use of precautionary and conservative sampling methodologies for living distribution applications. As Scott and Medioli (1980a) illustrated, however, total populations (living+dead) are relatively reliable as proxy indicators because they integrate temporal and large-scale spatial variations at a given site through the combined effects of biological mixing and physical redistribution processes. However, there is always the possibility that anthropogenic effects may create community changes for which there is no obvious precedent in the fossil record (e.g., Greenstein et al., 1998).

SPATIAL VARIABILITY OF FORAMINIFERA IN CORES

Given the degree of sediment mixing by bioturbators and the lateral redistribution of empty tests by tidal currents and storm-generated wave turbulence, it can be predicted that local foraminiferal spatial heterogeneity in sediment cores collected in shelf environments would be of little significance. Schafer and Mudie (1980) tested this idea using pairs of cores that were collected by SCUBA divers at a lateral distance of about 1 m at two 22-m-deep locations off the south shore of St. Georges Bay, Nova Scotia. They discovered about an order of magnitude difference in the average Foraminiferal Number (i.e., the number of foraminifera tests per cm^3 of wet sediment) between the two sites (Fig. 2.5). In addition, both pairs of cores also showed considerable variability in between-core differences of the Foraminiferal Number, which appears to reach a maximum within the 30–50 cm core interval. A comparison of the spatial patterns of prominent species in the respective core pairs based on the Berger–Soutar Similarity Index revealed distinctive differences in between-core similarity at the two coring sites. Nevertheless, comprehensive indices such as the calcareous/arenaceous species ratio (Rr) showed the distinctive and persistent character of the environment at each site

except for one short core interval near the 28 cm horizon (Fig. 2.5). In retrospect, this singular occurrence may, in fact, be meaningless since the data sets were not plotted in relation to time (i.e., the average sedimentation rate at each site was not determined).

Between-core comparisons based on pollen data also suggested greater spatial heterogeneity at the Georges Bay site characterized by relatively low between-core similarity based on foraminifera species abundances. These spatial differences accentuate the limitations of single-core sample nearshore foraminiferal data sets in regard to their suitability for use in some statistical models (e.g., transfer function analysis). Schafer and Mudie (1980) argue that maximum information on regional paleoecological events can only be obtained in these environments through the use of combinations of proxy indicators (i.e., sedimentological and paleontological) and that cores, whenever possible, should be collected from relatively low-energy (i.e., sheltered) settings in nearshore environments to try to avoid "noise" associated with high-energy transport mechanisms. The alternate strategy mandates replicate and temporal sampling, which may not be cost-effective. One advantage of the single-core sample approach is that subsamples can be averaged to produce a robust general profile of the indigenous total foraminiferal population that should be very useful as a baseline reference for future serial monitoring programs.

SOME DATA PRESENTATION OPTIONS

Data presentation techniques offer a much wider range of possibilities than is available in choosing an appropriate sediment sampler. However, key considerations in data presentation are usually linked to the objective of a particular survey. For foraminiferal applications, investigators are strongly encouraged to include raw counts in tabular form in their reports and publications so that these data can be considered by other researchers and be processed for reasons other than those that prompted their original collection. Statistical packages evolve, but original data remain the same and can be reevaluated as new quantitative methods appear. In addition to statistical techniques, which are useful for large data sets, good visual presentations of raw data (as shown in Chapter 3) are powerful tools to illustrate trends.

For routine contemporary environmental monitoring and mapping, there are several simple and conservative ways that foraminiferal data can be presented. Of the many available data presentation formats, the abundance ranking of species (e.g., Shaw et al., 1983) provides a

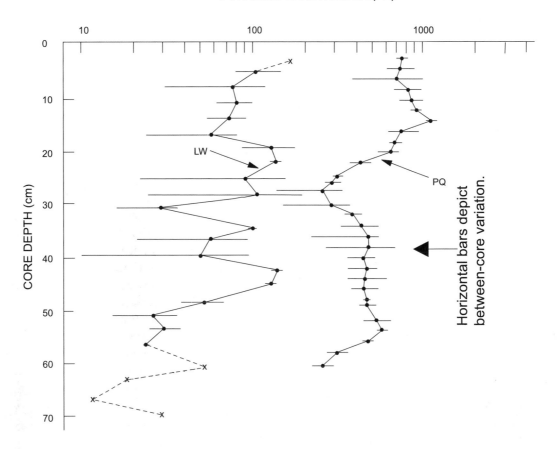

Figure 2.5. Variation of the foraminiferal number (number of specimens in a cubic cm of wet sediment) in two pairs of cores collected at two locations in St. Georges Bay, Nova Scotia. At each location, SCUBA divers forced two plastic core liners into the sediment; the cores were spaced 2 m apart (after Schafer and Mudie, 1980). Horizontal bars depict between-core variation at each location.

powerful first-order impression of community structure that almost always enhances an interpretation of commonly used diversity indices (e.g., Sokal and Sneath, 1963; Sanders, 1969). The level of influence of environmental disturbance on the indicator community can be gauged from the curvature and tail length of the ranking curve relative to curves from control sites or precontamination core intervals. Wilson (1988) noted that, for nonspecialists, this method offers a significant advantage in that the degree of taxonomic expertise, or time spent doing identifications, could be reduced because, in stressed environments, only the most abundant species need to be identified and plotted to obtain the basic shape of the curve. Rare species are of greater importance in normal, unimpacted settings (e.g., Yong et al., 1998).

The species-ranking technique has been applied to data from a core collected in the Saguenay Fjord where the pollution history is well known (Schafer et al., 1991). Major decreases in the flux of pulp mill contaminants to this marine basin occurred after 1970 as the result of the enforcement of new environmental legislation. Natural remediation of the most contaminated upper reaches of the fjord occurred as a consequence of a large landslide

in 1971 that effectively capped a large area of contaminated sediment with a relatively impervious layer of late glacial-age marine clay (Schafer et al., 1991). Ranking curves and associated data from a ^{210}Pb-dated core are shown in relation to a prepollution standard curve (Fig. 2.6). Departures from the shape of the standard curve can already be seen in the 1800–1850 core interval. Profound differences between the standard and the younger age interval curves first occur after 1928, or about ten years after the onset of increased organic matter discharges into the fjord/river system by the local pulp and paper mills. The most recent curves clearly show that the structure of the foraminiferal community indigenous to the fjord basin has still not recovered to that which existed before 1800. The technique also lends itself to defining zones within a variable nearshore environment (e.g., Fig. 2.7).

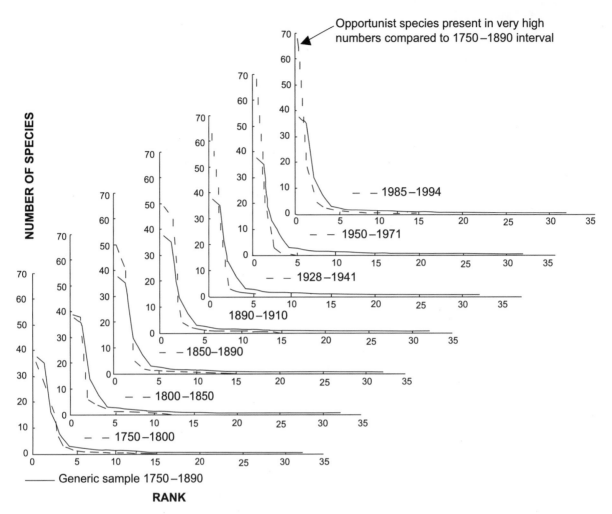

Figure 2.6. Ranking curves of foraminiferal assemblages for various eighteenth- to twentieth-century intervals for a core collected near the mouth of the north arm of the Saguenay Fjord (82008-39). The individual ranking curves (dashed lines) are shown in relation to a 1750–1890 average sample (solid line). The lowest species diversity is seen in the 1950–1971 period when industrial and municipal discharges were at their highest levels (after Schafer et al., 1991).

A variation of this graphical technique uses a log-normal plot (which is what one would expect for an unstressed assemblage) of the cumulative percentage of species versus the geometric class of individuals per species (e.g., Rygg, 1986). A plot of these two parameters on probability paper will give a relatively straight line if the species distribution is log-normal. Departures from a straight-line relationship can often be ascribed to an environmental stress effect. It is recommended that this technique be used in conjunction with a widely used diversity index such as "H" (Shannon and Weaver, 1963), and that data should be derived from a large sample of a species-rich community

whenever possible. This latter constraint places significant practical limitations on the use of this method for pollution-impact surveys. Rygg (1986) recommends that samples selected for this kind of graphical representation should contain at least sixteen species. This criterion tends to eliminate most samples collected proximal to contemporary sources of marine contaminants where species diversities tend to be very low (e.g., Schafer et al., 1975). The best application of this technique might be for assessing temporal changes in areas somewhat removed from a point source of contamination where pollution impact effects are more subtle and less variable.

For monitoring studies that involve the participation of local community organizations, the AMOEBA graphical representation provides an easily understandable presentation technique that is especially valuable for communicating the results of temporal monitoring surveys (e.g., Brink et al., 1991). The method has utility for illustrating differences between populations sampled for both temporal and spatial evaluations. Its use in defining environmental indicator assemblage

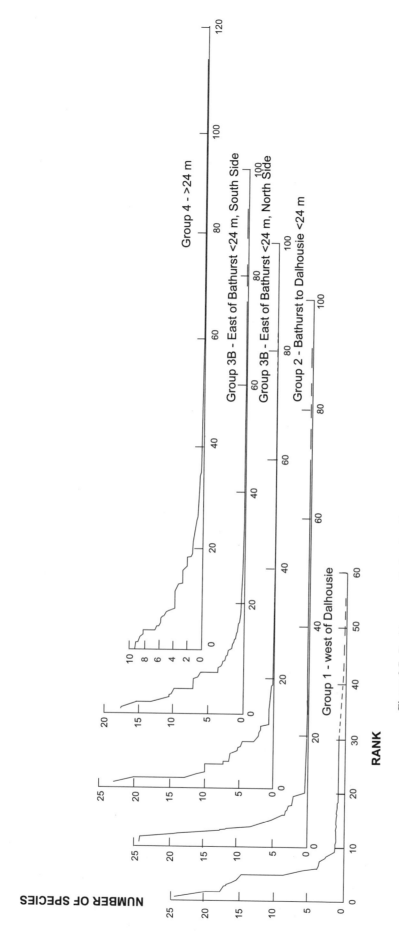

Figure 2.7. Ranking curves for key benthic environments in Chaleur Bay based on total population (living+dead specimens) percentage data (after Schafer and Cole, 1978).

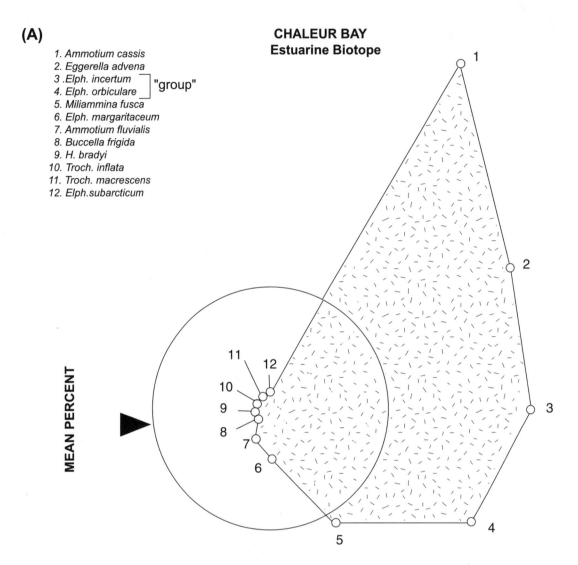

Figure 2.8. (A) An AMOEBA-like illustration of the Estuarine biotope of Chaleur Bay (Schafer and Cole, 1978) generated by ranking the twelve most abundant foraminifera species. Species percentage abundance approaches zero as less-abundant species are added to the diagram. The center of the mean percent circle is zero. Differences in the AMOEBA-like diagram are usually clearly distinctive in between-biotopes comparisons. (B) Diagrams of fossil populations from the same location will often show differences from the initial pattern as species react to changing environmental conditions (after Schafer et al., 1991).

characteristics for two areas of Chaleur Bay is shown in Fig. 2.8A. In a temporal context, the standard curve described in the Saguenay core-ranking curve example can be replaced by a reference AMOEBA-like illustration and compared to an assemblage from a particular time interval (Fig. 2.8B). In both examples, the radius of the reference circle has been set to the median percentage of the twelve most abundant species recorded in each of the samples. For the Saguenay core example, the temporal change in abundance of the two dominant species, and the loss or reduction in the number of sub-

ordinate species in the 1910–28 interval, are clearly reflected by the AMOEBA outline "fingerprint." In spatial monitoring applications, the reference AMOEBA can be derived from a composite average of previous surveys, or from sediment core microfossil data.

TAPHONOMIC CONSIDERATIONS

Although fossil assemblages of benthic foraminifera have been used successfully as a proxy indices to study a variety of paleoenvironmental problems (e.g., Vilks et al., 1975;

(B)

SAGUENAY FJORD
CORE

1. *T. earlandi*
2. *S. biformis*
3. *C. reniformis*
4. *R.catewata*
5. *R. subfusiformis*
6. *A. glomeratum*
7. *E. excavatum*
8. *I. helenae*
9. *S. atlantica*
10. *V. loeblichi*
11. *Q. stalkeri*
12. *I. islandica*

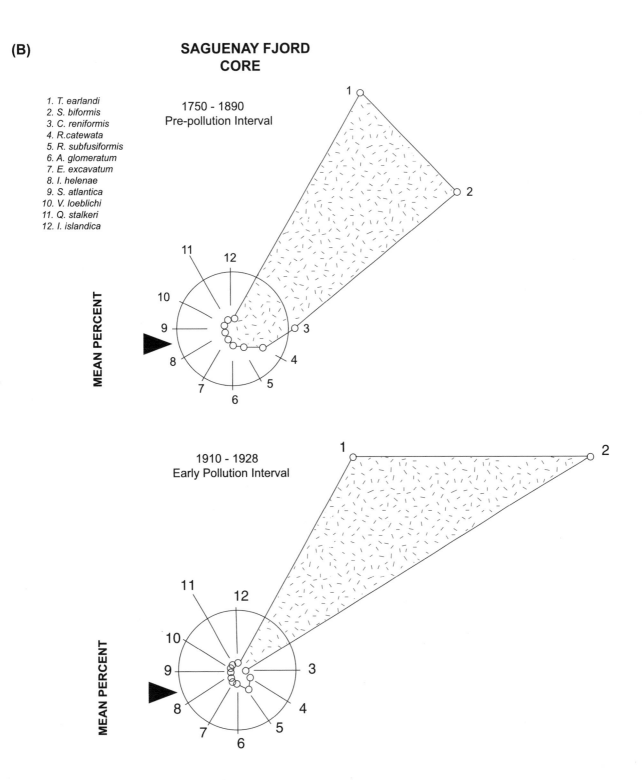

Wagner and Schafer, 1982; Scott and Medioli, 1986; Scott et al., 1987a; Collins, 1996), the transfer of surface total population (live+dead) distribution models to fossil assemblages, and the use of successively older fossil assemblages to establish paleoenvironmental trends, invokes a suite of precautionary subjects that must be considered on a case-by-case basis to maximize the flow of valid information. Bioturbation characteristics, sedimentation rate, geochemical effects, and foraminiferal test durability are among some of the more critical issues that must be considered.

All of these effects and processes can limit the resolution and reliability of proxy data. They must be balanced continuously against the countervailing power of proxy data that permit rapid and cost-effective evaluations of environmental trends in both the temporal and spatial domains.

Candidly stated, there will be situations in which the independent use of proxy microfossil data will be fraught with pitfalls that reflect our poor understanding of the effects of "overprinting" by post-depositional processes on fossil assemblage population densities and species compositions. Their net effect can reflect either the independent impact of one dominant mechanism or, more often, the synergistic effect of several concurrently operating biological, physical, and geochemical processes. An obvious consequence of the work of these overprinting mechanisms is that the profile of successively younger or older fossil assemblages may be interpreted as environmentally related variations (and rates) but may, in fact, partially mark changes in the local mix of physical and chemical overprinting processes.

Bioturbation

Bioturbation can mix high-frequency "paleosignals" (e.g., seasonal variations) and reduce their amplitude (Fig. 2.9) (Guinasso and Schink, 1975). This effect can be most limiting in high sedimentation rate areas where rates of accumulation are sufficiently high to actually record seasonal events. In areas of low sedimentation rates, the seasonal fossil record can often be averaged (mixed) over several years to decades as a total population. This effect is often termed "smearing" because the length of a discrete "paleosignal" may be mixed through a larger interval of time than was actually represented by the causal event itself. More than twenty years ago, Pemberton et al. (1975) observed a species of shrimp that had apparently burrowed to a depth of at least 3 m into the seafloor sediments of the Canso Strait (an overdeepened fjord-like inlet in eastern Canada). Despite the inferred high sedimentation rates observed in this inlet, the mixing of successively older and younger assemblages caused by the shrimp burrowing process was estimated to involve a time interval of as much as 300 years (Vilks et al., 1975). Risk et al. (1978) went on to point out that a population density of 18 specimens/m^2 of just one species of shrimp (*Axius serratus*) could rework (i.e., smear) approximately 30% of the upper 2 m of the strait's seafloor sediment column in only twenty years. The signal distorting effect of bioturbation is closely related to

ambient sedimentation rates. Flessa and Kowalewski (1994) have demonstrated that the median ^{14}C age of macroinvertebrate shells will often show the integrated effect of sedimentation and bioturbation processes. In nearshore and comparatively high sedimentation rate settings, they reported a median ^{14}C age for shells from a given horizon of about 2,400 years. This value, however, reached 8,800 years in more distal continental shelf environments where the rate of sedimentation is lower and the bioturbation effect more pronounced. Although their explanation of the median ^{14}C time interval difference invokes a "shell survival" interpretation, these results could also reflect similar bioturbation conditions under differing sedimentation rate regimes as might be expected in moving from proximal inshore to distal continental shelf settings. The point in focusing on this particular study is to emphasize that if macroinvertebrate shells can be mixed, then the probability of microfossil smearing is virtually certain. Depending on the type of bioturbator (e.g., shrimp versus polychaete worms), there may be size selective mixing that will affect only smaller shells but not larger ones, and mixing modes that are confined to near-surface sediments as opposed to deeper deposits. Part of the solution to this problem lies in achieving as complete an understanding as possible about the nature of local bioturbation processes (e.g., Smith and Schafer, 1984, 1998), recognizing of course that bioturbation regimes will also react to environmental forcing so that more than one mode of mixing may be encountered in the total interval represented by a single core.

The organic matter content of marine sediments plays an important role in the nature of bioturbation because of its role as a food source, or as a control of bottom water oxygen concentration (e.g., Sen Gupta et al., 1997). In continental slope sedimentological settings off Newfoundland, for example (Smith and Schafer, 1984), reduced bioturbation was found directly below the axis of the Western Boundary Undercurrent (WBUC), where the flux of low-density, organic matter–enriched particles to the seafloor was apparently at a minimum compared to relatively quiescent middle-slope and lower continental rise settings lying adjacent to the WBUC's fast-flowing core. These authors also noted that inclined burrow structures had introduced a significant lateral component to the downward transport of surficial sediments. Generally speaking, local bioturbation and sedimentation rate regimes will dictate the maximum theoretical temporal resolution of proxy paleosignals that can be derived from microfossil assemblages.

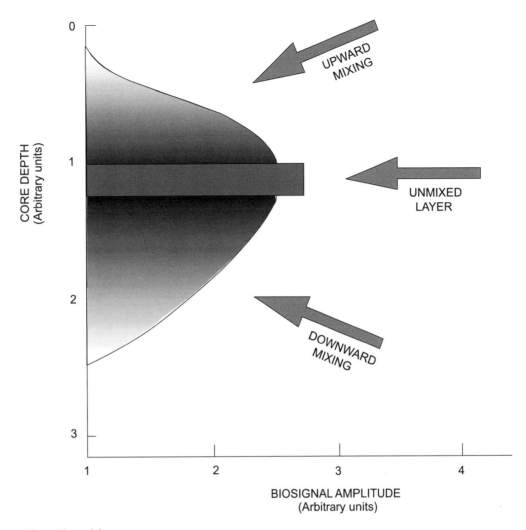

Living to Fossil Assemblage Transitions

Perhaps the most profound change in the transition from living to fossil assemblages is the destruction of fragile species through either mechanical, biological, or chemical mechanisms (e.g., Martin and Wright, 1988; Green et al., 1993). As such, fossil assemblages found in many depositional settings may be expected to be dominated by relatively thick-walled, robust forms or in low-pH environments by agglutinated forms (e.g., salt marshes and highly organic estuarine sediments that are contaminated by sewage). Because fossil-destroying diagenetic processes typically utilize a combination of physical, chemical, and biological mechanisms, there will be certain species that show intermediate levels of persistence (i.e., durability) in nearshore marine sediments (e.g., *Spiroplectammina biformis* and related arenaceous species; Elverhoi et al., 1980). Since many of these are slightly affected, agglutinated species are considered to be good index forms for mapping modern

Figure 2.9. As bioturbators dig through the unmixed layer, they promote "smearing" of unmixed layer material to subjacent deposits and may also transport it to younger overlying layers. The unmixed layer can be contaminated by both older and younger sediment through upward-mixing and burrow-infilling processes. This mixing leads to changes in the fossil information imprinted in the originally unmixed layer. Typical changes involve a reduction of peak percentage values of unmixed layer taxa and the intrusion of their "signal" into older and younger sediments (after Guinasso and Schink, 1975).

foraminifera biotopes (Schafer et al., 1975; Vilks et al., 1975; Scott et al., 1977; Schafer and Cole, 1978; Schafer et al., 1991) so that the rationale for their use in temporal studies is often very persuasive. Part of the problem rests in careful sample preparation – i.e., by not drying the sample so that organic inner linings that mark the dissolution of calcareous foraminifera or the breakdown of agglutinated tests can be detected.

The Dissolved Oxygen Factor

Laboratory experiments and field studies have demonstrated that the preservation potential of microfossil skeletons is enhanced under certain types of anoxic conditions (e.g., Sen Gupta et al., 1997). Low oxygen, however, in certain environments such as salt marshes, can also cause sulfide production and low pH (Phleger and Bradshaw, 1966). The preservation of macroinvertebrate fossil remains (including those species having skeletons constructed by secretion of $CaCO_3$) in estuarine settings has been inversely linked to the abundance of dissolved organic matter (DOM) in interstitial water more so than to relatively high sedimentation rates (Simon et al., 1994). High deposition rates could be expected to quickly isolate fossil remains from physical and biological destructive mechanisms found at the sediment/water interface. The DOM effect is apparently reduced in marine sediments deposited in shallow, relatively high energy settings where ambient sediment organic matter concentrations are relatively lower. The implications of these findings suggest both positive and negative aspects in regard to the completeness of the fossil record. One possible effect is that higher concentrations of organic matter in seafloor sediments can promote longer intervals of anoxicity, thereby enhancing preservation of fossil specimens by eliminating certain types of acid-generating bacteria. A secondary, well-recognized benefit of low oxygen conditions is that bioturbating species are effectively eliminated so that sediments can accumulate in an unmixed and sometimes continuously layered sequences. These deposits retain substantially more high-resolution information on natural process variations that can be seen in partially mixed deposits (e.g., Schafer et al., 1991).

Changes in ambient near-bottom dissolved oxygen concentrations appear to influence foraminifera microhabitat selection leading to active migration of taxa into deeper parts of the sediment column (e.g., Barmawidjaja et al., 1994). Consequently, some species may be epifaunal for part of the year but may revert to an infaunal habit at other times depending on ambient oxygen concentrations, predation, or other environmental stresses. Theoretically, their preservation potential might vary significantly from one habitat to another. Knowledge on changing bottom water oxygen and interstitial water oxygen concentrations may be particularly important in interpreting living data from seasonal surveys and points to the benefit of using "bioindicators" as one of several elements in a suite of physical and chemical parameters in assessing contemporary marine environmental dynamics.

$CaCO_3$ Dissolution

No introduction to taphonomic processes would be complete without mentioning several ideas about the potential effects of $CaCO_3$ dissolution processes on fossil foraminifera assemblage preservation. This physiochemical mechanism may operate on the test itself, or on the cement of certain arenaceous taxa (e.g., Elverhoi et al., 1980). Dissolution of $CaCO_3$ in deep-ocean environments is a well-known physical phenomenon that can be linked directly to hydrostatic pressure, salinity, and water temperature. However, it can apparently also be modulated by organic matter fluxes (e.g., Jahnke et al., 1994). In some anthropogenically impacted settings such as Long Island Sound, organic matter–driven dissolution becomes more important than its physically controlled deep-ocean counterpart, and may account for a significant loss of environmental proxy information that has been "imprinted" in calcareous assemblages (e.g., Green et al., 1993). According to Sayles (1985), enhanced $CaCO_3$ solubility is almost always observed at sediment depths greater than 10–15 cm. As suggested by Smith and Schafer (1984) and by several authors mentioned earlier (e.g., Simon et al., 1994), this sediment depth/dissolution relationship will be controlled to some degree by local organic matter flux conditions. For example, in recent studies of New Bedford Harbor, an estuary adjacent to Long Island Sound, high-sediment organic carbon has caused dissolution in the past (Latimer et al., 1997; Scott et al., 1997). However, the organic linings of some calcareous species could still be observed if the processed sediment was not dried. In these cases, the ratio of actual calcareous tests to inner linings can be used as a rough guide to environmental degradation and post mortem diagenesis. For further detailed information on this topic, and how it applies to foraminifera, the reader is referred to papers by Liddell and Martin (1989), Martin and Liddell (1989), and Smith (1987).

Seasonal changes can be a significant indirect factor in determining the fossil record of what was living at a given time in a marsh/estuarine systems. Scott and Medioli (1980a) observed that in the summer months, calcareous species dominated the living population of outer estuarine salt marshes in Nova Scotia, but were only minor components of the total population. This relationship was thought to indicate that calcareous species, while living, could resist the dissolution effect of the low pH of the marsh sediment (Phleger and Bradshaw, 1966). However, once the organism dies, its test dissolves, effectively removing it from the fossil assemblage. During the winter season, when temperatures drop below 0° C, the dominant living species in Nova Scotia salt marshes is *Miliammina fusca,* an agglutinated form. Because of its agglutinated siliceous test, which is insoluble in hydrochloric acid (Loeblich and Tappan, 1964), this species dominates total populations throughout the year. The total assemblage in any season is similar to what fossil populations look like at this location but with no trace of the seasonally dominant calcareous forms that are seen in the living population. In another instance, the highly dynamic T/S pattern of this environment has been linked to a pH effect that can alter the characteristics of total populations before they become part of the fossil record. In Mission Bay in southern California, where mainly living calcareous foraminifera were observed in the low marsh zone with few agglutinated forms present at any time, the subsurface populations were largely barren because calcareous forms dissolved in the low-pH marsh sediments (Scott, 1976a). In another marsh, 20 km to the south (Tiajuana Slough), organic content of the marsh sediments was even higher. This condition provided the agglutinated foraminifera with a competitive edge. As such, living populations were abundant and could then produce subsurface populations that were also numerous (Scott, 1976a). This is mentioned as an illustration of the profound effect that organic and oxygen content of the sediments can have on two assemblages from seemingly comparable environments.

SUMMARY OF KEY POINTS

- Surface samples should represent the upper 1 cm of sediment as closely as possible; many studies have indicated that benthic foraminifera live at depths up to 30 cm beneath the water/sediment interface. However, in most cases, 90% of the living fauna is included in the surface 1 cm; no studies have shown that foraminifera living at depth in the sediment affect or change the total population from what is observed at the surface. Consequently, the upper 1 cm of the sediment is representative of the time of deposition.
- Processing of soft sediments should always be done on wet sediment.
- Sediment sieve size used to process samples should be always at least 63 microns and sometimes as small as 45 microns.
- Samples should not be dried after sieving if there are large amounts of organic material present.
- Always use a standard sample size of wet sediment (e.g., 10 cm^3).
- Always be sure that there is sufficient data before attempting to use software programs to produce statistical indices and correlations.
- Taphonomic problems discussed here are concerns. However, in most cases, they can be mitigated if there is a good understanding of the environment under investigation.
- Remember that total populations integrate many of the high-frequency temporal/spatial variations that are seen in living populations. Living populations, in themselves, do not represent an overall, steady-state picture and therefore cannot be used as independent representative environmental indicators; however, they may be useful as monitors of remediation.
- Although micropaleontology may seem daunting at first, many undergraduate and graduate students from all over the world, with no prior experience, have been trained successfully within a matter of a couple of weeks to an acceptable level of proficiency. There are 10,000 described species of foraminifera, but only 20–30 are really needed on a case-by-case basis to gain the information that is required for most environmental studies.

3

Applications

This chapter is intended to facilitate an understanding of how foraminifera and thecamoebians can help in evaluating marine-related environmental questions. Many of the diagrams presented have been simplified from the original for demonstrative purposes.

SEA-LEVEL CHANGES

Definitive Assemblages

Many workers have used foraminifera as sea-level indicators (see Haynes, 1981, for a review) but, prior to 1976, their resolution was limited to plus or minus several meters, especially if offshore assemblages were used. The assemblages described here should provide an accuracy of plus or minus a few centimeters at best, and 50 cm at worst. In 1976, the absolute accuracy of salt marsh foraminiferal vertical zonations was verified in southern California (Scott, 1976a) and later compared on a worldwide scale (Scott and Medioli, 1978, 1980b). Since that time, much more work has been done to verify that the relationship exists everywhere (e.g., Petrucci et al., 1983; Patterson, 1990; D. K. Scott and Leckie, 1990; Jennings and Nelson, 1992; Gehrels, 1994; deRijk, 1995; Horton et al., 1999a,b). It appears that the same eight to ten species of marsh foraminifera are ubiquitous throughout the world's salt marshes, especially in the upper half of the marsh. The reason salt marshes in general, and marsh foraminiferal zones in particular, have been used widely for sea-level studies is that the entire marsh environment is confined to the upper half of the tidal range (Chapman, 1960). For most tidal ranges this means that the whole vertical range of the salt marsh deposit is 1 meter or less. This was adequate when sea level was first being investigated in relation to deglaciations. However, in investigating global-warming-driven sea-level movements of only a few centimeters, a ± 1 m resolution is of little value (Houghton et al., 1990; Scott et al., 1995b,c).

A walk on a salt marsh reveals that there is an obvious vertical plant zonation that is controlled by its elevation above sea level. Plants, however, are not consistent elevation indicators (Scott and Medioli, 1980b) and are difficult to identify in "peat" deposits. Foraminifera, on the other hand, do provide an accurate zonation related to mean sea level, which is consistent at least within regions. In addition, foraminifera are normally well preserved and easy to identify in fossil marsh deposits (Scott and Medioli, 1980b, 1986). The most typical marsh foraminifera are agglutinated – that is, they have an organic lining with a fine to coarsely agglutinated test or shell composed of silt and sand grains that the organism collects from the substrate and cements together to make a rigid shell. These tests – commonly characterized as "agglutinated" or "arenaceous" – are resistant to the low oxygen, low pH, reducing conditions that are common to all salt marsh deposits and hence are preserved in marsh sediments. Calcareous shells (molluscs, calcareous foraminifera), although often present as living organisms in most settings, are not usually preserved as fossils because of the inherent low pH conditions of marsh deposits (Scott and Medioli, 1980a). Arenaceous species appear to have been successful for a very long time – what appear to be the same species have been found in the Early Carboniferous (almost 400 million years ago) in Nova Scotia (Thibaudeau, 1993; Wightman et al., 1994) and most recently in the early Cambrian in Nova Scotia (Scott, 1996). What this means is that ancient sea levels potentially can be determined for most of the sedimentary geologic record.

In many cases "peats" have been used in the past as sea-level indicators (e.g., Emery and Garrison, 1967). In these cases, no attempt was made to ascertain whether the peat deposit was of marine or freshwater origin. Assuming, however, that they were of freshwater origin, the only information that the peat could supply was that it had been deposited above sea level, but these features could provide no indication of how far above sea level. On Sable Island (Nova Scotia), Scott et al. (1989a) were able to verify that freshwater peats formed up to 20 m above sea level by differentiating salt marsh peats from nonmarine ones using foraminifera and thecamoebian fossil assemblages.

In Nova Scotia studies, when the highest high marsh zone (zone IA) could be identified in a subsurface assemblage, Scott and Medioli (1978, 1980b) suggested that sea level could be determined with an accuracy of ± 5 cm (Figs. 3.1, 3.2). Except for one New Zealand marsh (Hayward et al., 1999), this particular zone has been identified in the northeastern part of North America only. It does not appear to occur in the Pacific coast or south of the state of Connecticut on the Atlantic side of the United States (Hayward and Hollis, 1994; Scott et al., 1996). Marsh foraminiferal distributions in eastern South America are a mirror image of those seen in the Atlantic region of the Northern Hemisphere (Scott et al., 1990). Thomas and Varekamp (1991) used a combination of marsh foraminifera and geochemical techniques to reconstruct a detailed late Holocene sea-level change in Connecticut, but to date similar investigations have been confined to areas of the South Carolina coast (Collins et al., 1995; Collins, 1996). The well-defined high marsh fauna observed between Nova Scotia and Connecticut is not present in South Carolina. However, in South Carolina and other locations where detailed studies have been conducted, it is possible to delimit high marsh zones that provide accuracies in the range of ± 10–20 cm vertically (Scott et al., 1991; Collins et al., 1995; Collins, 1996).

Applications

In the past five to ten years marsh foraminifera have become the method of choice when evaluating sea-level variations, especially for the late Holocene interval where changes are often less than 1 m. Generally speaking, it is not possible to detect sea-level changes of <1 m with other methods. Recently, sea-level studies have been used to address two important contemporary issues: rapid climatically induced sea-level changes and seismically induced changes where the land surface has been moved catastrophically either up or down by earthquakes.

■ Climatically Induced Changes

In two separate studies, Scott et al. (1995b,c; Gayes et al., 1992) investigated middle Holocene changes in sea level that took place in a timespan of less than 2,000 years. In a South Carolina study (Fig. 3.3), it was possible, using marsh foraminiferal zonations, to detect both a rise and a fall between 5,000 and 3,600 years ago – 2 m of rise followed by 2 m of fall, and then a slow rise that promoted

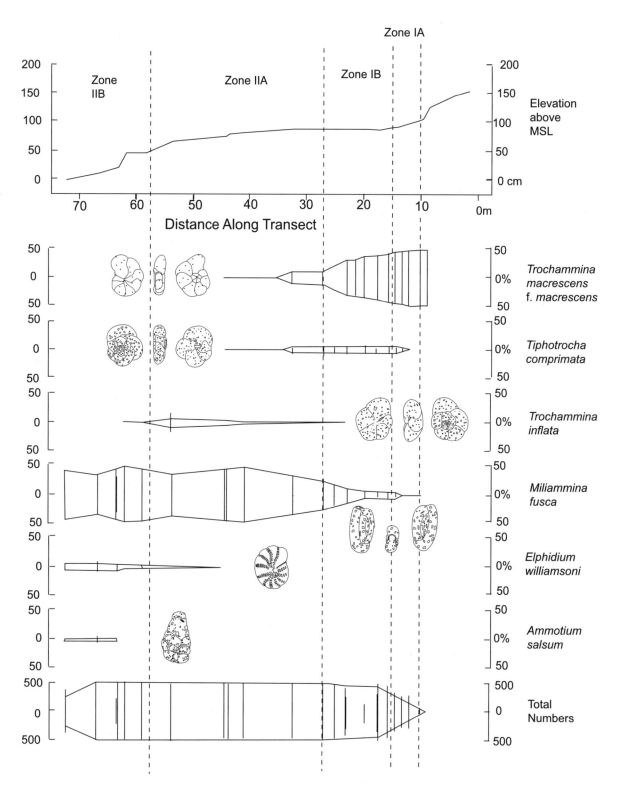

Figure 3.1. A transect across a typical marsh section from Nova Scotia, Canada, showing the vertical zonation displayed by marsh foraminifera (after Scott and Medioli, 1980b).

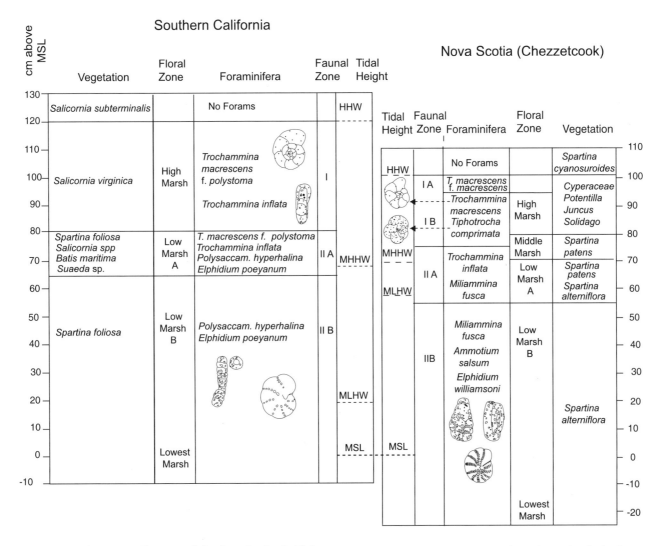

Figure 3.2. Comparative diagram of marsh species (both plants and foraminifera) illustrating how high marsh foraminiferal species from two locations are almost always similar, while their plant species counterparts are often completely different (after Scott and Medioli, 1978).

deposition that eventually covered the deposits that held the record of earlier variations (Scott et al., 1995b). Detection of these changes (Fig. 3.3) was only possible using marsh foraminiferal zonations that, in South Carolina, are sensitive to ± 30 cm sea-level changes. Figure 3.3A shows a sequence prior to detailed microfossil analysis. Interpreted primarily on the basis of lithology, it suggests a broad band of freshwater peat extending across the channel (Gayes et al., 1992). After detailed foraminiferal analyses, the interpretation is altered significantly. To amplify this point, examine Figure 3.3B closely. In the sequence of cores 100 to 103, the thickness of the late Holocene freshwater marsh (Cypress) varies from 1.5 m in core 100 to 0.5 m in core 103 – the only way to differentiate the freshwater marsh from the underlying freshwater sandy material/salt marsh was by using foraminifera. It can be seen that cores 101 and 102 had no underlying salt marsh peat while cores 100 and 103 did – sedimentologically these were all identical. On

the other side of the channel in core 106, sedimentological data indicated that a 3,716-year-old peat was freshwater. Foraminiferal data proved that it was a salt marsh deposit, which completely changed the interpretation, in that these deposits now become sea-level indicators rather than just freshwater peats that provide only limited sea-level information. This is an extreme case of high sea-level variability that, without foraminiferal zonations, would have yielded only limited information on sea-level history. There are many sequences similar to this in the literature that remain problematic because micropaleontological analysis was not part of the study.

(A)

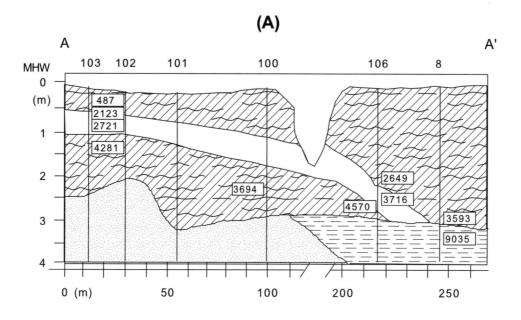

(B)

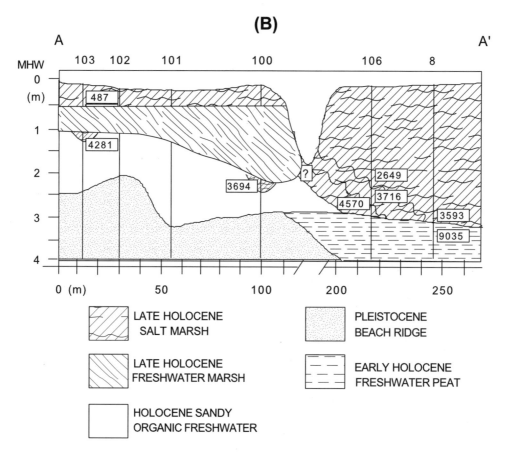

Figure 3.3. (A) Cross section through a marsh in Murrells Inlet, South Carolina, showing horizons of marsh and freshwater peats and underlying older peats (after Gayes et al., 1992). (B) The same cross section based on results from microfossil analysis reveals a much more refined stratigraphy providing a different interpretation that emphasizes the benefit of foraminiferal analysis for classifying nearshore sequences. Numbers in boxes are Carbon-14 dates (after Scott et al., 1995b).

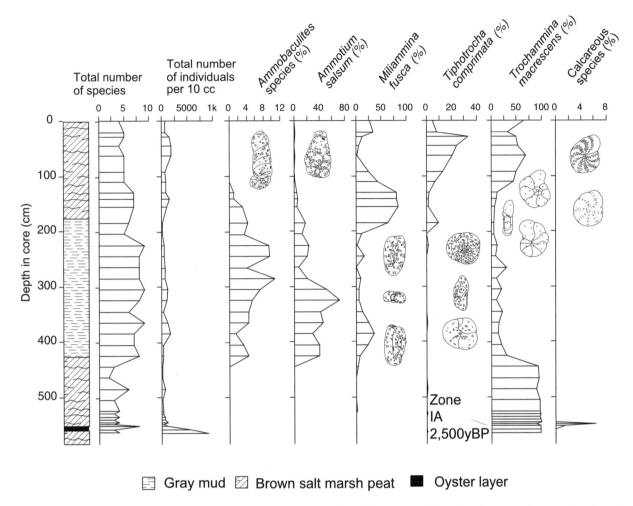

Total number of species — Total number of individuals per 10 cc — *Ammobaculites* species (%) — *Ammotium salsum* (%) — *Miliammina fusca* (%) — *Tiphotrocha comprimata* (%) — *Trochammina macrescens* (%) — *Calcareous* species (%)

Depth in core (cm)

Zone IA 2,500yBP

▤ Gray mud ▨ Brown salt marsh peat ■ Oyster layer

Figure 3.4. Core 12 from Chezzetcook Inlet, Nova Scotia, showing the horizon dated for sea level at ~550 cm. Foraminiferal distributions in this core relate back to Fig. 3.2 with the monospecific fauna at ~530–550 cm indicating Zone IA. This zone provides a measure of sea level relative to higher high water with a resolution of ± 5 cm. The oyster layer at 5.5 m appears to be an ancient native shell midden with shells deposited by Atlantic coast natives that traded with groups from the Northumberland Strait; oysters were not living on the Atlantic coast of Nova Scotia at 2,500 yBP (after Scott et al., 1995c).

In Nova Scotia, an event roughly synchronous to the South Carolina event was observed, but with different characteristics (Scott et al., 1995c). In Chezzetcook Inlet (Nova Scotia), the sedimentary sequence was considerably thicker (11 m of section vs. 3 m in South Carolina) but it represented essentially the same time frame (Figs. 3.4, 3.5, 3.6). In the Chezzetcook case, at least a 6 m, and possibly up to a 10 m, rise in relative sea level was interpreted, for the same time interval that an apparent 2 m rise was occurring in South Carolina

(Fig. 3.7). In the Nova Scotia case, the contribution of high-resolution marsh foraminiferal zonations (± 5 cm) is clearly evident. In the cores from Chezzetcook Inlet, the 8.23 m, 10.09 m, 10.20 m, 10.68 m, and 11.6 m horizons were all ^{14}C dated; the ^{14}C dates on the 10–11.6 m levels were all within 200 years of each other. Without very independent evidence that these sediment intervals were in fact caused by various heights of relative sea level, they probably would have been interpreted as one deposit forming at the same time. Because of the unique characteristics of marsh zone 1A, which has a well-defined vertical range of ± 5 cm (Scott and Medioli, 1980b), it was possible to determine that sea level was rising at a rate of almost 1 m per century between 4,247 and 3,833 years ago (i.e., 3.4 m in 350 years). This rate is five times the present rate of 20 cm per century in this area, and it occurred at the same time as the sea-level variation observed in South Carolina sequences. Without the zonation provided by foraminiferal indicator assemblages, this relationship could not have been resolved.

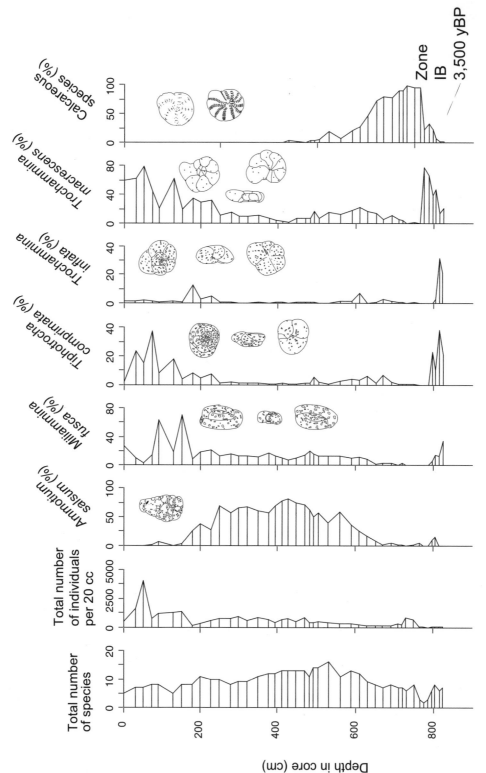

Figure 3.5. Core 15 from Chezzetcook Inlet indicates the same type of zonations as those shown in Fig. 3.4. There are more diversified estuarine environments in core 15 above the marsh sequence that are indicated particularly by calcareous species in the 600–800 cm zone. The basal Carbon-14 date is from the 850 cm horizon (after Scott et al., 1995c).

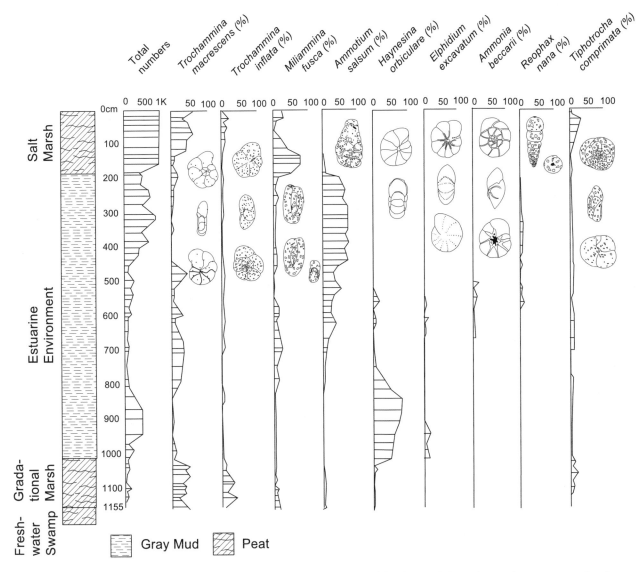

Figure 3.6. Core 5 from Chezzetcook Inlet. This is one of the longest marsh/estuarine sequences ever collected from a single locality on the eastern seaboard of North America; it contains a 4,000-year record. What separates this record from others in the area is the presence of *Ammonia beccarii* in small numbers at the midpoint of this core. This species marks a warm interval in the middle Holocene. The entire sequence from 10.7 to 1.7 m is an essentially featureless gray mud that can only be differentiated into different estuarine and marsh zones using foraminifera. The 4,000-year Carbon-14 date marks a sea-level point that is 11.5 m below present mean sea level (after Scott et al., 1995c).

■ Seismic Events

Increased interest in earthquake activity, particularly in coastal Pacific areas, has prompted innovative researchers to study tidal marsh deposits for clues (Atwater, 1987, 1992). One of the reasons tidal marshes were selected as sites for study is that rapid 1 to 2 m level changes could be reliably detected in salt marsh sequences in those instances where there were sudden lithologic changes from, for example, forest peat to intertidal mud. It was also necessary, however, to be able to subzone the marsh deposits, a task for which the foraminifera, and to some extent diatom data, are crucial (e.g., Jennings and Nelson, 1992; Nelson, 1992; Clague and Bobrowsky, 1994a,b; Hemphill-Haley, 1995). It is not overstating the case to say that, without microfossil evidence, the arguments for possible earthquake periodicity would be incomplete. There are many studies from Chile (Jennings et al., 1995) to British Columbia (Clague and Brobrowsky, 1994b) documenting various seismic uplift/subsidence events that rely on microfossil evidence, principally foraminifera. This section summarizes two types of studies – one on paleoperiodicity and one possible precursor earthquake event.

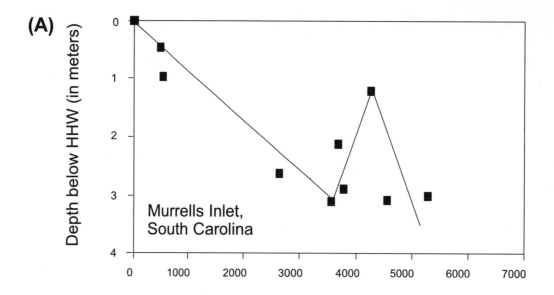

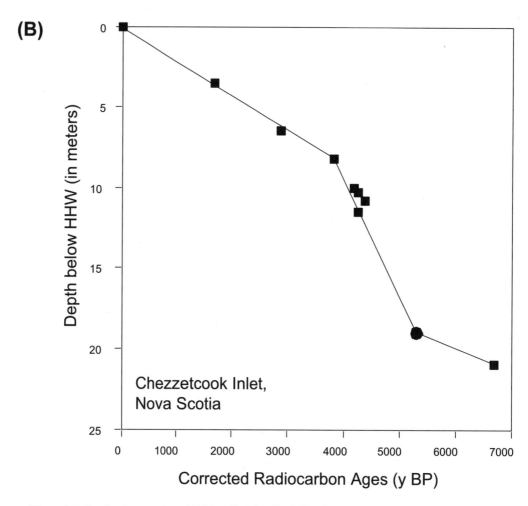

Figure 3.7. Sea-level curves from (A) Murrells Inlet, South Carolina, and (B) Chezzetcook Inlet, Nova Scotia, covering the same time period. These curves are based on points from Figs. 3.3–3.6. The degree of resolution shown would not be possible without marsh foraminiferal zonation data (after Scott and Collins, 1996).

Paleoperiodicity. Probably the most detailed use of fossil foraminifera assemblages to reconstruct seismic events to date was done in a study by Nelson et al. (1996) (Fig. 3.8). In one core from coastal Oregon, they were able to identify several "steps" in the sea-level variation "curve," but not all these "steps" could be linked with seismic events. The abrupt changes at couplet 3, 4 (180 cm) and couplet 1, 2 (50 cm), however, were interpreted as very strong signals of rapid elevation change from a high marsh fauna *(Trochammina macrescens)* to low marsh fauna *(Miliammina fusca)* in just a 20-cm-long section. These data indicated an almost instantaneous 50 cm rise in relative sea level (i.e., a drop of the land) and are interpreted as seismic events at 1,700 years before the present (yBP) and 300–400 yBP, respectively. It should be noted that although there are lithologic changes at these boundaries, it is the foraminiferal zones that provide the data needed to estimate the actual changes in elevation associated with the seismic event (Jennings and Nelson, 1992). Diatoms were also examined in these cores but did not seem, in our opinion, to be as useful as the foraminiferal assemblages in resolving this type of problem.

Besides actual land movement from seismic events, tsunami deposits have been identified, in part, by means of foraminifera (Clague and Bobrowsky, 1994a,b). A tsunami layer is generally assumed to be a sandy layer that is "out of place" in a salt marsh environment. In one instance, Clague and Bobrowsky (1994a,b) encountered a high marsh interval *(Trochammina macrescens),* a sand layer with few foraminifera, and a low marsh interval *(M. fusca),* all included in about a 10-cm-thick layer. They interpreted this sequence as being suggestive of both a tsunami and a concurrent subsidence event.

Precursor Events. In addition to documenting paleoperiodicity, some interesting events prior to major earthquakes have also been recognized. Shennan et al. (1996, 1998) had observed some events in sediments from prehistoric earthquakes on the Oregon coast that they thought were occurring prior to large megathrust quakes. However, because the quakes were prehistoric, it was difficult to know the exact timing of the events. Shennan et al. (1999) had the opportunity to visit sites of exposed sedimentary sequences that represented the great 1964 Alaska earthquake (the second largest ever measured, at 9.2 on the Richter Scale). There were exposed sections of submerged forest where the contact between the prequake forest and postquake intertidal sediments was exceptionally clear, and the microfossils in this case were absolutely vital to obtain the record described below.

The forest zone (from 18 cm to 13 cm), represented by dark brown peat (Fig. 3.9) is dominated by *Centropyxis aculeata* and *Difflugia oblonga,* with lower frequencies of *Pontigulasia compressa* (Fig. 3.10). The latter two species are typical of nonmarine environments, while *Centropyxis aculeata* is a freshwater species that can tolerate low salinities arising from infrequent tidal inundation. Since *D. oblonga* and *P. compressa* cannot tolerate even these mildly saline conditions, *Centropyxis aculeata* occurs at the transition between high marsh and fully freshwater environments. This feature can be seen in foraminiferal data from a marsh/forest transect at Portage Flats and has previously been documented in several other places (e.g., Scott et al., 1981). *Centropyxis aculeata* also dominates in an intermediate zone that comprises the two uppermost samples (12 cm and 11 cm) of the peat, and in four samples from the overlying silt. In the top peat sample (11 cm), *Centropyxis aculeata* reaches almost 100% and a maximum concentration of 3,480 individuals per 5 cc. This extreme dominance and high abundance is fairly typical of areas just above any tidal influence, where infrequent salt spray and storm tides eliminate most freshwater species but do not allow colonization by any foraminifera species. Although the numbers of *Centropyxis aculeata* throughout transects at Portage Flats are low (Shennan et al., 1999), immediately after the earthquake the site became intertidal (e.g., Plafker, 1969; McCulloch & Bonilla, 1970) and too saline for *Centropyxis aculeata* to live. It is believed that many of the individuals of *Centropyxis aculeata* within the silt layer above the peat are allochthonous. The typical low marsh foraminifera *Trochammina ochracea* gradually increases in abundance in the upper part of the marine silt unit. The uppermost two samples are characterized by the low-marsh foraminiferal species *Trochammina ochracea,* the high-marsh foraminiferal taxon *Trochammina macrescens,* and by declining frequencies of *Centropyxis aculeata.* The low numbers in the two tidal flat samples are identical to modern transects across the marsh surface near this location (Shennan et al., 1999).

Numerous studies have demonstrated that land subsidence and sediment consolidation have resulted in subsequent tidal flat clastic sedimentation over preexisting forest following large megathrust earthquakes (e.g., Plafker, 1969; McCulloch & Bonilla, 1970; Nelson et al., 1996, as shown in previous section). These flats are soon colonized by marsh and, in some locations, by freshwater communities as the land rebounds following the quake (e.g., Bartsch-Winkler & Schmoll 1987; Combellick, 1991, 1994, 1997).

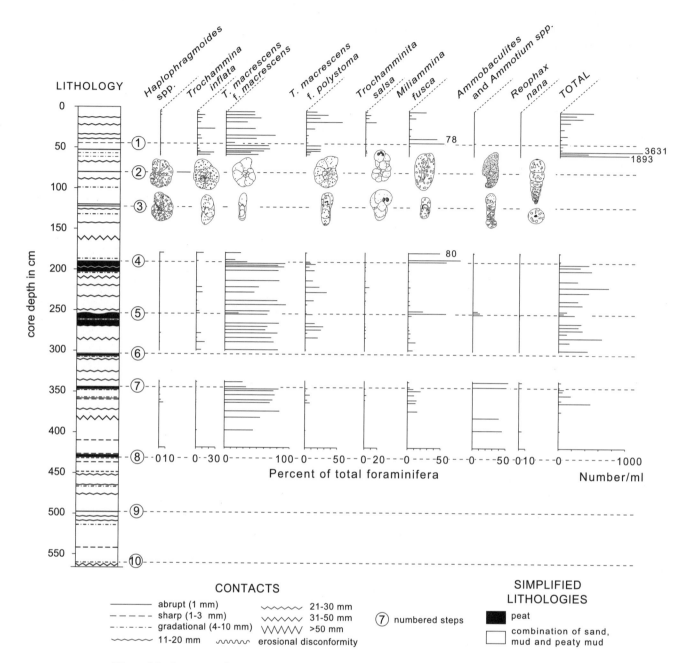

Figure 3.8. A sequence from coastal Oregon (U.S.A.) that illustrates a series of "steps" marking abrupt level changes as indicated by rapid shifts from high marsh to low marsh assemblages. The shifts suggest a ~70 cm level change over a short core interval. These variations are interpreted as earthquake-related crustal movements and are readily defined using foraminiferal assemblages (after Nelson et al., 1996).

However, few investigations have shown much indication of prequake subsidence events except for some ancient earthquake horizons in Oregon (Shennan et al., 1996, 1998). The 1964 Alaska earthquake depositional sequence is most important because, unlike prehistoric events recorded in Oregon, the chronologic sequence in the Alaska case is known precisely.

The accepted sequence of events for Girdwood Flats, Alaska, is (1) prequake emergence (relaxation after the previous prehistoric earthquake), followed by (2) rapid 1.7 m subsidence on March 26, 1964. What can be shown using microfossil evidence is that there was a pre-1964 quake subsidence event that was recorded by the presence of a *Centropyxis aculeata* association at 11 cm (i.e., just

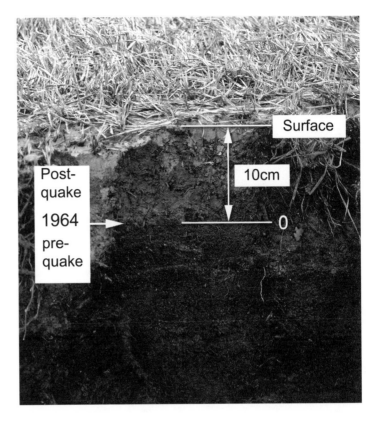

Figure 3.9. Cliff section from Girdwood Flats, Alaska, that exposes the contact between the forest and intertidal sediments created during the great Alaska earthquake of March 27, 1964 (after Shennan et al., 1999).

before the quake). This association could not be reestablished after the quake because conditions suddenly became mid-intertidal. Specimens of *C. aculeata,* which were no longer living there, were reworked by tidal currents from the underlying peat, which explains their relatively high abundance in the overlying gray-mud sequence. Salt influence did not persist long enough to kill the trees at Girdwood Flats before the quake, but the time interval was long enough for the "brackish" taxon *Centropyxis aculeata* to dominate temporarily until the earthquake subsidence occurred. The high abundance of this species also shows that the prequake subsidence event must have occurred at least as early as the previous summer. This is because the *Centropyxis* population could not have flourished in the dead of the Alaska winter. In other cores, not shown here, this sequence is repeated both for the 1964 section and for an older quake that occurred 1,800 years ago (Combellick, 1997; Scott et al., 1998). Hence, successive seismic events in coastal sections along the west coast of North America can be detected using foraminiferal zones as elevation markers. It also appears that the same techniques have the capacity to record, perhaps several months to a year in advance, rheological conditions that precede large magnitude, megathrust earthquakes. The implications of this finding are significant for decision makers charged with

responsibilities for determining safety protocols based on signals from local earthquake-monitoring networks. These data provide the basis to interpret the physical tilt detected by tilt meters that might be set up strategically across critical zones.

■ General Changes

The preceding examples represent instances where high vertical resolution is needed to determine sea-level changes. Marsh foraminiferal zonations, however, are also useful for other slow-occurring changes (e.g., Scott et al., 1987b). Because foraminiferal zonations take one of the variables (elevation) to a new level of resolution, it is only necessary to deal with the other critical variable, which is timing. Given a detailed historical documentation for a particular area, it is often possible to establish dated "calibrated" horizons that are useful for confirming extrapolations based on ^{14}C dating alone (e.g., volcanic ash or forest fire ash deposits).

The presence or absence of foraminifera in isolated offshore peat deposits can now be used to confirm or refute its marine or nonmarine origin, and to ascertain the elevation of the deposit to less than ± 1 m if the peat is marine. If it is not marine, it can provide only a maximum position of relative sea level (i.e., sea level

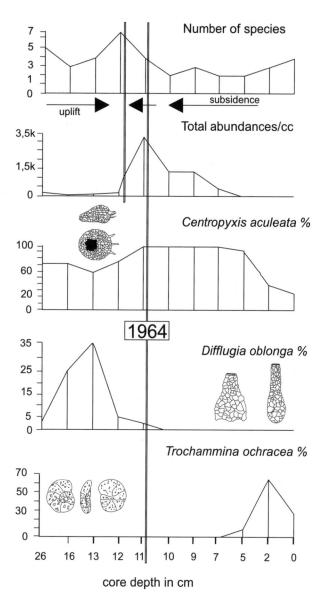

Figure 3.10. Results from samples collected from the cliff section shown in Fig. 3.9. The top 10 cm of this core equates to the top 10 cm of the cliff section. The zero cm horizon shown in Fig. 3.9 equals the 1964 line shown on this figure. The small left-pointing arrow indicates subsidence just before the 1964 quake. Subsidence is indicated by an increase in *C. aculeata* specimens and by total testate rhizopod abundance changes in the centimeter interval below the 1964 earthquake horizon (after Shennan et al., 1999).

■ Other Cases

There are many cases where the preservation potential of marsh deposits is low. This is particularly true where the coastline is being uplifted and exposed to subaerial erosive forces. In Scandinavia and eastern Canada, where postglacial isostatic adjustment ("rebound") is or has taken place, methods have been devised using microfossils to obtain records of past sea-level variations (Berglund, 1971; Alhonen et al., 1978; Scott and Medioli, 1980c; Honig and Scott, 1987). These techniques rely on formerly marine basins, now raised above sea level by glacial isostatic rebound.

These archives of past sea-level changes are sampled by coring the lake basins (see coring methods for lakes, Livingstone corer, Fig. 2.1), examining the core for microfossils and determining the freshwater/marine transition (Fig. 3.11). This horizon is ^{14}C dated, and that date is considered as the time of emergence of the sill or inlet of the basin above mean sea level. In Scandinavian areas, diatoms have been used as indicators (Berglund, 1971; Alhonen et al., 1978); in eastern Canada, however, foraminifera were found to be much more precise proxies of this process because they pinpoint the marine cutoff to within a few centimeters section of the core. Diatom data, on the contrary, spread this transition over a wide (100 cm) range and do not provide a definitive cutoff point (Berglund, 1971; Alhonen et al., 1978). In both cases, the information generated using these techniques represents the only way of obtaining a sea-level curve for these areas, as opposed to single sea-level highstand information that marks the high point but nothing in between.

The basins act as sediment traps that record the marine/freshwater transition. Conversely, the record of relative sea-level change in other open marine coastal areas is being lost because as sea level drops, erosion destroys the record. The basins selected for this type of study must be chosen carefully such that the transition point can be predicted to be virtually instantaneous (i.e., a small, shallow basin where freshwater inflow quickly obliterates the marine influence) (Scott and Medioli, 1980c; Figs. 3.12, 3.13). In the example from Gibson Lake, New Brunswick (Fig. 3.12), marine conditions indicated by calcareous foraminiferal species of glacial marine origin *(Elphidium* sp. and *Cassidulina)* in the 550 to 425 cm segment of the core are abruptly replaced over a 2 cm interval (425 cm in Fig. 3.12) by a sparsely populated brackish thecamoebian zone. The brackish stagnant zone persisted for several thousand years so that sea-level information could only be

could not have been higher but it could have been a lot lower). The absence of this determination in some early sea-level papers (e.g., Emery and Garrison, 1967) may explain the point scatter seen in some of the early sea-level curves.

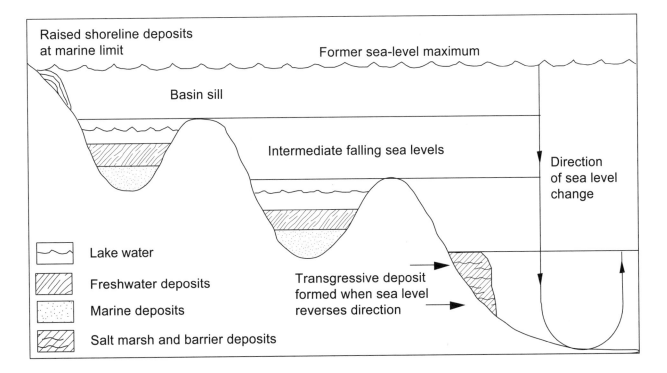

Figure 3.11. Simplified model of how to use formerly marine basins, now raised above sea level, to obtain a sea-level curve from an emergent coastline. Foraminifera delineate marine versus freshwater sediments. The transition between these two types of deposits can be dated to provide the timing of when sea level dropped below the sill elevation of the lake basin (after Scott and Medioli, 1980c).

determined from the organic-rich stagnant zone just above the last foraminifera occurrence. This horizon was dated at ~12,000 years ago and provided a point that was +35 m above present sea level. In Norse Pond, Maine (Fig. 3.13), the situation was much the same as for Gibson Lake except that there were macrofossils available for ^{14}C dating. As in Gibson Lake, the foraminifera clearly marked the nonmarine transition (at 450 cm in Fig. 3.13), which was dated at ~12,000 years ago at an elevation of +35 m (almost identical to nearby Gibson Lake). There was also a long time lag between marine and fully freshwater conditions comparable to that seen in Gibson Lake. This phenomenon seems to occur in periglacial environments in northern Canada. It is also observed in lakes that are still emerging above sea level but that are able to maintain a stagnant brackish bottom water mass for several thousand years after emergence, apparently as a consequence of poor drainage (R. T. Patterson, pers. comm., 1993).

RECONSTRUCTION OF COASTAL MARINE PALEOENVIRONMENTS

Classification of Estuaries and Embayments

Classification of modern estuarine/lagoonal systems can be carried out using several different types of criteria: physiochemical, geomorphological, or origin of basin type, to name a few. Any of these criteria can be used unambiguously for classifying a modern system where everything is laid out to see – but what about ancient systems? For physically defined classifications such as basin type, this characteristic can usually be determined through time by reconstructing valley fill sequences. Classification, however, may be more difficult in regard to physiochemical criteria, such as salinity, temperature, organic loading, and turbidity, because these variables leave a preserved physical "signature" that may be modified by postdepositional, diagenetically driven overprinting processes. Foraminifera can serve as proxies for these variables and, when used in conjunction with sedimentological indices, can provide a first-order picture of past watermass conditions in a variety of estuarine/ lagoonal settings. The successful application of benthic foraminifera as indicators relies on good groundtruthing of modern environments so that the relationship of species occurrence and abundance is quantitatively linked to specific environments to the greatest possible degree.

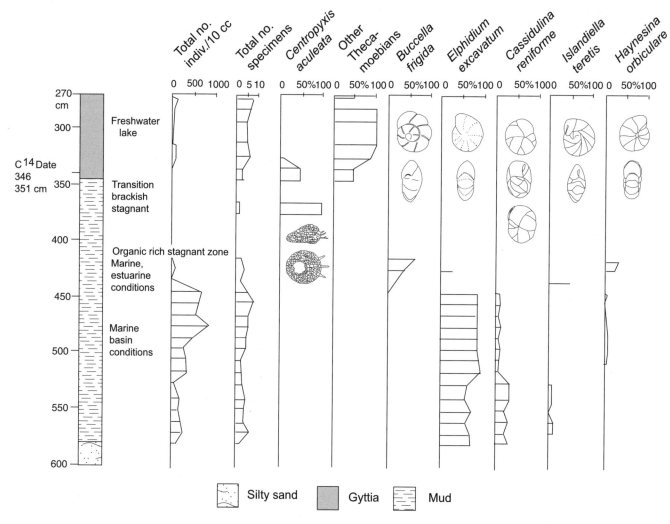

Figure 3.12. Distribution of thecamoebians and foraminifera from a core in Gibson Lake, New Brunswick (Canada). The lake is a raised basin in which the transition from marine to nonmarine is defined by the abrupt disappearance of foraminifera at 420 cm. They are replaced by a brackish "stagnant" sequence that often lasted a few thousand years in these isolated pond environments. The core record shows a transition to freshwater conditions at 340 cm as indicated by the presence of a full range of thecamoebian species. The Carbon-14 date is from the stagnant brackish sequence just above the last occurrence of foraminifera (after Patterson et al., 1985).

There are many studies on estuarine foraminifera, especially on the east coast of North America. Nichols (1974) was among some of the first researchers to suggest that foraminifera could be used as a tool in estuarine classification. Subsequently, Scott et al. (1980) developed an estuarine classification framework based on the extensive work done by several investigators in eastern Canada. The framework, once established for a particular region, can be put to work to interpret ancient (or not so

ancient) core sections. Freshwater thecamoebians are important elements of this framework model because they help in mapping sources and pathways of freshwater input. The presence of few thecamoebians often indicates input from freshwater runoff or ground water, while high numbers usually mark strong inflow from a river (where thecamoebians live and hence are transported from). The following sections illustrate how thecamoebians and foraminifera can be used as proxy indices to determine a number of parameters in estuarine paleosequences.

Salinity/Temperature Indicators

It has been established for some time that estuarine foraminifera assemblages are useful as markers of past salinity and temperature conditions (e.g., Murray, 1973). An early benchmark study on estuarine foraminifera by Höglund (1947) more or less defined the indicator species that are now reported worldwide, although he did not provide much detail on relationships between specific

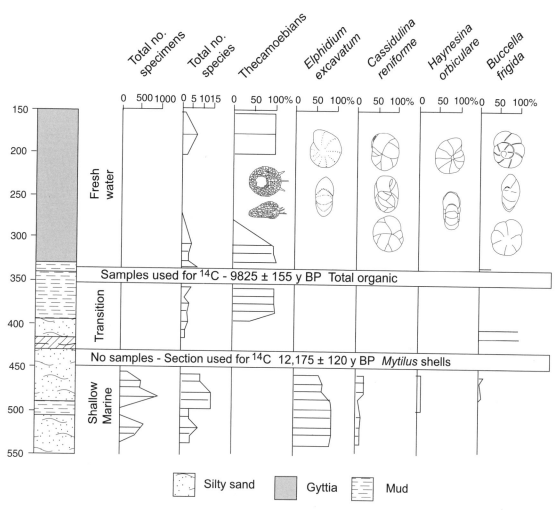

Figure 3.13. A sequence similar to that shown in Fig. 3.12 from a lake in Maine (U.S.A.) just across the border from Gibson Lake, New Brunswick. Norse Pond is at the same elevation as Gibson Lake now, and the Carbon-14 date of a similar assemblage sequence is also very close, which shows that the same amount of emergence has taken place at this location in Maine as for Gibson Lake. At Norse Pond, the time interval of transition from marine to completely freshwater is manifested by almost 3,000 years of "brackish stagnant" conditions which are indicated by the dominance of *Centropyxis aculeata* (after Scott and Medioli, 1980c).

physical parameters and foraminiferal distributions. In the 1950s and 1960s, in a series of papers on the Gulf of Mexico and later on the Gulf of California, Phleger and colleagues published a rich data set that defined the environments of estuarine foraminiferal assemblages from that area (Phleger and Walton, 1950; Phleger, 1951, 1954, 1965a–c, 1967; Phleger and Ewing, 1962). Unfortunately, in much of this pioneering work, information on physical parameters was still comparatively weak. Nevertheless, these studies were central to later investigations that proceeded to refine the results of Phleger's earlier work. Another benchmark study was carried out by Ellison and Nichols (1974). They presented an extremely detailed account of foraminiferal distributions in the James River estuary system which is part of the larger Chesapeake Bay system. Their data showed strong assemblage zonations within the estuary that could be closely tied to salinity variations. In eastern Canada, inshore surveys were started in the 1960s and 1970s with the work of Bartlett and his students on many small estuarine and lagoonal systems within the Gulf of St. Lawrence system, and by Schafer and colleagues in the 1970s and 1980s. These investigations were integrated in Scott et al. (1980) through their establishment of an estuarine framework classification system that was partly based on salinity indicators. In the latter half of the 1980s and early 1990s there have been major contributions on coastal settings from Norwegian researchers (Alve and Nagy), who have completed a large body of work in relation to pollution in northwestern European fjord systems (see Alve, 1995, for a review). In a number of these anthropogenic impact studies, the factors controlling the systemwide distribution of foraminifera were concluded to involve temperature/salinity variations (hereafter referred to as T/S variations).

In considering estuarine foraminiferal distributions, it is difficult to separate salinity and temperature, because the approach relies heavily on a ratio of agglutinated versus calcareous forms, and this ratio covaries with T/S (Greiner, 1970). In relatively warm settings (over 20° C), calcareous foraminifera are often found in salinities as low as 10‰. Conversely, in cold temperate environments, the salinity threshold seems to be higher, and typically calcareous foraminifera are not observed in salinities lower than 20% (Scott et al., 1980). A practical application of this kind of information is shown by the foraminiferal distributions of Chezzetcook Inlet (Nova Scotia) in relation to salinities measured in 1974 (Fig. 3.14). In the 4,000-year history of the upper part of the estuary and in the vicinity of station 31 in Fig. 3.14, it can be seen that bottom water characteristics in this inlet have changed significantly since that time (Fig. 3.6). A case that includes the earliest part of the postglacial sea-level transgression shows that basal salt marsh deposits formed, but that these were quickly drowned by a rapidly rising relative sea level (Fig. 3.6). The initial proxy indicator of this process is a 100% calcareous fauna dominated by *Haynesina orbiculare.* Somewhat higher in the section, *Ammonia beccarii* makes its first appearance. Above that, at about 6 m depth in the core and corresponding to about 2,500 yBP, the fauna changes from calcareous to agglutinated and, at 200 yBP (1.7 m core depth), it changes back to a marsh assemblage dominated by *Miliammina fusca.* These variations (except at 1.7 m) are responses to relative sea-level controlled T/S changes that have occurred in the inlet over the past 4,000 years (Scott et al., 1987b, 1995c). Assemblage data show that water temperatures seem to have been warmer and salinities were very slightly higher 4,000 yBP along this part of the coast (Scott et al., 1989b), or the calcareous fauna would not have colonized this location. In this instance, however, it is not certain that salinities were higher since it is known that bottom waters were warmer. Higher bottom water temperature would have allowed the calcareous species to colonize habitats with lower salinities than they can tolerate today. At present, salinities at this coring site and at low tide can be as low as 0‰ but proxy evidence shows that this was probably not the case 4,000 yBP. The lithologic log of the core shows a homogenous, featureless gray mud from 10 m to 1.7 m. Without corresponding foraminiferal information, this entire sequence would cer-

tainly have been interpreted as "estuarine" throughout, which is technically true but not very informative. Using foraminiferal data, it was possible to obtain a detailed paleoenvironmental record at this location along with an evolutionary picture of the inlet that could not be resolved in the lithological record itself.

Another area on the coast of the Northumberland Strait (Baie Verte, on the Nova Scotia/New Brunswick border, southern Gulf of St. Lawrence) shows a similar and even more dramatic record (Fig. 3.15). At 4,000 yBP there was a foraminiferal population occupying this site similar to that living today in coastal habitats of Virginia or further south (Scott et al., 1987a). Subsequently, the Northumberland Strait foraminiferal population changed to an agglutinated one at about the same time as it did in Chezzetcook Inlet. The presence of *Ammonia beccarii,* in the sediments deposited in the formerly shallow subtidal Chezzetcook Inlet, is important because this is one of the few taxa for which the ecological limits of the species have been determined experimentally (Bradshaw, 1957, 1961; Schnitker, 1974). Although there is some disagreement among various authors, the reproductive interval of *Ammonia beccarii* can be set between 15 and 20° C. This bottom water temperature does not occur in present-day Chezzetcook Inlet, except in intertidal marshes close to the ocean – i.e., no *A. beccarii* are found in subtidal sediments on the Atlantic coast of Nova Scotia. They are found, however, to the west, in the Northumberland Strait where shallow bottom water temperatures reach 15–20° C and higher during the summer because of local oceanographic stratification related to the St. Lawrence River discharge. At several Prince Edward Island coastal locations, the work of Bartlett indicates that, in shallower water where summer temperatures exceed 20° C, *Ammonia beccarii* is present, unlike the present-day situation in the Miramichi estuary (New Brunswick) or on the Atlantic coast of Nova Scotia (see summary in Scott et al., 1980). These observations accentuate the strong relationship between T/S changes and the presence of some calcareous species, and emphasizes why the two variables cannot be discussed independently, especially in north temperate latitudes.

Another estuary for which strong T/S control was established is the Miramichi (Bartlett, 1966). Here the upper estuarine agglutinated fauna, dominated by *Miliammina fusca,* and the open bay assemblage, dominated by *Elphidium excavatum* and *Haynesina orbiculare,* are sharply divided just where the river widens into the bay (Fig. 3.16). This very sharp boundary is clearly related

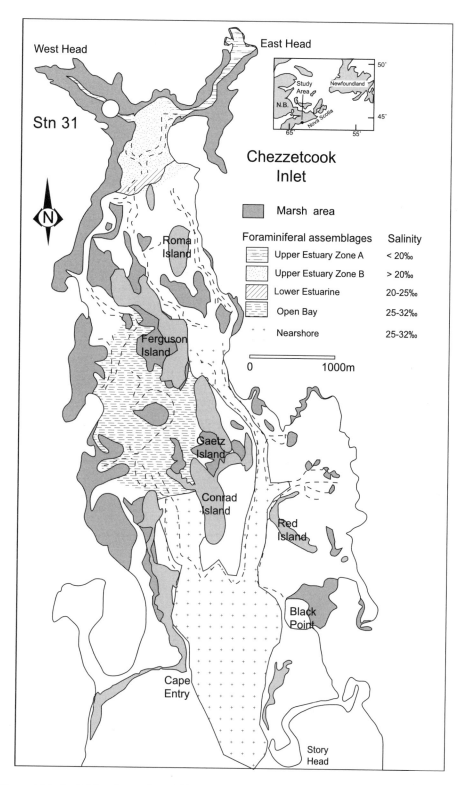

Figure 3.14. Surficial sediment foraminiferal distributions from Chezzetcook Inlet, Nova Scotia, showing upper estuarine to open bay (nearshore) faunas. Upper estuarine assemblages tend to be dominated by agglutinated species, while open bay assemblages are usually dominated by calcareous species. Station 31 is the position of core 5 in Fig. 3.6 (after Scott et al., 1980).

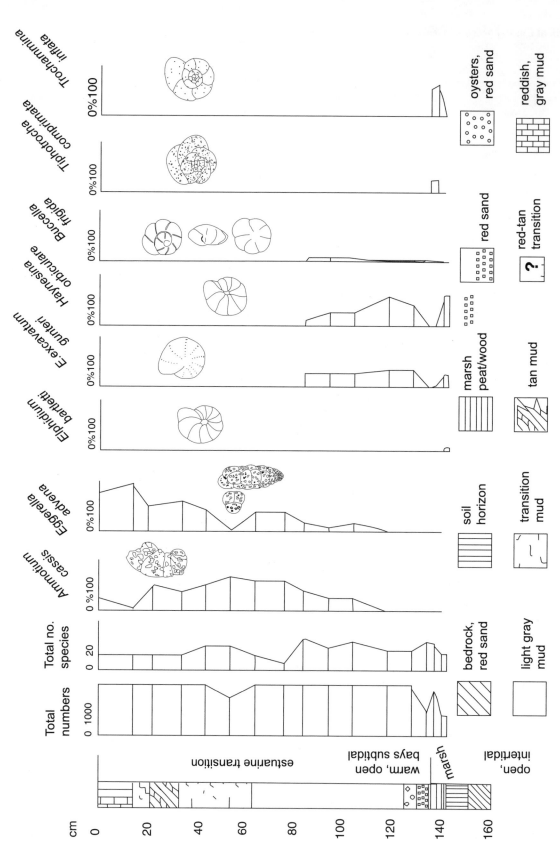

Figure 3.15. A piston core from Baie Verte, New Brunswick (Canada) showing an open bay/marsh/open bay/transitional fauna. This core is unique for this area because it contains a fauna from ~100–140 cm that indicates temperatures that no longer occur north of Virginia. This interpretation implies that these coastal waters were much warmer 4,000 years ago (date from marsh sediments, after Scott et al., 1987a).

46

to salinity. Bottom water salinities in the upper river average less than 20‰, while those in the Outer Bay (lower estuary) average over 23‰ under essentially similar temperature conditions. Examples described in the next section show that this type of salinity pattern may not be a stable one.

A general statement can be made about north temperate upper estuarine species; they are almost always dominated by *Miliammina fusca* and/or *Ammotium* and *Ammobaculites* spp. Except for some low marsh systems (Scott and Medioli, 1980b), these taxa typically indicate lower than normal salinities. Debenay et al. (1998) describe some South American systems where salinity variation was a major influence, both horizontally as seen in the Miramichi and vertically as documented for some constricted lagoon areas where there are small depressions in which high-salinity water can be trapped. The trapping of relatively high-salinity water creates a localized "high-salinity" zone where one observes calcareous foraminifera living in the deeper, high-salinity depressions and more typical agglutinated foraminifera living in shallower, low-salinity environments.

Turbidity Maxima

In the post–World War II era, the conventional way to define an estuarine foraminiferal distribution pattern was the one based on salinity (e.g., Nichols, 1974). There are, however, many other characteristics of estuaries to which foraminifera respond, and these features may sometimes be detected or mapped more readily and inexpensively by means of bioindicators than through physical measurements (Scott et al., 1980). Physical measurements are often limited in scope, especially in a temporal context – i.e., they tend to be expensive if continuous monitoring over a long period of time is needed. As Esteban Boltovskoy, one of the preeminent micropaleontologists of the twentieth century, once pointed out in a lecture at Dalhousie University, benthic foraminifera monitor 24 hours/day, 365 days a year, year after year. Understanding their local contempo-

Figure 3.16. Foraminiferal distribution reported for Miramichi Bay, New Brunswick (Canada) by Bartlett (1966) showing the sharp boundary between upper estuarine (riverine) and open bay that existed in 1964 (after Scott et al., 1977).

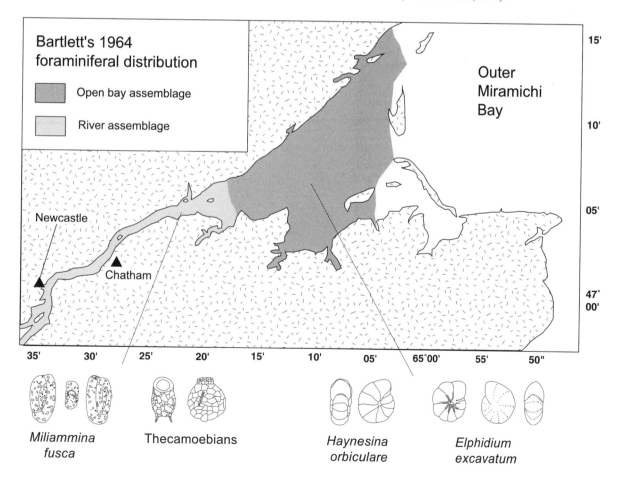

rary distribution patterns permits exploitation of their monitoring capabilities both in modern situations and, perhaps in retrospect, to reconstruct climatic and environmental conditions that existed in the near and distant past.

One important distribution pattern characteristic of benthic foraminifera is associated with the position of the turbidity maximum in estuaries, or that location where river discharge first meets and mixes with ocean water. This is a critical environment because fine muds, typically characteristic of the suspended particles comprising the turbidity maximum, are often enriched in toxic trace metals (e.g., Menon et al., 1998). Depending on the relative strength of opposing tidal and river currents, the turbidity maximum will either be wide or be nonexistent. Almost equal and opposite forces produce a wide mixing zone, while extremely unequal forces appear to create a dynamic barrier and a nonmixing zone setting in which the dominant aqueous force basically overwhelms the other. In an estuary, the "mixing zone" typically can be highly variable depending on tidal stage, annual runoff patterns, and many other natural and anthropogenic factors. Consequently, physically measuring its extent can be very difficult. There are, however, some foraminifera species that have an affinity to high-turbidity concentrations, and these can be used to measure and record its configuration and temporal variation. So while it may not be easy to continuously monitor the entire mixing zone of a particular estuary, the foraminifera register a time-integrated signal that should reveal the extent of the "footprint" of that zone to at least an annual level of resolution.

One helpful example of turbidity maximum definition using foraminifera is found in the Miramichi Estuary (Scott et al., 1977). Bartlett (1966) collected samples in this location in 1964 that showed only two populations: (a) an upper estuarine one and (b) an open bay fauna comprising mostly calcareous species (Fig. 3.16). By 1974, this situation had changed and a *transition* fauna had become established in the Inner Bay between the *open bay* and *upper estuarine* foraminifera assemblages (Fig. 3.17). The dominant species of the transition assemblage was the agglutinated species *Ammotium cassis.* Wefer (1976) had previously linked this species to the high concentrations of suspended particulate matter (SPM) that characterize turbidity maxima. Salinity measurements made between 1964 and 1974 (Scott et al., 1977) showed no major shifts that could explain the almost 100% turnover of species in the inner bay of the estuary. Diver observations (Schafer, pers. comm.) at the time (1974) reported a distinctive 1 m thick turbid layer developed on the bottom of the inner bay area. Precipitation records had been provisionally linked to higher stream

flows between 1964 and 1974 and could account for the intensification of the turbidity zone. By 1974, the modal flow of the river appears to have increased to almost equal that of the incoming tidal flow. This condition could be responsible for broad turbidity maximum area seen in the inner bay in 1974 that apparently had not existed in 1964 (Fig. 3.17). Physical measurements of salinity had not detected this phenomenon, but it was clearly shown by the complete turnover of foraminiferal species within the turbidity maximum part of the inner bay.

The discovery of the turbidity maximum foraminifera distribution pattern led to the development of a new classification scheme for estuaries in eastern Canada (Scott et al., 1980) based on the presence or absence of a high-turbidity, transition zone marked by high ambient bottom water turbidity conditions (Fig. 3.18A). In this framework, Miramichi Estuary fell into two categories because of the distinctive temporal and spatial variation of its turbidity zone (Scott et al., 1980). The relationship between species and turbidity has the potential to yield new information on the historical precipitation record of this area over the past several thousand years. Possibly more important than its potential as a proxy of paleoprecipitation, the foraminiferal approach can be used to quickly map the time-integrated extent of turbidity zone deposits in any given year. Other species that also appear to be useful as transition environment indicators in north temperate estuaries are *Hemisphaerammina bradyi* (agglutinated) and *Haynesina orbiculare* (calcareous but present in an agglutinated capsule in transition zones); these two species occur in shallow intertidal to shallow subtidal estuarine settings (Fig. 3.14).

In deep estuarine settings, *Reophax arctica,* together with *Ammotium cassis,* seem to have potential as a turbidity zone indicator. Why is turbidity zone information important? One reason is that high SPM concentrations may cause damage to commercial shellfish beds. The SPM signal may also mark modal contamination pathways. Its detection and delineation in space and time might therefore be of value to harbor engineers charged with the planning of dredged channels, sewage outfalls, and offshore dump sites.

Organic Matter Deposition

This subject is closely related to the preceding turbidity maximum discussion because particulate organic matter deposition often occurs within transition zones. Some of the same species used to track turbidity maxima are also useful in mapping either natural or anthropogenic organic matter (OM) deposition patterns. In some cases (e.g., fish

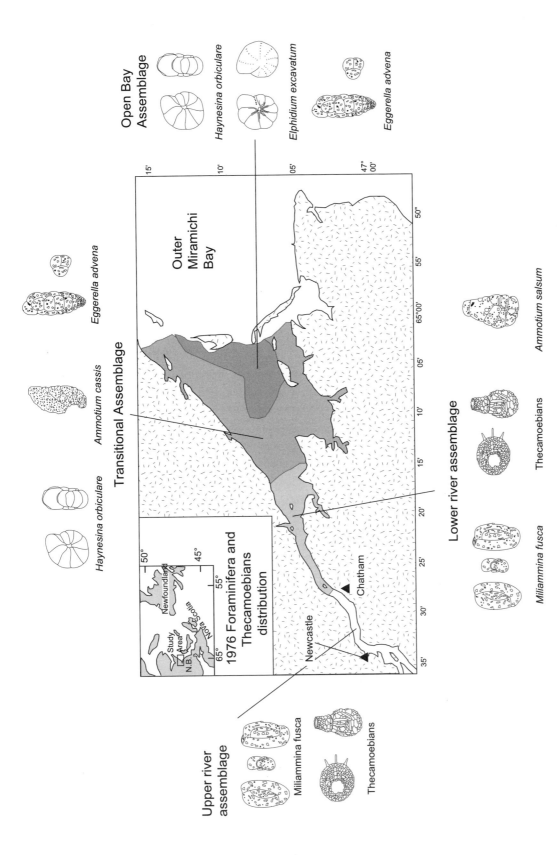

Figure 3.17. The same area of Miramichi Bay as shown in Fig. 3.16. Foraminiferal distributions reflect conditions in the bay in 1974 (ten years later). Notice that the large inner bay area that was formerly occupied by an open bay calcareous fauna in 1964 is now occupied by an agglutinated fauna dominated by *Ammotium cassis*. This species marks relatively high suspended particulate matter conditions that appear to be related to an expanded mixing or transition zone that was not observed in the 1964 study (after Scott et al., 1977).

49

(A)

Transitional and nontransitional estuaries in Maritime Canada

Transitional*
Miramichi (after 1975)
Chezzetcook inlet
Restigouche Estuary
Halifax Harbour
Mahone, St Margaret's
Bay estuaries
La Have estuary

Nontransitional
Miramichi estuary (before 1975)
Prince Edward Island
and Northumberland
Strait estuaries

* Defined by presence or absence of transitional fauna, not by geographical size of zone.

(B)

Species composition of estuarine zones for each environment

Assemblage zone

Environment	Upper Estuary	Transitional	Open Bay
Intertidal (from Chezzetcook)	Miliammina fusca Ammotium salsum Ammobaculites dilatatus Thecamoebians	Miliammina fusca Elphidium williamsoni Haynesina orbiculare Ammotium salsum Hemisphaerammina bradyi Ammonia beccarii	Eggerella advena Miliammina fusca Haynesina orbiculare Elphidium excvataum Ammonia beccarii
Intermediate (from Prince Edward Island)	Miliammina fusca Thecamoebians		Elphidium spp. Eggerella advena Haynesina orbiculare Ammonia beccarii Ammotium cassis
Shallow subtidal (from Miramichi)	Miliammina fusca Thecamoebians Ammotium salsum	Ammotium cassis Eggerella advena Hemisphaerammina bradyi Miliammina fusca	Elphidium excavatum Haynesina orbiculare Eggerella advena Buccella frigida
Deep subtidal (from Restigouche and Halifax Harbour)	Miliammina fusca Thecamoebians	Eggerella advena Ammotium cassis Reophax artica Fursenkoina fusiformis plus an array of others	Elphidium excavatum Eggerella advena Buccella frigida plus many more oceanic forms

Figure 3.18. (A) Some transitional versus nontransitional estuaries in eastern Canada. The size of the transitional zone can vary from a large proportion of the inlet as depicted for Miramichi Bay (1974) to a relatively small area such as the one seen in Halifax Harbour. The size of the transition zone is mostly a function of the river discharge versus tidal prism magnitude relationship. (B) A list of estuarine faunae based on water depth with species composition is given for each zone. Notice that the most diagnostic species are those associated with transitional zones (after Scott et al., 1980).

aquaculture sites) the foraminiferal signal associated with exceptionally high OM concentrations under aquaculture operations may actually be a function of bottom and interstitial water O_2 concentrations (Grant et al., 1995; Schafer et al., 1995).

In many estuaries organic "loading" is naturally high, due to high river inputs of OM that settles quickly as it comes in contact with relatively static marine water. OM deposition usually takes place in the upper estuarine zones, upstream from the more normal marine salinities of high-turbidity transition zones. In these areas, however, the range of ambient OM concentration can be so high that it is often difficult to detect if there has been an impact from anthropogenic OM. Upper estuarine foraminifera faunae may be helpful in these situations because they occur over a broad range of OM concentrations (e.g., Schafer et al., 1975).

Hurricane Detection in Estuarine Sediments

Liu and Fearn (1993) were likely among the first to show that there was a long (several thousand years) record of hurricane strikes recorded in coastal sediments. They investigated nontidal coastal ponds on the Alabama

(U.S.A.) coast, reasoning that nontidal inlets would record the transported sand layers associated with hurricanes without later being reworked by subsequent tidal action. A similar technique was applied in the coastal zone of South Carolina; both tidal and nontidal coastal embayments were investigated.

Sites were selected on the basis of whether they might have a well-preserved record of recent hurricanes, most notably Hugo, which occurred in September 1989 (Collins et al., 1999). Price's Inlet is a nontidal intrabeach ridge area that was directly in the path of the eyewall of Hugo. Sandpiper Pond is a coastal nontidal pond near Murrells Inlet, about 50–75 km north of where the main landfall of hurricane Hugo occurred, but still within the area of high storm surge (Fig. 3.19). Cores were analyzed for percentage OC, visual observations, structure, and microfossils. The microfossils were used to differentiate marine/nonmarine sequences in the inlets, and to identify reworked sediments by means of displaced benthic foraminifera. Cores were dated using ^{210}Pb techniques that provide chronological information for the past hundred years. In Price's Inlet, Hugo's impact was marked by an 8-cm-thick sand layer containing many nearshore foraminifera, implying transport from offshore areas (Fig. 3.20). In Sandpiper Pond, the effect of Hugo was detectable from the offshore foraminifera contained in sediments sandwiched between freshwater intervals deposited before and after the hurricane; in neither the structure nor the sedimentology of this core, however, was there detectable evidence indicating a storm event (Fig. 3.21). Hence, a range of responses for hurricanes in the form of different types of sediment layers and microfossil assemblages sampled in these nontidal areas could be recognized, depending on the location of the storm's impact point on the coast. In the more peripheral location (Sandpiper Pond, Fig. 3.21) the storm layer could not have been detected without foraminifera. Hence at least two types of signal from the same storm were discerned, which has significant implications for detecting and correctly interpreting these events in the prehistoric record. Instead of only detecting a direct eyewall hit, peripheral hits can also be detected. This capability potentially increases the number of paleostorms that can be observed at any one site, providing a better estimate of paleoperiodicity.

FORAMINIFERA AND POLLUTION

The use of benthic foraminifera as marine pollution indicators is, for the most part, a post–World War II phenomenon. It is not the intent of this section to review the large number of studies on this subject that have appeared, and continue to appear, in the scientific literature. Instead, the reader is referred to several recent comprehensive treatments on this subject (Murray, 1991; Alve, 1995; Culver and Buzas, 1995). This section covers several practical relationships and techniques that can provide coastal researchers with a range of approaches and tools for dealing with specific marine contamination-assessment problems using foraminiferal indicators. Care must be exercised continuously to design monitoring programs that can (1) resolve natural from contaminated-related benthic population changes (see Ferraro et al., 1991), (2) test for time lags between natural and anthropogenic disturbances (3) define the natural variability of local benthic foraminifera populations in space and time (Schafer, 1968, 1971; Schafer and Cole, 1976; Schafer et al., 1995), and (4) link foraminifera results to appropriate physical and chemical data sets (e.g., Buckley et al., 1974).

Species Sensitivity

The ubiquitous distribution of benthic foraminifera in a broad range of modern coastal marine environments attests to the relatively wide spectrum of sensitivities that can be found among the species belonging to this group of shelled protozoans. Clues on the specific nature of foraminiferal sensitivity to environmental and anthropogenic "forcing" are appearing with ever-increasing frequency in scientific publications (e.g., Alve, 1991; Lee

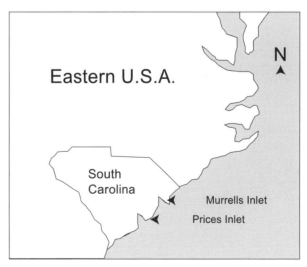

Figure 3.19. Regional map of South Carolina (U.S.A.) showing two inlets used for the study of hurricane traces (after Collins et al., 1999).

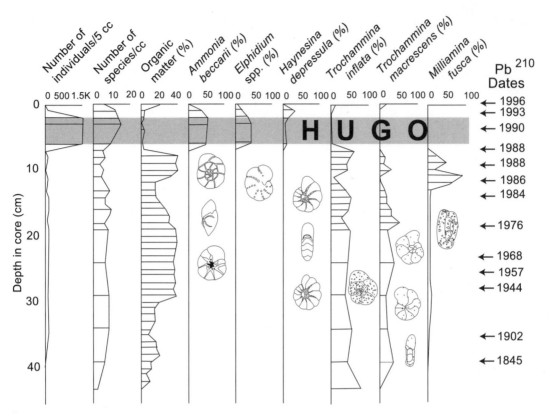

Figure 3.20. Profile of foraminiferal and Pb[210] data from Price's Inlet, South Carolina (U.S.A.). Note the large presence of calcareous, offshore foraminifera in the hurricane Hugo layer that was deposited in September 1989; these foraminifera are sandwiched between marsh layers, thereby confirming their transported origin (Collins et al., 1999).

and Anderson, 1991). In many instances, species sensitivity will be inversely related to environmental variability. Consequently, only relatively hardy and adaptable taxa are likely to be found in most nearshore habitats. Among the foraminifera, the more sensitive, or "biologically accommodated," taxa tend to be restricted to comparatively stable low-latitude nearshore environments, or to deep-sea habitats that are buffered from the day-to-day processes operating in the coastal zone. This ecological relationship has shaped many of the strategies that have been devised to adapt benthic foraminifera for biomonitoring applications (see following section). A corollary to this general relationship is that the restricted (i.e., local) environmental conditions that characterize many nearshore habitats often make it difficult to separate natural population distributions and species associations from those formed as a consequence of contamination effects (e.g., colonization rate; Alve, 1999). This impediment has resulted in the

establishment of general models, but has also produced discrete contemporary empirical assemblage models for each environmental situation. Empirical models are useful especially when attempting to trace temporal changes that are believed to be modulated by anthropogenic contamination (e.g., Alve, 1995; Culver and Buzas, 1995) (Fig. 3.22). Perhaps the most appropriate guiding principle for foraminiferal biomonitoring applications has been noted by Ricci (1991), who pointed out that the marine environment, although often well described and understood in overall terms, is at the stage of a Gordian knot that scientists are still a long way from unraveling, at least in regard to its protozoan components.

Benthic Foraminifera and Oxygen

Many of the anthropogenic contamination situations that affect benthic foraminifera assemblages can be linked directly to reduced dissolved oxygen concentrations in bottom and interstitial waters (e.g., Grant et al., 1995). From their investigations in Drammensfjord, Norway, Bernhard and Alve (1996) found that species respond to (and survive) anoxia using different strategies including dormancy and as-yet-unidentified anaerobic metabolic pathways. One of these responses may even involve some species' taking in chloroplasts (Bernhard and Bowser, 1999). The onset of depressed levels of dis-

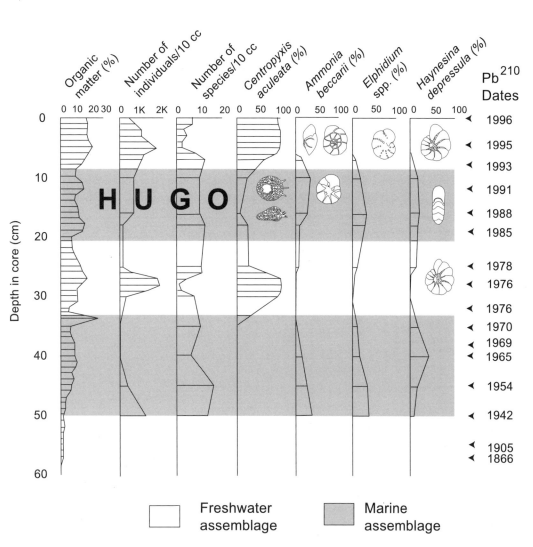

Figure 3.21. Profile of core 8 from Sandpiper Pond (Murrell's Inlet), South Carolina. There are two marine zones in this core, one of which relates to the incursion by hurricane Hugo. The other is a pre-1970 event that occurred when this pond was more exposed to marine conditions. The pond was isolated from the ocean after 1960, except for a short period when the storm surge of Hugo carried in a large amount of offshore calcareous species (after Collins et al., 1999).

solved oxygen in bottom water seems to be marked by a decrease in the number of calcareous species and by the dominance of one or more arenaceous taxa (e.g., Alve, 1991; Schafer et al., 1991). In some north temperate coastal marine environments, the arenaceous taxon *Spiroplectammina biformis* appears to be a useful indicator of depressed oxygen levels. It usually replaces comparatively ubiquitous calcareous forms such as *Elphidium*. In those marine environments marked by an annual oxygen stress, or hypoxia, as has been observed for example on parts of the Louisiana continental shelf, a ratio of species has been used successfully by Sen Gupta et al. (1996) to map affected areas. Their A-E index, given as $[N_A/(N_A + N_E)] \times 100$ (where N_A and N_E are respectively the numbers of *Ammonia parkinsoniana* and *Elphidium excavatum*), increases directly with the intensification and frequency of bottom water hypoxia; this suggests indirectly that *A. parkinsoniana* is more tolerant of anoxia than *E. excavatum*. Oxygen depletion in this offshore setting can be related in turn to elevated

total sedimentary organic carbon concentrations and fluxes that have been linked to phytoplankton blooms. The rise in the A-E index observed in Louisiana shelf cores covering the latter part of the twentieth century is especially pronounced (Fig. 3.23). Sen Gupta et al. (1996) suggest that the phytoplankton blooms may denote a response to nutrient inputs in the form of commercial fertilizers to the Gulf of Mexico; records show that the use of these chemicals increased markedly between 1930 and 1980.

(A)

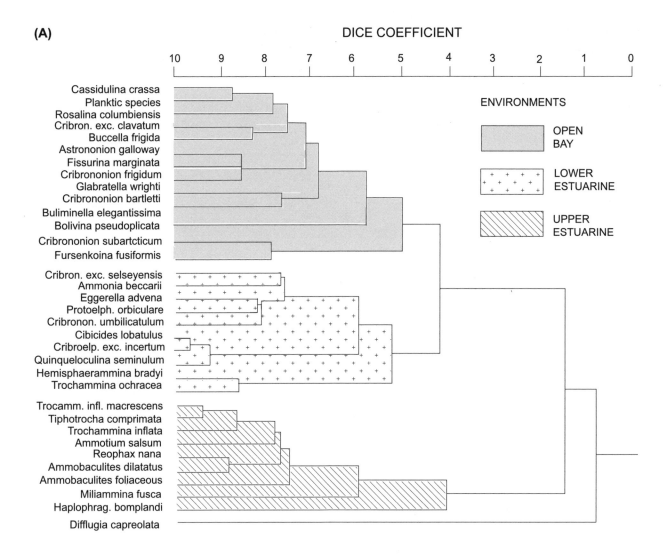

Figure 3.22. Examples of spatial empirical assemblage models created using a cluster analysis routine on total population data. The three-assemblage model (A) is for Chezzetcook Inlet on the south coast of Nova Scotia. The four-assemblage model (B) relates to environments identified in the Miramichi Estuary, which discharges into the southern Gulf of St. Lawrence (Scott et al., 1980). (C) Example of a general model showing predicted changes to a benthic foraminiferal community that has been impacted by contamination (after Alve, 1995).

Data from other investigations suggest that infaunal species of foraminifera may be more tolerant to reduced oxygen concentrations than their epifaunal counterparts (e.g., Moodley and Hess, 1992), which may explain why they are among the first and more successful colonizers of the soft bottom habitat (Alve, 1999). On the contrary, some epifaunal taxa (e.g., *Ammonia*

beccarii, Elphidium excavatum, Quinqueloculina seminulum) were shown to be able to survive at least twenty-four hours without oxygen, suggesting a capability for facultative anaerobic metabolism. The range of oxygen concentration sensitivities among foraminifera has potential as a tool for serial monitoring of oxygen-depletion effects. More importantly, it points to the benefits of calibrating local assemblages in regard to ambient oxygen concentration variation through appropriate laboratory and field experiments (e.g., Alve, 1990). Dissolved oxygen variation in bottom water may also cause indigenous species to migrate into and out of the sediment in order to maintain their exposure to some particular threshold level of O_2 (Alve and Bernhard, 1995). Exploitation of this migration process has several implications for monitoring applications, such as in the design of appropriate sediment sampling techniques and sampling schedules.

(B)

DICE COEFFICIENT

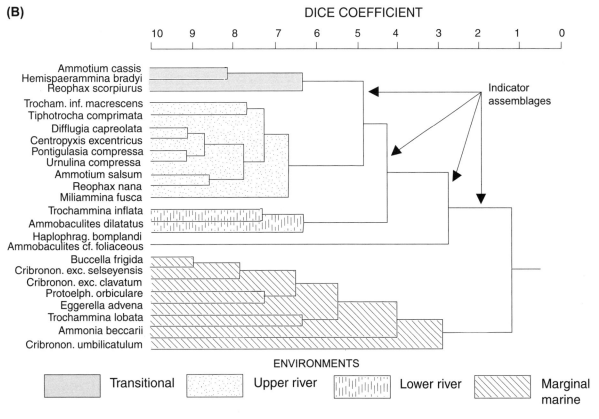

Ammotium cassis
Hemispaerammina bradyi
Reophax scorpiurus
Trocham. inf. macrescens
Tiphotrocha comprimata
Difflugia capreolata
Centropyxis excentricus
Pontigulasia compressa
Urnulina compressa
Ammotium salsum
Reophax nana
Miliammina fusca
Trochammina inflata
Ammobaculites dilatatus
Haplophrag. bomplandi
Ammobaculites cf. foliaceous
Buccella frigida
Cribronon. exc. selseyensis
Cribronon. exc. clavatum
Protoelph. orbiculare
Eggerella advena
Trochammina lobata
Ammonia beccarii
Cribronon. umbilicatulum

Indicator
assemblages

ENVIRONMENTS

Transitional   Upper river   Lower river   Marginal
marine

(C)

ORGANIC POLLUTION

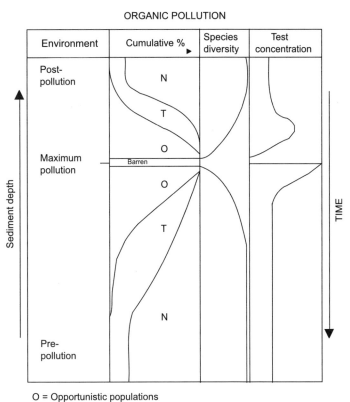

O = Opportunistic populations
T = transitional populations
N = Natural populations

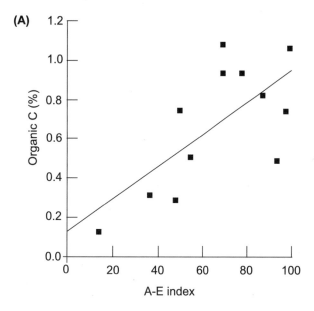

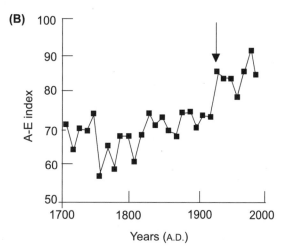

Figure 3.23. A-E index plotted against organic carbon (A) and with respect to time (B) in a core from the Louisiana continental shelf. Because of the small size of the foraminiferal subsamples needed for this study, each value represents a 2-cm-thick interval. The increase in organic carbon deposition after 1900 A.D. is marked by an increase in A-E index values (after Sen Gupta et al., 1996).

Foraminifera/Organic Matter Interactions

Organic matter (OM) comes in a broad variety of textures and compositions depending on its source, and on the processes that control its sedimentation to the seafloor; it can also occur in dissolved form. Although its origins may be natural, its impact on benthic foraminifera populations nonetheless may be as profound as that noted for anthropogenically contaminated sites. For example, Smart et al.

(1994) showed that in the open northeast Atlantic, a spring bloom of phytoplankton produced a seasonal pulse of "phytodetritus" that settled to the ocean floor where an opportunistic benthic foraminifera species *(Epistominella exigua)* was able to rapidly colonize this new food resource. *E. exigua* population density rose to levels above ambient values as a result of the increased flux of phytodetritus, giving rise to an abundance peak of this species that has been preserved in the sedimentary record as an index of natural organic matter flux variation.

Anthropogenically sourced OM has also been shown to produce fields of above-background foraminiferal population densities. However, the size, location, and configuration of these zones relative to the OM source reflect both the integrated effect of local environmental conditions (e.g., oxygen concentrations) and the type and texture of organic matter reaching the seafloor (e.g., Schafer and Frape, 1974). Anthropogenically derived OM usually consists of either domestic sewage or organic compounds from agriculture (fertilizers) and aquaculture (fish feces). These three categories of OM are all relatively biodegradable in contrast, for example, to pulp and paper mill effluents, which are composed of relatively refractory substances such as cellulose and lignin (wood fiber material). Differences in OM oxidation rates and input amounts, in relation to tidal flushing and watermass mixing, will often explain the reasons behind the modal (interseasonal) spatial pattern of a high foraminiferal population density zone (e.g., Seiglie, 1971; Schafer and Frape, 1974). In a weakly flushed and relatively quiescent (sheltered) environment receiving easily biodegradable OM from a point source (e.g., a sewage outfall), a high-density foraminiferal population zone may occur at some distance from the point source itself because oxidation of organic matter in proximal areas may be high enough to cause local anoxia (e.g., LeFurgey and St. Jean, 1976). In areas with strong tidal currents, such as the Bay of Fundy, local high concentrations in OM may be a seasonal phenomenon that causes no permanent habitat degradation (Schafer et al., 1995, Scott et al., 1995a). In one of the few studies to examine the record of temporal changes of OM fluxes at a finfish aquaculture site located in a coastal area having a 10 m tidal range, Scott et al. (1995c) observed a dramatic increase in OM sedimentation under the salmon cages that they related to a reduction in total abundances of foraminiferal populations. In this instance, the population reduction appeared to reflect a simple dilution, and there was no obvious change in assemblage composition (Fig. 3.24). One major change that could be detected in the fossil record was a large influx of the pelagic tintinnid *Tintinnopsis rioplatensis,* which appeared to respond to the large increase in suspended particulate matter that had developed in this relatively dynamic tidal current setting. Under shellfish sites, there is only an increase in fecal material, unlike the finfish case where there is also deposition of excess fish food. In the shellfish case, there was virtually no change in species composition of local foraminifera populations even though there was a small increase in OM (Fig. 3.25). This stability may be partly attributable to where these operations have been sited. In upper estuarine environments, where the indigenous taxa have a wide tolerance to high OM concentration in the sediment, the effect of increased OM deposition from shellfish aquaculture on indigenous foraminifera populations appears to be minimal. Local populations of polychaete worms observed at the shellfish aquaculture sites appeared to be more sensitive to lowered oxygen concentrations than their foraminiferal counterparts (Pocklington et al., 1994; Schafer et al., 1995), but they can undoubtedly rapidly recolonize foul substrates if the conditions that are promoting depressed O₂

are removed. Unfortunately, the poor preservation of polychaetes as fossils renders them unsuitable for paleoenvironmental reconstruction. The avoidance of hypoxic benthic habitats by polychaetes is thought to provide a setting in which foraminiferal population densities could increase significantly above those occupying distal substrates where natural OM concentrations would allow grazing by predator species (e.g., Buzas, 1982; Lipps, 1983).

Figure 3.24. Distribution of foraminifera and tintinnids in a core from the seafloor adjacent to a finfish (salmon) aquaculture site in Bliss Harbour, New Brunswick (Canada). Relatively little change is observed except that *Reophax scottii* increases towards the upper part of the core. Tintinnids also show an increase up core that heralds the onset of aquaculture operations, and a contemporaneous increase in the amount of suspended organic material. Tintinnids are planktonic protozoans not closely related to foraminifera but in the same general size range. They are very useful in characterizing areas that are experiencing high suspended particulate organic loads that may not be settling out at that location. The Bliss Harbour study area was not directly below the fish cages so that the sediment, even during the aquaculture period, was not highly organic (after Scott et al., 1995a).

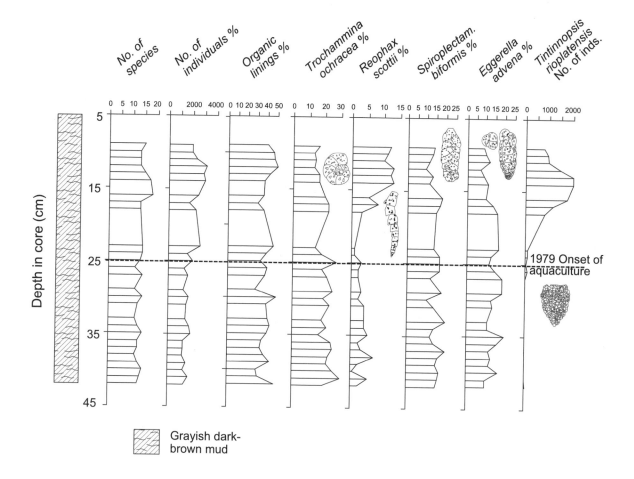

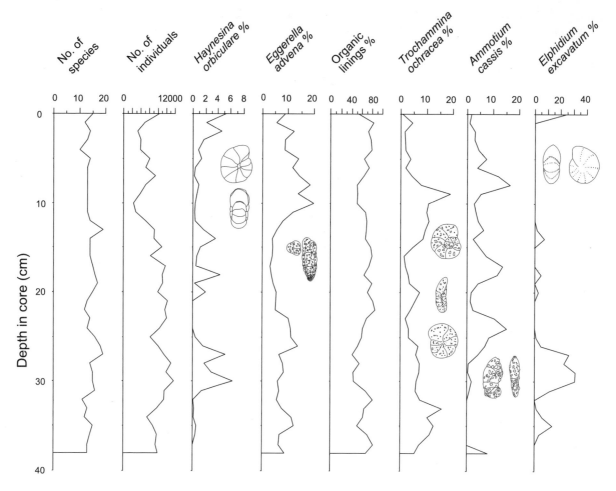

Figure 3.25. Distribution of foraminifera under a shellfish aquaculture site in Cardigan Bay, Prince Edward Island (Canada). There is evidence of cycling of faunas here that predates any aquaculture operations, suggesting that environmental changes observed here started to occur as a result of mechanisms that are not directly related to aquaculture. These data accentuate the requirement to be able to reconstruct precursor depositional environments before making decisions on what caused contemporary faunas to occupy a site (after Scott et al., 1995a).

Organic matter–controlled population density effects are sometimes demonstrated using diversity indices that account for the number of specimens of each species (e.g., Schafer, 1973; Schafer and Frape, 1974; Bates and Spencer, 1979) (Fig. 3.26). The spatial pattern and amplitude of high-population density zones defined by these kinds of indices, or by contoured primary data such as the number of foraminifera per cm³ of wet sediment, might be monitored to (a) evaluate seasonal variation of OM impacts, (b) test for effects of sewage treatment/discharge regulations, (c) determine the enrichment interval

(i.e., stabilization or substrate conditioning period) of dumped solid wastes (e.g., contaminated dredge spoils, processed municipal wastes/garbage), and (d) evaluate the impact of changes in tidal circulation on local OM sedimentation and transport that may be expected as a consequence of dredging or channelization projects (e.g., Wang et al., 1986), or from changes in the location, number, and cross-sectional area of inlets to bays, estuaries, and fjords. The typically heterogeneous characteristics of natural living foraminiferal population density patterns in coastal marine sediments (Schafer, 1971) and sediment cores (Schafer and Mudie, 1980), and the human resources needed to count reliable numbers of specimens per unit volume of sediment, augers for an initial evaluation of simple species number patterns for obtaining comparable (i.e., mappable) information. Species number (both living and total) is a much more conservative feature of indigenous foraminifera populations and has been shown to be applicable to the study of a broad variety of OM impact problems (e.g., Schafer, 1973; Schafer et al., 1991).

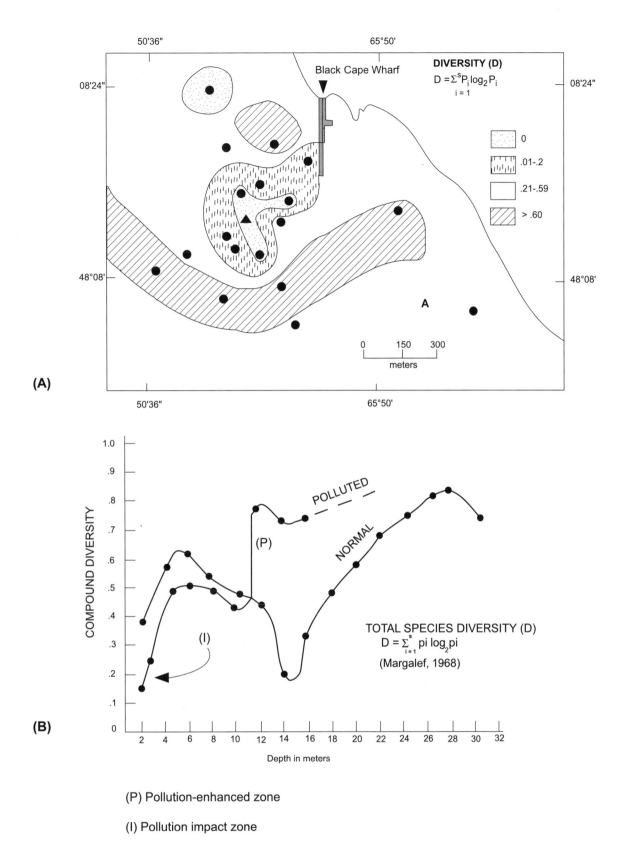

Figure 3.26 (A) Species diversity index variation of benthic foraminifera around the Grand Rivière pulp mill subtidal industrial waste outfall. The species distribution pattern is controlled primarily by organic matter depositional conditions near the outfall's mouth (Schafer and Frape, 1974). (B) Diversity index profiles for contaminated versus normal benthic habitats observed along the coasts of Chaleur Bay (Schafer, 1973).

Foraminifera and Trace Metal Contamination

Information on the direct sensitivity of foraminifera to elevated trace metal concentrations is not as well constrained compared to other parameters such as oxygen and organic matter. Usually, OM contamination increases the food supply, which tends to provoke a rise in population density, or it may depress oxygen levels, causing a reduction in both population density and species diversity. Trace metal contamination, in contrast, does not increase the food supply so that structural changes in the local benthic foraminiferal community caused by toxic trace metals would be expected to differ from those caused by OM (Rygg, 1985, 1986). Effects of toxic trace metal and organic matter contamination can be expected to show differing intervals of persistence in the marine environment and thus modulate substrate reconditioning times (e.g., Gustafsson and Nordberg, 1999). In addition, trace metals such as mercury may undergo chemical transitions in the marine environment that enhances their retention in the tissues of various organisms (e.g., Schafer and Cole, 1995), thereby giving rise to multiple effects.

In most instances, the correlation between trace metal concentration and foraminiferal community structure appears to mark the effect of concurrent inputs of OM and trace metal contaminants. Some researchers have tentatively concluded that trace metals, in themselves, are of relatively minor importance as a modulator of benthic foraminifera population characteristics (e.g., Alve, 1991). In their study of pollution effects in Canso Strait, Nova Scotia, Schafer et al. (1975) found that correlations between certain trace metals and foraminifera species may actually have been indicative of "remote" causal factors such as sediment texture and OM concentration. Conversely, Rygg (1986) has pointed out that, for larger marine organisms (>1.0 mm), copper pollution of sediments appears to have been directly responsible for a reduction in species diversity in some Norwegian fjords such that the number of macrofaunal species was roughly halved for each tenfold increase in the copper concentration. These observations demonstrate the utility of using foraminifera in combination with other organisms in pollution monitoring and assessment work (see following subsection).

Determinations of acute toxicity (i.e., LC 50 results) of some epiphytic foraminifera species (Bressler and Yanko, 1995a) have shown that when these taxa are attached to seaweeds, they appear to be less sensitive to the acute toxicity of cadmium, copper, and mercury than their detached counterparts living on the sediment. More important, the dissolved organic carbon produced by decomposition of seaweeds in experimental aquaria was observed to decrease acute toxicity of cadmium, copper, and mercury for both attached and sedentary foraminifera in a dose-dependent manner. These relationships also provoke questions on the influence of "remote" causal factors on species/trace metal correlations. In her evaluation of foraminifera/heavy metal relationships in two cores from Sørfjord, Alve (1991) suggested tentatively that heavy metal contamination has had a detrimental effect on species abundance compared to what has been reported from areas characterized by OM enrichment. She interpreted slight decreases in species diversity between relatively uncontaminated and contaminated sediments as the result of a general impact of trace metals on the entire assemblage. In summary, "remote" causal factor effects, in conjunction with the paucity of research data on direct relationships between species occurrence/abundance and trace metal concentration, suggest that foraminifera should not be used independently for inorganic contamination biomonitoring applications. Alve (1995) observed similarly that "heavy metals and chemicals are unlikely to favor any particular species of foraminifera." Further laboratory work and field observations on this problem should help to confirm or refute this idea.

A unique study that examined a site many years after its initial contamination by mainly municipal discharge, and where previous foraminiferal data were available, was done off the coast of California at an outfall site known to have been polluted nearly forty years ago (Bandy et al., 1964; Stott et al., 1996). The pioneering work initiated by Orville Bandy and his students tried to link foraminiferal populations with pollution effects, in this case thought to be mostly heavy metal contamination, from municipal discharge that occurred in the early 1960s. These studies provided baseline data for Stott et al. (1996), who returned to the site thirty years later after remediation was supposed to have taken place. They tried to determine if there was a change in foraminiferal fauna in response to decreased concentrations of contamination. Records of heavy metal releases showed a steady decrease from 1970 to 1992 as well as a decrease in suspended solid release. Stott et al. (1996) concluded that in fact the foraminiferal populations had shown a marked recovery around the site. In particular, there were no "dead zones" around the outfall as Bandy et al. (1964) had reported, while diversity and total abundance had returned to almost normal shelf conditions. Unfortunately there is no core data to determine if the decrease in emissions and foraminiferal recovery took place simultaneously. However, this study does illustrate how foraminifera can be used to assess both pollution impacts and remediation effects.

Combined Pollution Effects

Winyah Bay, South Carolina, is one of the most heavily polluted estuaries in the United States. It is contaminated by discharges from steel and pulp and paper mills, which have supplied a mixture of domestic sewage and heavy metal contamination (Collins et al., 1995). There is also a large freshwater input from the intracoastal waterway, but pollution effects are felt well outside the estuary to the edge of a visible plume that extends several km into the open ocean; it is only outside that plume that a normal marine foraminiferal fauna can be found (Fig. 3.27). This distribution may be partially due to the high freshwater input, but heavy metal contamination also appears to play a part in accounting for the observed decrease in diversity. The two most common species, *Elphidium excavatum* and *Ammonia beccarii,* are two well-known pollution indicator taxa.

Two diver-collected cores from Bedford Basin, Halifax Harbour (Nova Scotia), one from a domestic sewage outfall and one from an industrial outfall, show several apparently noteworthy contamination responses of local species (Figs. 3.28–3.30; Asioli, unpubl. data). At the domestic outfall, specimens typical of organic loading, such as tintinnids, *Reophax scottii,* and *Reophax arctica,* as well as *Ammotium cassis,* which is a marker of high suspended particulate matter (SPM), are all present. After 1996, with the doubling of sewage output, foraminifera became almost absent as a result of the dilution effect of the discharged OM, a relationship that is also suggested by total organic carbon (TOC) data (Fig. 3.29). At the industrial site, the two *Reophax* spp. were not common, but *Eggerella advena,* which is known to tolerate industrial waste, was the dominant species except at the sediment surface where high OM concentrations were at their highest (Fig. 3.30). Typical faunae at both sites prior to impacts would have contained several calcareous species *(Elphidium, Haynesina)* as documented by Gregory (1970).

Water Temperature Impacts

There are a number of studies in which benthic foraminifera have been used to map the extent of thermal pollution. The degree to which these investigations have yielded useful results has been strongly influenced by background temperature. Bamber (1995) points out that the direct effects of thermal discharges on marine organisms fall into several categories. These include (a) the mean temperature in relation to "normal" temperature, (b) the absolute temperature, which may approach lethal levels, and (c) short-term temperature fluctuations. Temperature variations tend to favor eurythermal species (i.e., those inhabiting the littoral zone or taxa that dominate in warmer latitudes) while inhibiting stenotherms or cooler-water species. In an in situ heated substrate field experiment, Schafer et al. (1996) found that the most statistically significant response of the north temperate shallow water foraminiferal population occupying a subtidal location in Halifax Harbour, Nova Scotia, was one of avoidance of above-normal temperatures. The two most abundant foraminifera species in the natural environment at the experiment site *(Eggerella advena* and *Trochammina ochracea)* preferred unheated sediments. One species *(Reophax scottii)* showed a preference for sediments heated to +4° C above ambient during the colder seasons. These results reflect an exploitable range of temperature preferences of these nearshore temperate species that should be useful for monitoring and survey purposes, but only if sufficient background information on seasonal variation is available from nearby control sites.

In the highly eurythermal environments of Guayanilla Bay, Puerto Rico, both test deformation and heat avoidance effects have been documented (Seiglie, 1975). For example, *Quinqueloculina rhodiensis* developed a specific morphologic response to thermal pollution involving chamber deformation and chamber arrangement distortions. *Elphidium poeyanum,* the dominant form during prethermal pollution times, was found to be virtually absent in modern assemblages. Moving north to a relatively stenothermal setting in Chaleur Bay, Gulf of St. Lawrence, Schafer (1973) found that the percentage of living species versus total species (living+dead specimens) decreased with distance from a power plant outfall during August and increased in November. Among the local population, arenaceous taxa such as *Ammotium cassis* and *Eggerella advena* showed increased percentage abundances at some distance from the outfall, whereas a number of calcareous species (e.g., *Buccella frigida, Elphidium excavatum* "group") appeared to be attracted to the warmer bottom water conditions found in areas closer to the outfall during the cooler seasons as might be expected since calcareous species are characteristic of warmer water. These calcareous taxa usually included the dominant members of the local population. This relationship could be advantageous in a monitoring

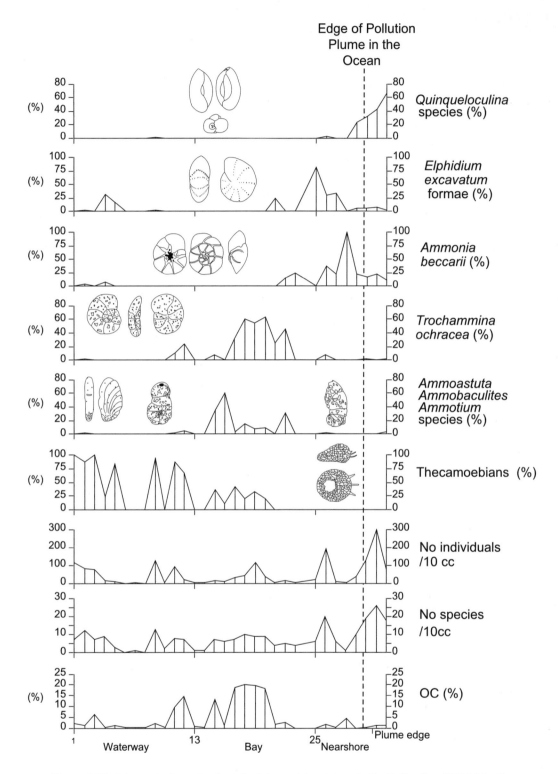

Figure 3.27. A transect of samples from the intracoastal waterway in South Carolina (U.S.A.) leading into Winyah Bay, which is exposed to several types of municipal and industrial contamination (both chemical and heavy metals). The pollution-tolerant species observed here are *A. beccarii* and *Elphidium* spp. which persist out to the edge of the waterway plume. They are replaced by less-tolerant Miliolid species in the more open marine and less contaminated parts of the bay (after Collins et al., 1995).

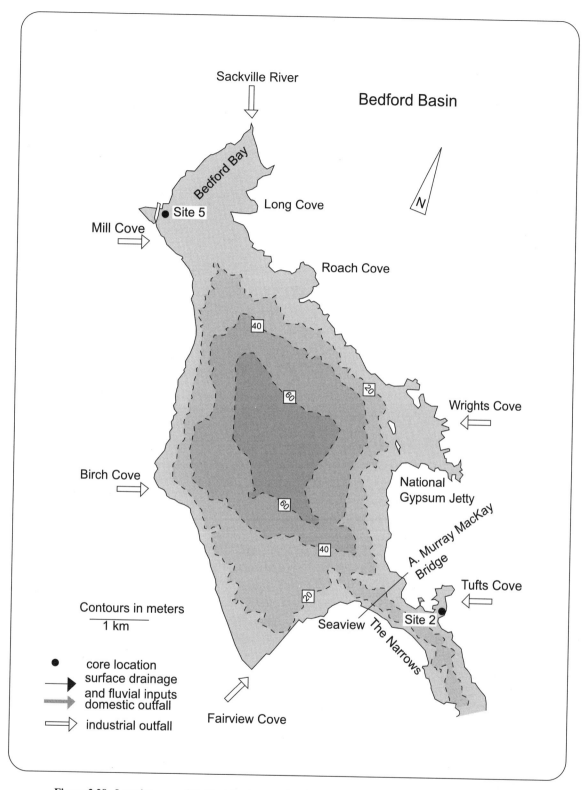

Figure 3.28. Location map of Bedford Basin core sites from 1996 (inner Halifax Harbour), Nova Scotia. The figure shows coring sites and point sources of both domestic and industrial sewage (from Asioli, unpublished).

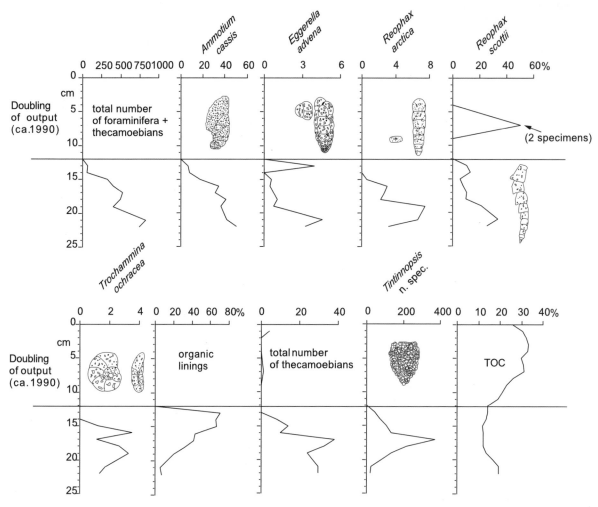

Figure 3.29. Foraminiferal and tintinnid distributions from a core collected at site 5 in Bedford Basin. This is a domestic outfall site. The upper 13 cm of the core is almost barren of microfossils because in 1996, when this core was collected, the sewage plant feeding this site pumped several times more than its usual capacity and literally buried everything (i.e., the upper 13 cm of the core represents one year). Below this layer tintinnids are abundant together with other pollution indicators. Thecamoebians are also comparatively abundant, being redeposited in this marine environment by freshwater runoff discharged by the outfall, which is also connected to storm drains. Since this core was collected, the site has started to remediate and calcareous species have "pioneered" the surface layer (Asioli, unpublished, 1997, Williamson, 1999).

situation since spatial changes in the abundance ratio of prominent calcareous species might provide a more conservative measure of the extent of thermal effluent influence than could be obtained from mapping living population densities, or the spatial distribution pattern of some of the relatively sensitive but less abundant taxa.

Deformed Foraminifera Tests as Pollution Indicators

Above-background percentages of deformed tests, and a relatively high number of species exhibiting deformities, are features of foraminifera populations inhabiting intensely contaminated environments (see Boltovskoy et al., 1991). However, Alve (1991) pointed out that these test abnormalities are not only linked to contamination effects, but can also mark environmental stress arising from either anthropogenic or natural forcing. The test deformation parameter yields best results when used in conjunction with other population indices and with environmental data that independently define pre- and post-contaminated intervals. Caution must be exercised in distinguishing between test abnormalities and intraspecific variation. Expressions of test deformation noted in Sørfjord, Norway (Alve, 1991), are typical and include double apertures, reduced chamber size, protuberances on chambers, twisted chamber arrangements, aberrant chamber shapes, and twinned specimens. Many of these

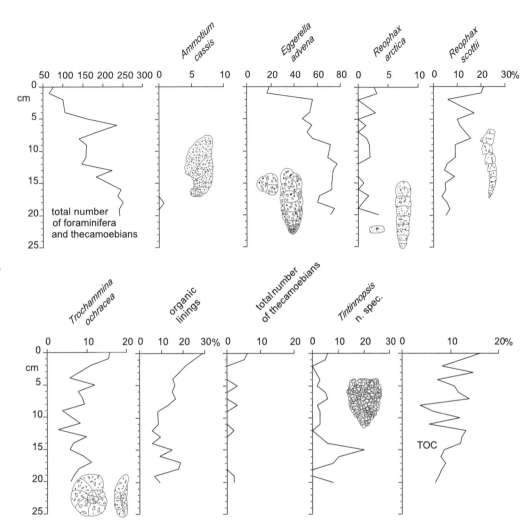

Figure 3.30. Foraminiferal distribution from site 2, core A, in Tufts Cove, Bedford Basin. This is an industrial site sampled the same time as the core shown in Fig. 3.29. Note that the species are quite different, with *Eggerella advena* being one of the dominant taxa and tintinnids present in only low numbers. Organic matter concentrations are also less here. The chronology of this core is not well constrained and it probably does not recover preimpact intervals (from Asioli, unpublished data, 1997).

features are linked to particular species (Fig. 3.31). Deformed specimens usually comprise less than 10% of the total population inhabiting contaminated environments. Seiglie (1975) noted that about 5% of the benthic foraminifera populations observed in chemically contaminated and thermally altered environments of Guayanilla Bay, Puerto Rico, were deformed. Such low percentages usually limit the treatment of test abnormality data to semiquantitative methods.

Test abnormalities in Guayanilla Bay included more pronounced spiraling in *Ammonia catesbyana* under stressed conditions provoked by organic matter contamination. The species *Quinqueloculina rhodiensis* was shown to develop two abnormal forms. Specimens having a thin and transparent last chamber occurred in areas contaminated by OM. Conversely, individuals with deformed chambers and a distorted chamber arrangement were associated with lagoonal environments described as thermally polluted. Between 10% and 30% of living *Q. rhodiensis* found in these environments exhibit the abnor-

malities mentioned earlier. Seiglie (1975) concluded that, in the Guayanilla Bay case, test abnormalities appear to be of greater significance than the species composition of indigenous assemblages in establishing differences among closely similar contaminated environments. As such, the power of this technique may be realized in those environments where species diversity is too low to allow the effective application of mapping and monitoring strategies that exploit this fundamental community structure parameter. In a preliminary study of some estuaries in the southern United Kingdom, Stubbles (1997)

Figure 3.31. Three examples of deformed tests collected from a western Norwegian fjord contaminated by heavy metals (after Alve, 1991).

reported direct correlations between heavy metal contamination and test deformities, even assigning percentages above and below natural limits; any instance of deformed tests exceeding 5% was defined as contaminated.

Combined Use of Foraminifera and Other Organisms

The total number of organism types included in contamination mapping and monitoring is clearly a function of financial and human resources, although Ferraro and Cole (1995) argue that, in certain instances, taxonomic identifications can be held at the family level to reduce survey and monitoring costs. In contemporary environmental surveys, the suite of species may include both soft-bodied and fossil-forming taxa (e.g., Seiglie, 1971; Grant et al., 1995). The strategy of multiple group surveys reflects the benefits derived from increasing the total range of organism sensitivities, response times, and species interactions resulting from contamination effects (e.g., Ros and Cardell, 1991; Ives, 1995). In general, the sensitivity range will be a function of the variety of organism biological complexity included among the set of selected indicator species. Comparatively complex marine organisms will usually show greater sensitivity and shorter response times because they are found, more often than not, among the biologically accommodated types (e.g., Josefson and Widbom, 1988). In contrast, comparatively simple organisms such as bacteria and

protozoans tend to occur more often in the physically accommodated category and typically are members of relatively hardy and adaptable pioneer communities. For serial studies of changing environments, the principal approach should be to opt for organism types that are well represented in the study area and to augment these with other taxa that extend the range of sensitivities and response times to levels appropriate for meeting the objectives of the study.

Initial investigations of pollution impact after the fact must rely on fossil-forming taxa since their signal can be used for both spatial and temporal analysis. As such, when considered in connection with possible postdepositional taphonomic effects, the contemporary empirical assemblage distribution model will often provide the framework needed to interpret the historical record in semiquantitative rather than simply relative terms. However, virtually every case of contamination is unique in some way, and combinations of organisms that work well in one environment may yield little useful information in other, seemingly similar settings (e.g., Danovaro et al., 1995).

Industrial contamination effects in Canso Strait, Nova Scotia, were assessed spatially and temporally using a combination of benthic foraminifera, ostracods, and molluscs (Schafer et al., 1975; Vilks et al., 1975). The tidal flushing of the Strait was severely curtailed in 1954 as a consequence of the construction of a causeway linking the mainland to Cape Breton Island. Because of its deep-water characteristics, the shores of the Strait have attracted a suite of petrochemical and pulp/paper industries during the following several decades. Discharges from these facilities, and from local municipalities, eventually produced a significant impact on the adjacent, poorly ventilated benthic marine environment. Among the three groups of organisms used to map the integrated pollution effect in 1973, ostracods appeared to be the most sensitive to the anthropogenically induced conditions that had developed in the Strait (Fig. 3.32). This conclusion was reached based on the large aerial extent of their barren zone, a feature that is consistent with results obtained in similar comparative studies (e.g., Seiglie, 1975). The indigenous mollusc population observed in the Strait in 1973 described a barren zone that was intermediate in size relative to the barren zones of foraminifera and ostracods. In the more intensively polluted areas of the Strait (i.e., near point sources of industrial contamination) foraminifera population densities were relatively low. However, the high tolerance of some of the species in this group to the effects of contamination was marked by a relatively small foraminiferal barren zone. In this instance, the comparatively robust nature of the foraminifera pro-

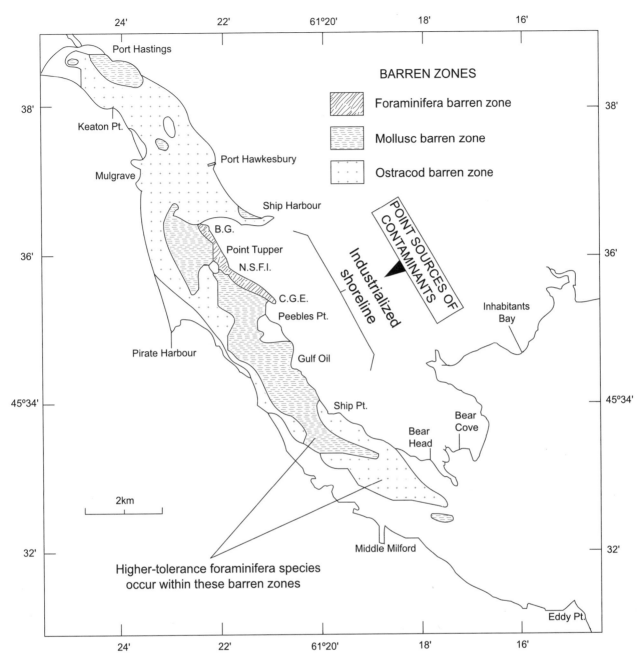

Figure 3.32. Spatial extent of foraminifera, molluscs, and ostracod barren zones along the industrialized shoreline of Canso Strait. These data illustrate the apparent relative sensitivity of three distinctive invertebrate groups to the mix of contamination and environmental conditions found in this fjord-like inlet. The barren zone distributions point to the value of multi-organism monitoring and mapping approaches (after Schafer et al., 1975).

vided useful data on environmental variability within the larger mollusc and ostracod barren zones.

The relatively strong tolerance of estuarine foraminifera to pollution forcing can be seen in a variety of studies (e.g., Josefson and Widbom, 1988), making this group an effective "end member signal" when used in conjunction with more sensitive organisms in pollution assessment and monitoring. One advantage provided by the foraminifera is their utility for mapping some of the more intensely contaminated areas near sewage and waste outfalls that have been abandoned by other benthic organisms. Stressed environments near contamination

sources in the strait are characterized by large numbers of "physically dominated" species such as *Eggerella advena, Elphidium excavatum* "group," the mollusc species *Modiolus modiolus,* and several ostracods including *Baffinicythere emarginata* and *Muellerina canadensis*. The concurrent evaluation of this larger spectrum of organism types produces data that reflect both direct physical effects (e.g., low oxygen concentrations) and the consequences of positive and negative feedbacks between physical and biological regimes that control the ultimate response of population densities to environmental changes (Ives, 1995). Species interaction factors appear to be more pronounced in the case of long-term environmental trends where there is sufficient time for interspecific contacts to have strong effects (e.g., Yodzis, 1989).

In the Saguenay Fjord, Quebec, Schafer et al. (1991) studied foraminifera and thecamoebians in gravity cores and grab samples collected between 1976 and 1988. These samples contained a physical record of OM contamination of benthic habitats, attributable primarily to discharges by local pulp and paper mills. In surface samples, the abundance of the dominant arenaceous foraminifer, *Spiroplectammina biformis*, decreased between 1982 and 1988. The authors concluded that this decrease marked the recolonization of the upper reaches of the fjord by several other arenaceous taxa, following an interval of reduced industrial discharge. In the same interval, the dominant living calcareous species showed a threefold increase in relative abundance. This recolonization could have been due to the combined effect of the regulations imposed by the Canadian government on industrial polluters in the early 1970s and the capping of a large area of contaminated fjord basin sediment by a clayey late glacial sediment layer derived from a catastrophic landslide that occurred in May 1971.

The 1982 thecamoebian population of the fjord usually comprised four species, of which *Centropyxis aculeata* was the most abundant. Generally, thecamoebian percentages more than doubled between 1982 and 1988. In 1988 samples, thecamoebians showed increased percentages (relative to benthic foraminifera) at all stations. Their temporal change in distribution pattern is comparable to that noted for the total number of foraminifera/cc of wet sediment. Distinct differences are observed in the foraminifera and thecamoebian assemblages associated with "potentially stressed" and "mildly contaminated to normal" benthic environments.

Both the concentration and diversity of the thecamoebian population were noted as being higher in presumed stressed intervals of cores. In these stressed core sections, total population values (foraminifera+thecamoebians) were lower than seen in mildly contaminated to

normal environments. Based on these findings, the authors suggested that a ratio of thecamoebians/total foraminifera may be helpful in describing the temporal variation of pollution impact on the benthic foraminiferal community of this particular marine setting. They suggested further that thecamoebian habitat in Saguenay River nearshore environments might also have been influenced by the influx of various contaminants. Although little difference in diversity was observed in core subsamples characterized by relatively high organic matter content, thecamoebian specimen concentrations were double that observed in intervals with low organic matter percentages. It was tentatively suggested that higher concentrations of organic matter in the Saguenay River may have provided a more abundant food supply for indigenous thecamoebian populations.

FORAMINIFERA AS TRACERS AND TRANSPORT INDICATORS

Foraminifera as Sediment and Transport Tracers

There are many coastal developmental, environmental, and scientific problems for which marine sediment transport information is of key importance (e.g., Hayes, 1980; Riedel, 1985; Thorn, 1987). Most field methods used to gather sediment transport data are inherently expensive (e.g., dyed sands or glass beads doped with radioactive materials). Under certain conditions, however, foraminifera can be used in conjunction with other natural tracer methods (e.g., Solomons and Mook, 1987), or as a precursor to more quantitative physical measurement programs, to obtain an understanding of the general nature and pathways of sediment transport processes. One advantage of foraminiferal sediment tracers is that their size and test morphology cover a broad range of hydrodynamic energies so that it is often possible to associate the occurrence of a species with a particular hydrodynamic process. The most likely candidates for sediment tracer work are those species whose distribution is restricted to a particular environment from which they can be passively transported by either steady-state (e.g., tidal currents) or non-steady-state (e.g., storms) processes (Li et al., 1997). This section reviews several applications that demonstrate the potential of foraminifera as sediment tracers.

The foraminiferal tracer technique gives best results when used in conjunction with other physical observations (e.g., grain size distributions, surficial tidal current patterns, terrestrial organic matter distribution patterns) that can provide both complementary and confirming evidence about the nature of those transport processes under investigation. This survey strategy reflects the fact that the very watermass that may be responsible for the passive transport of foraminifera tests is also among the key elements controlling active species distributions. A species distribution pattern is essentially an integrated "signal" that may have several explanations in addition to passive transport (e.g., different levels of locomotion, predation patterns). It is also noteworthy that while living (i.e., stained) specimens can be expected to yield the most conservative results in sediment transport applications, their independent use depends on significant understandings of the local nature of reproduction patterns (e.g., Buzas, 1965; Jorissen and Witting, 1999). Total population distributions (stained plus unstained specimens), on the other hand, may be biased toward the impact of individual non-steady-state transport events or may be indicative of the proximity of older source deposits from which particles are being resuspended. To give the reader a sense of the limitations of this methodology, the following case histories are drawn from a variety of physical settings that utilize a suite of investigative strategies that often include multidisciplinary elements.

Coulbourn and Resig (1975) used foraminifera tracers as an aid in defining sand sources and sand transport pathways in Kahana Bay, Oahu (Hawaii). In their study, foraminiferal distribution patterns represented one of a suite of physical and oceanographic measurements that were deemed necessary to adequately define the physical and oceanographic setting of the bay. Foraminiferal species were subdivided into several groups according to constraints derived from associated physical measurements (mean grain size of the sediment, weight percent of terrigenous material, and location). For example, their "estuarine" group was closely associated with relatively high percentages of terrigenous material and included a significant representation of brackish-water species. Other groups were differentiated based on differences in grain size distributions resulting from winnowing, or from inputs of relatively coarse particles from proximal sources (e.g., reef-derived material). Fossil beach ridges were recognized by their organic swamp mud content. In general, low foraminiferal numbers (i.e., the number of specimens per gram of dried sediment) distinguished high-energy reef flat environments from quieter wave and tidal current regimes of adjacent channels. Foraminiferal number (FN) results were augmented by species distribution data. Brackish-water species distributions followed the pattern of stream-derived sediment that was deposited in an adjacent bay.

In the Kahana Bay study, small species showed a close relationship to large FN values, to fine-grained sands, and to high percentages of terrigenous material. Collectively, these features were explained as a function of sorting during transport down the stream channel. Information related to the energy of transporting forces was derived from the percentage occurrence of small tests (e.g., their percentages were generally inversely related to wave energy magnitude because wave turbulence effectively winnowed out smaller tests and facilitated their transport to lower-energy environments). Conversely, relatively large species were associated with high-energy reef flat environments and were transported downdrift to adjacent channels and nearshore high-energy environments in a pattern opposite that found for small species (Fig. 3.33). Specimens of one relatively robust, thick-walled species of *Amphistegina* were found to be too large to be transported to low-energy central bay environments and thus were useful for estimating areas characterized by continuously low current speeds. Coulbourn and Resig (1975) noted that many species were determined to be unsuitable as sediment transport indicators in this setting because of their ubiquitous distribution. In contrast, conclusions drawn from the distributions of typically restricted species were borne out by data derived from physical measurements in the bay.

In another study, Schafer et al. (1992) employed foraminiferal assemblages in a tidal inlet that was scheduled for redevelopment into a large harbor. Foraminiferal data were helpful in defining modal tidal circulation and particle transport patterns. In that study, species occurrence data were processed using factor analysis, and statistical assemblages were plotted as summed percentages of the three or four highest of the factor score species for each factor. Species percentage data could be separated into four factors. Factor 1 was interpreted as a general suspended particle transport factor that apparently reflected the processes and conditions that focused deposition of foraminifera-sized particles in relatively deep and sheltered outer-harbor environments (Fig. 3.34). Stations with high loadings on Factor 2 were confined primarily to the outer harbor navigation channel and to the main tidal channel (Fig. 3.35). The assemblage associated with this factor helped in illustrating the extent of bidirectional sediment transport along the main tidal channel of the inlet, and a depositional pattern attributable to the ebb tidal flushing of sediment from the inner harbor (lagoon).

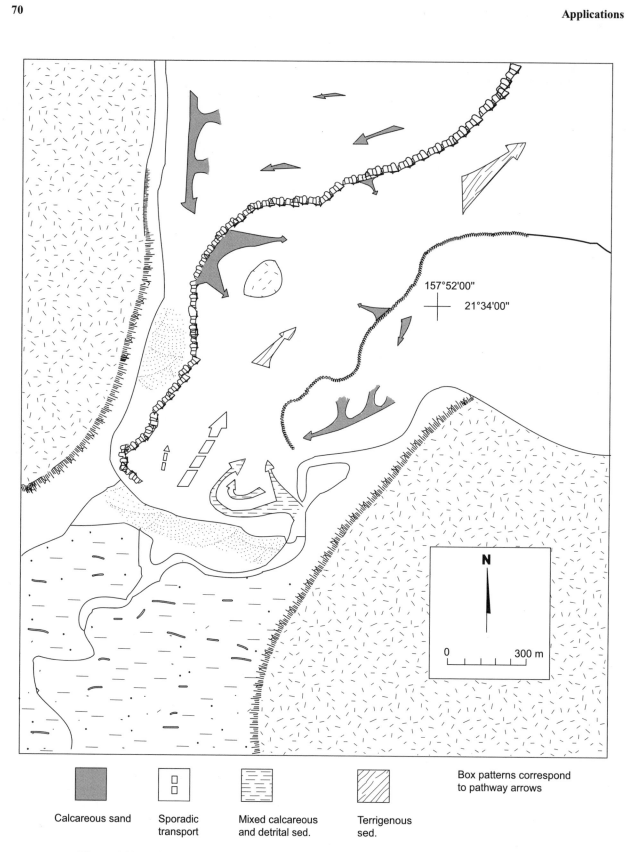

157°52'00"
21°34'00"

N

0   300 m

Calcareous sand   Sporadic transport   Mixed calcareous and detrital sed.   Terrigenous sed.   Box patterns correspond to pathway arrows

Figure 3.33. Sediment transport pathways defined using sixteen species of benthic foraminifera (redrawn and simplified from Coulbourn and Resig, 1975).

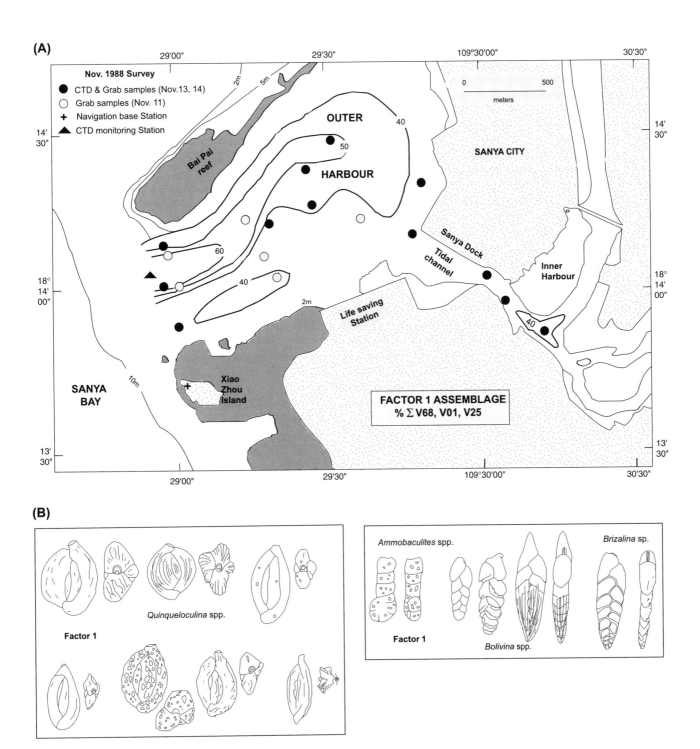

Figure 3.34. (A) Spatial distribution of foraminifera factor 1 values (thickened contour lines) in outer Sanya Harbour. Data reflect the occurrence of the foraminifera indicator assemblage in a part of the outer harbour where deposition of suspension-transported material predominates during the ebb tide (after Schafer et al., 1992). (B) Representatives of the factor 1 assemblage including *Quinqueloculina* spp., *Ammobaculites* spp., and *Bolivina/Brizalina* spp.

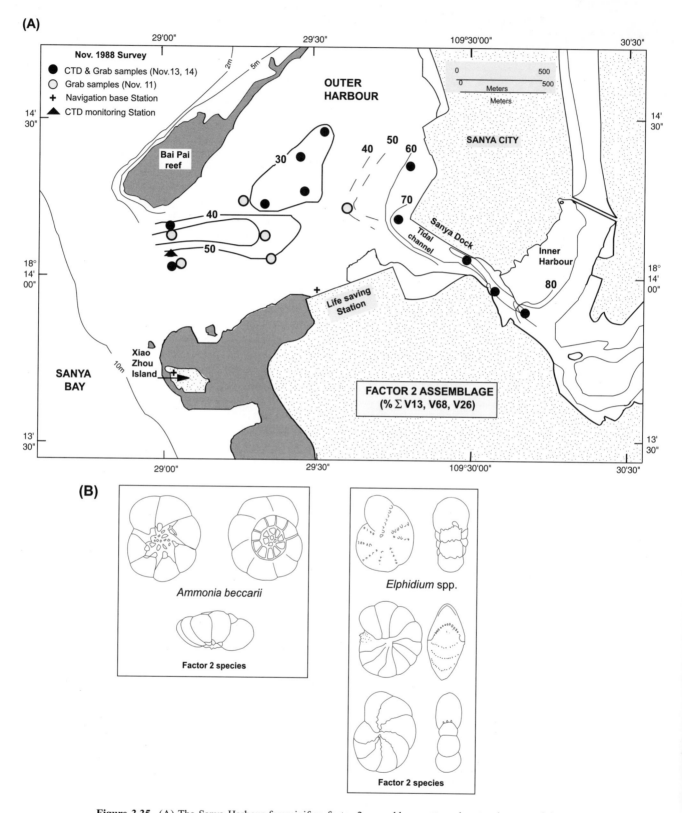

Figure 3.35. (A) The Sanya Harbour foraminifera factor 2 assemblage pattern denotes the area of the inlet that is influenced by tidal transport. Traction transport appears to be relatively intense at either end of the channel that separates the inner (lagoon) and outer (bay) harbor (after Schafer et al., 1992). (B) The factor 2 assemblage *(Ammonia, Elphidium* spp.) is dominated by calcareous taxa that are probably transported along the channel floor as saltating or as continuously suspended particles depending on tidal current strength. Deposition occurs at both ends of the narrow channel in response to a pronounced reduction of tidal current speed at these two locations.

The characteristic species of Factor 2 are rounded calcareous types. Ebb tidal currents appeared to carry trochospiral taxa such as *Ammonia beccarii* from inner-harbor environments seaward to less constricted and relatively low tidal current energy areas of the outer harbor such as the dredged turning basin adjacent to the present main dock. The Factor 3 assemblage consisted mostly of marginal marine calcareous species that described the general circulation of inner shelf marine water that enters the outer harbour during the flood stage of the tide. The distribution of key Factor 3 species (*Nonionella sp.* and *Florilus* spp.) appeared to represent both passive transport effects and water-mass characteristics. Factor 4 species accounted for a very small percentage of the total variance (5.5%). The percentage abundance pattern of the four key species of this factor described several local transition areas of the outer harbour where diagnostic taxa of Factors 1, 2, and 3 showed an exceptionally strong association. Reworked or relic benthic foraminifera tests derived from the erosion of penecontemporaneous or older sediment deposits are typically characterized at these locations by slight petrifaction and by a white or yellowish-brown color. Relic specimens were also often observed in the tidal channel and in the outer harbour navigation channel. As Thorn (1987) points out, numerical sedimentation models (that might be used to predict the impact of harbour expansion on flushing patterns and sediment fluxes) need empirical information from the site before they can be adapted to the unique environmental settings of individual coastal inlets and estuaries. Foraminiferal "proxy" data can represent a utilitarian element of the requisite data set required for these kinds of calibration exercises.

There are several interesting examples of how foraminifera have been used for large-area sediment transport studies in offshore environments. The Western Approaches and western English Channel are shelf sea environments that are strongly influenced by tidal currents, storms, and waves. To evaluate the transport impact of these hydrodynamic effects, Murray et al. (1982) collected suspended particles from 40 m below the sea surface and from 5 m above the seafloor using plankton nets. They used these samples, which earlier studies had shown to be rich in dead foraminifera tests of both benthic and planktic species, to map the movement of water currents and to determine residual transport directions. Their study highlighted the role of suspension transport (as opposed to traction transport) processes, and also considered the importance of waves generated in exposed shelf environments on the entrainment of relatively large particles of up to 0.3 mm in diameter (which includes many foraminifera species) and their transport to water depths of as much as 200 m. In those areas characterized by relatively intensive erosion processes, the number of specimens per liter of water increased at both the –40 m and –5 m depths. Most specimens showed little evidence of damage or abrasion, and those that showed damage were among the relatively larger specimens.

Planktic foraminifera data presented in the Murray et al. (1982) study demonstrated that the maximum size of specimens in this group (0.40 to 0.57 mm) occurred on the outer shelf of the Western Approaches where exposure to large sea waves and storms would be expected to be relatively high. Approaching the western end of the English Channel, the maximum size of planktic tests decreased to 0.40 mm and size distribution data showed a much greater degree of specimen sorting than had been seen in the Western Approaches area. Sorting characteristics were ascribed to the increased influence of tidal currents flowing into the relatively constricted and sheltered channel environment. Murray et al. (1982) pointed out that the western section of the channel is distinguished by its relatively high numbers of benthic foraminifera tests in all parts of the water column; this feature suggested extensive erosion resulting from relatively intense vertical turbulence and mixing.

Net sediment transport in this inner shelf environment was estimated using different species as tracers. For example, the water column distribution of the benthic outer shelf species *Brizalina difformis* was selected to infer net transport of suspended material from the outer shelf into the western English Channel. Two inner shelf benthic species (*Ammonia beccarii* and *Nonion [=Haynesina] depressulum*) showed water column distributions near the coast which appeared to mark limited offshore transport. In an earlier paper, Murray (1980) showed that passive suspension transport of benthic foraminifera in the Exe Estuary was manifested by forty-three species that are not known to inhabit that environment. Thirty-two of these were among the group collected in water column samples in the western English Channel study. Most of the forty-three species fall within the 0.14–0.18 mm size range, which is included in the size interval of most easily erodible solid quartz spheres (Hjülstrom, 1939). Detrital foraminifera tests thrown into suspension cannot settle out until energy conditions are reduced significantly. This settling lag mechanism was used by Murray et al. (1982) to explain the penetration of outer shelf foraminifera into estuaries where they can be redeposited in low-energy environments. The spatial patterns observed in bottom sediment data can be used to describe the geographical aspects of these processes. Perhaps more importantly, spatial patterns of foraminifera collected from the water column provide a means of explaining the details of particle transport from the area of resuspension to the point of deposition, which gives additional clues regarding the comprehensive picture of local particle transport processes. For example, in the western Channel study, Murray et al. (1982) were able to infer the presence or absence of a thermocline (i.e., watermass stratification) during various seasons of the year based on the absence of certain resuspended benthic species in upper water column samples. The presence or absence of this key watermass structural feature would be expected to have a significant effect on the spatial distribution pattern of certain types of suspended particles because of its inhibiting effect on vertical mixing processes. The Murray et al. (1982) study has two important aspects. It demonstrated the utility of foraminifera in evaluating (tracing) watermass dynamics, and it showed how water column data can be used to explain the intermediate steps in the process controlling test displacement patterns revealed in seafloor sediment data.

■ Submarine Slides

Although it is often relatively easy to describe terrestrial landslide deposits based on lithological, textural, and proximity considerations, understanding the sources of submarine slide sediments may be more difficult because of (1) their relatively long transport "pathways" and (2) the fact that the original slide material may be reworked considerably during its transport in water. In certain geologic settings, such as the one that characterizes the watershed of the Saguenay Fjord in Quebec, it was possible to utilize microfossil data from a well-documented twentieth-century submarine slide to create an empirical model that could be used to detect and interpret older slide events (Schafer et al., 1990).

Most of the landslides that have occurred near the head of the Saguenay Fjord have involved the displacement of sensitive marine clays that were raised above sea level during the course of the postglacial crustal rebound process in this area of Canada (Chagnon, 1968). A widely publicized landslide of these raised marine clays occurred in the early morning of May 4, 1971. The slide began after a period of heavy rainfall and eventually displaced an estimated 6.8 million m³ of sediment, of which about 5.3 million m³ was carried into the north end of the fjord basin by the Saguenay River. In undermining the town of St. Jean Vianney, the terrestrial component of the slide caused the death of thirty-one residents and the destruction of forty homes. Slide sediments deposited in the fjord formed an exponentially thinning tongue of gray clayey silt that extended more than 10 km along the floor of the basin. This deposit was marked by its distinctive color and its content of tiny clay pellets, and by a redeposited calcareous benthic foraminifera assemblage (Schafer et al., 1979, 1983). The calcareous assemblage contrasted markedly with the predominantly arenaceous foraminifera population that inhabits this comparatively estuarine upper part of the fjord.

Subsequent studies of sediment cores collected in the Saguenay Fjord basin revealed information on an apparently earthquake-triggered landslide that is believed to have taken place in February 1663 and that formed the valley in which the 1971 slide occurred (Schafer and Smith, 1987a,b). The 1663 slide was about thirty times larger than the 1971 event. Evidence that it had actually flowed as far as the Saguenay River channel was discovered during a dam construction project in the early 1940s (Leggett, 1945). Data from a gravity core collected at a relatively distal site in the main basin of the fjord indicated the top of a landslide-like deposit at a core depth of 64 cm. This horizon corresponded to an estimated age (based on ^{210}Pb) of between 1667 and 1686. The slide sediments contained a familiar redeposited calcareous assemblage similar to that known to occur in the upper sections of the local raised marine clay sequence (Hillaire-Marcel, 1981). The assemblage included relatively large numbers of planktic foraminifera specimens that are not found in contemporary fjord environments (Fig. 3.36). Their preservation appeared to reflect their rapid transport and burial during this seventeenth-century mass flow event. Furthermore, their co-occurrence with relatively high numbers of thecamoebian specimens pointed to the possibility that the slide material may have included both shallow nearshore estuarine and deep-water marine facies of the raised clay source material. Using a mixture of microfossil, lithological, textural, radiographic, and historical documentary evidence, it was possible to piece together a sequence of events that included the apparent earthquake-triggered displacement of local raised marine clays, their transport to the main fjord basin as a cohesionless mass flow, and the subsequent resuspension and deposition of the fine fraction of the slide sediment by river and tidal currents for at least six weeks after the event itself. A continuous examination (i.e., cm by cm) of foraminifera assemblages in the core section overlying the 1663 slide layer showed that there were no other local marine clay slide events of comparable scale between the mid-seventeenth century and 1971.

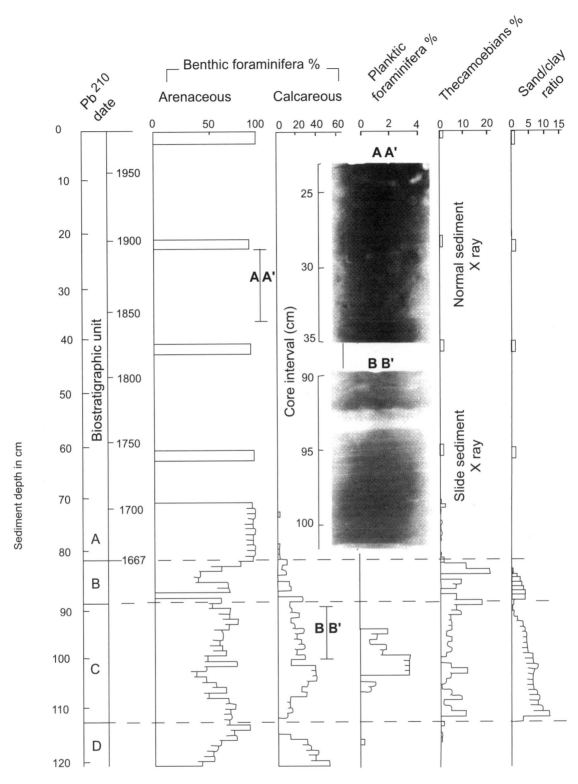

Figure 3.36. Core from the main channel of the Saguenay Fjord showing the presence of redeposited planktic and benthic calcareous specimens in the 80 cm+ interval. The planktic specimens are believed to be associated with raised marine deposits that were displaced during an earthquake-triggered landslide that occurred near the head of the Saguenay Fjord in 1663 A.D. (after Schafer and Smith, 1987b).

■ Foraminiferal Test Features
as Transport Indicators

Up to this point, we have reviewed several field studies that focus on integrated data sets. It is also appropriate, however, to examine how foraminifera tests themselves can be helpful in documenting the nature of sediment transport processes.

Minas Basin, Bay of Fundy, Nova Scotia (Canada). When benthic foraminifera are eroded and passively transported by wave turbulence and bottom currents, the evidence of the transport process is often etched onto their tests. One location on the east coast of Canada that lends itself particularly well to the broader study of foraminiferal test transport is the Bay of Fundy. The Minas Basin is situated at the head of the bay. The basin is a unique environment for several reasons, including its exceptionally large tide range (16.3 m; Dawson, 1917). Surface water tidal currents can exceed 2.0 m/s and reach values of more than 1.0 m/s at the seafloor (Amos and Joice, 1977). These comparatively high velocities are well in excess of those required to erode and transport foraminifera tests (e.g., Sternberg and Marsden, 1979; Shu and Collins, 1995). Bottom sediments in the Minas Basin range from muddy sands and sands – in the extensive tidal flat areas – to sandy gravel and gravel in deeper offshore environments that are exposed to the full force of local tidal currents (Amos and Long, 1980). In general, suspended material is transported into the basin from the bay and is eroded and redistributed during each tidal cycle.

Three foraminiferal associations, comprising a total of forty species, were identified in basin sediment samples (Thomas and Schafer, 1982). One of these assemblages was restricted to nearshore or intertidal environments and consisted mostly of relatively small species *(Miliammina, Lagena, Bolivina,* and *Oolina).* These forms are characterized generally by comparatively fragile tests and, except for the arenaceous taxon *(Miliammina),* most exhibited some degree of abrasion and damage on their test surface. A second estuarine association included both arenaceous *(Trochammina)* and calcareous taxa *(Islandiella, Trifarina, Rosalina, Buccella,* and *Elphidium).* Many of these forms have relatively robust tests that showed little evidence of abrasion. Transport of the species in the estuarine association was presumed to have occurred in suspension, thereby avoiding the test surface abrasion that could result from bedload transport (see Loose, 1970). The occurrence of unabraded planktic specimens in the Avon River Estuary, where the estuarine association dominates, was cited as supporting evidence for suspension transport of the members of this relatively diverse association. The mean maximum diameter of planktic specimens observed in basin sediments is 0.23 mm, a size that is relatively easily eroded (Hjülstrom, 1939; Shepard, 1963).

A third association observed in the basin consisted of ubiquitous taxa *(Quinqueloculina, Pyrgo, Ammonia, Eggerella,* and *Elphidium)* that have relatively large and/or thick-walled tests. Thomas (1977) speculated that the apparent widespread distribution of ubiquitous species in the basin may be controlled largely by the resiliency of their tests. A*mmonia beccarii* is one of the largest of the calcareous foraminifera found in the basin (mean ∅. = 0.58 mm). Its thick-walled test is often heavily abraded (Fig. 3.37B). Commonly, the ultimate and/or penultimate chamber is missing from its test, suggesting intervals of bedload transport (e.g., Boltovskoy and Wright, 1976). *Quinqueloculina seminulum* is also a relatively large calcareous species with a distribution similar to that of *A. beccarii.* In basin environments, it often displayed evidence of pronounced test abrasion comparable to that noted for *Pyrgo williamsoni* (Fig. 3.37C). *P. williamsoni* is regarded generally as a deep bay form that is usually associated with muddy substrates and comparatively high salinities (e.g., >29‰; Bartlett, 1964). Its presence and distribution pattern was considered to be indicative of sediment scouring and bedload transport from high to relatively low energy environments that are situated around the rim of the basin (Fig. 3.38A). *Cibicides lobatulus* is an attached species that is often associated with relatively high energy environments (Bartlett, 1964). Many of the specimens of *Cibicides lobatulus* collected in the basin showed extensive test abrasion (Fig. 3.37A). Some specimens had their entire dorsal surfaces removed, suggesting long intervals of bedload transport or abrasion by other detrital particles while the test was still attached to a hard substrate lying in the path of the tidal flow (Fig. 3.38B).

The *Elphidium excavatum* "group" is the most ubiquitous foraminiferal taxon inhabiting the basin and often exhibits abrasion damage comparable to that noted for *C. lobatulus.* Schafer (1976) reported that the *E. excavatum* "group" was among the most transport-susceptible member of the shallow-water assemblage observed in St. Georges Bay, Nova Scotia. The general distribution of the *E. excavatum* "group" in the basin mirrors that of several other key calcareous species *(Pyrgo williamsoni, C. lobatulus, Elphidium margaritaceum,* and *E. frigidum)* and points to a modal transport pattern of foraminifera tests covering environments of relatively high tidal current

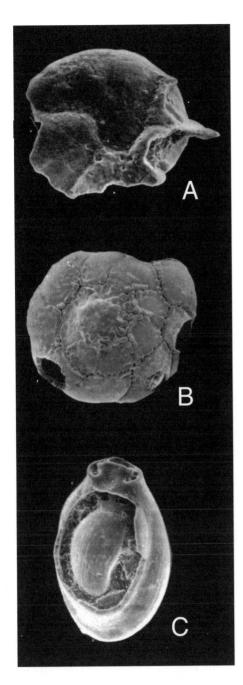

Figure 3.37. SEM photos of abraded foraminifera from the Minas Basin in the Bay of Fundy. (A) *Cibicides lobatulus,* (B) *Ammonia beccarii,* and (C) *Pyrgo williamsoni* (after Thomas and Schafer, 1982).

areas during earlier phases of the flood cycle, and at later phases of the ebb cycle. A scour lag effect enhances the probability that specimens would not be eroded from nearshore shallow water areas during the ebb portion of the tidal cycle.

The empirical foraminiferal model is reinforced by the bathymetric distribution of sediment textures seen throughout the basin (e.g., Amos and Long, 1980). Thomas and Schafer (1982) speculated that the absence of abrasion features on certain species (e.g., *M. fusca* and *E. margaritaceum*) may have denoted their nearshore and intertidal habitat preferences, which would not be subject to the relatively strong and prolonged tidal current activity found in deeper offshore basin settings. The hydraulic equivalent diameter (i.e., the diameter of a quartz grain having the same settling velocity) of the *E. excavatum* "group" is in the 0.10 to 0.16 mm range for specimens with an average diameter of 0.35 mm (Haake, 1962; Grabert, 1971). Since the modal diameter of the *E. excavatum* "group" in the basin is only slightly larger (0.40 mm), Thomas and Schafer (1982) concluded that there was a strong possibility that most specimens of this species would be included in the equivalent diameter range of the most easily eroded particle sizes.

The qualitative model information that emerged from the Thomas and Schafer (1982) study consisted of two elements. One of these considered bedload transport of large, robust-test species such as *A. beccarii.* This process produces extensive damage to the test wall and its associated surficial ornamentation. The other element was related to the suspension transport of relatively small and fragile forms such as *E. frigidum.* This transport mode is associated with significantly fewer abrasion features. Actual perforation of the test wall appears to be confined to relatively large and robust specimens. Observations reported in the literature, however, suggest that the destruction of foraminiferal tests on sandy beaches involves both small and large species (e.g., Murray, 1973). A conservative conclusion that can be drawn from all of these data is that the successful application of this technique is strongly tied to careful calibration studies of indigenous populations in areas under investigation, and that noncalibrated extrapolation of locally calibrated models to other inshore systems could yield erroneous results.

Washington State Continental Shelf (U.S.A.). A more general approach to the application of foraminifera data to sediment transport studies is seen in the research of Snyder et al. (1990). In their investigation of particle transport processes on the Washington State continental shelf, they estimated the traction velocity of the thirty-

energies to lower-energy nearshore settings (e.g., Figs. 3.38A and B). This distribution pattern is consistent with the general nature of tidal cycle dynamics, which are marked by decreasing current velocities as the tide approaches its maximum height. Consequently, its maximum erosion potential would be felt in deeper subtidal

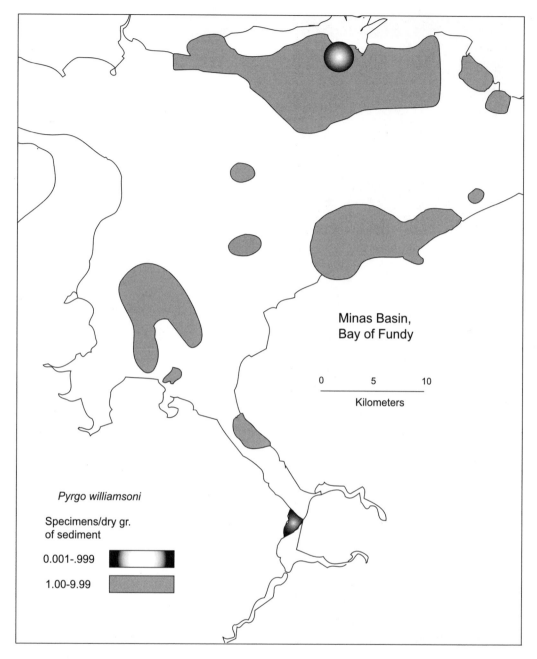

Minas Basin,
Bay of Fundy

0   5   10

Kilometers

Pyrgo williamsoni

Specimens/dry gr.
of sediment

0.001-.999

1.00-9.99

(A)

Figure 3.38. (A) Distribution of *Pyrgo williamsoni* within the Minas Basin, Bay of Fundy, showing higher concentrations around the rim of the basin, which suggests scouring and redeposition (after Thomas and Schafer, 1982). (B) Distribution of *Cibicides lobatulus* within the Minas Basin, Bay of Fundy. This shallow-water attached species shows more of a nontransported distribution (after Thomas and Schafer, 1982).

one most common benthic foraminifera species found in their study area with a view to identifying species that would be transported under similar energy conditions. Common species were arbitrarily defined as those taxa that occurred in more than fifteen samples, or in two or more samples with a relative abundance of

more than 5%. The authors were able to recognize three "traction velocity" groups. Maximum projection sphericity (MPS) was then calculated for each specimen in a species category. MPS is the cube root of $S^2/L(I)$, where S is the short dimension of the particle (specimen) and L and I are the long and intermediate dimensions,

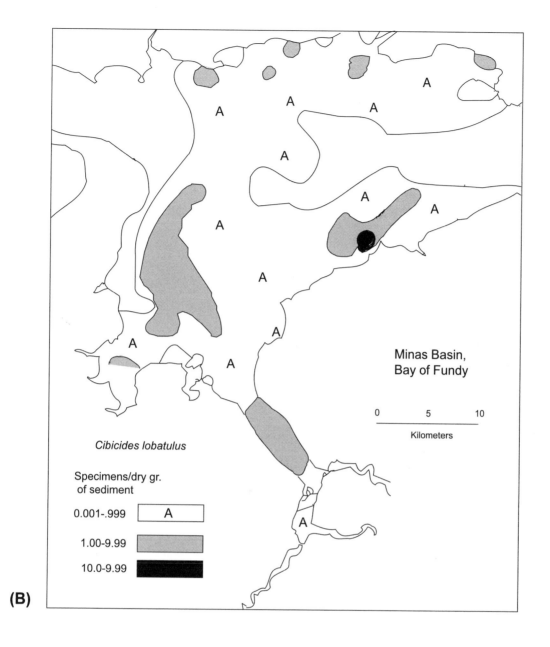

respectively. One group consisted of four species having generally equidimensional tests (e.g., *Eggerella, Adercotryma, Nonion*) that were susceptible to transport at mean erosion velocities in the range of 4–6 cm/s. At the other end of the spectrum were species with elongate, highly compressed or coiled, discoidal tests (e.g., *Trochammina, Spiroplectammina, Bolivina*) that were characterized by mean traction velocities in the 10.0–13.5 cm/s range. Traction velocity for each species was estimated using the regression equation $Y = 22.3 - 19.8$ (MPS) where Y is the estimated traction velocity and 22.3 is the intercept of the Y axis. Mean traction velocity was then calculated for each of the thirty-one selected species

based on 20 MPS measurements per species. The rationale of Snyder et al. (1990) was that, depending on the magnitude of bottom current velocities, one of the traction velocity groups might be expected to numerically dominate a particular current-sorted assemblage.

Students of coastal and nearshore marine systems, however, are always learning. Nearshore marine environments are inherently heterogeneous both temporally and spatially, and nature invariably poses surprises that reflect this dominating feature. In the Washington shelf investigation, Snyder et al. (1990) went on to compare their traction group "tracers" with several major foraminiferal faunal associations that had been defined using cluster analysis on grab sample data collected in the study area. They reported that each of the statistical associations was composed of mixtures from all three traction velocity groups and went on to show that direct measurements of bottom currents indicated that their velocities at the sediment-water interface were generally too low and erratic in direction to effectively sort the species into the traction velocity groups that they had defined. Nevertheless, their approach has merit because it can easily be transferred to a wide range of environments where their particular calibrated traction velocity species occur. The method can also be used to define the traction velocity threshold of other species that may be potentially useful as "monitors" of hydrodynamic conditions in other situations. Perhaps the most important feature of this approach is that the traction velocity groups are not only potentially useful as tracers of tidal current patterns, but can also provide quantitative estimates of the geographic patterns of bottom current maximum velocity fields (grab sample surveys), and of temporal changes (sediment core studies) in bottom current power that may point to changes in basin geometry, or in relative sea level or barrier bar inlet position (e.g., Wagner and Schafer, 1982).

Glacial Marine/Fluvial Transport – Missouri (U.S.A.) and Scotian Shelf (Canada). The problem of reworking older material is particularly severe along former glacial ice margins because glaciers grind up preexisting older sediments and redeposit them in outwash deposits. This section presents two examples from very different settings that have been impacted by the same mechanism and that have suffered similar results – a high amount of reworking of Mesozoic foraminifera into Pleistocene sediments. The material is exceptionally well preserved, in some cases more "pristine" looking than the contemporary fauna that lived at the time that the Pleistocene sediments were deposited. The first example is from eastern Missouri, where Thompson (1983) found high percentages of Mesozoic foraminifera in fluviolascustrine deposits that occur in the central part of the continent. In this case, there was no question that these taxa were reworked because they were marine fossils deposited in a nonmarine environment. The striking thing about these reworked fossils was their almost perfect preservation (see plate in Thompson, 1983), which was perhaps better than might have been obtained by processing the original rock for microfossils. It appears that subglacial grinding action and subsequent resuspension by glacial meltwater might be less harmful than some of the more rigorous laboratory processing techniques used to separate and concentrate specimens.

In a similar study, Scott and Medioli (1988) evaluated glacial marine sediments from the Scotian Shelf and found large numbers (sometimes exceeding 4,000/10 cm^3) of Mesozoic foraminifera mixed in with a relatively sparse Quaternary marine assemblage. Because accurate seismic profiles and other controls were available, it was clear that this material was Quaternary in age. The Mesozoic fossils, as in the Missouri case, were exceptionally well preserved. However, unlike the Missouri example, the Scotian Shelf is in a marine environment relatively close to where Mesozoic sediments could have been outcropping. The Scotian Shelf sediments in question were clearly not Mesozoic, but they were marine. Scott and Medioli (1988) suggested that the amount of reworked material could be used as an index of glacial activity because, in the period of most intense glaciation, reworked material comprised over 95% of the assemblage while, near the end of the glacial cycle, the proportions were closer to 10%. Concentrations were highest in fine sand layers (as opposed to silt layers) which would have had a similar traction velocity as foraminifera (see Snyder et al., 1990, above). These sand layers were interpreted as either small turbidities or ocean current deposits associated with sediment overloading at the marine face of a grounded glacier. Hence, the more reworked material, the more intense the glacial erosion activity.

MARINE–FRESHWATER TRANSITIONS

Identifying marine–freshwater transitions in the geologic record requires familiarity with the fossilizable biota present in modern marginal marine environments. These include such diverse environments as coastal wetlands (salt marshes, mangrove swamps), coastal ponds, lagoons, estuaries, and deltas. Studies of the modern distribution of foraminifera and thecamoebians in various marginal marine environments have illustrated a number of general trends (e.g., Schafer and Frape, 1974; Scott et al., 1977, 1980, 1991; Haman, 1990; Patterson, 1990; Collins, 1996). Marginal marine environments are usually characterized by assemblages containing both relatively euryhaline (i.e., tolerant of a wide salinity range) foraminifera and thecamoebians. Because of the inherently high degree of environmental stress, marine-freshwater transitions are usually characterized by low-diversity assemblages.

Bedford Basin, Nova Scotia (Canada)

Various studies in Atlantic Canada have identified marine–freshwater transitions using a modern analog approach (e.g., Scott and Medioli, 1980c). Miller et al. (1982a) identified different degrees of marine influence in Bedford Basin, which was once a deep, freshwater coastal pond, isolated from the sea by a sill during the early Holocene (Figs. 3.39 and 3.40). High percentages of *Centropyxis aculeata* in early Holocene sediments (core 79-11) indicated slightly brackish conditions, followed by freshwater conditions that were recorded by a *Difflugia oblonga*–dominated thecamoebian assemblage (Fig. 3.41). Around 5,830 ± 230 yBP, this assemblage was replaced by a foraminiferal fauna recording marginal marine conditions (i.e., low populations, low species diversity, and assemblages dominated by *Elphidium excavatum, Elphidium bartletti, Eggerella advena,* and *Haynesina orbiculare*). These are similar to faunae found in the seaward portions of modern estuaries, such as the Miramichi River estuary (Scott et al., 1977, 1980). A subsequent rise in sea level is recorded by an increase in foraminiferal

populations and species diversity, and by the establishment of an assemblage dominated by *Reophax* spp. and *Fursenkoina fusiformis.* Similar faunae are found in modern deepwater coastal inlets in Atlantic Canada, such as Chaleur Bay and the Saguenay Fjord (Schafer and Cole, 1978, 1995). A resurgence in *Centropyxis aculeata* in core 79-11 just prior to the mid-Holocene marine transition may also record slightly brackish conditions, since this interval also contains low abundances of marine dinocysts and foraminifera, although freshwater microfossils remain dominant. It is possible that occasional incursions of marine water (e.g., during storms) may

Figure 3.39. Bathymetric map of Bedford Basin, Nova Scotia, which is separated from Halifax Harbour and the Atlantic Ocean by a 22-m-deep sill. The location of core 79-11 is in a water depth of ~55 m (after Miller et al., 1982a).

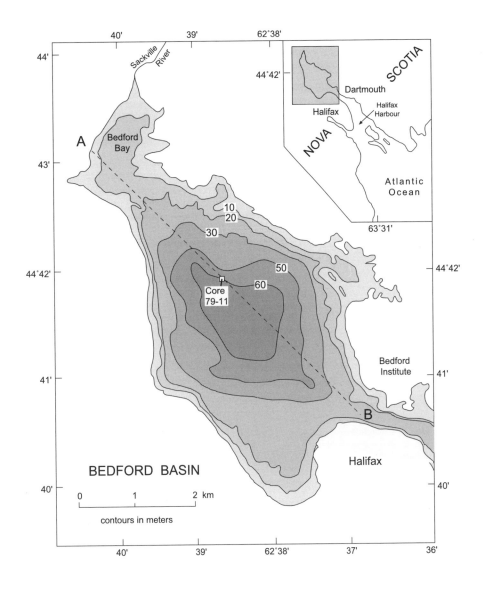

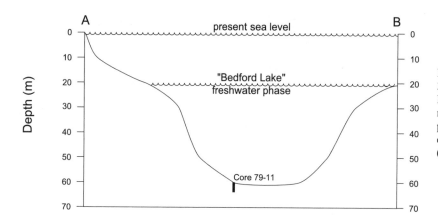

Figure 3.40. Cross section A-B from Fig. 3.39 of Bedford Basin showing the early Holocene freshwater lake level in relation to modern sea level. The top of the sill is in a present-day water depth of 22 m. The lake environment existed prior to 6,000 years ago (Miller et al., 1982a).

have transported marine dinocysts and foraminifera across the sill into the lake that eventually evolved into the Bedford Basin marine inlet.

Raised Basins in New Brunswick (Canada)

Foraminiferal and thecamoebian data have been used to identify the transition from marine to freshwater conditions in several lakes on the New Brunswick coast (Patterson et al., 1985; Honig and Scott, 1987), allowing construction of a sea-level curve of emergence for New Brunswick (Honig and Scott, 1987). In Big Pond (elevation 5 m above sea level), a foraminiferal assemblage recording marginal marine conditions (dominated by *Elphidium excavatum, Cassidulina reniforme,* and *Islandiella teretis*) was deposited during the late Pleistocene (top of the marine sequence dated ~14,040 ± 485 yBP) and was succeeded by a thecamoebian assemblage dominated by *Difflugia oblonga* and *Pontigulasia compressa* by 7,370 ± 400 yBP (Fig. 3.42). The transitional interval was barren, and a long hiatus is suggested by the associated radiocarbon dates. In nearby Gibson Lake (elevation 35 m above sea level), a very sparse thecamoebian association dominated by *Centropyxis aculeata* (see Fig. 3.12) marks the transition from coastal marine conditions (recorded by a foraminiferal fauna) to lacustrine conditions (recorded by a diverse and abundant thecamoebian association).

Porter's Lake, Nova Scotia (Canada)

Laidler and Scott (1996) studied the assemblages of foraminifera and arcellaceans in surficial sediments collected in this lake. Porter's Lake is a unique estuarine environment, open to the ocean at one end and to a fresh-

water source at the other end. It comprises four distinct basins that have restricted communication with the ocean, resulting in a range of marine to freshwater basin environments. The bottom water salinity, along the lake's longitudinal axis, varies from 0‰ at the north end to 25‰ at the south end. Estuarine systems are in permanent transition (regression or transgression); faunal data are very helpful in understanding these dynamics (Fig. 3.43). In the Maritimes provinces, in particular, where complex postglacial rebound phenomena are active at present, estuaries are in various states of evolution. Porter's Lake–like situations are likely to have occurred in the past. The dynamic assemblage model presented in this section is aimed at recognizing similar paleoenvironmental fluctuations and for determining the time lags between sea-level rise and the onset of marine conditions in restricted basins.

In the four basins of the lake, the indigenous assemblages indicated a strong gradient from fresh to marine water (Fig. 3.43). Transitions from fresh to marine water are abrupt; presently there is no evidence of intermediate arcellacean assemblages as observed in many cores from other areas of the Maritime provinces (Scott and Medioli, 1980c). The present connection of Porter's Lake with the sea is by a channel that has a maximum depth of 3 m below higher high water. Its sill must have become tidal almost 1,500 years ago (based on sea-level curves from nearby Chezzetcook Inlet; Scott et al., 1995c).

The evolution of the lake was studied through cores collected in three of its major basins (Fig. 3.43). Core 3 (2.35 m long) was collected at the north end of Basin 2. Two ^{14}C dates provided ages of 7,590 (± 255) yBP at the 2.1–2.15 m level, and 2,110 (± 240) yBP at the 0.95–1.0 m level (Fig. 3.44). Thecamoebian specimens (seven individuals/cm³) first appear at 2.2 m with *Difflugia oblonga* (dominant), *Pontigulasia compressa,* and *Centropyxis*

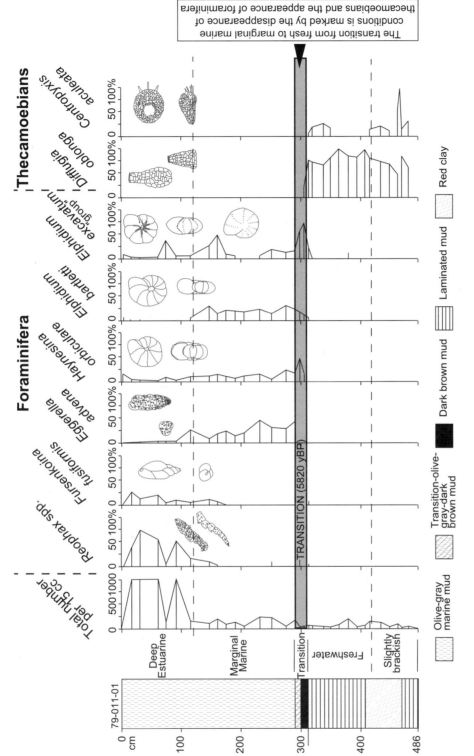

Figure 3.41. High percentages of the thecamoebian *Centropyxis aculeata* record slightly brackish conditions during the early Holocene. Freshwater conditions are indicated by the dominance of *Difflugia oblonga* until 5,800 years ago when a marine incursion started. The incursion is recorded by the resurgence of *C. aculeata* followed by the establishment of a marginal marine foraminiferal fauna (after Miller et al., 1982a).

83

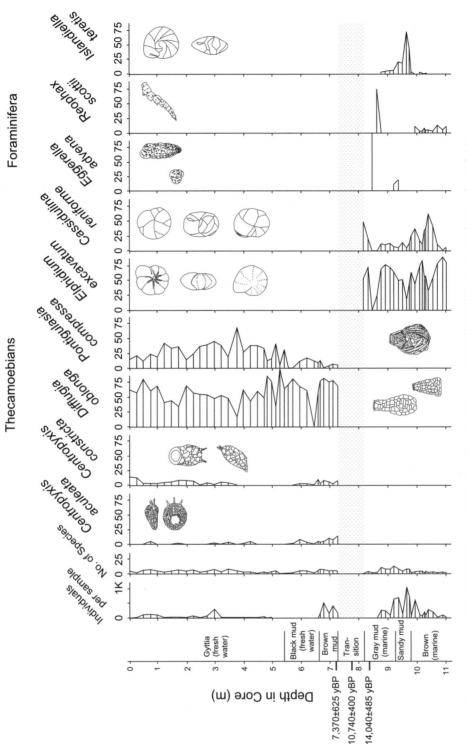

Figure 3.42. Barren sediments are found at the unconformable transition from marginal marine to fresh-water conditions in Big Pond on Deer Island, New Brunswick (Canada) (stippled pattern). The *Elphidium/Cassidulina* fauna, which is typical of "warm" ice margin conditions in the North Atlantic, is found in older sediments that were deposited when the area had a semipermanent ice cover. The existence of a diverse thecamoebian fauna above the barren zone confirms the interpretation of a hiatus, which was initially suggested by the time spans between the radiocarbon dates shown on the left side of the diagram (after Honig and Scott, 1987).

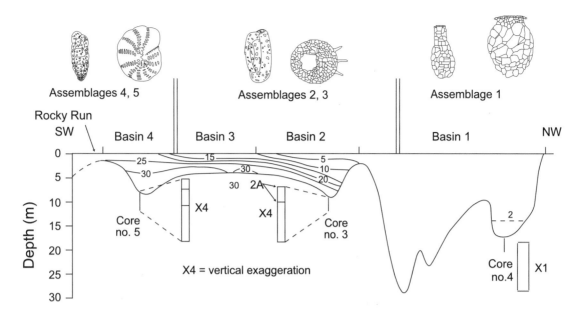

constricta. *D. oblonga* remains dominant throughout the entire core. At about the 2.1 m horizon, the sediment becomes more organic and total numbers climb to 592 individuals/10 cm³. The following species appear: *Difflugia urens, D. urceolata, D. urceolata* f. *elongata,* and *Centropyxis aculeata.* At 1 m (2,110 yBP), a foraminifer, the well-known brackish water–tolerant species *Miliammina fusca,* appears. This species identifies a short-lived transition from a lacustrine to an estuarine interval that took place at 2,110 yBP, corresponding to a similar interval in core 5, which is located closer to the ocean (Fig. 3.45).

Core 4 (10.4 m long) was collected at the southernmost end of Basin 1. Thecamoebian abundance and assemblages remain constant throughout the length of the core (dated at the base at 12,000 yBP) until the present, indicating a rather stable environment. The association was dominated by *Difflugia oblonga* and *Pontigulasia compressa,* with all other thecamoebians being of negligible importance. This core illustrates that even though the sill of this basin is below sea level, the marine water apparently has not penetrated to this location at any time during the Holocene.

Core 5 (3.17 m long) was collected in the central part of Basin 4. One ¹⁴C analysis provided an age of 1,675 (± 235) yBP at the 0.67–0.70 m level (Fig. 3.45). The bottom 2.2 m contain a varied estuarine foraminiferal assemblage dominated by *Eggerella advena* and *Trochammina ochracea,* with a substantial but irregular presence of the *Elphidium excavatum* "group" and *Haynesina orbiculare.* This association is easily explained by the proximity of the Atlantic Ocean. The sudden disappearance of *Eggerella advena* and *Trochammina ochracea* – both moderately tolerant of brackish conditions – at 0.7 m, preceded

Figure 3.43. Vertical salinity profiles in Porter's Lake, Nova Scotia, with associated foraminiferal/thecamoebian assemblages (after Laidler and Scott, 1996). Basin 1 is still mostly freshwater even though sea level has been above the level of the sill at Rocky Run for at least the past 1,500 years. Cores are shown in detail in Figs. 3.44 and 3.45.

by the rather gradual disappearance of the less tolerant *Elphidium excavatum* "group" and *Haynesina orbiculare* starting at about 1.2 m, indicates the end of communication between the lake basin and the ocean at 1,675 yBP. This change was caused by infilling of a channel now buried near a barrier beach. There is a short sequence of freshwater conditions (70–45 cm) where "Difflugids" and *Centrpyxis* dominate. The modern estuarine sequence starts at 45 cm and is marked by a peak in the abundance of the low-salinity indicator foraminifer *Miliammina fusca.* At the top of the core, *Eggerella advena,* a more marine species, replaces *Miliammina fusca* as the dominant species.

The method of Scott and Medioli (1980c) appears to be able to achieve sea-level reconstructions accurate to within ± 1 m in silled coastal lakes in Atlantic Canada (see Fig. 3.11). However, Laidler and Scott (1996) demonstrated that a considerable lag existed (and still exists) between sea-level rise to the elevation of the top of the sill in Basin 1 of Porter's Lake and the incursion of marine water into that basin. This feature is evidenced by the absence of a contemporary marine influence that core 4 data shows has persisted for at least 1,500 years (Fig. 3.43). This is most likely as a result of an overwhelming freshwater head over the narrow sill that holds the seawater back from the upper reaches of the lake. In the previ-

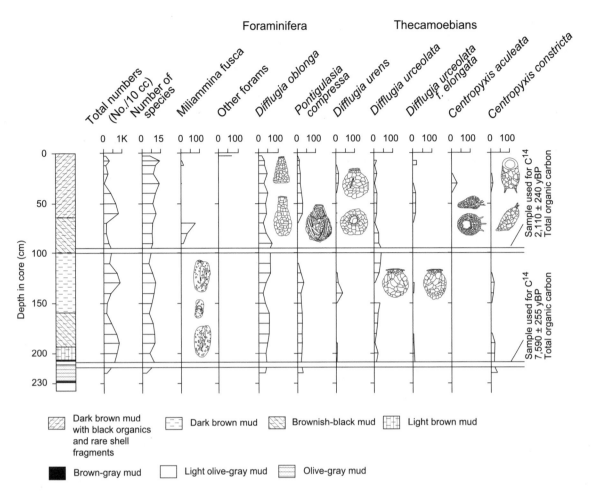

Figure 3.44. Core 3 from basin 2 of Porter's Lake records a persistence of freshwater conditions until recently, except for a brief marine incursion about 2,110 years ago. The brief incursion of seawater corresponds to a breach of the barrier beach near the entrance of the present-day inlet (not Rocky Run from Fig. 3.43) that presently connects the lake to the ocean (after Laidler and Scott, 1996).

ous example from Bedford Basin, the situation may have been exactly the same 6,000 years ago when Halifax Harbour was almost identical in configuration to the present-day Porter's Lake. The recent transition from freshwater to marine microfossils is abrupt near the tops of cores 3 and 5, which are closer to the mouth of the lake, which in turn is in close proximity to the ocean (Figs. 3.44 and 3.45).

PALEOCEANOGRAPHIC ANALYSIS

Although this book is largely concerned with coastal environments, many also consider continental shelves to be marginal marine. Physical/chemical conditions of shelf environments are much more variable than their open ocean counterparts, which is why most typically open ocean planktonic organisms such as planktonic foraminifera and radiolarians occur in reduced numbers on the shelf. Shelf areas can be considered "buffer zones" between the open coast and the open ocean. These zones may be wide or narrow depending on the geologic setting of individual continental margins. Some pollution studies discussed in this book were actually carried out on the California borderland (shelf). Given the initiation of offshore oil drilling on many continental shelves, and destructive techniques used by some commercial fisheries, shelf environments are likely to come under much greater stress in the future. Paleoceanography is not emphasized very much in this book because it is thought to be largely the domain of "deep-sea" investigators. However, the shelf offers some advantages for paleo-climate work that may be germane to understanding modern environments. Where there is sediment accumulation (e.g., in intrashelf basins), the deposition rates are often higher than in deep-sea areas. This feature offers the possibility for high-resolution records not obtainable in deep-sea settings. It is much easier to make a land–sea climate connection using shelf records because they usually can

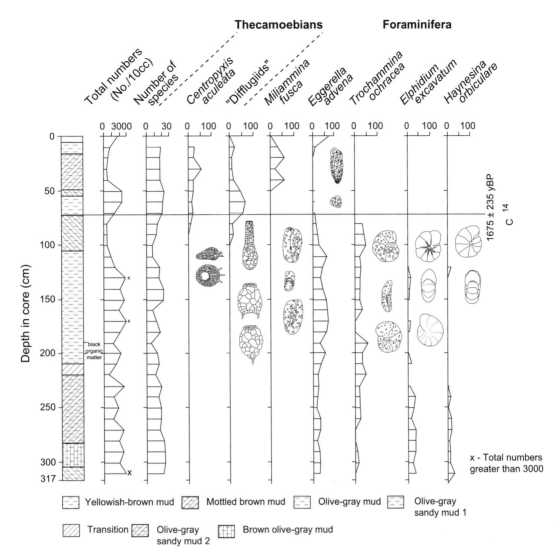

Figure 3.45. Core 5 in Porter's Lake basin 4 (Fig. 3.43) shows that this environment, which is fully marine at present, only recently achieved its marine character as Rocky Run became more submerged. Prior to 1,600 years before present, the barrier beach just seaward of this area was an open channel that subsequently closed. Barrier beach dynamics are marked by the freshwater fauna at 75 cm in this core. Sea level was over the sill at Rocky Run soon after 1,500 years ago (data from nearby Chezzetcook Inlet, Scott et al., 1995c). This is indicated by the reintroduction of marine conditions shortly above the freshwater interval in core 5 at 50 cm (after Laidler and Scott, 1996).

be linked directly with onshore pollen records. Although this section does not deal specifically with impacts, it will provide an insight on how much natural variability exists in these areas and, as such, offer useful ancillary information for the increasing level of baseline monitoring work that is predicted for these important commercial resource areas.

It is assumed that conditions at the ocean's surface will be reflected by the distribution of organisms that inhabit surface water masses, but in shelf environments, where water depths do not exceed 300 m, the benthic foraminifera also reflect surface water/climatic conditions. Unfortunately, most shelf areas are erosional, but some formerly glaciated shelves, such as the Scotian Shelf off eastern Canada, feature intrashelf basins that are depositional and contain sediment accumulations that record local paleoceanographic conditions that correspond closely with local climate. One example from a shelf area off eastern Canada has a well-known

present-day circulation pattern (Fig. 3.46). In addition, surficial foraminiferal data are well constrained (Fig. 3.47; Williamson, 1983, and Williamson et al., 1984) and correspond closely with the distribution of local watermasses. Over 400 data points from the study area facilitate the use of these results as accurate indicators of watermass changes in a core sequence that includes a detailed record of the paleoceanography of this part of the Scotian Shelf over the past 20,000 years.

Scott et al. (1984) found that benthic foraminifera in cores from shelf environments on the Canadian Atlantic margin reflect the late Pleistocene–Holocene paleoceanographic transition that drives, and is driven by, climate change. Immediately following deglaciation, benthic foraminifera assemblages indicate bottom waters warmer and more saline than today, followed by substantial

warming around 7,500 yBP, and then subsequent cooling at about 2,500 yBP (Fig. 3.48). This pattern closely mirrors pollen-derived reconstructions of the climate of northeastern North America, with hypsithermal conditions during the middle Holocene followed by marked cooling over the past 2,000 years (Livingstone, 1968). The *Nonionellina labradorica–Islandiella teretis–Cassidulina reniforme–Globobulimina auriculata* fauna in sediments older than ~11,500 yBP in Emerald Basin, on the Nova Scotia outer continental shelf (Fig. 3.49), is similar to the fauna associated with the modern outer Labrador Current (2–4° C, 34–35%). This association is also present in early-middle Holocene sediments in the Notre Dame Channel core (Fig. 3.50). The abundance of *Cassidulina laevigata* in Emerald Basin between ~7,500

Figure 3.46. Present-day ocean surface current patterns on the continental shelf of eastern Canada (after Williamson et al., 1984). The cores from the two locations shown are illustrated with foraminiferal results in Figs. 3.49 and 3.50.

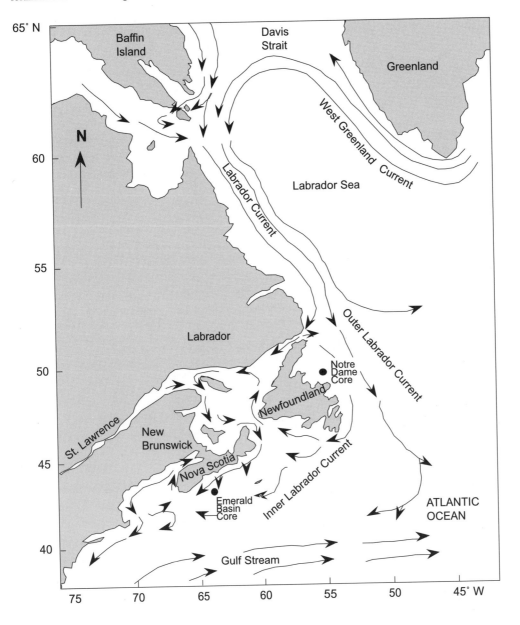

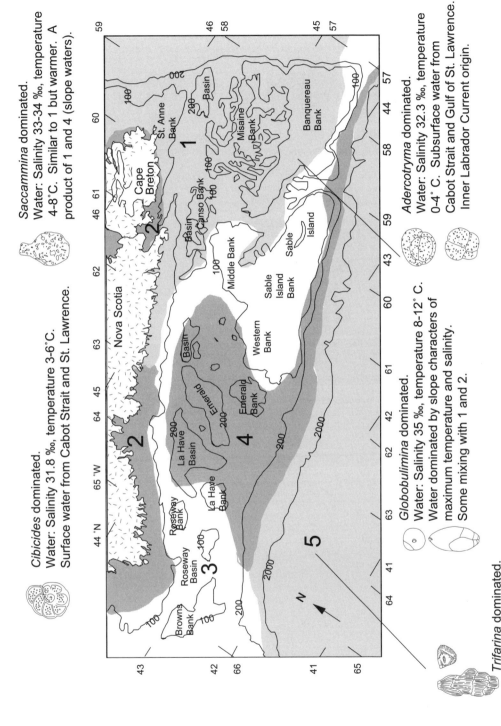

Cibicides dominated.
Water: Salinity 31.8 ‰, temperature 3-6˚C.
Surface water from Cabot Strait and St. Lawrence.

Saccammina dominated.
Water: Salinity 33-34 ‰, temperature 4-8˚C. Similar to 1 but warmer. A product of 1 and 4 (slope waters).

Adercotryma dominated.
Water: Salinity 32.3 ‰, temperature 0-4˚ C. Subsurface water from Cabot Strait and Gulf of St. Lawrence. Inner Labrador Current origin.

Globobulimina dominated.
Water: Salinity 35 ‰, temperature 8-12˚ C. Water dominated by slope characters of maximum temperature and salinity. Some mixing with 1 and 2.

Trifarina dominated.
Water: Salinity 34.5-35 ‰, temperature 4-6˚ C. Deep Atlantic water.

Figure 3.47. Present-day benthic foraminiferal faunal distributions on the Scotian Shelf, eastern Canada, in relation to watermass patterns. Substrate type also influences foraminiferal distributions on shallow bank areas with the attached species, *Cibicides lobatulus*, dominating shallower high-wave energy environments (after Williamson et al., 1984).

89

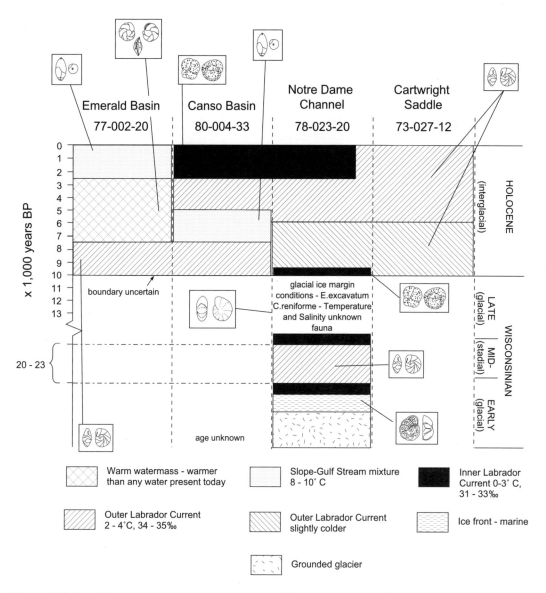

Figure 3.48. Late Pleistocene to recent bottom water conditions on the eastern Canadian margin, inferred from benthic foraminiferal distributions in cores from intrashelf basins (after Scott et al., 1984). Synchronous changes in benthic foraminiferal assemblages reflect major changes in watermass characteristics that may be related to global climate variations, such as the mid-Holocene hypsithermal, the last glacial maximum, and late Holocene cooling trend. All of these events are observed in the microfossil record on the eastern margin of Canada and correspond to onshore pollen stratigraphies (after Scott et al., 1984).

and 2,500 yBP, records the existence of water warmer than is found anywhere on the Atlantic eastern Canadian margin today (excluding the Gulf of St. Lawrence). This species presently is not abundant north of Cape Cod. The existence of a *Bulimina marginata–Brizalina subae-* *nariensis–Elphidium excavatum* fauna in the upper 2 m of core records the establishment of modern bottom water conditions around 2,500 yBP (7–10° C, 33.5–34%, Williamson, 1983). In the highly condensed Holocene record of a core from Notre Dame Channel on the Newfoundland shelf (Fig. 3.50), middle Holocene warming is recorded by an increase in the percentage of calcareous benthic foraminifera, which established a fauna similar to that associated with the modern outer Labrador Current. Abrupt cooling in late Holocene time is indicated by the establishment of a totally agglutinated fauna similar to that associated with the modern inner Labrador Current (0–3° C, 31–33%). In the context of this book, the point that needs to be stressed is that natural variation, even on the relatively stable (by marginal marine standards) continental shelf, has been high over the past 10,000 years,

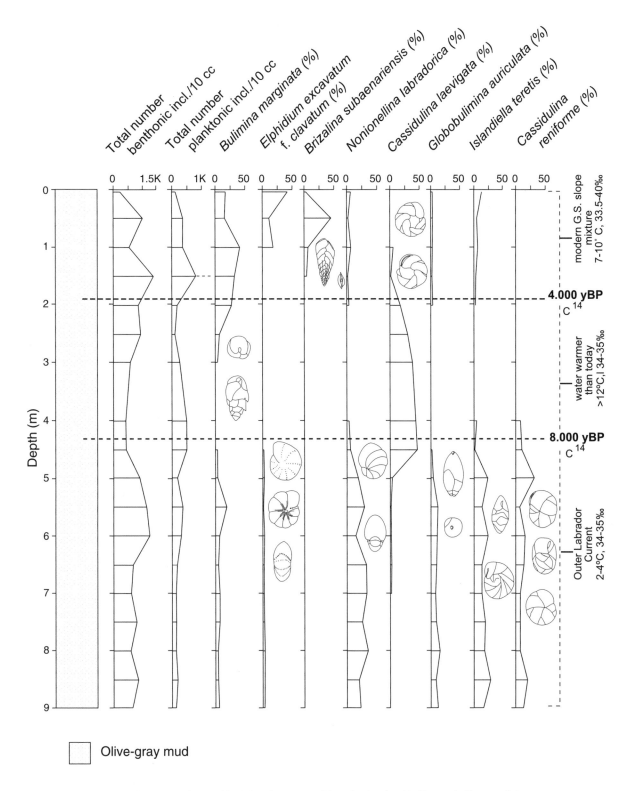

Olive-gray mud

Figure 3.49. Benthic foraminiferal data from Emerald Basin, Scotian Shelf. Note indicators of the presence of water that was warmer than occurs in this area today. This mid-Holocene condition is denoted by the presence of *Cassidulina laevigata,* which does not inhabit the modern basin environment (after Scott et al., 1984).

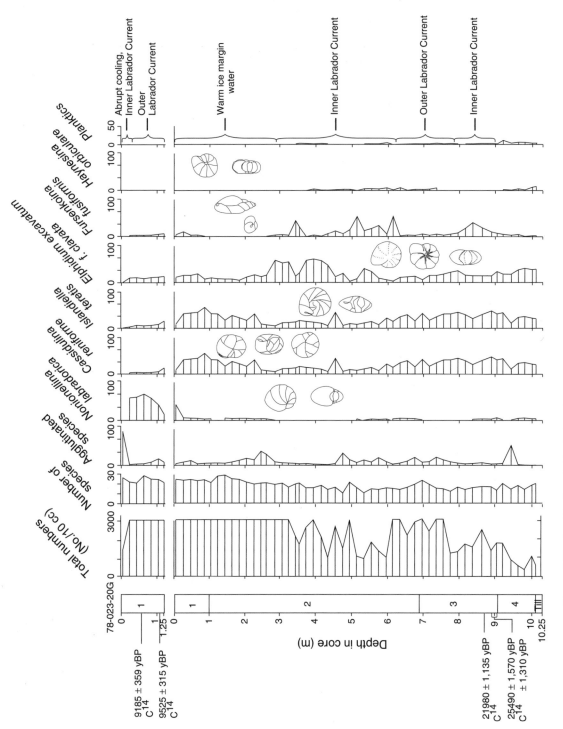

Figure 3.50. Benthic foraminiferal data from Notre Dame Channel off Newfoundland (east coast Canada). Note the warmer-than-present water indicators in the early to mid-Holocene section. Below ~3 m in the piston core, palynological data indicate glacial conditions onshore; the species *Fursenkoina fusiformis* suggests low bottom water oxygen at this time, suggesting year-round ice cover and poor circulation conditions (after Scott et al., 1984).

92

especially on the Scotian Shelf. To examine anthropogenic impacts in these areas, one must first understand the scope and magnitude of variability that may be expected from natural processes.

SUMMARY OF KEY POINTS

- Marsh foraminifera provide the most cost-effective and high-resolution technique of determining former sea levels in many different situations – from those that are climatically driven to others that have resulted from rapid seismic shifts.

- Estuarine foraminifera can be used in a variety of ways to reconstruct environmental changes in relation to both natural and antropogenic forcing – they are often the only tool available for extracting an environmental signal from otherwise featureless muds.

- Foraminifera can be used as tracers in a variety of ways, from reworking of fossil material into a modern sediment to detection of transport of sediment in both onshore and offshore directions.

- The combination of foraminifera and thecamoebians provides one of the more utilitarian techniques for quickly determining freshwater–marine transition intervals in both the space and time domains.

- Foraminifera proxies are one of the few means of determining paleocirculation regimes in continental shelf and estuarine settings because most of the typical marine markers (e.g., planktonic foraminifera, radiolarians) are absent in marginal marine settings.

- As a general rule, microfossils often provide the only way to reconstruct "a priori" baseline conditions. Most impact situations occur in areas for which serial data are sparse or nonexistent. Historical time series are absolutely critical for understanding the nature and extent of any type of anthropogenic or natural impact.

4

Research on
New Applications

Methods to detect and monitor environmental change using indigenous species are in demand more and more each day as they become recognized as important tools in resource management and in situ monitoring (e.g., Goldberg, 1998). The benthic foraminifera continue to emerge as an important and unique type of indicator organism. As was illustrated in Chapter 3, they are abundant, provide statistically significant populations in small samples, have rapid reproductive cycles, are preserved as fossils, and have many types of applications to monitoring programs. This chapter provides a taste of some recent developments aimed at improving the utility of this group of shelled marine protozoans.

PALEOPRODUCTIVITY

Unlike the organic matter (OM) record, which essentially registers the amount of refractory organic carbon (C-org) that has bypassed the sediment/water interface, the Benthic Foraminifera Accumulation Rate (BFAR), which is defined as the number of specimens/unit area/unit time, fluctuates in relation to the downward (i.e., exported) flux of labile OM which is consumed in the benthic ecosystem. Where bottom water oxygen concentrations remain above 0.5 ml/l, the BFAR may be useful as an estimator of "export productivity" (Jorissen, 1998). Relatively productive intervals are marked by opportunistic faunae that are able to produce high numbers of offspring per gram of labile OM arriving at the seafloor. For example, phytodetritus flux (= labile OM) has been shown to trigger the rapid opportunistic reproduction of some shallow infaunal taxa (*Textularia kattegantensis, Fursenkoina* sp.) in Sagami Bay, Japan (Kitazato et al., 1998).

In some Arabian Sea settings, low oxygen benthic environments (O_2 = >2 mM) occur at midwater depths in highly productive upwelling areas. The intensity and persistence of these low O_2 zones (OMz's) vary as a function of changes in summer monsoon productivity that can be traced temporally using benthic foraminifera. A high-diversity and high-equitability fauna reflecting relatively oxygenated bottom water is associated with minima in summer monsoon–related productivity. Low O_2/high OM flux conditions are, in contrast, marked by a low-diversity/low-equitability fauna that consists of a few dominant species (Den Dulk et al., 1998). This fauna proliferates during precession-driven maxima in summer monsoon productivity in the Arabian Sea area. Laboratory experiments and field observations suggest that O_2 itself is not a limiting factor, although this idea is still somewhat contentious (e.g., Alve, 1995). Interspecific competition may play a more critical role than previously thought. For example, the microhabitat position of a species, and thus its access to the most labile OM, depends (apart from the redox state of the sediment) on the presence of other species.

In comparatively deep offshore environments, the BFAR responds not only to average OM flux but also to its temporal heterogeneity. A strong fluctuating food supply of labile OM promotes the development of low-diversity faunae dominated by opportunistic species such as *Epistominella exigua*. Consequently, benthic foraminiferal faunae that include abundant phytodetritus-exploiting species can be distinguished from those (e.g., *Uvigerina spp., Melonis spp.*), which mark a high continuous flux of OM to the seafloor. A ratio of pulsed OM-responsive species to high steady-state flux species seems to be valuable for identifying the part of the total OM flux that is deposited as a consequence of non-steady-state deposition (Jorissen, 1998).

There is speculation that individual foraminiferal species may have several different feeding strategies depending on their life mode (epifaunal versus infaunal), and that foraminifera living in low-food-abundance environments will tend to be opportunistic generalists, while those occupying abundant food settings will tend to be specialists. This idea is offered as a working hypothesis to try to explain some of the assemblage distribution patterns seen under various environmental (i.e., OM loading) conditions.

Gooday and Rathburn (1999), in review of the subject, suggest that population dynamics of some deep-sea foraminifera might be controlled by two factors: flux of organic carbon to the seafloor and oxygen in the pore water of the sediments. There are many types of organic matter input, from seasonal phytoplankton blooms to dead whale carcasses, causing a local organic "oasis." Gooday and Rathburn (1999) point out that most of these processes are not fully predictable and they are likely to be less predictable in the shelf/nearshore than in deep-sea settings. This question remains to be tested.

FORAMINIFERA POPULATIONS AS INDICATORS OF CORAL REEF HEALTH

Hallock et al. (1995) and Cockey et al. (1996), among others, have recognized changes in both the nature of reef foraminiferal tests and the assemblages found over time in coral reef communities. "Bleaching" of reefs has been well known for some time (e.g. Ginsburg and Glynn, 1994). However, it appears that reef-dwelling foraminifera also show evidence of bleaching that results in loss of color, symbiont loss, and weakening of the test, which may allow easier access for boring organisms. In addition to bleaching, they detected many deformities in the tests of these reef forms, chiefly in the genus *Amphistegina,* which is associated with many symbiotic diatoms (Hallock et al., 1995). Field and laboratory evidence suggest that UV-B radiation may be a contributing factor, but, in the Florida reefs studied, pollution could also be an important factor. Whatever the cause, Hallock et al. (1995) suggested that the implications for coastal sedimentation are severe, considering that foraminifera often make up a large part of the reef sediment load (Maxwell, 1968). Some coral bleaching has been attributed to water temperature increases, but foraminifera exhibited bleaching long before water temperatures started to warm up to current summer values (Hallock et al., 1995). Cockey et al. (1996) also recognized changes in the assemblage composition of reef foraminiferal faunae. Studies of the Key Largo, Florida, reef showed that there were many large symbiont-bearing foraminifera present during the 1959–61 period. In contrast, specimens collected in 1990–91 featured smaller Rotaliidae and Miliolidae (small and lacking symbionts) as the dominant taxa. This size change suggested a less favorable environment for symbionts, and for the secretion of thick carbonate tests. As pointed out by Hallock et al. (1995), if the photosynthetic symbionts are sensitive to increased UV radiation, the phenomenon could have serious implications for worldwide carbonate production. Foraminifera may be a useful frontline tool as a detector of these effects.

CHEMICAL ECOLOGY IN BENTHIC FORAMINIFERA

This is a relatively new field, which has only recently started to receive the attention of some Israeli researchers (Bresler and Yanko, 1995b). They studied defense mechanisms used by foraminifera against "xenobiotics." Xenobiotics are any chemicals not used by organisms for metabolic processes. They can include natural products that may or may not be detrimental to the organism, or they may be manmade compounds that are possibly toxic. Bresler and Yanko's (1995b) initial investigation considered the response of foraminifera to various xenobiotics and found that they have various defense mechanisms for these compounds, such as (1) formation of membranes, (2) secretion of different types of chemicals that can counteract the effects of xenobiotics, or (3) systems for the elimination of the compounds.

This type of study is important because it could provide vital information for coastal monitoring in at least two crucial areas: (1) The production of certain chemicals by foraminifera in a natural setting may supply an early proxy warning that toxic chemicals are building up in the water, and (2) the chemical response of foraminifera to xenobiotics may provide clues on how to chemically counteract toxic wastes by using the same chemicals that are manufactured by the organism.

CHEMICAL TRACERS IN FORAMINIFERAL TESTS

This is a very large, complex, and specialized field, which has been mentioned only occasionally in this book; it includes the study of stable isotopes (C, O), which have been used extensively in paleoclimatic research along with trace elements and their ratios.

One of the most useful isotope ratios applicable to coastal/shelf settings is [87]Strontium/[86]Strontium ([87]Sr/[86]Sr). It has been used as a paleosalinity proxy in marginal marine environments (Schmitz et al., 1991, 1997; Ingram and Sloan, 1992; Ingram and DePaolo, 1993; Bryant et al., 1995; Holmden et al., 1997a,b; Reinhardt et al., 1998a,b). Biogenic carbonates, such as those found in calcareous foraminifera inhabiting marginal marine environments, incorporate and record the Strontium ratio in their crystal lattice which, in turn, records the salinity at the time of formation of the foraminiferal test. This relationship, however, has some limitations; the concentration of Sr in seawater is so much higher than in freshwater that there has to be substantial dilution by freshwater to detect the salinity effect. This circumstance has limited the technique to moderately brackish situations (Palmer and Edmond, 1989). One place where this method became crucial was in the Nile River Delta (Reinhardt et al., 1998b), where it was known that seasonal flooding of the Nile River had caused large salinity fluctuations. The foraminiferal fauna, however, was basically unchanged throughout the sequence due to the fact that the dominant species, *Ammonia beccarii,* is not sensitive to salinity changes under the high-temperature conditions of the delta's shallow water environments. Only the Strontium ratios could detect them, and by combining geochemistry and the study of foraminiferal assemblages, Reinhardt et al. (1998b) were able to define the environment so precisely from Sr proxy data in core sequences that they could detect the increase in freshwater discharge into the Nile Lagoon following the construction of the Aswan Dam in 1965.

SUMMARY OF KEY POINTS

- Some foraminifera react to high organic matter fluxes and can be used as markers of paleoproductivity events.
- Reef foraminifera react more quickly than coral reefs themselves to bleaching effects and may therefore provide an early-warning mechanism of potential reef deterioration.
- Recent research suggests that the foraminifera may be useful in demonstrating how marine organisms cope with chemical contamination from a biogeochemical perspective.
- Chemical, isotopic, and elemental tracers observed in certain foraminifera species tests appear to be able to provide enhanced information on various environmental factors over and above that provided by the assemblages themselves.

5

Freshwater Systems Applications

The previous parts of this book use the general and informal term "testate rhizopods" to indicate both foraminifera and thecamoebians. Up to this point, however, the discussion has focused almost exclusively on foraminifera. This is because of the enormous body of information available on these organisms, which have been a key tool of micropaleontologists for either commercial or environmental applications for more than a century. Thecamoebians, on the other hand, have been the exclusive domain of geneticists, biologists, and taxonomists; no attempt has been made to use them as geological proxies until very recently. These organisms are not a familiar subject for most environmental managers. The literature concerning them is mainly in nongeological journals and is not always readily available. Although they inhabit mainly freshwater bodies, thecamoebian tests, either transported or indigenous, are also found in marginal marine environments. For these reasons, it was deemed appropriate for this book to summarize some of the relevant general information on these organisms in somewhat greater detail than was done for foraminifera.

THECAMOEBIANS

General Considerations

"Thecamoebians," although morphologically similar and taxonomically close to foraminifera, are mainly freshwater organisms; very few forms tolerate mildly brackish conditions. The term "thecamoebians" (= amoebae with a test) is an informal one used to characterize a very diverse "group" of organisms belonging to two different classes within the subphylum Sarcodina (Fig. 1.1).

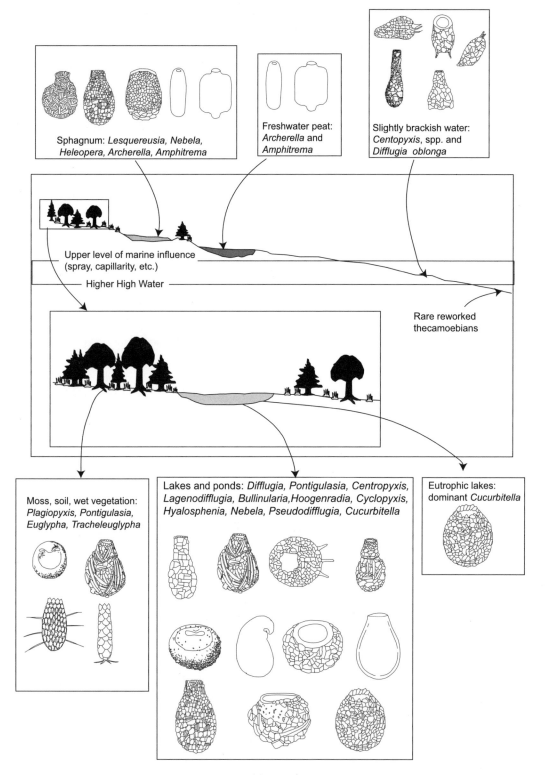

Figure 5.1. Idealized transect of a "typical" forest/lake/wetland area with diagnostic thecamoebian species indicated.

The common element of all thecamoebians is the presence of a very simple, mainly unilocular test that is very similar to that of some monothalamous foraminifera. Thecamoebians live in all types of freshwater bodies (lakes, rivers, springs, and temporary ponds) and in a variety of moist environments such as mosses, wet soils, or bark of trees; a few can survive in brackish water. However, almost all the empty tests found in sediments are of lacustrine and brackish origin and are limited largely to the superfamily Arcellacea with minor components from other groups. For more details on generalities see Medioli and Scott (1988) and Medioli et al. (1994).

Thecamoebian assemblages preserved in sediments have proven to be easy-to-use and very inexpensive tools for (a) the detection of fresh invasions (Scott and Medioli, 1980c), (b) eutrophication (Scott and Medioli, 1983; Medioli et al., 1987; Asioli and Medioli, 1992; Parenti, 1992; Asioli et al., 1996; Patterson et al., 1996; Burbidge and Schröder-Adams, 1998), and (c) heavy metal pollution (Asioli and Medioli, 1992; Asioli et al., 1996; Patterson et al., 1996). As they are almost invariably among the first colonizers of periglacial lakes formed immediately after glacial retreats, they are usually present at the bottom of lacustrine sequences in northern latitudes where they record pristine conditions and, as such, provide an ideal baseline for the detection of subsequent environmental changes (Fig. 5.1).

In the literature, the record of pre-Pleistocene fossil thecamoebians has hardly been discussed. Recently, however, thecamoebians have successfully been used for paleoecological reconstructions of Cenozoic, Mesozoic, and Paleozoic deposits (see following sections).

This chapter is not intended to review all thecamoebians, but rather to supply basic, practical information on those forms that are often found as fossils and that are usable as environmental and paleolimnological proxies.

Biology of Thecamoebians

■ Test Composition and Morphology

Like the foraminifera, thecamoebians can either secrete their test *(autogenous test)* or build it by agglutinating foreign particles *(xenogenous test)* (Fig. 5.2). A few taxa (Hyalosphenidae) can build either type, depending on circumstances and availability of foreign material.

Autogenous Tests. These tests are secreted by the organism and can be solid organic, solid calcareous, siliceous vermicular, or made of siliceous or calcareous plates *(idiosomes)*. Purely autogenous tests are seldom found fossilized.

Xenogenous Tests. The vast majority of fossilizable thecamoebians are aquatic and possess a xenogenous test built of mineral particles cemented together *(xenosomes)*. The composition of xenosomes is exceedingly variable, often including diatom frustules. In general the material included in their tests appears to parallel the distribution of particle types in bottom sediments (i.e., the material available in the immediate surroundings) (Medioli and Scott, 1983; Medioli et al., 1987).

Mixed Tests. Some forms of the family Hyalosphenidae can produce either purely autogenous or partly or entirely xenogenous tests, depending on circumstances. Some forms have an organic test loosely covered with xenosomes.

Morphology. Despite obvious limitations imposed by their unichambered architecture, and regardless of the composition of their test, thecamoebians have developed an amazing array of different shapes that can be grouped into three broad categories:

(1) the beret-shaped group *(Arcella, Centropyxis, –* Fig. 5.3), with an often invaginated aperture developed on a more or less flattened ventral side

(2) the sack-shaped group *(Difflugia, Pontigulasia, –* Fig. 5.3), with their aperture located more or less at the tapered end of the test structure

(3) the others, with a variety of shapes. The test of *Mississippiella,* for instance, is more or less a flat disk with numerous apertures arranged in a crescent on the ventral side; that of *Amphitrema* is shaped like a hot-water bottle with two apertures at both ends, and so forth. A few forms *(Lagenodifflugia, Pontigulasia, Lesquereusia)* have a sort of second chamber in the form of an enlarged collar separated from the rest of the test by a distinct external constriction. Internally, this constriction often corresponds to a diaphragm, or what is left of it, which may be related to a previous cystic stage (Fig. 5.3).

■ Growth

The test, which is built at the time of reproduction, does not grow after the original division (Penard, 1902), and the organism is unable even to repair accidental damages to it (Jennings, 1937).

■ The Living Organism

The thecamoebian soft parts are represented by an amoeba. General information on the living organisms, cytological characteristics, feeding habits, methods of reproduction, morphological variability, and so forth, can be found in Ogden and Hedley (1980), Medioli et al. (1987), and Valkanov (1962a,b, 1966). It is important to

EXAMPLES OF AUTOGENOUS TESTS

1a, b, *Mississippiella,* solid calacareous; 2, *Hyalosphenia,* solid organic; 3, *Lesquereusia,* siliceous vermicular;
4, *Euglypha,* siliceous plates; 5, *Paraquadrula,* calcareous plates

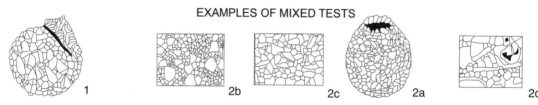

EXAMPLES OF MIXED TESTS

1, *Lesquereusia,* neck siliceous vermicular, main body xenogenous; 2a, agglutinated *Cucurbitella*; 2b, detail
of partially xenogenous test; 2c, completely xenogenous test; 2d, completely autogenous test

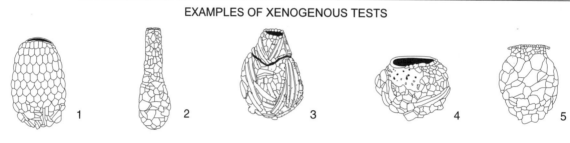

EXAMPLES OF XENOGENOUS TESTS

1, *Heleopera,* the xenosomes of the upper part of the test are autogenous plates scavanged by *Heleopera,* those
at the fundus are mineral particles; 2, *Difflugia oblonga,* xenosomes entirely of mineral origin; 3, *Pontigulasia,* the
xenosomes are partly of mineral origin, the large ones are diatom frustules; 4, *Pseudodifflugia,* the xenosomes
are a mixture of mineral grains and diatom frustules, notice the organic liner in the part near the aperture where
the xenosomes cover is missing; 5, *Difflugia urceolata,* the xenosomes are entirely of mineral origin

Figure 5.2. Test types of thecamoebians. Unlike foraminifera, some thecamoebians can change their test type from agglutinated to autogenous.

explain here, however, that under unfavorable conditions, the thecamoebian protoplasm may contract and surround itself with a spherical solid enclosure (cyst). The aperture of the test is blocked by a sort of cork-like structure, and the cyst floats in liquid inside the test. Encystment is used as a mechanism of rest, dormancy, and defense (Ogden and Hedley, 1980). The cyst appears to be capable of withstanding extreme environmental conditions such as desiccation, freezing, lack of food, lack of oxygen, extreme pH values, and so forth. This feature probably explains why

these organisms are able to migrate all over the world and quickly colonize new habitats (Fig. 5.4).

■ Dispersal

It is very important to elaborate on the mechanisms of dispersal of thecamoebians to explain their potential for evaluating freshwater environments. Deflandre (1953) was of the opinion that thecamoebians are cosmopolitan, but probably not ubiquitous – an opinion held by many other thecamoebian workers. Probably what he meant by this was that, provided that sufficient moisture was available, thecamoebians might be predicted to migrate to all parts of the world, but with different species occupying different continents. However, available information on the mechanisms of dispersal and the factors controlling it

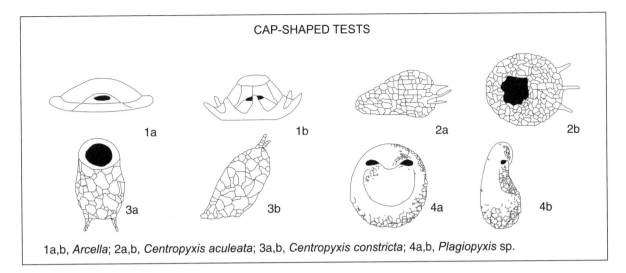

CAP-SHAPED TESTS

1a,b, *Arcella*; 2a,b, *Centropyxis aculeata*; 3a,b, *Centropyxis constricta*; 4a,b, *Plagiopyxis* sp.

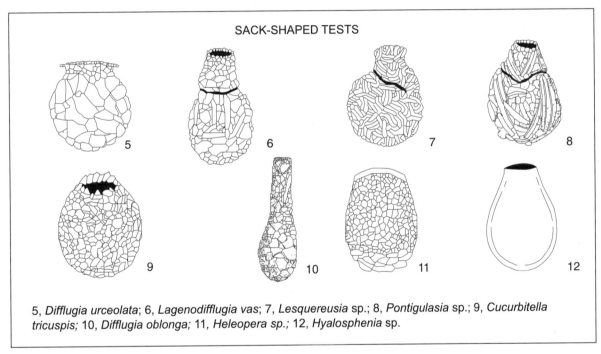

SACK-SHAPED TESTS

5, *Difflugia urceolata*; 6, *Lagenodifflugia vas*; 7, *Lesquereusia* sp.; 8, *Pontigulasia* sp.; 9, *Cucurbitella tricuspis*; 10, *Difflugia oblonga*; 11, *Heleopera* sp.; 12, *Hyalosphenia* sp.

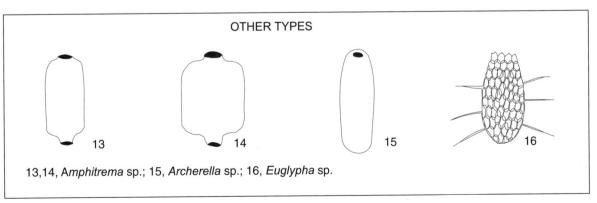

OTHER TYPES

13,14, *Amphitrema* sp.; 15, *Archerella* sp.; 16, *Euglypha* sp.

Figure 5.3. Various morphologies exhibited by thecamoebian species.

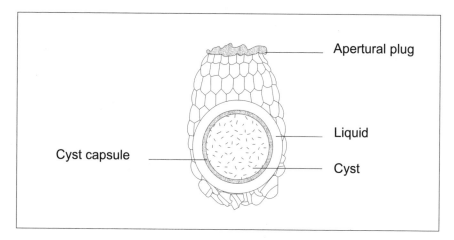

Figure 5.4. Encystment occurs in some thecamoebians; cysts allow "resting" stages and long-distance transport of living individuals.

suggest otherwise. According to Decloître (1953), the two main mechanisms of dispersal of encysted individuals appear to be wind and migratory birds.

Wind Transport. The main agent of transport, according to Decloître (1953), who refers back to an old idea of Penard (1902), is wind. He argues that an encysted thecamoebian of 30 microns in diameter (thus falling well within the 62–4 micron limits of silt) cannot weigh more than 54×10^{-6} mg. Such an object, once made airborne by turbulent winds, can remain aloft long enough to cover substantial distances. Decloître's hypothesis is confirmed by evidence supplied by Ehrenberg (1872), who found eleven species of *Arcella* and twelve species of *Difflugia* in atmospheric dust samples collected in Australia, Asia, Africa, and Europe, thus suggesting that the phenomenon occurs on a regular basis all over the world. Since the cysts can survive almost any natural conditions, it is not surprising that thecamoebians were able to achieve worldwide distribution, and that they are able to colonize any new available niche in what, geologically speaking, is an instantaneous event. Wind alone, however, cannot be the only agent of transport for lacustrine Arcellacea. The desiccated cysts of these organisms are not exposed to wind action often enough, and when they are it is only in relatively small areas and under extreme circumstances. In addition, prevailing wind patterns would make it very difficult for encysted thecamoebians to cross the equatorial trough. Wind transport seems to be efficient only when assisted by another mechanisms.

Transport via Migratory Birds. Decloître (1953) suggested that migratory birds may be as important as – or even more important than – wind as a mechanism for transporting live thecamoebians. In this instance, cyst transport might occur by attachment to the bird's outer surface, or via incorporation in the excrement. Although this mechanism may not account for the large numbers involved in the migration process, it would explain how thecamoebians manage to cross the equatorial trough on a regular basis.

While the first hypothesis was verified by Ehrenberg (1872) who found thecamoebian tests from North Africa in muddy rain falling over Naples, the second one was conjectured by Decloître (1953) by comparing birds' migratory routes and thecamoebian distributions. In any case, thecamoebians seem to be able to translocate rapidly to all parts of the earth and to colonize any suitable aquatic environment.

THE FOSSIL RECORD

Unlike foraminifera, pre-Holocene thecamoebians have never really attracted the attention of micropaleontologists. The more or less clearly stated or implied explanations for this peculiar state of neglect were virtually self-fulfilling prophecies: (1) thecamoebian tests do not fossilize well, and (2) thecamoebians (despite the fact that, from Pliocene on, the fossil record is plentiful) developed only very late in the history of life (late Pleistocene or even later). Loeblich and Tappan (1964) suggested that one of the factors was that not enough thecamoebian work had been done on freshwater deposits and they correctly predicted that, if more work were to be done, the number of reports of pre-recent occurrences would increase.

This suggestion was generally ignored until several Canadian investigators (Thibaudeau and Medioli, 1986; Thibaudeau et al., 1987; Medioli et al., 1990a,b; Wightman et al., 1992a,b, 1993, 1994; Thibaudeau, 1993; Medioli, 1995a,b; Tibert, 1996) started a deliberate search for thecamoebians in older freshwater and marginal marine deposits. Fossil thecamoebians were discovered exactly where they would be expected to be found.

In addition, the presence of the *Cucurbitella*-like *Difflugia robusticornis* (Bradley, 1931) in association with *Spirogyra* (Davis, 1916) in mid-Eocene Green River oil shale strongly suggested that the strict relationship between *Spirogyra* and the large array of morphotypes that Medioli et al. (1987) grouped under *Cucurbitella tricuspis* still holds true today, and that the ecological requirements of the group have not changed significantly, at least since Eocene time. It therefore seems very likely that the information that is been gathered on the ecology of modern thecamoebians will become a vital source of paleoecological information applicable to fossil material.

Medioli et al. (1990b) reviewed and evaluated the still scarce and uneven record of fossil thecamoebians starting from the Namurian and reaching to the upper Pleistocene (see Cushman, 1930a; Bradley, 1931; Frenguelli, 1933; Miner, 1935; Kövary,1956; Vasicek and Ruzicka, 1957; McLean and Wall, 1981; Medioli et al., 1986, 1990a; Thibaudeau and Medioli, 1986; Thibaudeau et al., 1987). Thibaudeau (1993) reported and partly illustrated *Difflugia, Heleopera,* and other unidentified thecamoebians from carboniferous coal-bearing deposits of the Sydney Basin (Nova Scotia); from the same Carboniferous deposits, Wightman et al. (1992a, 1992b) reported and illustrated forms with unmistakable affinities with the modern genera *Cucurbitella, Centropyxis,* and *Nebela* and other unidentified thecamoebians. Based on foraminiferal as well as thecamoebian evidence, these researchers were able to reconstruct the marginal marine environments of the Sydney coal deposits. Other unidentified fossil forms were reported and illustrated by B. Medioli (1995a) from the Eocene marginal marine deposits of the Pyrenees, and by Tibert (1996) from the Lower Carboniferous Blue Beach deposits of Nova Scotia. Recent studies have extended the range of thecamoebians back to Lower Cambrian (Scott and Medioli, 1998) and the Neoproterozoic (Porter and Knoll, 2000).

EVOLUTION

Deflandre (1953) remarked that there was no evidence that any thecamoebian evolution had taken place since upper Miocene. Based on our experience, we would be inclined to extend Deflandre's remark back at least to Carboniferous and, possibly, to the Lower Cambrian.

Considering that these organisms can apparently sur-

vive almost any natural calamity using their encysting capability, it is hardly surprising that they have been under no evolutionary pressure throughout their history. If this is true, the group would have little stratigraphic significance. Knowledge of the ecology of modern forms, however, could prove to be invaluable for the paleoecological reconstructions of many ancient freshwater and marginal marine deposits.

THECAMOEBIAN METHODOLOGY

The methods used for the collection, processing, and data presentation of thecamoebians do not differ significantly from those used for foraminifera. Thecamoebians, however, are usually – but not always – smaller than the average foraminifer. Consequently, the smallest standard sieve that we normally used in concentrating thecamoebians tests has a 44 micron opening (i.e., 19 microns smaller than the 63 micron opening used for foraminifera).

Another important difference between thecamoebians and foraminifera relates to the structure of the test, which, in many thecamoebian species, is much thinner. Solid organic types, when dried, tend to collapse and shrivel irreversibly. In some cases, it is necessary to prepare key slides with dried material for comparative studies because, in fossil material, the shriveling process often has already taken place before the sample is collected. In these cases, only an experienced specialist may be able to identify the most highly deformed specimens. As a general rule, however, washed residues from recent and Pleistocene waterlogged sediments (such as peat from bogs) should not be allowed to dry.

PALEOECOLOGICAL RELATIONSHIPS

In freshwater sediments, where foraminiferal tests are not present, thecamoebian tests replace them; in transitional (e.g., estuarine) areas, the two types of tests are found mixed together in various proportions that have paleoecological significance. Unfortunately, the ecology of thecamoebians has not been studied as exhaustively as that of foraminifera. Consequently, it is prudent to be conservative in evaluating some of the following statements.

Various authors have described species associations characteristic of special niches. They are listed here in summary forms and are presented as possible environmental indicators for recent and Pleistocene deposits. The reader is cautioned that these lists are still both incom-

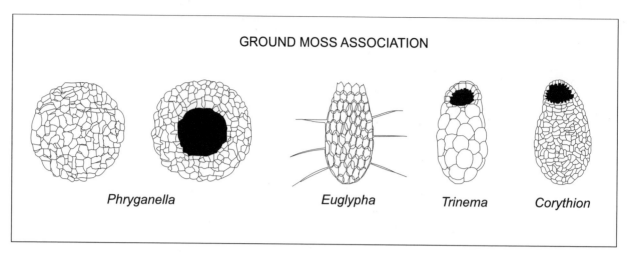

Figure 5.5. Association of thecamoebians often seen in ground moss (*Sphagnum* sp.).

plete and tentative. They are essentially only a starting point for future research.

Wet Niches

■ Ground Mosses

Phryganella and *Euglypha,* at times associated with *Trinema, Heleopera,* and *Corythion* a (Fig. 5.5).

■ Forest Mosses

Difflugia, Euglypha, Centropyxis, Corythion, Nebela, Sphenoderia (Fig. 5.6).

■ Sphagnum Bogs

Amphitrema, Archerella, Sphenoderia, Arcella, Bullinularia, Heleopera, Hyalosphenia, Nebela, Phryganella, Lesquereusia, Pontigulasia, and rare *Difflugia oblonga* (Fig. 5.7).

Lacustrine Niches

■ Spirogyra Mats

Various authors place a variety of species of *Difflugia* into this particular niche; all of them have been grouped into the single species *Cucurbitella tricuspis* (Medioli et al., 1987). The vast majority of *C. tricuspis* tests formed in this niche typically are autogenous (Fig. 5.8).

■ Deep Water

Difflugia lemani, D. praestans, D. urceolata, D. proteiformis (Fig. 5.9).

■ Gyttja

Arcella hemispherica, Difflugia proteiformis, D. urceolata, D. avellana, D. elegans, D. fallax, D. globulus, D. urceolata, D. oblonga, D. bidens, D. corona, Cucurbitella tricuspis, Lagenodifflugia vas, Pontigulasia compressa, Heleopera sphagni, Centropyxis aculeata, C. constricta,

Figure 5.6. Forest moss assemblages of thecamoebians are typically a mixture of autogenous and xenogenous types.

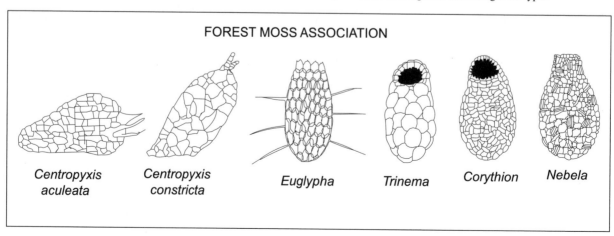

Euglypha acanthophora (Fig. 5.10). Empty autogenous tests of *Cucurbitella tricuspis* are found in the gyttja of eutrophic lakes because after the attached pseudoplanktic stage, or after death, thecamoebian tests will eventually settle into the gyttja. Xenogenous tests actually live and probably reproduce in the gyttja itself during the periods of the year when the algal mats are not floating (Medioli et al., 1987).

Brackish Water

Some thecamoebians appear to be able to survive and thrive in slightly brackish water. However, a sharp distinction must be made between forms capable of surviving temporary brackish water invasions and those capable of reproducing in a predominantly brackish environment. The first group probably includes most aquatic thecamoebians that, through the process of encystment, are able to temporarily survive almost anything. The second group, as far as it is known and excluding forms never reported as fossils, can be restricted to the genus *Centropyxis* and to the species *Difflugia oblonga.*

Estuaries

Estuaries can be quite varied in topography and physiochemical characteristics. Some rivers broaden to form lakes or a lake-like features and can be connected with the sea by a more or less restricted channel (Laidler and Scott, 1996); others are wide open and are influenced substantially by tidal action (Bartlett, 1966). In either case, there is a substantial amount of reworking of thecamoebian tests. The fossil signature of estuarine deposits is often a discontinuous distribution of a mixture of foraminiferal and thecamoebian tests (Bartlett, 1966). Typically, the genus *Centropyxis,* which is well

Figure 5.7. *Sphagnum* moss thecamoebian assemblage.

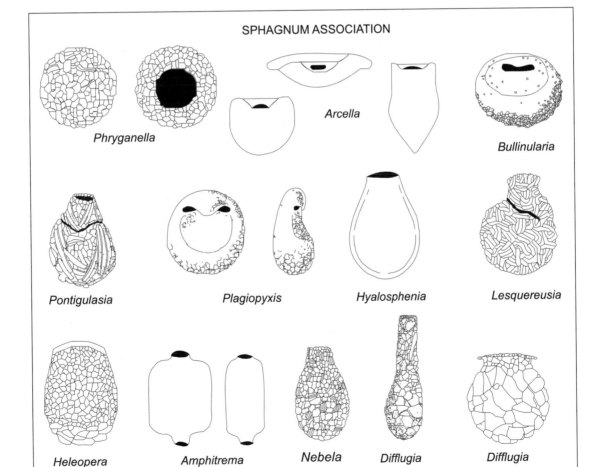

SPIROGYRA MAT ASSOCIATION

Autogenous or mixed specimens of *Cucurbitella tricuspis* with a collar usually dominate this habitat. *C. tricuspis* is a polymorphous species that can be autogenous, mixed, or xenogenous and with a very variable apertural structure. The number of teeth in the aperture vary; a collar may or may not be present. The xenogeous forms without a collar are probably the benthic version of the species which develops after the floating stage of *Spirogyra* ends.

Figure 5.8. *Spirogyra* algal mat thecamoebian assemblage commonly observed in eutrophied lakes typically feature a high abundance of *Cucurbitella tricuspsis*.

Figure 5.9. Deep-water lake assemblage.

EXAMPLES OF LACUSTRINE ASSEMBLAGE SPECIES

Difflugia proteiformis

Difflugia urceolata

Variety of morphotypes of *Difflugia proteiformis* and *D. urceolata* found in lake waters together with other species.

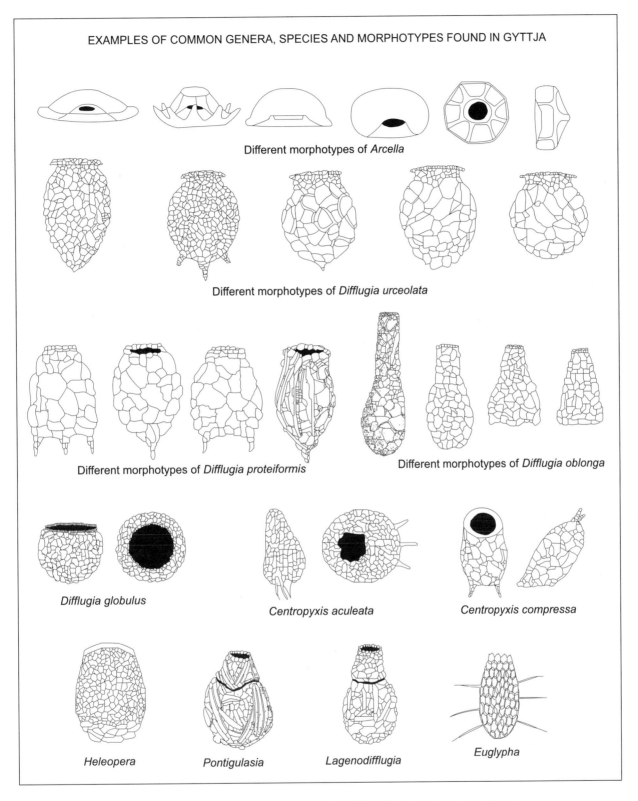

EXAMPLES OF COMMON GENERA, SPECIES AND MORPHOTYPES FOUND IN GYTTJA

Different morphotypes of *Arcella*

Different morphotypes of *Difflugia urceolata*

Different morphotypes of *Difflugia proteiformis*

Different morphotypes of *Difflugia oblonga*

Difflugia globulus

Centropyxis aculeata

Centropyxis compressa

Heleopera

Pontigulasia

Lagenodifflugia

Euglypha

Figure 5.10. Typical association found in gyttja deposits in lakes with a low clastic deposition rate.

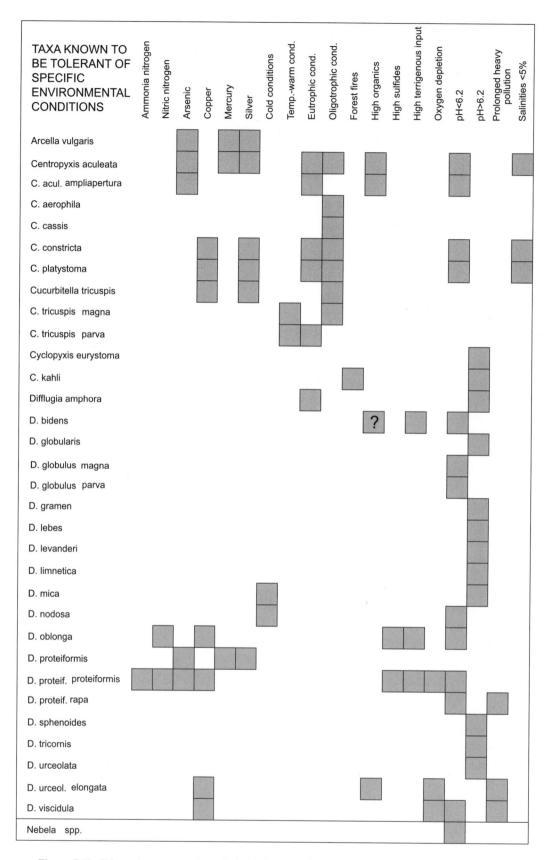

Figure 5.11. Schematic representation of what is known about the environmental tolerance of various thecamoebian species.

adapted to low levels of salinity, tends to dominate the thecamoebian assemblage.

ECOLOGICAL INDICATORS

Although most attempts to correlate thecamoebian taxa to ecological variables are relatively recent, some environmental indicators have been identified, often tentatively, at the generic, specific, and strain levels. For instance, Ellison (1995) grouped a number of species into two categories: (1) those found in water with pH >6.2 and (2) those found in water with pH <6.2. These pH values, established in one single study, could be circumstantial but suggest that the idea is worthy of further investigation.* The information available thus far, still subject to evolution and improvement, is listed next and tabulated in Fig. 5.11.

Arcella vulgaris: This species has been reported by Patterson et al. (1996) as being relatively abundant in sediment moderately to heavily contaminated by Ag and Hg. It would appear that *A. vulgaris* can thrive in marginally brackish, shallow pools such as those of the Canadian prairies (Loeblich and Tappan, 1964; Scott and Medioli, 1980c; Burbidge and Schröder, 1998).

Centropyxis spp: Found mainly in waters having pH >6.2 (Ellison, 1995); some species can thrive in marginally brackish water (Scott and Medioli, 1980c; Patterson et al., 1985).

Centropyxis aculeata and *Centropyxis constricta:* Both species of *Centropyxis* seem to be very tolerant of extreme conditions (see Fig. 5.11) and usually are dominant in coastal lakes occasionally affected by salt spray. Norse Pond (Maine; Fig. 3.13) was once submerged by seawater and was subsequently raised above it. *C. aculeata* and *C. constricta* were the first pioneering forms observed in the core. They dominated the thecamoebian population in the interval representing the transition from marine to fresh water (Scott and Medioli, 1980). Similar transitional associations were observed in cores from other New Brunswick lakes (Patterson et al., 1985; see Fig. 3.12). These two species appeared to possess a particularly efficient dispersal mechanism, as they are often the first pioneer

forms appearing in oligotrophic periglacial lakes, immediately after deglaciation. They also seem to be well adapted to eutrophic conditions.

Centropyxis aculeata: Often found dominant in marginally brackish coastal ponds affected by salt spray (<5‰) during windstorms (Scott and Medioli, 1983; Patterson et al., 1985). This species is quite tolerant of low algal productivity (Burbidge and Schröder, 1998) because it appears to feed on bacteria (McCarthy et al., 1995). McCarthy et al. (1995) and Schönborn (1984) considered *C. aculeata* to be a useful indicator of oligotrophic conditions.

Centropyxis aculeata morph "ampliapertura": Parenti (1992) reported *C. aculeata* "ampliapertura," in association with *Cucurbitella tricuspis,* from Lake Mantova (northern Italy) as indicators of eutrophic conditions.

Centropyxis constricta: Often found dominant in marginally brackish (<5‰) coastal ponds affected by salt spray during windstorms (Scott and Medioli, 1980c; Patterson et al., 1985).

Centropyxis aerophila (= Centropyxis *aculeata?*): Found mainly in oligotrophic water (Ellison, 1995).

Centropyxis cassis (= Centropyxis *aculeata?*): Found mainly in oligotropic water (Ellison, 1995).

Centropyxis platystoma: (= Centropyxis *aculeata?*): Found mainly in oligotropic water (Ellison, 1995).

Cucurbitella tricuspis: Scott and Medioli (1983) were the first to report large populations of *C. (Difflugia) tricuspis* from Lake Erie, relating them to high nutrient input. Medioli et al. (1987) have shown that *C. tricuspis* infests floating filamentous algae (particularly the various species of the genus *Spirogyra)* that flourish best in eutrophic conditions. It follows that high-concentration populations of *C. tricuspis* would be expected to occur in eutrophic lakes, although noneutrophic lakes may have low concentrations of large xenogenous specimens. Medioli et al. (1987) suggested that this species produces abundant autogenous tests during *Spirogyra's* floating season. During the floating phase, *C. tricuspis* is apparently able to find plenty of food and seems to reproduce very rapidly, producing numerous small tests. For this phenotype, Parenti (1992) proposed the trinomial nomenclature *C. tricuspis* "parva." Among the *Spirogyra* mats, however, mineral particles to use as xenosomes are scarce, so the living organism is forced to produce autogenous tests, at best occasionally agglutinating diatom frustules. For the rest of the year the species is a bottom dweller, producing scarce and large xenogenous tests. For this phenotype Parenti (1992) has proposed the nomenclature *C. tricuspis* "magna." This

---

*The Ellison (1995) paper simply listed binomina without figuring the species. As it is impossible to ascertain with any degree of confidence what those names actually represent, whenever possible they are supplemented with the subjective and more comprehensive equivalent binomen used in this book; ex.: *Difflugia amphora (= D. urecolata).*

observation has been confirmed by Collins et al. (1990) in their study of a transect along the eastern North American coast, Parenti (1992) in the eutrophic Lake Superior of Mantua (northern Italy), Asioli et al. (1996) in Lake Varese (northern Italy), Patterson et al. (1996) from deposits in eutrophic lakes in Ontario, and Torigai (1996) and Torigai et al. (2000) in a study of Lake Winnipeg. Interestingly, Davis (1916) found fossil remains of *Spirogyra* in the middle Eocene Green River oil shales of Colorado and Utah. Fifteen years later, Bradley (1931) found, in the same oil shales, fossilized thecamoebians very similar to *C. tricuspis* (Medioli et al., 1990a,b). These two observations appear to confirm that the relationship between *Spirogyra* and *C. tricuspis* extends as far back as at least middle Eocene.

Cyclopyxis arcelloides (= Centropyxis *aculeata* strain?): Found mainly in waters with pH <6.2 (Ellison, 1995).

Cyclopyxis eurystoma (= Centropyxis *aculeata* strain?): Found mainly in waters with pH >6.2 (Ellison, 1995).

Cyclopyxis kahli (= Centropyxis *aculeata* strain?): Found mainly in oligotrophic waters with pH >6.2 (Ellison, 1995).

Difflugia acuminata (= *D. proteiformis?*): Found mainly in oligotrophic waters with pH >6.2 (Ellison, 1995).

Difflugia amphora (= *D. urceolata?*): Found mainly in eutrophic waters (Ellison, 1995).

Difflugia bidens: From a study of New Brunswick lake cores (Patterson et al., 1985), it seems that the abundance of *D. bidens* is related to high terrigenous input. As this species tends to agglutinate exceptionally small xenosomes, the presence of fine-grained particles is likely to be particularly critical in controlling the presence and abundance of this taxon. In one of the New Brunswick lakes, *D. bidens* was recorded as abundant only in the surficial sediment. It was later discovered that the area around that lake had been affected by a major forest fire twenty years prior to the study. It is speculated that the fire may have caused an increase in fine-grained terrigenous inflow in the form of wood ash and soil mineral particles. This species was also found in Lake Erie, but only after 1850 when clearcutting of the forests would have exposed the soil and increased the terrigenous clastic input (Scott and Medioli, 1983). The presence of *D. bidens* in Holocene sediments, although not yet convincingly documented, may prove to be helpful in defining the local impact of forest fires on lacustrine sedimentation.

Difflugia difficilis (= *D. oblonga?*): Found mainly in waters with pH <6.2 (Ellison, 1995).

Difflugia elegans (= *D. oblonga?*): Found mainly in waters with pH <6.2 (Ellison, 1995).

Difflugia globularis (= *Difflugia globulus?*): Found mainly in waters with pH <6.2 (Ellison, 1995).

Difflugia globulus: Collins et al. (1990) suggested that the presence of abundant large specimens of *D. globulus* may be indicative of cold climate. It would appear, in fact, that under conditions of high latitude and relative short summers, reproduction slows down, resulting in the formation of large-size individuals. As a working hypothesis, we suggest that the converse may also be true: Abundant specimens of small *Difflugia globulus* may prove to reflect short reproductive periods and low-latitude conditions. Burbidge and Schröder-Adams (1998), however, pointed out that this species feeds mainly on green and yellow-green algae and its value as a cold-water indicator is questionable, although they did not discuss the relative size of their specimens.

Difflugia gramen (= *Cucurbitella tricuspis*): Found mainly in waters with pH >6.2 (Ellison, 1995).

Difflugia lebes (= *Cucurbitella tricuspis*): Found mainly in eutrophic waters with pH >6.2 (Ellison, 1995).

Difflugia levanderi: Found mainly in waters with pH >6.2 (Ellison, 1995).

Difflugia limnetica (= *Cucurbitella tricuspis*): Found mainly in waters with pH <6.2 (Ellison, 1995).

Difflugia manicata (= *Difflugia oblonga?*): Seems to feed mainly on Cyanophytes and diatoms, like *Difflugia oblonga,* and it is usually present in high percentages in sediment with high organic content. *D. manicata* is seldom reported in the literature. It is very small and is not retained in the commonly used 63 micron sieve; its study requires the use of the less common 44 micron sieve (Burbidge and Schröder-Adams, 1998).

Difflugia mica: Found mainly in waters with pH <6.2 (Ellison, 1995).

Difflugia nodosa: Found mainly in waters with pH >6.2 (Ellison, 1995).

Difflugia oblonga: Found mainly in waters with pH <6.2 (Ellison, 1995). Kliza (1994) reported this species in high percentages in arctic lakes with organic matter-enriched sediment, where it replaced *D. globulus* when the organic content of the sediment increased. Kliza's observation was subsequently confirmed by Patterson et al. (1996) in their Ontario lakes investigation, and by Burbidge and Schröder-Adams (1998) in their Lake Winnipeg study.

McCarthy et al. (1995) reported that, in lakes in the Canadian Maritimes, the accelerated climatic warming of the early postglacial resulted in increased organics in the sediment, and the percentages of *D. oblonga* increased at the expense of *Centropyxis aculeata*. It would appear that this species may be connected with the presence of gyttja in which it presumably lives (Patterson et al., 1985; McCarthy et al., 1995).

Difflugia proteiformis: Asioli et al. (1996), in a study of thecamoebians in three sediment cores collected in three northern Italian lakes, observed the following:

1 *D. proteiformis* "proteiformis" is well adapted to environments rich in organic matter, sulfides, sulfites, and low oxygen.

2 *D. proteiformis* "rapa" appears to be particularly resistant to increases in concentration of ammonia nitrogen and nitric nitrogen, and well adapted to habitats with lower pH, oxygen depletion, and high concentration of copper. Asioli et al. (1996) concluded that this morph is an indicator of environments strongly polluted for a long period of time.

Difflugia pyriformis (= *D. oblonga*): Found mainly in waters with pH >6.2 (Ellison, 1995).

Difflugia rotunda: Found mainly in waters with pH <6.2 (Ellison, 1995).

Difflugia sphenoides: Found mainly in waters with pH >6.2 (Ellison, 1995).

Difflugia tricornis (= *D. proteiformis*): Found mainly in waters with pH >6.2 (Ellison, 1995).

Difflugia urceolata: Found mainly in eutrophic waters with pH >6.2 (Ellison, 1995).

Difflugia urceolata "elongata": Patterson et al. (1996) reported this species from lakes in Ontario, where it was present in moderately high percentages in sediment characterized by high organic matter concentrations.

Difflugia viscidula: This species has been found by Asioli et al. (1996) associated, under the same environmental conditions, with both *D. proteiformis* "rapa" and *D. proteiformis* "proteiformis."

Lesquereusia **spp.:** Found mainly in waters with pH >6.2 (Ellison, 1995).

Nebela **spp.:** Found in waters with pH <6.2 (Ellison, 1995).

APPLICATIONS IN VARIOUS FIELDS

To date, only a few paleolimnological studies based on thecamoebians have appeared in the scientific literature. Despite the scarcity of information, it has already become obvious that thecamoebians have value for reconstructing the history of environmental changes recorded in recent as well as very old freshwater and lacustrine deposits. Due to the durable nature of their

tests, most thecamoebians found fossilized, even in very recent deposits, belong to the superfamily Arcellacea, whose mainly siliceous or organic tests are preserved in almost any freshwater sedimentary environment, no matter how low the pH conditions. Other, more delicate thecamoebian tests seldom fossilize and are not dealt with here.

Relocation of Paleo-sealevels

In a micropaleontological study of the classical Pyrenean cyclical sequences (Mutti et al., 1988), B. Medioli (1995a,b) focused on the micropaleontological content of a number of lignite lenses interbedded in these deposits. The lignites were generally assumed to be of freshwater origin and had been ignored by micropaleontologists. Medioli's (1995a) study showed that these lignites contained large numbers of older, reworked open marine foraminifera, marsh foraminifera, and thecamoebians. The areal distribution of in situ forms revealed patterns essentially identical to the modern patterns of distribution of marginal marine forms, and to those distributions reported in various papers by McLean and Wall (1981), Wall (1976), and Wightman et al. (1992a,b, 1993, 1994). Based on her results, Medioli (1995a) was able to use these faunae collectively to provisionally interpret the complex interplay of eustatic and tectonic sea-level changes recorded in the Pyrenean sequence.

Forensic Studies

In Belgium in 1975, a man was arrested for the murder of a girl. The man always maintained that he had never been in the area where the body had been found. However, the study of the soil thecamoebians contained in the dirt attached to the defendant's shoes suggested that he was lying. In December 1976, the Court of Assizes of Liège found the defendant guilty and sentenced him to life in prison (Lambert and Chardez, 1978).

There does not appear to be any other anecdote of this nature, but this one demonstrates that these organisms have a comparatively broad range of potential as indicators that has yet to be fully realized.

Freshwater Influence Detection

The first few practical applications of thecamoebians to paleoecological studies were limited to the use of these organisms as indicators of freshwater influence in estuarine settings (Bartlett, 1966; Ellison and Nichols, 1976; Scott et al., 1977, 1980; Scott and Medioli, 1980b). However, these studies were concerned primarily with marine foraminifera and regarded arcellaceans essentially as reworked organic material. See Chapter 3 for more detail under "Marine/Freshwater Transitions."

PALEOECOLOGICAL STUDIES OF LACUSTRINE DEPOSITS

Lakes in North America

■ Lake Erie

In cores from Lake Erie, Kemp et al. (1976) established the 1850 A.D. horizon, which corresponds to the beginning of industrialization, and consequent contaminant discharge into the lake. Scott and Medioli (1983) were able to correlate changes in arcellacean assemblages with such historical events. In all three basins of Lake Erie there were detectable changes at the 1850 boundary. In the western basin, total thecamoebian numbers dropped sharply just below the 1850 boundary (Fig. 5.12), while *Cucurbitella tricuspis* percentages decreased slightly. In the central basin, total numbers also dropped sharply (Fig. 5.13) before the 1850 horizon. This decrease was paralleled by a pronounced assemblage change compared to that observed in the western basin; *Difflugia oblonga* was virtually entirely replaced by *Difflugia urceolata*. In the eastern basin, the assemblage did not change, but total numbers decreased sharply below the 1850 level (Fig. 5.14).

Similar assemblages, characterized by low numbers, occur at the base of all Lake Erie cores. They are comparable to the present-day assemblage living at the deepest station in Lake Erie. At present, the environment of the deep station is marked by high sedimentation rates and by comparatively high oxygen values. The occurrence of this "deep-water" assemblage in all three basins of the lake, in sediment less than 1,000 years in age, suggests that the strong environmental gradients existing today are a comparatively recent phenomenon. Some conclusions and hypotheses, as well as some general considerations, were also inferred from some individual species: (1) high percentages and total numbers of *Cucurbitella tricuspis* presently in the western basin appear to be related to eutrophication; (2) presence of *Difflugia bidens* seems to reflect the present high terrigenous input that presumably is connected with anthropogenic influence; and (3) higher total thecamoebian numbers seen generally in the modern sediment proba-

bly reflect an increase in nutrient input since 1859, following human settlement around the lake (Scott and Medioli, 1983).

■ Small Lakes in New Brunswick and Nova Scotia

Scott and Medioli (1980c), Honig and Scott (1987), and Patterson et al. (1985) studied surficial as well as core material from a number of small New Brunswick (Canada) coastal lakes that have been uplifted by postglacial crustal rebound. In some instances, they have been able to illustrate the rebound-induced transition from salt- to freshwater conditions, and the intermediate and temporary brackish water phase.

Core data from Gibson and Journeays lakes (Nova Scotia) (Patterson et al., 1985) revealed brackish-water sequences near the bottom. This was established in Gibson Lake by the presence of foraminifera-bearing marine sediments underlying the freshwater ones. The marine deposit relates to a time when the basin was below sea level (Fig. 3.12). The environment of that interval supported high percentages of *Centropyxis aculeata* and *Centropyxis constricta* (Scott and Medioli, 1980c). Using this simple association, it was possible to trace the brackish episode in other nearby lakes where marine deposits were either absent or had not been penetrated by the core sampler. In Journeays Lake there are no marine indicators at the base of the core. However, a lowered total number of thecamoebians, in conjunction with comparatively high percentages of *C. aculeata* and *C. constricta,* was considered to be indicative of slightly brackish-water conditions (Fig. 5.15).

Aside from the increase in *C. tricuspis* and the transition to brackish conditions that is seen at the base of each core, there are relatively few assemblage changes over a relatively long period of time (12,000 years in Gibson Lake; 11,000 years in Journeays Lake). It is known from pollen studies that the climate changed sharply during this period (Mott, 1975). Nevertheless, the indigenous thecamoebians assemblages in these lakes do not appear to have been particularly sensitive to climatic parameters, such as temperature, compared to their response to salinity. Contemporary assemblages in these lakes are quite different from those of Lake Erie in that the eutrophication indicator *Cucurbitella tricuspis* is absent. This species, however, becomes prominent just below the sediment surface in Journeays Lake. The reason this lake was eutrophic in the past and not now remains, for the time being, an unanswered question.

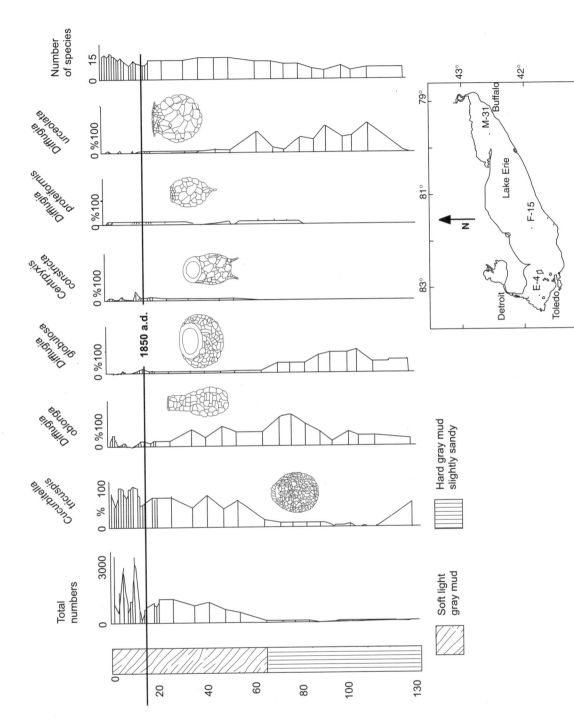

Figure 5.12. Core taken in the early 1980s from the western end of Lake Erie, Ontario (Canada) in ~10 m of water. The 1850 horizon marks the initiation of contamination flux into the lake. The response to contamination is seen as an increase in thecamoebians, especially *Cucurbitella tricuspis* (after Scott and Medioli, 1983).

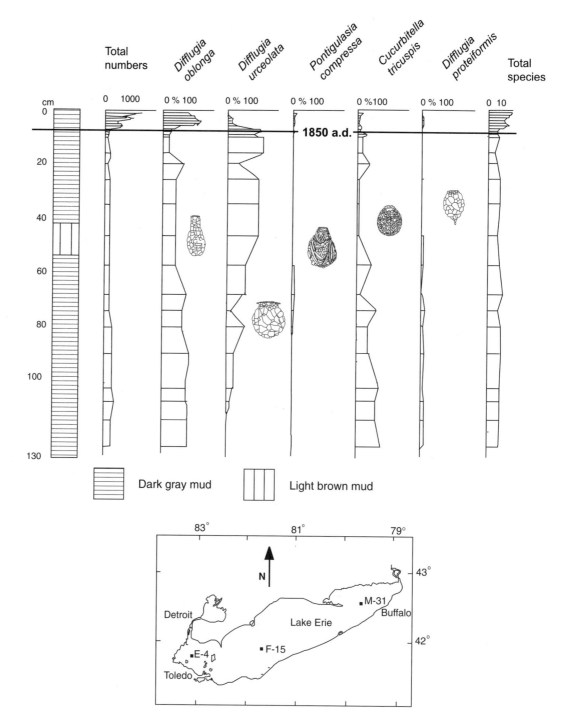

Figure 5.13. Core collected from central Lake Erie in ~15 m water depth at the same time as the one shown in Fig. 5.12. Although not shown on this diagram, because of its low relative abundance, *Difflugia bidens is* observed in post-1850 core samples from this part of the lake, suggesting an increase in clastic input (after Scott and Medioli, 1983).

■ **Thecamoebian Assemblages and Pollen Successions in Atlantic Canada**

McCarthy et al. (1995) studied pollen and arcellaceans in cores, dating back to the last deglaciation. The samples were collected from two lakes, one in New-foundland and one in Nova Scotia. Based on pollen analysis, they interpreted a sudden warming at around 10,000 yBP that was followed by a general warm-ing to the mid-Holocene Hypsithermal. The post-Hypsithermal interval record showed a decrease in tem-perature and an increase in precipitation to the present.

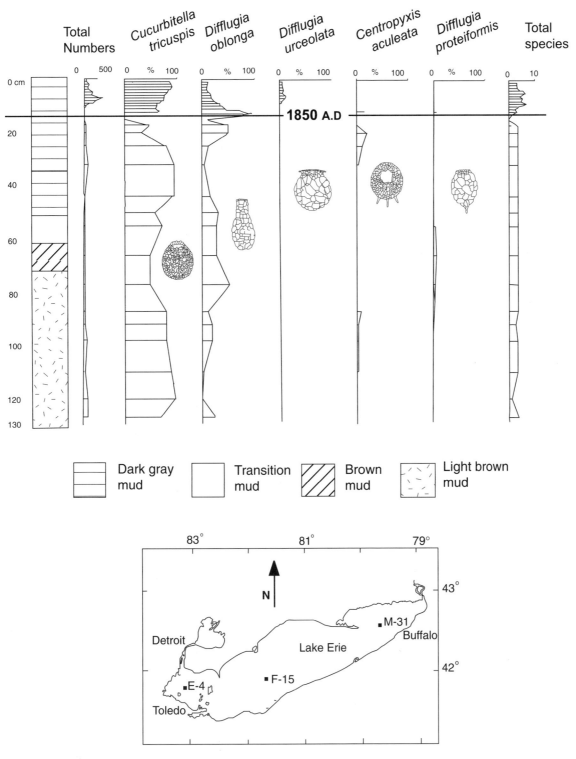

Figure 5.14. Core collected from ~50 m water depth in eastern Lake Erie at the same time as those shown in Figs. 5.12 and 5.13. The major effect seen here was a large increase in total numbers of thecamoebians but little change in relative species abundances (after Scott and Medioli, 1983).

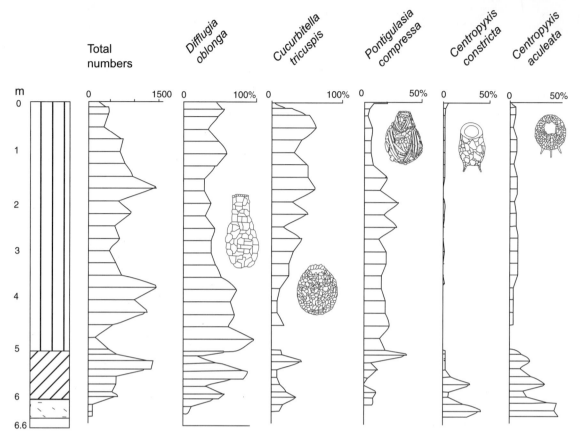

Figure 5.15. A typical thecamoebian fauna occurs throughout the Journeays Lake, Nova Scotia, core until near the base of core. It changes to what is thought to be a brackish fauna, with *Centropyxis aculeata* only, marking lifting of the basin above ambient sea level. There is no evidence of foraminifera at this site (after Patterson et al., 1985).

Comparable thecamoebian associations were found in the three lakes in late glacial (13–10 ka), early Holocene (10–8 ka), mid-Holocene (8–4 ka), and late Holocene (4–0ka) sections. In all three lakes, immediately following the retreat of the ice sheet, *Centropyxis aculeata, C. constricta, Difflugia oblonga, D. urceolata,* and *D. corona* were common. The latter part of the late glacial age core section was marked by sparse assemblages dominated by the opportunistic species *C. aculeata.* For Atlantic Canada, this occurrence suggested a climatic reversal (11.5 ka–10,000 yBP) analogous to the Younger Dryas, which apparently was not recorded by the pollen results at these particular sites. Pollen analysis (Ogden, 1987) suggested a sudden warming in both areas at around 10 ka BP. The warming trend was signaled by a change of pollen composition from open tundra to closed boreal forest. This transition was followed by a general warming starting at 9 ka, with a peak temperature interval (mean July temperatures of over 20° C) between 8 ka and 2 ka BP, that is marked by peaks in the percentages of the thermophilous taxa *Pinus* and *Tsuga* (Ogden, 1987). Pollen data also indicated that the 2 ka BP to present interval witnessed a decrease in temperature and an increase in precipitation to the present (July mean temperature of 18.2° C). McCarthy et al. (1995) reported five distinct and comparable thecamoebian assemblages in all three lakes (Fig. 5.16) roughly corresponding to the five climatic episodes just described. They concluded that, due to their quick generation time, thecamoebians responded rapidly to climatic changes and appeared to be better suited than pollen, at least in these lakes, for recording multi-millennial climatic events. This study, unlike previous studies in similar lakes (e.g., Patterson et al., 1985), was able to establish connections between climate and thecamoebian assemblages.

■ **Small Lakes in Ontario**

Patterson et al. (1996) and Patterson and Kumar (2000) studied thecamoebian populations in three small lakes (two of which were heavily contaminated by mine tailings) near the town of Cobalt in northeastern Ontario (Fig. 5.17).

Vegetation (terrestrial climate) vs. Arcellacean assemblages in Eastern Canada

Years BP	Vegetation		Arcellaceans	
	NS	**Nfld**	**NS**	**Nfld**
0 **Post Hypsi-thermal**	More spruce and alder	Alders, sedges, ferns and grasses	**A** *Centropyxis aculeata* *Difflugia oblonga* *Pontigulasia compressa*	**A** *Centropyxis aculeata* *Difflugia oblonga* *Pontigulasia compressa*
2,000 I 4,000	More birch, less pine		**B** *Difflugia oblonga* *Pontigulasia compressa* *Difflugia bacillifera*	
Mid-hypsi-thermal		Spruce, fir, pine, birch		**B** *Difflugia oblonga* *Pontigulasia compressa* *Difflugia bacillifera*
6,000	Max. pine, hemlock	Spruce, birch, fir, alder	**C** *Difflugia oblonga*	**C** *Difflugia oblonga*
8,000				
Early warming **10,000**	Increasing birch, then pine		**D** *Centropyxis aculeata*	**D** *Centropyxis aculeata*
"Younger Dryas" **12,000** **Late Glacial**	Sedges, grasses, spruce	Sedges, grasses, heather, birch, willow, alder	**E** *C. aculeata* *D. urceolata* *C. constricta* *D. oblonga* *D. corona*	**E** *C. aculeata* *D. urceolata* *C. constricta* *D. oblonga* *D. corona*

Figure 5.16. Summary of pollen vs. thecamoebian data from eastern Canada showing parallel climatic trends detected by both proxies (after McCarthy et al., 1995).

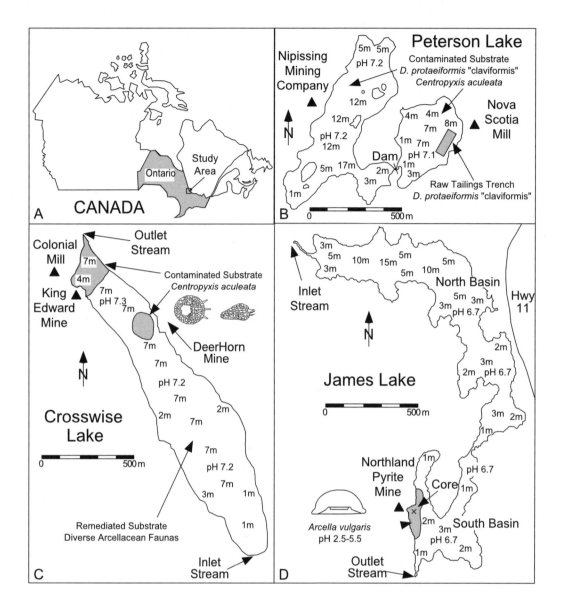

Figure 5.17. Some northern Ontario lakes which are characterized by heavy metal surface sediment contamination (after Patterson et al., 1996).

Mine waste and mill tailings had been dumped into Crosswise Lake until 1970, and a leaking dam continued to release contaminated water into Peterson Lake after that year. Natural sedimentation is slowly burying the tailings, but several highly toxic areas remain exposed. In Crosswise Lake, levels of As and Hg contamination in the substrate are, respectively, over 140 and 25 times the maximum acceptable concentrations for aquatic life. In Peterson Lake, these values are even higher. Patterson et al. (1996) and Patterson and Kumar (2000) identified five distinct faunal assemblages that they correlated to environmental conditions.

(1) Contaminated Substrate Assemblage. This assemblage dominated very contaminated mine tailings in the south-central part of Crosswise Lake, the western basin, and the dam area of Peterson Lake. Grab samples from these areas were fetid and, although no chemical analysis was performed, were presumed to be highly contaminated because these silver-bearing muds permanently stained the collection bottles. The thecamoebian assemblage living on these substrates was dominated by:

Centropyxis aculeata (27.5%)
Centropyxis constricta (13.5%)
Arcella vulgaris (9.7%)

(2) Mine Tailings Assemblage. This assemblage is very similar to the previous one, but is restricted, in Crosswise and Peterson lakes, to samples consisting of white, muddy to silty, mine tailing material that seems to be very similar to

the samples with very high levels of As and Hg that had previously been studied in these lakes. The thecamoebian assemblage living on this substrate is dominated by:

Cucurbitella tricuspis (21.6%)

Difflugia oblonga (18.2%)

Centropyxis aculeata (13.1%)

Difflugia proteiformis (11.3%)

(3) Muddy Substrate Assemblage. This assemblage characterized organic-rich substrates in all three lakes. Samples containing this assemblage were all composed of mud and/or gyttja, and were found at water depths from 3.9 to 18.0 m. The thecamoebian assemblage living on these substrate is dominated by:

Difflugia oblonga (40.9%)

Difflugia urceolata phenotype "elongata" (18.3%)

Centropyxis aculeata (9.8%)

(4) Diatom Mud Assemblage. This assemblage was restricted to diatomaceous mud (6.7–6.8 m) associated with lake weeds along the margins of Crosswise Lake. There was no physical evidence of tailings at these sites. The thecamoebian assemblage living on this substrate was dominated by:

Cucurbitella tricuspis (6.9%)

Difflugia proteiformis (13.1%)

Difflugia oblonga (14.1%)

Centropyxis aculeata (5.6%)

(5) Transported Fauna Assemblage. Sediments characterized by this assemblage vary in composition from silt to mud to gyttja and typically are found in deep water (15–37 m), well beneath the thermocline and in an environment of minimal oxygen concentration. The thecamoebian assemblage living on these substrates was dominated totally by:

Cucurbitella tricuspis (90.3%)

The interpretation of this assemblage as being the result of transport, however, seems open to questions. The conditions of "minimal oxygen concentration" seem comparable, very approximately, to euxinic conditions. Under such conditions, planktic organism remains usually vastly outnumber those of the rare organisms adapted to live at the bottom (e.g., Graptolites in Ordovician black shale; Cooper et al., 1990). *C. tricuspis*, as explained briefly before, is endemic on floating algae. Consequently, it can prosper at the surface totally unaffected by the lethal conditions at the bottom. After the tests become empty, they fall to the bottom where, thanks to the scarcity of other organisms, they can dominate the fossil assemblage.

A core in Crosswise Lake (Fig. 5.18) illustrates thecamoebian variability through time at one of these lakes and suggests that climate plays an important role in controlling the species composition of these faunae. From the ^{14}C dates on this core, it is clear that it penetrates into the early Holocene when it was colder in northern Ontario than today. The colder climate seems to have limited the fauna seen in the lower part of the core. Also, it is easy to see the onset of the heavy metal contamination with the appearance of *Arcella vulgaris* near the top of the core. This one example illustrates the importance of looking not only at present but past faunae because, in this case, the climate appears to have had an even more profound effect on the total faunae than the heavy metal contamination.

■ Lake Winnipeg

Burbidge and Schröder-Adams (1998), in a study of cores collected in Lake Winnipeg, came to the general conclusion that biologic productivity, and consequently the type of organic material in the sediment, is the main factor controlling the distribution of thecamoebian populations. Secondary factors seem to be water chemistry and turbidity, while inorganic sediment geochemistry and temperature do not seem to significantly influence these organisms.

Based on variations in abundance of key species, they divided Lake Winnipeg into three distinct areas:

(1) The North Basin: which seems relatively unchanged since the final retreat of Lake Agassiz (~7,500 yBP), as indicated by the consistent dominance of *Difflugia manicata* from the Agassiz unconformity to the top of the cores.

(2) The Narrows: in which high turbidity hinders the production of algal food, as demonstrated by several phytoplankton surveys. Here *Centropyxis aculeata* replaces *Difflugia manicata* as the dominant species.

(3) The South Basin: in which three distinct assemblages were identified above the Agassiz unconformity:

(a) A *Centropyxis-Arcella* assemblage characterized the base of the core and dominated by *Centropyxis aculeata* (*Centropyxis aculeata* "aculeata" and *Centropyxis aculeata* "ecornis") and *Arcella vulgaris*. *Centropyxis* repeatedly has been reported as an opportunistic genus, adaptable to ephemeral and severe conditions such as marginally brackish, oligotrophy, eutrophy, and so forth (Scott and Medioli, 1980c; Patterson et al., 1985). The various strains of *Centropyxis* have been cultured successfully in bacteria-rich pond water devoid of algae (Kerr, 1984), demonstrating that this genus is well adapted to environments poor in those nutrients usually associated with testate rhizopods (such as other protists, metazoans, and organic detritus; Lipps, 1993).

A. vulgaris has also repeatedly been reported as capable of withstanding marginally brackish conditions (Loeblich and Tappan, 1964; Scott and Medioli, 1980b). In the

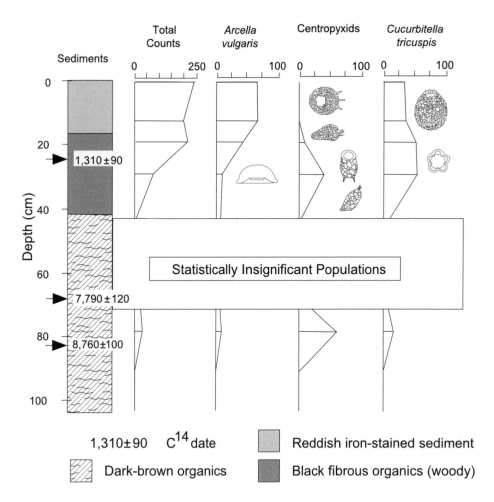

Figure 5.18. Example of a core from one of the Ontario lakes studied by Patterson and Kumar (2000). Crosswise Lake shows contamination of its sediment surface. Sediment changes into organic mud in pre-historical time and finally into a "gyttja" that contains few thecamoebians, possibly because the climate was too cold at that time (after Patterson and Kumar, 2000).

ancient South Basin, marginally brackish conditions are suggested by the occurrence of fossil plants at the base of the Lake Winnipeg sequence (Vance, 1996) that are similar to modern ones living in shallow, hyposaline lakes in the Canadian prairies. In conclusion, the presence of the assemblage seems to be controlled by an early phase in which an oligotrophic (OC in the sediment varies from 5 to 6.2%), slightly brackish, shallow pool developed in the depression originally occupied by the South Basin.

(b) A *Difflugia globulus* assemblage characterizing the central part of the core and dominated by *Difflugia globulus* and by low abundances of *D. manicata*, *D. oblonga* "linearis," *D. ampullula* and *D. urceolata* "lebes." No chemico-physical explanation for the existence of this assemblage was suggested.

(c) *Cucurbitella tricuspis* assemblage characterizing the upper part of the core and dominated by *C. tricuspis* and marked by the decline of *Centropyxis aculeata* "aculeata" and *Difflugia globulus*. This assemblage correlates to an OC signal that marks the natural eutrophication of the lake, a process that seems to have started approximately 450 yBP. This finding supports the conclusions of other investigations that have described the proxy value of this species as an indicator of eutrophic conditions (Medioli et al., 1987; Collins et al., 1990; Parenti, 1992; Asioli et al., 1996; Patterson et al., 1996; Torigai, 1996).

■ Lakes in Richards Island (Northwest Territories, Canada)

A study of the climatic gradient on Richards Island lakes was carried out by Dallimore et al. (2000). On this island, due to the contrasting influences of the cold Beaufort Sea to the north and the warm waters of the Mackenzie River to the south, lake water temperatures can vary by as much as 12° C across the island. Dallimore et al. (2000) found that the thecamoebian assemblage was composed of *Centropyxis aculeata,*

Cucurbitella tricuspis, Difflugia oblonga, Difflugia urceolata "lebes," *Difflugia globulus, Difflugia proteiformis, Pontigulasia compressa, Arcella vulgaris, Lagenodifflugia vas,* and *Lesquereusia spiralis,* with a minimum of five species represented in each lake. Assemblages were dominated by *Difflugia oblonga, Difflugia urceolata* "lebes," *Difflugia globulus, Centropyxis aculeata,* and *Cucurbitella tricuspis.* The species *Difflugia oblonga* and *Centropyxis aculeata* were represented in each lake. The most northern lake was strongly dominated by *Centropyxis aculeata,* representing 50% of the assemblage. The more southern lakes were characterized by more even species abundances.

Arctic conditions did not seem to have an appreciable effect on population abundances or the number of species, since assemblages on Richards Island are essentially comparable to temperate and semitropical faunal assemblages (Scott and Medioli, 1983; McCarthy et al., 1995; Burbidge and Schröder-Adams, 1998). However, certain morphological characteristics, such as large and coarse agglutinated tests and the dominance of assemblages by one or two species – particularly in the colder lakes – appeared to be diagnostic of arctic conditions. Temperature data showed a short six-week "window" of relatively warm-water temperatures rising above 10° C, and peak temperatures of 15 to 20° C – which presumably brackets the reproductive temperature interval – for only days or weeks each year during the summer. This seems to confirm the hypothesis proposed by Collins et al. (1990) that the presence of abundant large specimens may be indicative of cold climate, due to a short reproductive season.

The study of lake water conductivity (related to lake water dissolved minerals) showed that very slight changes in conductivity triggered a change in the assemblage, with the percent abundance of *Centropyxis aculeata* usually increasing with conductivity, at the expense of other taxa. This further strengthens the conjecture that *Centropyxis* is tolerant of low-level salinity as proposed by Scott and Medioli (1980c) and confirmed by Patterson et al. (1985).

During the winter, some of the lakes freeze right to the bottom for about nine months each year (Dallimore et al., 1999), which confirms what has been suspected all along (i.e., that encysted thecamoebians can survive freezing).

Studies of core material revealed that thecamoebians have difficulties colonizing proglacial lakes immediately after deglaciation, perhaps because of high turbidity, turbulence, or alkalinity, and, above all, lack of food.

Organic carbon data, from a core representing 11,000 of deposition, showed that a minimum organic content is required before thecamoebian populations can become established.

Lakes in Europe

■ Northern Italy

Lake Mantova. In a master's thesis on the thecamoebians of Lago Superiore di Mantova (Mantua, Italy), Parenti (1992) identified only ten species. The author, however, using informal trinomial nomenclature, separated and illustrated twenty-three distinct morphs in the hope of being able to connect them with contemporary environmental factors. She reached the conclusion that *Centropyxis aculeata* (holotypic morph), *Centropyxis aculeata* "ampliapertura," and *Cucurbitella tricuspis* (holotypic morph) were the most competitive ones. Based on some of the characteristic natural features of the lake sediment (such as clay and sand content, organic-carbon, and nitrogen), she concluded that all three of these morphs were indicators of eutrophic conditions.

■ Lakes Orta, Varese, and Candia

Asioli and Medioli (1992) and Asioli et al. (1996) studied the thecamoebians in three cores, each one collected in one of the northern Italian lakes of Orta, Varese, and Candia (Fig. 5.19).

Lake Orta. The contamination of this lake started around 1927 with the dumping of copper and ammonium sulfates by the Bemberg Co. (Monti, 1930). A recent study indicated that although the dumping of copper was substantially reduced in 1958, a strong increase in average content of ammonium nitrogen and nitrite nitrogen and persistent acidity of the water, with pH values declining between 3.9 and 4.5, continued due to the emplacement of electrogalvanic factories along the lake shores after 1958 (Calderoni and Mosello, 1990). Between 1958 and 1986, values of primary production were typical of mesotrophic lakes. Zooplankton, which before 1926 was typical of an oligotrophic lake, disappeared completely in response to the pollution process, only to reappear some years later in the form of small and unbalanced communities; this situation had not changed in the early 1990s (Bonacina, 1990).

The lower part of the core collected in this lake consisted of a lower 78 cm (89–11 cm) section of light brown silty clay, changing sharply to black silty clay in the top 11 cm (Fig. 5.19). Three thecamoebian assemblages were identified:

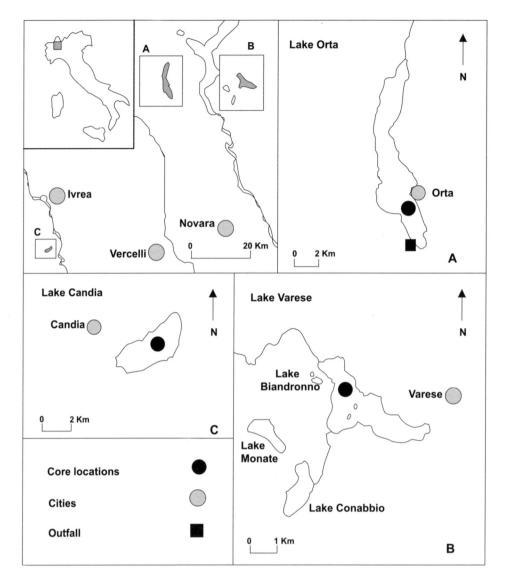

Figure 5.19. Location map of lakes studied in Northern Italy by Asioli et al., 1996. All of these lakes exhibit varying degrees of environmental impact that are described in detail in the text (after Asioli et al., 1996).

(1) *Difflugia globulus* assemblage (84.5–64.5 cm). Dominated by *Difflugia globulus, D. oblonga* (represented mainly by *D. oblonga* "magna"), and *Pontigulasia compressa;* among other species present is small numbers, noteworthy are *D. proteiformis* and the sporadic presence of *D. viscidula.*

(2) *Difflugia oblonga* assemblage (62.5–5 cm). Dominated by *D. oblonga* "parva," *D. proteiformis* "crassa," and *D. viscidula.* In this interval the percentage of *D. globulus* drops dramatically. At 12.5 cm *D. proteiformis* "proteiformis" increases suddenly, and from there on, the assemblage grades into the overlying *D. proteiformis* "rapa" assemblage with the

progressive disappearance of all taxa, except for *D. proteiformis* "crassa" and *D. viscidula.* At the 5 cm horizon, these two species represent 90% of the assemblage.

(3) *Difflugia proteiformis* "rapa" assemblage (1.5 cm). Characterized only by *D. proteiformis* "rapa" (80%) and *D. viscidula* (20%).

The three zones identified in Lake Orta seem to correspond to three ecologic events. As mentioned earlier, Collins et al. (1990) suggested, for *D. globulus,* that the dominance of large-sized individuals of this species may be indicative of cold conditions at high latitudes. DeLaca et al. (1980) and Hallock et al. (1981) made similar conjectures for benthic foraminifera. If this idea can be generalized, the decrease in size of *D. oblonga* and the decline in frequency of *D. globulus* could be interpreted as a response to climatic warming. However, the decrease in size could also be due to scarcity of food, as Bradshaw

(1961) and Hallock et al. (1981) observed for foraminifera. The ²¹⁰Pb dates provided by Alvisi et al. (1996) indicate that the 1926 sediment is located approximately 13 cm below the core top, while the top 5 cm represents the period 1963–66. The 1926 level is characterized by the disappearance of phytoplankton (Guilizzoni and Lami, 1988) and by a sudden pronounced increase of *D. proteiformis* "proteiformis." This occurrence suggests that this strain of *D. proteiformis* may be particularly well adapted to low oxygen and high levels of organic matter and sulfites. The top 5 cm of the core, representing the post-1963 period (Alvisi et al., 1996), was deposited while the lake was affected by increasing concentrations of ammonia and nitric nitrogen, by decreasing pH and oxygen in the water, and by increased concentrations of copper at the bottom (Calderoni and Mosello, 1990). Yet, this core section is characterized by high numbers of *D. proteiformis* "rapa" and *D. viscidula,* which are obviously well adapted to this type of environment.

Lake Varese. In the 1950s the watershed of Lake Varese was the site of a dramatic demographic and industrial expansion. The consequent continuous dumping of untreated industrial and domestic sewage directly into the lake increased the phosphorous and nitrogen salt content, which produced an abnormally large biomass of algae. This drastically affected both zooplanktic and zoobenthic populations, which partly disappeared. Populations of these two groups became restricted to shallow water as oxygen concentrations of the hypolimnion became lethal. The lake, already eutrophic before the beginning of the pollution process, eventually became hypereutrophic (Ruggiu et al., 1981), a feature that was reflected in the complete disappearance of benthic organisms in the deepest part of the lake basin (Bonomi, 1962).

Asioli et al. (1996) studied the thecamoebian distribution in an undated 1 m core (Varese 1). They correlated this core with a dated 90 cm core studied by Lami (1986) and used some of Lami's data to interpret the thecamoebian distribution in core Varese 1 (Fig. 5.19). The bottom 60 cm interval of this core is dominated by *Centropyxis* spp. and *C. tricuspis* "parva." According to the correlation with the Lami (1986) core, this section was deposited prior to 1945. The presence of strictly anaerobic sulfur bacteria indicates that, at the time, the lake was already naturally eutrophic (Guilizzoni et al., 1986). As the process of increasing eutrophication continued (60–25 cm), *Centropyxis aculeata* and *Cucurbitella tricuspis* "parva" increased their dominance. When hypereutrophication began (about 25 cm), all thecamoebians decreased in number, except for *Difflugia proteiformis*

"proteiformis." This taxon reached its peak of abundance in the 30 to 20 cm interval. The upper 20 cm of core Varese 1 confirm the final hypereutrophication of the lake with the disappearance of all thecamoebians. From these observations, the authors suggested that *Centropyxis aculeata* spp. and *Cucurbitella tricuspis* "parva" are particularly well adapted to environments with high organic content – thus confirming the ideas of Medioli et al. (1987) and Parenti (1992). They surmised further that *Difflugia proteiformis* "proteiformis" is well adapted to high organic content and/or reducing conditions.

Lake Candia. This lake is located at an altitude of 226 m above mean sea level. It is part of the watershed of the river Dora Baltea and has a maximum depth of about 7 m (Fig. 5.19). The lake is relatively small and eutrophic, rich in littoral vegetation, and densely populated by phyto- and zooplanktic organisms (Guilizzoni et al., 1989; Giussani and Galanti, 1992). It is frozen in January and February and has a very low concentration of oxygen in its hypolimnion (0.5–3.0 mg/l). Thecamoebian assemblages collected from Lake Candia are quite different from those observed in the other two northern Italian lakes. Guilizzoni et al. (1989) reported the presence in the sediment, as well as in the water, of okenone, which is indicative of the presence of H₂S and of anaerobic conditions. These conditions appear to have existed frequently during the past 200 years. The consistent dominance of *Difflugia proteiformis* "proteiformis" from about 90 cm to the top of the core is consistent with the apparent tolerance of this form to high organic content and/or reducing conditions (i.e., oxygen deficiency).

■ English Lake District

Ellison (1995) studied bottom sediments from 33 tarns in the English Lake District and found a relationship between the distribution of thecamoebians and the physico-chemical parameters of the tarn water. Two discrete groups of species were identified: one preferring pH values of <6.2, the other preferring pH values of >6.2. The specific pH proxy values of the taxa discussed in this study are listed in an earlier part of this book. From a 6 m core, the author was able to reconstruct, by means of thecamoebian distribution, the past 11,000 years of paleolimnological history of Ullswater Lake and its uneven increase in acidity.

Ellison also remarked that the genera *Euglypha, Placosista, Hyalosphenia,* and *Cyphoderia,* although sparsely present in the tarns' surficial samples, are not preserved in the core, which confirms similar general observations reported by various authors (Medioli and Scott, 1983, 1988).

OTHER POTENTIAL APPLICATIONS

In cases such as that of the Everglades (Florida), where saltwater invasion has become a hot political issue, the study of shallow cores might help to establish unequivocally the extent of any freshwater body at any given time within the reach of ^{14}C. This could be done accurately in a fraction of the time and at a fraction of the cost required by other techniques such as chemical, sedimentological, or other analyses.

In Venice, where subsidence has become an immensely expensive Europe-wide concern, the combined study of marsh foraminifera and thecamoebians in the numerous cores already collected might clarify a very crucial point that seems to have escaped everybody so far. That is: Has this phenomenon been going on for millennia, as the general instability of the northeastern Italian coast strongly suggests, or did it start only recently (as politicians like to believe) after heavy industrialization of the Marghera area started to overexploit the groundwater and methane pock-

ets? If a long-term process were to be proven, then the many millions of dollars siphoned into engineering studies over the past thirty years would have to be considered a complete waste of resources. If the second case were to be demonstrated, then there might be hope of controlling the subsidence, and further investments of public funds in the project could be justified.

SUMMARY OF KEY POINTS

- Relatively little is known about the distribution patterns of thecamoebians. Consequently, new areas of investigation often require baseline studies. However, their distribution in freshwater environments is widespread and they often provide the only proxy indicator of benthic conditions.
- As in the case of foraminifera, thecamoebians can be employed as environmental indicators in a variety of freshwater and brackish settings because of their universal occurrence and sensitivity to environmental change.

6

Conclusions
and Final Remarks

A glossary and some basic taxonomy on all of the species used in this book have been provided, as an appendix, for those readers who want to go a step further. The bibliography is also in the appendix and includes all the text references as well as those only in the taxonomy section of the appendix; this should provide a good literature base for further study.

A variety of applications have been shown here, such as:

- Climatic (including sea-level)
- Pollution impact, monitoring, mitigation
- Seismic activity "fingerprints"
- Sediment transport phenomena (tracers)
- Storm activity tracers
- Paleoproductivity indicators
- Classification and characterisation of estuaries
- Freshwater–marine transitions

There are also remarks on several other subjects. Biostratigraphy, which is the most widely known of all microfossil applications, has been excluded as it was felt that it has been already documented in great detail elsewhere; the type of applications discussed in this book represent the future of micropaleontology and will likely be the most often used in the coming decades.

It is clear that there are almost as many applications for microfossils as there are environmental problems. The authors have discussed a few examples derived from their own experience, but new types of problems arise almost daily. The readers of this book should consider these examples as just that – examples – whereas the techniques discussed in the book can be applied to any type of problem that may be encountered in aquatic environments. The emphasis throughout this book has been on ease of methods and cost effectiveness, as well as on the quality of data needed to provide reliable results.

Due to space constraint, some of the issues dealt with

in this book may have been oversimplified; this should not cause major problems since exactly the same conditions seldom reoccur. Two crucial points, however, must constantly be kept in mind:

(1) Data must be of good quality and carefully collected.

(2) A moderate amount of experience must be acquired.

The first point can be dealt with readily; all that is required is good working habits. The second point is not so easy to fulfill; it needs patience and time. However, in times varying from two weeks to two months, the authors have repeatedly trained students with no experience to deal with these problems (for example, the pollution of Halifax Harbour) and to produce, with a minimum of supervision, rather elaborate B.Sc. Honour theses. Students from various universities have been trained to identify marsh foraminifera over a two-week period. Hence, although experience is rather essential, it is possible for anyone with a moderate scientific background to acquire the necessary skill set in a relatively short period of time and then proceed to successfully design experiments and surveys that exploit the approaches described in this book.

Appendix

GLOSSARY

The terms, as defined below, refer specifically to how they are used in this book. In a different context, many of the same terms may have different meanings not defined here. For example, **Smearing** means: *"the blurring of a sediment record due to the disruption of the normal layering of a sediment sequence caused by bioturbation."* In the Oxford dictionary it has nine different meanings, ranging from "staining" to "defame," and none of them is the one indicated here. **Evolute** means: *"Tending to uncoil; chambers nonembracing."* The dictionary defines the term as a curve that is the center of curvature of another curve.

Adventitious (refers to foraminifera) Formed under unusual conditions.

Agglutinated *(= arenaceous)* (refers to foraminifera and thecamoebians) Composed of foreign material bound together to form a skeletal covering, as in the tests of some foraminifera and thecamoebians, and the lorica of some tintinnids.

Algal mats Floating masses of filamentous algae. Algal mats are discussed here in relation to lake eutrophication and the distribution of some thecamoebians.

AMOEBA-like graphical representation A graphical technique that can be used to portray changes in the species composition of a foraminiferal assemblage in either a spatial or temporal context. This technique is especially useful for public presentations to a nonscientific audience.

Anaerobic metabolism The metabolism of organisms that are capable of living in the absence of free oxygen.

Anaerobic Refers to environments or conditions characterized by a severe lack of free oxygen.

Anoxia An environmental condition characterized by complete lack of oxygen.

Anthropogenic Caused by human activity.

Aperture (refers to foraminifera and thecamoebians) Opening (or openings) from chamber of test to exterior.

Arenaceous (See *agglutinated*).

Attached (refers to foraminifera) Forms living attached to a substrate are referred to as attached. Usually at least one side of the test is deformed to adapt to the surface of attachment; often the entire test becomes deformed, which has been the cause of much taxonomic confusion.

Autogenous (refers to thecamoebians) Term indicative of a test secreted by the organism (as opposed to exogenous or xenogenous).

Baseline data Data collected prior to impacts or events that occur in the environment being studied. Baseline data are important for the accurate comparison of pre-event and post-event conditions.

Bedload The part of sediment transported by a stream that is moving near the channel bottom.

Benthic Refers to organisms that live on the bottom, either in the ocean or in lakes.

Berger–Soutar Similarity Index One of several kinds of statistical indices that have been used to quantify the degree of similarity between two or more foraminiferal assemblages.

Bifid (refers to foraminifera) Divided into two branches, usually used to describe apertural teeth.

Bilateral symmetry The symmetry of a test in which one side is roughly the mirror image of the other one.

Biodegradable Capable of being rendered harmless upon exposure to the elements and organisms of soil and water.

Bioindicators Species, strains, and morphotypes whose presence in the sediment is indicative of specific conditions, such as the presence of heavy metals, high organic content, low oxygen concentration, etc.

Biologically accommodated types Species that occur within a community mostly as a consequence of the presence of other species, and whose distribution often reflect predator/prey or symbiotic relationships.

Bioturbation The burrowing and disruption of sedimentary deposits by organisms.

Biserial (refers to foraminifera) Having chambers arranged in two rows, usually in a linear fashion.

Biumbonate (refers to foraminifera) Having two raised umbonal bosses (e.g., *Lenticulina).*

Brackish Water with a salinity between that of normal fresh water and normal sea water.

C^{14} A carbon isotope with a half-life of 5,730 years and a dating range of 500–40,000 years.

CCD (= carbonate compensation depth) The depth below which no carbonate in solid form is found. The CCD is controlled by a combination of depth, temperature, salinity, and sometimes organic matter, which may lower the pH with consequent dissolution of carbonates.

Calcareous/arenaceous species ratio The ratio, in terms of total percentages, of calcareous to agglutinated species in a sample. This ratio can supply information about water temperature, pH, $CaCO_3$ availability, etc.

Carina (refers to foraminifera) Keel or flange that occurs around the periphery of some species.

Carinate (refers to foraminifera) Having a carina.

Chamber (refers to foraminifera) Test cavity and its surrounding wall, formed in a single growth stage in multilocular forms. Chambers may be variously shaped and are interconnected by various types of passages.

Ciliates A protozoan with cilia and belonging to the phylum Ciliophora.

Closed boreal forest Closely spaced northern forest trees with rare open bog areas.

Clumped spatial pattern Species occurring in discrete clumps, as opposed to being uniformly dispersed within an environment.

Cluster analysis A multivariate statistical method that is used to quantify relationships between species or samples (i.e., R versus Q mode analysis) used to develop assemblage models.

Coefficient of variation Standard deviation of the mean value of an entity divided by its mean and multiplied by 100%. This statistic can be used to interpret either temporal or spatial variability of a species.

Coil (refers to foraminifera) The type of spiral along which the foraminiferal chambers are arranged (e.g., trochospiral, planispiral, etc.).

Compressed (refers to foraminifera) Refers to the shape of foraminiferal test and often used as "laterally compressed," which means a more or less flattened, pancake-shaped test.

Copepods A small aquatic crustacean of the class Copepoda; copepods are a source of food for many foraminifera species.

Cosmopolitan Distributed in all parts of the world; not restricted to specific areas but not necessarily present everywhere (as opposed to "ubiquitous").

Cyst (for foraminifera) A resistant cover over the entire organism, commonly formed of agglutinated debris, for protection during chamber formation or asexual reproduction. (for thecamoebians) Spherical solid enclosure into which the protoplasm of an organism contracts. Usually the cyst floats in liquid inside the test, but in some cases it can form outside the aperture. Some cysts may give rise to uniflagellate spores which may conjugate. Encystment is used as a mechanism of protection against unfavorable conditions.

Diagenetic processes, or diagenesis All the physical, chemical, and biologic changes undergone by sediment or the skeleton of any organism after its initial deposition, exclusive of weathering and metamorphism.

Diatoms Microscopic unicellular algae with a siliceous cell wall (frustule).

Distal Situated away from the center of the subject under discussion; antonym of proximal.

Diversity Variety of species. In paleoecology, it can be defined as the total number of different species present in a particular area. The term is often defined quantitatively with a variety of mathematical indices.

DOM Dissolved organic matter.

Dormancy The temporary suspension of biological activities; suspended animation.

Dorsal (in foraminifera) Refers to spiral side of test in trochospiral forms where all the chambers can be observed; opposite of ventral.

Ecophenotype A distinct intraspecific morphotype (often going under the names of "forma," "strain," "morph," etc.) for which the environmental causes that induced the different morphology are known.

Encysted   In a cyst stage; or refers to an organism that has formed a cyst.

Endemic   An organism restricted to a particular geographic region or environment.

End member signal   An informal term that refers to an extreme value. Often used to describe an assemblage found under very unstable (e.g., polluted) or very stable (e.g., pristine) conditions.

Environmental indicators   Taxa that are indicative of a specific environment, such as upper estuarine, shelf, etc.

Epifauna   The complex of animals living on the surface of a substrate.

Epiphytic   Refers to organisms living on or attached to a plant.

Estuary   The zone of mixing of fresh and sea water (e.g., the mouths of rivers) where freshwater input is sufficient to lower salinity below oceanic values.

Eurythermal   An organism with a wide range of tolerance for temperature changes.

Eustatic sea level   A term used to denote actual water level of the ocean; antipathetic to land movements causing "apparent" or relative sea-level changes that are often difficult to distinguish from eustatic changes.

Eutrophic   An environmental condition caused by nutrient overloading by nitrogen, phosphorous, and other plant nutrients. Eutrophication can be caused by natural aging of an aquatic system. More commonly, however, it is caused by increase in nutrients by agricultural runoff or municipal/industrial discharges. Eutrophic environments often experience excessive blooms of algae that prevent light penetration with consequent reduction of the oxygen needed for a healthy system.

Evolute (refers to foraminifera)   Tending to uncoil; chambers nonembracing.

Exogenous   See *xenogenous*.

Eyewall (Refers to hurricanes or typhoons)   The most intense leading edge of a tropical depression where the pressure differential and winds are the highest.

Factor analysis   A multivariate statistical technique that has been used to establish relationships between species identified from a suite of samples and to test assemblage linkages to certain environmental parameters (e.g., water depth, salinity, sediment texture).

Factor score   A statistical value that indicates how strongly a particular species or sample is linked to a factor. Factor score data are often mapped to show the spatial influence of a particular set of physical and chemical characteristics.

Fission   The asexual reproduction of protists by cell division.

Foraminiferal number (FN)   The number of foraminifera tests per cm^3 of wet sediment. Some authors define it as the number of specimens per gram of dried sediment.

Forcing   A factor (or series of factors) that causes an environment to change.

Forma (pl. formae)   A term denoting infrasubspecific rank for those individuals of a species consistently morphologically different from other individuals of the same species. Often the development of the characteristic morphological differences are environmentally controlled and, when the cause is known, formae are considered ecophenotypes.

Fundal (refers to thecamoebians)   Pertaining to the fundus.

Fundus (refers to thecamoebians)   The rounded part of the test roughly opposite the aperture.

Geometric class of individuals per species   Refers to the abundance of individuals per species expressed as a geometric function of their population density (e.g., 2, 4, 8, 16 specimens per species).

Gyttja   Amorphous organic accumulation of sediment at the bottom of temperate lake systems surrounded by forests.

Habitat   The locality (and obviously the set of environmental conditions) in which a plant or an animal lives naturally.

"H" Diversity Index   A statistical index based on the sum of the abundances of species composing a living or total population, where species abundance is defined as the product of the number of specimens and the log of that number. Values of "H" can vary from <0.0 to >1.0, where 0.1 might be indicative of a very low diversity assemblage and 1.5 might reflect a stable, moderately diverse assemblage.

Heterotroph   An organism that obtains its energy by ingesting a variety of organic material, alive or dead; herbivores, carnivores, and scavengers are heterotrophs.

Holocene   The time period from 10,000 years ago to the present; it is usually subdivided into early Holocene (8,000–10,000 yBP), middle Holocene (8,000–4,000 yBP), and late Holocene (0–4,000 yBP).

Holotype   A single specimen designated as the name-bearing type of a species, or the single specimen on which such species was based.

Holotypic morph   A morph with the characteristics of the holotype.

Hyaline (refers to foraminifera)   Glassy, clear, transparent; in this book it refers to the calcareous tests of the foraminiferal superfamily Rotaliidae.

Hypereutrophic   The maximum level of eutrophication; occurs in areas where hydrogen sulphide and other byproducts of microbial metabolism accumulate, and where the addition of inorganic nutrients does not enhance productivity.

Hypersaline   Waters with a salinity greater than normal sea water.

Hypertrophic   Abnormal increase in size or overdevelopment of one part of the body; in the case of this book, generally caused by some environmental stresses.

Hypolimnion   The water of the deepest part of a lake, below the mixed upper layer of relatively constant temperature.

Hyposaline   Water with a salinity considerably lower than normal sea water.

Hypoxia   See *anoxia*.

Idiosomes (refers to thecamoebians)   Secreted particles (vermicular, or in the form of more or less regular plates) forming the test of autogenous thecamoebians.

Imperforate (refers to foraminifera) Without pores; sometimes used for porcellaneous tests (e.g., Miliolids) and in describing ornamentation of normally perforate forms.

Infauna The complex of animals living within the sediment.

Inner linings (refers to foraminifera) An organic, inner layer present in many foraminifera tests. The inner lining is the base of agglutinated or calcareous tests.

Involute (refers to foraminifera) Strongly overlapping; in enrolled forms, later whorls completely enclosing earlier ones.

Ka 1,000 years.

Keel (refers to foraminifera) A synonym of carina.

Lacustrine Of or relating to lakes.

Lagoon A body of salt water separated from the sea by a barrier; usually characterized by anomalous salinity.

Latitudinal gradient Usually refers to species or assemblage changes that vary in a north-to-south direction and indicative of changes per degree of latitude.

Lc 50 results Refers to the time interval needed for 50% of a sample of living organisms to die as a consequence of being exposed to a specific chemical or physical condition (e.g., oxygen concentration).

Lenticular (refers to foraminifera or thecamoebians) Lens-shaped.

Lorica The "test" of Tintinnids; also used by some authors to describe the test of thecamoebians.

Macrofauna Animals >1,000 microns in length.

Marsh (salt) See *salt marsh.*

Megalospheric test (refers to foraminifera) Foraminiferal test having large first chamber, commonly representing asexual generation. The root *megalo-* refers to the first chamber; in fact, the adult test is smaller than its microspheric counterpart. (See *microspheric test.*)

Meiofauna Animals from 50 microns to 1,000 microns in diameter; foraminifera are an important component of this group.

Microfauna Animals 10 to 50 microns in diameter. In this book, the term is used informally to include all microscopic organisms.

Microhabitat A small habitat within a larger one. The existence of a microhabitat is controlled by any number of small-scale environmental variables.

Microspheric test (refers to foraminifera) A foraminiferal test with a small proloculus formed by the fusion of gametes during sexual reproduction. The root *micro-* refers to the first chamber; in fact, the adult test is larger than its megalospheric counterpart. (See *megalospheric test.*)

Mid-Holocene hypsithermal The mid-Holocene interval that was warmer and wetter than present.

Modal (interseasonal) A term sometimes used to describe those species of a foraminiferal population that are observed most often throughout the year. These taxa usually form the "core assemblage" of a living population.

Modal contamination pathways A term used to describe how contaminants move through an environmental system, such as an estuary, under normal circumstances. The modal pathway may have both physical (e.g., river runoff) and biological (e.g., food web) elements.

Modal diameter The diameter represented by the largest number of grains in a grain size distribution plot.

Morph A term informally used as a synonym of "forma" and referring to different morphologies within the same species.

Morphotype A term used as a synonym of "forma," "strain," and "morph."

MPS (maximum projection sphericity) A cross-sectional area calculation that was used by Snyder et al. (1990) in their estimate of the traction velocity of certain foraminiferal species. They used this technique to distinguish between in situ and allocthonous foraminiferal assemblages as part of a sediment transport study.

Multiple fission See *fission.*

Niche All the ecologic factors affecting or potentially affecting a single species or group of species. Often discussed in terms of a "species" niche.

Nomen nudum A species name introduced in the literature without an original description; it is invalid.

OC Organic carbon as opposed to total carbon.

Okenone an organic compound indicative of the presence of H_2S and of anaerobic conditions.

Oligotrophic Parts of the ocean or a lake characterized by a low nutrient level.

OM Organic matter. (See also *OC.*)

Open tundra Subpolar and polar regions containing open vegetation, with few or no trees. The open tundra is generally frozen in the winter and boggy and wet in the summer; it is also frequently associated with permafrost.

Opportunist species Species that usually are the first colonizers of a new environment because either of their rapid dispersal, their tolerance to stressed conditions unfavorable to other species, or their ability to use a broad range of food types.

Organic matter flux In this book, it represents the rate of organic carbon transport to the seafloor from the water column per unit area and per unit time.

Paleoecology The study of ancient environments; paleoecology deals with the relationships between ancient organisms and their environment and with one another.

Paleoenvironment An ancient environment.

Pb^{210} A lead isotope used for dating recent events; Pb^{210} dating range is 1–100 yBP.

Peat An organic deposit formed from dense vegetation such as occurs in marshes or bogs. A strict biologic classification puts limits on the percentage of organic matter a deposit must have to qualify as "peat." In this book, the term is often used informally to refer to highly organic salt marsh deposits although, according to our classification, they do not always qualify as "peat."

Pelagic Living in the water column, as opposed to living on the seafloor.

Perforate (refers to foraminifera) The term refers to walls of test pierced by numerous pores that are distinct from apertures, foramina, and canals; characteristic of calcareous hyaline tests, although some other test types may exhibit it.

pH The negative logarithm of the hydronium ion concentration, and a measure of the acidity or alkalinity of a liquid. Values of less than 7 indicate acidity, while values of more than 7 indicate alkalinity.

Physically dominated species   Those species whose distribution is largely controlled by physical parameters rather than by more subtle biological ones, such as competition, symbiosis, and predation. Most species thought of as physically dominated are those living in areas of low diversity and high stress, such as marshes or contaminated marine environments.

Phytodetritus   The detritus produced by phytoplankton.

Phytoplankton   Mostly planktic, photosynthetic protists.

Phytoplankton blooms   The blooming of phytoplankton as a consequence of high-nutrient conditions. Blooms can be caused by eutrophic conditions but can also occur naturally in spring and fall when nutrients are highest and there is sufficient sunlight.

Planispiral (refers to foraminifera)   Test coiled in a single plane.

Planktic   Refers to organisms that float in open waters. (See *pelagic.*) The term is used mainly for foraminifera and is synonymous with the more widely used term "planktonic."

Plankton   Organisms that live in the open waters of the ocean or a lake and that are usually moved by water currents rather than by self-locomotion.

Planoconvex (refers to foraminifera)   Test flat on one side and convex on the other, thus resulting in a roughly hemispherical overall appearance.

Pollution forcing   An environmental change caused by contamination.

Polychaete worms   A common taxon of marine annelid worms often used as pollution-impact indicators.

Porcelaneous (refers to foraminifera)   Having a calcareous, white, shiny, and commonly imperforate wall resembling porcelain in surface appearance. Porcellaneous tests may include extraneous material incorporated in the wall structure. Although some porcellaneous genera, such as *Pyrgo,* are adapted to live below the CCD, this type of wall is more prone to dissolution than all other the calcareous wall types.

Postglacial crustal rebound   Vertical crustal uplift caused by the removal of the ice load after deglaciation. This vertical movement is very slow and continues today in deglaciated areas. Along the eastern shore of Hudson Bay, the uplift, as of now, seems to be several hundred meters above sea level.

Primary producers   Photosynthetic organisms that are capable of converting light energy into organic matter.

Primary productivity   The amount of organic material synthesized by organisms using photosynthesis in a specified volume of water.

Proximal   Situated close to the subject under discussion (antonym of distal).

Proxy   A tool (either fossil or chemical) from which paleoenvironmental conditions can be inferred in the absence of actual measurements.

Pseudochitin (refers to foraminifera)   Chitin-like proteinaceous material that makes up some protozoan tests; similar to keratin in that it contains sulfur but including inframicroscopic granules of opaline silica.

Quinqueloculine pattern (refers to foraminifera)   A test with chambers coiled 72° apart so that characteristically four chambers are visible from one side and three from the other.

Relative sea level   Sea level measured relative to the land. Relative sea level combines both water and land vertical movements; neither component can be measured independently using a sea-level proxy.

Remediation   Actions taken to bring an environment back to its natural state.

Rhizopoda (= the informal term Rhizopods)   A superclass of naked or shelled unicellular organisms of the phylum Sarcodaria; the superclass includes the order Foraminiferida and the Thecamoebians (orders Thecolobosa and Testaceofilosa).

Salt marsh   A coastal area developed in the upper half of the tidal range, between higher high water and mean sea level in protected coastal locations. Salt marshes are vegetated by a group of salt-resistant plants often distributed in vertical zones corresponding to tidal levels.

Serial baseline data set (see also *baseline data*)   Data collected over a time interval to provide a reference measurement of temporal variation.

Smearing   In this book, the term signifies the blurring of a sediment record due to the disruption (mixing) of the normal layering of a sediment sequence caused by bioturbation. Smearing can decrease the time resolution that the record would otherwise provide.

Spiral side (refers to foraminifera)   Part of test where all whorls are visible (e.g., trochospiral forms); also commonly called the dorsal side.

SEM   Scanning electron microscope.

SPM   Suspended particulate matter, often an index of turbidity in coastal environments.

Stenothermal   An organism with a narrow range of tolerance for temperature changes.

Strain   A population of genetically identical cells derived from a single cell. While individuals of the same strain tend to be morphologically identical, they may differ substantially from other strains of the same species.

Suture (refers to foraminifera)   Line of union between two chambers or between two whorls (spiral suture).

Swarmers (refers to foraminifera)   A noncommittal term to designate what are presumed to be gametes emitted by foraminifera during sexual reproduction.

Symbiont   An organism that derives benefits from and provides benefits to another organism, without harm to either one.

Symbiosis   A life association mutually beneficial to both organisms; in foraminifers it commonly refers to green or blue green algae or yellow cryptomonads.

Synonym   Each of two or more scientific names of the same taxonomic rank used to denote the same taxon.

Synonymy   (1) The relationship between synonyms. (2) A list of synonyms.

Synoptic spatial distribution   The pattern of spatial distribution at an instant in time.

Taphonomy The branch of paleontology concerned with the death, burial, and fossilization of organisms.

Tarn A small mountain lake, associated with alpine glaciers.

Taxon (pl. taxa) Any taxonomic unit, whether named or not; a taxon includes its subordinate taxa and individuals.

Taxonomy The science of the classification of living and extinct organisms, governed by the International Code of Zoological (and Botanical) Nomenclature (ICZN).

Terrigenous Land-derived material, such as a sediment that comes from land.

Testate Rhizopods Rhizopods with a test.

Test deformation parameter A parameter referring to percentages of deformed foraminifera in a sediment sample; the parameter can sometimes be related to certain types of pollution.

Thermocline A relatively thin zone lying beneath the surface zone; the thermocline is characterized by a marked change in water temperature per unit of depth.

Thermophilous Refers to organisms that can survive relatively high temperatures.

TOC Total organic carbon. (See *OC*.)

Tooth (refers to foraminifera) Projection in the aperture of a test; may be simple or complex, single or multiple.

Triserial (refers to foraminifera) Chambers arranged in three columns; high trochospiral with three chambers in each whorl.

Trochospiral (refers to foraminifera) Chambers, evolute on one side of test, involute on the opposite side.

Trophic position The level at which an organism lives in the food chain.

T/S pattern Temperature/salinity pattern.

T/S variations Temperature/salinity variations.

Tuberculate (refers to foraminifera) Covered with tubercles or small rounded projections.

Turbidity maximum A zone in an estuary where the turbidity of the water is at a maximum due to intense mixing at the fresh/saltwater interface.

Turbidity zone The area defined by the presence of the turbidity maximum; it varies in size depending on the balance between fresh- and saltwater input.

Type species The species on which a genus is based; the typical species for the genus.

Ubiquitous Present everywhere pervasively; as opposed to "cosmopolitan."

Umbilicus (pl. umbilici) (refers to foraminifera) More or less wide depression formed between inner margins of umbilical walls of chambers belonging to same whorl; may be restricted by other structures.

Unilocular Monothalamous, single-chambered.

Uniserial (refers to foraminifera) Chambers arranged in one single column.

Ventral (refers to foraminifera) Pertaining to the underside of the test – commonly the umbilical side; opposite of dorsal – commonly the apertural side.

WBCU Western Boundary Contour Undercurrent; a current that occurs in the western North Atlantic at depths of 2,000–3,000 m.

Winnowing Erosion that leaves a layer of relatively larger particles on the sediment surface.

Xenogenous (refers to thecamoebians) Test formed of cemented foreign particles (xenosomes).

Xenosomes (refers to thecamoebians) Foreign particles of various nature (usually mineral grains, diatom frustules, etc.) cemented together to form a test.

Younger Dryas A cold period that occurred 11,000 to 10,000 yBP (radiocarbon years) after a slight warming at 13,000 to 11,000 yBP.

Zoochorelles Symbiotic green algae living in the digestive system of some animals.

Zooplankton Nonphotosynthetic organisms that live in the water column.

Zygote Result of fusion of two gametes in process of sexual reproduction; zygote (diploid) containing twice as many chromosomes as each gamete (haploid).

TAXONOMIC LIST OF SPECIES

This is a synopsis of essential information for the identification and ecological interpretation of benthic foraminifera and thecamoebians mentioned or occurring in figures in this book. The suprageneric classification of the foraminifera follows that of Loeblich and Tappan (1964, 1988); the suprageneric classification of the thecamoebians follows that of Medioli and Scott (1983) and Medioli et al. (1987). Genera, and species within genera, are listed in alphabetical order. Each synonym includes the original reference, some generic changes for some species, and references to papers discussed in the text of the book. References cited in this synopsis, if they are not already in the main bibliography, are listed at the end of this section.

This synopsis is intended to be used, in combination with the figures of the plates, for initial assessment. For accurate identifications, readers should make use of the sources cited – if possible, the original one.

Because literature on thecamoebians is substantially scarcer and harder to find than for foraminifera, the authors decided to supply proportionally more detailed information than was supplied for foraminifera; this required a discrete change in style. Since the dimensions of thecamoebians vary exceedingly from population to population and even within the same population, it was decided to supply, when available, the most common approximate dimensions, with the caveat that substantial departures from such values must be expected. Consequently, no specific dimensions are given in the tables and figures.

Benthic foraminifera

Adercotryma glomerata (Brady)

Plate I, Figs. 1a,b

Lituola glomerata Brady, 1878, p. 433, pl. 20, figs. 1a–c.

Adercotryma glomerata (Brady). Barker, 1960, pl. 34, figs. 15–18; Williamson et al., 1984, p. 224, pl. 1, fig. 1.

Remarks: Test agglutinated and irregularly coiled with elongated chambers. This species characterizes many types of estuarine as well as shelf environments; it is also is one of the dominant forms in the deepest part of the ocean. This species appears to be common only in areas where there is no competition from calcareous species – i.e. below the carbonate compensation depth in the deep sea and in the cold, reduced-salinity environments seen in polar regions; it also characterizes deep estuarine areas where salinity is relatively stable but slightly lowered, and where high organic matter concentrations lower the pH of the sediments, reducing or eliminating the presence of calcareous species.

Ammoastuta inepta (Cushman and McCulloch)

Plate I, Figs. 2a,b

Ammobaculites ineptus Cushman and McCulloch, 1939, p. 89, pl. 7, fig. 6.
Ammoastuta salsa Cushman and Brönnimann, 1948a, p. 17, pl. 3, figs. 14–16.
Ammoastuta inepta (Cushman and McCulloch). Parker et al., 1953, p. 4, pl. 1, fig. 12; Phleger, 1954, p. 633, pl. 1, figs. 1–3; Scott et al., 1991, p. 384, pl. 1, fig. 15.

Remarks: Test finely agglutinated, probably initially coiled, then with rapidly broadening chambers in curved semi-enrolled series; main aperture – seldom visible – a slit at center of terminal face; secondary apertures – in the form of perforation at lower end of final chamber. The latter differentiate this species from the superficially similar *Ammotium*-like species. This species lives only in very brackish marshes, sometimes fresh water, and only in warmer climates; the authors did not find it north of Chesapeake Bay on the Atlantic coast of North America.

Ammobaculites dilatatus Cushman and Brönnimann

Plate I, Fig. 3

Ammobaculites dilatatus Cushman and Brönnimann, 1948b, p. 39, pl. 7, figs. 10, 11; Scott et al., 1991, p. 384.
Ammobaculites c. f. *foliaceus* (Brady). Parker, 1952, p. 444, pl. 1, figs. 20, 21.
Ammobaculites foliaceus (Brady). Scott and Medioli, 1980b, p. 35, pl. 1, figs. 6–8.

Remarks: Test agglutinated, initially planispirally coiled, later two to several chambers uniserial with a single terminal aperture. This species lives typically in low marsh and shallow upper estuarine environments where salinities do not exceed 20%. It appears to have a worldwide occurrence.

Ammobaculites exiguus Cushman and Brönnimann

Plate I, Fig. 4

Ammobaculites exiguus Cushman and Brönnimann, 1948b, p. 38, pl. 7, figs. 7, 8; Scott et al., 1991, p. 384; Scott et al., 1995d, p. 292, fig. 6.1.
Ammobaculites dilatatus Cushman and Brönnimann; Scott et al., 1977, p. 1578, pl. 2, fig. 6; Scott and Medioli, 1980b, p. 35, pl. 1, figs. 9, 10.

Remarks: Test agglutinated, initially planispirally coiled, later several chambers uniserial; similar to *A. dilatatus* but much narrower in outline; when broken, it can often be confused with *Ammotium salsum*. Its occurrence is similar to *A. dilatatus*.

Ammonia beccarii (Linné)

Plate 1, Figs. 5a–c

Nautilus beccarii Linné, 1758, p. 710.
Ammonia beccarii (Linné). Brünnich, 1772, p. 232; Scott and Medioli, 1980b, p. 35, pl. 5, figs. 8, 9.

Remarks: Test calcareous, trochospiral; morphologically highly variable, which has led to the erection of a large number of specific and subspecific names. Schnitker (1974) demonstrated, through laboratory cultures, that many of the described forms are ecophenotypic variations of *Ammonia beccarii,* and no attempt is made here to distinguish the various forms described in the literature. This species is very useful because it is one of the few species with some known ecological parameters – i.e., it requires 15–20° C to reproduce (Bradshaw, 1959, 1960; Boltovskoy, 1963).

Ammotium cassis (Parker)

Plate I, Figs. 6a,b

Lituola cassis Parker, in Dawson, 1870, pp. 177, 180, fig. 3.
Haplophragmium cassis (Parker). Brady, 1884, p. 304, pl. 33.
Ammobaculites cassis (Parker). Cushman, 1920, p. 63, pl. 12, fig. 5.
Ammotium cassis (Parker). Loeblich and Tappan, 1953, p. 33, pl. 2, figs. 12–16; Scott et al., 1977, p. 1578, pl. 2, figs. 1, 2; Miller et al., 1982a, p. 2362, pl. 1, fig. 8.

Remarks: Test agglutinated, initially planispirally coiled; later chambers tend to uncoil, forming a wide uniserial pattern with slanting suture lines, aperture terminal and rounded. This estuarine species is indicative of increased levels of suspended particulate matter.

Ammotium salsum (Cushman and Brönnimann)

Plate I, Fig. 7

Ammobaculites salsus Cushman and Brönnimann, 1948a, p. 16, pl. 3, figs. 7–9; Phleger, 1954, p. 635, pl. 1, figs. 7, 8.
Ammotium salsum (Cushman and Brönnimann); Parker and Athearn, 1959, p. 340, pl. 50, figs. 6, 13; Scott et al., 1977, p. 1578, pl. 2, figs. 4, 5; Scott and Medioli, 1980b, p. 35, pl. 1, figs. 11–13; Scott et al., 1991, p. 384, pl. 1, figs. 11–13.

Remarks: Test agglutinated, similar to *A. cassis* but with chambers not as broad. This is an upper estuarine species but, unlike *A. cassis,* it can also be found in lower marsh sediments.

Amphistegina gibbosa d'Orbigny

Plate I, Figs. 8a,b

PLATE I

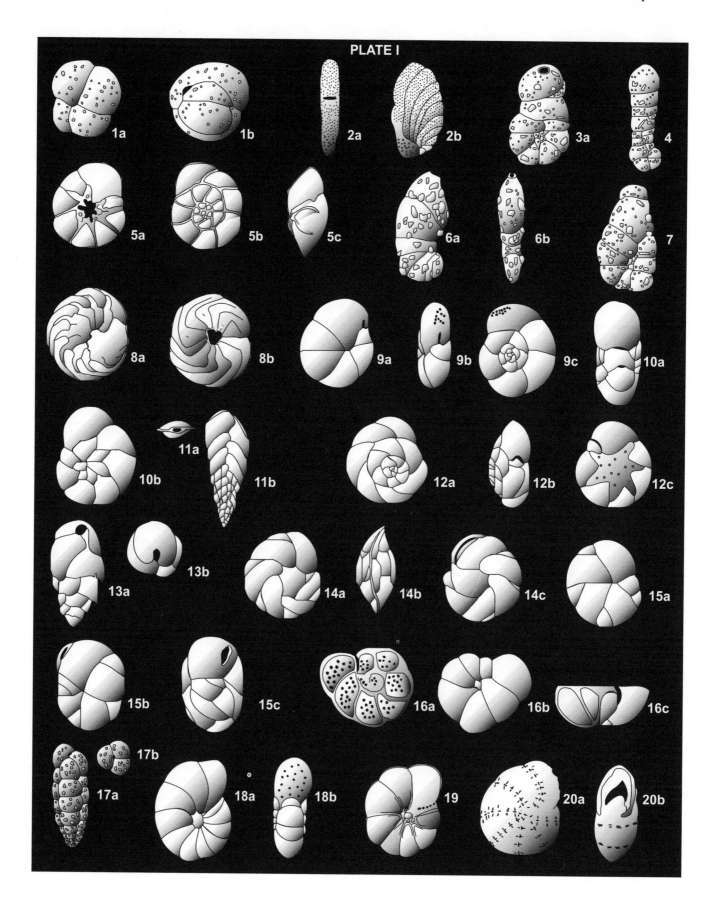

Amphistegina gibbosa   d'Orbigny, 1839a, p. 120, pl. 8, figs. 1–3.

Remarks: Test calcareous, planispiral, often inhabited by symbiotic algae. This species is common in reef environments worldwide and requires warm, high-salinity water.

Arenoparella mexicana   (Kornfeld)

Plate I, Figs. 9a–c

Trochammina inflata (Montagu) var. *mexicana* Kornfeld, 1931, p. 86, pl. 13, fig. 5.

Arenoparella mexicana (Kornfeld). Andersen, 1951, p. 31, fig. 1; Phleger, 1954, p. 636, pl. 1, figs. 12–14; Scott and Medioli, 1980b, p. 35, pl. 4, figs. 8–11; Scott et al., 1990, p. 729, pl. 1, figs. 7a–c; Scott et al., 1991, p. 384, pl. 1, figs. 16, 17.

Remarks: Test agglutinated, trochospiral with supplementary apertures on the apertural face which differentiate the genus from other trochospiral forms. This species is typical of high marsh environments.

Astrononion gallowayi   Loeblich and Tappan

Plate I, Figs. 10a,b

Astrononion gallowayi Loeblich and Tappan, 1953, p. 90, pl. 17, figs. 4–7; Schafer and Cole, 1978, p. 27, pl. 9, fig. 3; Scott et al., 1980, p. 226, pl. 4, fig. 5.

Remarks: Test calcareous, planispiral; the species is easily identified by its star-shaped umbilical area (Greek astron = star). This species is characteristic of polar and temperate inner-shelf and outer estuarine environments.

Brizalina subaenariensis   (Cushman)

Plate I, Figs. 11a,b

Bolivina subaenariensis Cushman, 1922a, p. 46, pl. 7, fig. 6.

Brizalina subaenariensis (Cushman); Williamson et al., 1984, p. 224, pl. 1, fig. 8; Scott, 1987, p. 327, pl. 1, fig. 11.

Remarks: Test calcareous, biserial, much compressed laterally, characterized by ribbing on the lower part of the test. This species appears to live in relatively warm water (>10° C) and is a good indicator of the break between cold-temperate and warm-temperate shelf waters.

Buccella frigida   (Cushman)

Plate I, Figs. 12a–c

Pulvinulina frigida Cushman, 1922b, p. 144.

Eponides frigida (Cushman) var. *calida* Cushman and Cole, 1930, p. 98, pl. 13, figs. 13a–c; Phleger and Walton, 1950, p. 277, pl. 2, fig. 21.

Eponides frigidus (Cushman). Cushman, 1941, p. 37, pl. 9, fig. 16.

Buccella frigida (Cushman). Anderson, 1952, p. 144, figs. 4a–c, 5, 6a–c; Schafer and Cole, 1978, p. 27, pl. 8, figs. 1, 2; Scott et al., 1980, p. 226, pl. 4, figs. 10, 11; Miller et al., 1982a, p. 2364, pl. 2, figs. 9, 10.

Remarks: Test calcareous, trochospiral; granular material on the sutures of the umbilical area distinguishes this species from other similar ones. This species is characteristic of temperate to cold outer estuarine and inner-shelf environments.

Bulimina marginata   d'Orbigny

Plate I, Figs. 13a,b

Bulimina marginata d'Orbigny, 1826, p. 269. pl. 12, figs. 10, 11.

Remarks: Test calcareous, triserial, usually characterized by spines or similar structures hanging down from the sutures. This species is characteristic of upper-slope marine environments, but it can also inhabit low-oxygen deep-shelf environments, such as those off Nova Scotia.

Cassidulina laevigata   d'Orbigny

Plate I, Figs. 14a–c

Cassidulina laevigata d'Orbigny, 1826, p. 282, no. 1, pl. 15, figs. 4, 5; Scott, 1987, p. 327, pl. 2, fig. 10.

Remarks: Test calcareous, hyaline, smooth, lenticular; chambers alternating on each side of its periphery and alternating in regard to their extension either partway or completely to the center, often with a distinct peripheral keel. This species appears to prefer relatively warm water (>12–13° C) in open-shelf environments; it is found only off eastern Canada in warm-water mid-Holocene deposits.

Cassidulina reniforme   Nørvang

Plate I, Figs. 15a–c

Plate I. (1) *Adercotryma glomerata* (Brady): 1a, end view; 1b, lateral view. **(2)** *Ammoastuta inepta* (Cushman and McCulloch): 2a, apertural edge view; 2b, side view; notice the cluster of supplementary apertures at the base of both views. **(3)** *Ammobaculites dilatatus* Cushman and Brönnimann: side view. **(4)** *Ammobaculites exiguus* Cushman and Brönnimann: side view. **(5)** *Ammonia beccarii* (Linné): 5a, umbilical view; 5b, dorsal view; 5c, edge view. **(6)** *Ammotium cassis* (Parker): 6a, side view; 6b, edge view. **(7)** *Ammotium salsum* (Cushman and Brönnimann): side view. **(8)** *Amphistegina gibbosa* d'Orbigny: 8a, dorsal view; 8b, ventral view. **(9)** *Arenoparella mexicana* (Kornfeld): 9a, dorsal view; 9b, apertural view; 9c, ventral view. **(10)** *Astrononion galloway* Loeblich and Tappan: 10a, apertural view; 10b, side view. **(11)** *Brizalina subaenariensis* (Cushman): 11a, side view; 11b, top apertural view. **(12)** *Buccella frigida* (Cushman): 12a, umbilical view; 12b, dorsal view; 12c, apertural view. **(13)** *Bulimina marginata* d'Orbigny: 13a, side view; 13b, apertural view. **(14)** *Cassidulina laevigata* d'Orbigny: 14a, dorsal view; 14b, edge view; 14c, opposite side view. **(15)** *Cassidulina reniforme* Nørvang: 15a, side view; 15b, apertural view; 15c, opposite side view. **(16)** *Cibicides lobatulus* (Walker and Jacob): 16a, flat side view; 16b, edge view; 16c, opposite side view. **(17)** *Eggerella advena* (Cushman): 17a, side view; 17b, apertural view. **(18)** *Elphidium bartletti* Cushman: 18a, side view; 18b, apertural edge view. **(19)** *Elphidium excavatum* (Terquem): 19a, apertural edge view; 19b, side view. **(20)** *Elphidium frigidum* Cushman: 20a, side view; 20b, apertural edge view (aperture broken).

Cassidulina crassa var. *reniforme*   Nørvang, 1945, p. 41, text-figs. 6c–h.

Cassidulina reniforme (Nørvang). Scott, 1987, p. 327, pl. 2, figs. 11, 12.

Remarks: The test arrangement of this species is very similar to that of *C. laevigata* except that the chambers are more inflated and there is no trace of a keel. This species, together with *Elphidium excavatum f. clavata,* is an indicator of "warm" ice margin conditions all over the North Atlantic and North Pacific.

Cibicides lobatulus (Walker and Jacob)

Plate I, Figs. 16a–c

Nautilus lobatulus Walker and Jacob, in Kanmacher, 1798, p. 642, pl. 14, fig. 36.

Truncatulina lobatula (Walker and Jacob). d'Orbigny, 1839a, p. 134, pl. 2, figs. 22–24; Brady, 1884, p. 660, pl. 92, fig. 10, pl. 93, fig. 1; Cushman, 1918, p. 16, pl. 1, fig. 10, p. 60, pl. 17, figs. 1–3.

Cibicides lobatulus (Walker and Jacob). Cushman, 1927b, p. 170, pl. 27, figs. 12, 13; Cushman, 1935, p. 52, pl. 52, figs. 4–6; Parker, 1952, p. 446, pl. 5, fig. 11; Schafer and Cole, 1978, p. 27, pl. 9, figs. 1, 2; Scott et al., 1980, p. 226, pl. 4, figs. 8, 9; Williamson et al., 1984, p. 224, pl. 1, fig. 14.

Remarks: Test attached, calcareous, usually planoconvex, spiral side coarsely perforate and flat to irregular; aperture extending characteristically from convex side along the suture of the first few chambers of the flat side. Like most attached forms, this species, due to the shape of the surface of attachment, exhibits a high degree of variability that often has resulted in taxonomic chaos. This species lives in high-energy nearshore environments, usually attached to rocks or plants.

Eggerella advena (Cushman)

Plate I, Figs. 17a,b

Verneuilina advena Cushman, 1922b, p. 141.

Eggerella advena (Cushman). Cushman, 1937, p. 51, pl. 5, figs. 12–15; Phleger and Walton, 1950, p. 277, pl. 1, figs. 16–18; Scott et al., 1977, p. 1579, pl. 2, fig. 7; Scott and Medioli, 1980b, p. 40, pl. 2, fig. 7; Scott et al., 1991, p. 385, pl. 2, figs. 1, 2.

Remarks: Test finely agglutinated, later chambers triserial, roughly triangular in cross section; aperture a small slightly protruding slit at the base of the last chamber. This species occurs worldwide in outer estuaries and appears to be more tolerant to pollution impacts than most species.

◼ Genus ELPHIDIUM   de Montfort, 1808

The identification of some of the species of the genus *Elphidium,* which is an important genus in defining marginal marine environments. It has been the center of controversy among taxonomists for about a century and, in order to facilitate the comprehension of this thorny issue, what follows is a brief and general description of the genus and what makes the various relevant species and formae unique. Technical descriptive terms are defined in the glossary.

Type species: *Nautilus macellus* var., B Fichtel and Moll, 1798, p. 66; *Elphidium,* de Montfort, 1808, p. 14.

Test lenticular, planispirally coiled, involute to partially evolute, biumbonate, occasionally with umbilical plug on both sides, seven to twenty chambers in the final whorl; the test sometimes displays deeply incised sutures. Surface at times showing a complex ornamentation that varies between species and even within species; periphery carinate; wall calcareous, finely perforate, surface with pores in the plugs and along the sutures; aperture a single or multiple pore. L. Eocene to Recent; cosmopolitan.

Remarks: some of the species included in *Elphidium* in this book have been reported in the literature under *Cribrononion* or *Cribroelphidium,* even by the authors themselves. The typical morphological variability within the genus *Elphidium* is so exceptional that the validity of the other two genera is debatable and, in any case, it is based on internal structures. Consequently, it was decided to group all species under the genus *Elphidium.*

Elphidium bartletti   Cushman

Plate I, Figs. 18a,b

Elphidium bartletti   Cushman, 1933, p. 4, pl. 1, fig. 9; Schafer and Cole, 1978, p. 27, pl. 10, fig. 4.

Cribrononion bartletti (Cushman). Scott et al., 1980, p. 226, pl. 2, fig. 7.

Remarks: This is a calcareous, planispiral species. It appears to be restricted to the North Atlantic in outer estuarine and shelf environments; it is not tolerant to many types of stress.

Elphidium excavatum (Terquem)

Plate I, Figs. 19a,b

Polystomella excavata   Terquem, 1876, p. 429, pl. 2, fig. 2.

Elphidium excavatum (Terquem), formae Miller et al., 1982b, throughout.

Remarks: This calcareous, planispiral species has been one of the most contentious in the history of foraminiferal study and the controversy is still active.

The species is listed here as "*E. excavatum* formae" because it includes several (maybe as many as ten) morphotypes or ecophenotypes that appear as "species" in the literature. Ecophenotypes, while they may have great ecological significance, have little taxonomic value and fall outside of the International Code of Zoological Nomenclature. Consequently, this species is subdivided here into "formae," which are considered to have ecological significance. Consequently, it is extremely useful to keep them separated because they often can provide all the salinity and temperature information needed to study an estuary. For example: *E. excavatum* forma *clavata* occurs by itself in polar regions; *E. excavatum* forma *lideoensis* and several others are found in temperate and subtropical areas. *E. excavatum* forma *clavata,* together with *Cassidulina reniforme,* characterizes "warm" ice margins. *E. excavatum* forma *clavata,* alone, can also be found living on the Scotian Slope in

1,000–2,000 m of water, which suggests its extreme versatility. To be able to make full use of this species "group" as a paleoecological proxy, it would be necessary to peruse the paper by Miller et al. (1982b). For most practical purposes, however, it will suffice to say that, as the water temperature increases, the number of formae increases, and the ornamentation and pore sizes become larger. This group, as a whole, is also tolerant of anthropogenic contamination, but sometimes the specimens occurs only as organic inner linings where the calcite has been dissolved by the low pH.

Elphidium frigidum   Cushman

Plate I, Figs. 20a,b

Elphidium frigidum   Cushman, 1933, p. 5, pl. 1, fig. 3; Schafer and Cole, 1978, p. 27, pl. 10, figs. 2a, b.
Cribrononion frigidum (Cushman). Scott et al., 1980, p. 228, pl. 2, fig. 8.

Remarks: This species, as the name implies, appears to prefer polar waters and is not tolerant to pollution.

Elphidium gunteri   Cole

Plate II, Figs. 1a,b

Elphidium gunteri   Cole, 1931, p. 34, pl. 4, figs. 9, 10; Phleger, 1954, p. 639, pl. 2, figs. 3, 4.
Elphidium excavatum (Terquem), forma *gunteri*   Cole. Scott et al., 1991, p. 385, pl. 2, fig. 15.

Remarks: This species is listed as separate from the other *E. excavatum* formae simply because, in the opinion of the authors, it is the warm-water end of the *E. excavatum* group occurring in subtropical and tropical areas.

Elphidium margaritaceum   Cushman

Plate II, Figs. 2a,b

Elphidium advenum Cushman var. *margaritaceum* Cushman, 1930b, p. 25, pl. 10, fig. 3.
Elphidium margaritaceum   Cushman. Van Voorthuysen, 1957, p. 32, pl. 23, fig. 13.

Remarks: This is another temperate warm-water species of *Elphidium*. It is not part of the *E. excavatum* group, from which it can be separated because it is more ornamented; it seems to be more restricted, but not entirely, to the Mediterranean Sea.

Elphidium poeyanum   (d'Orbigny)

Plate II, Fig. 3

Polystomella poeyana   d'Orbigny, 1839b, p. 55, pl. 6, figs. 25, 26.
Elphidium poeyanum (d'Orbigny). Cushman, 1930b, p. 25, pl. 10, figs. 4, 5; Phleger, 1954, p. 639, pl. 2, figs. 8, 9; Hansen and Lykke-Andersen, 1976, p. 13, pl. 9, figs. 9–12; pl. 10, figs. 1–5.
Elphidium translucens   Natland. Scott, 1976a, p. 170.

Remarks: This species is similar in distribution to *E. margaritaceum* but is different and distinct morphologically (see Pl. II, fig. 3). On the west coast of North America it has been called *E. translucens* Natland.

Elphidium williamsoni   Haynes

Plate II, Fig. 4

Polystomella umbilicatula   Williamson, 1858, p. 42–44, figs. 81, 82.
Elphidium williamsoni   Haynes, 1973, p. 207–9, pl. 24, fig. 7, pl. 25, figs. 6, 9, pl. 27, figs. 1–3.
Cribroelphidium excavatum (Terquem). Scott et al., 1977, p. 1578, pl. 5, fig. 4.
Cribrononion umbilicatulum (Williamson). Scott and Medioli, 1980b, p. 40, pl. 5, fig. 4.
Cribrononion williamsoni (Haynes). Scott et al., 1980, p. 228.

Remarks: As can be seen in the taxonomic list above, there has been confusion with this important intertidal *Elphidium* species in the past. Normally the oldest name would be the correct one, but the oldest name in this case turned out to be a "nomen nudum," which made it invalid, as pointed out by Haynes (1973), and consequently it could be renamed. It is an important temperate intertidal species that often dominates low-marsh-living populations but leaves no fossil record there because it is dissolved in the low pH sediments shortly after it dies.

Epistominella exigua   (Brady)

Plate II, Figs. 5a–c

Pulvinulina exigua Brady, 1884, p. 696, pl. 103, figs. 13, 14.
Epistominella exigua (Brady). Parker, 1954, p. 533; Scott, 1987, p. 327, pl. 2, figs. 8, 9.

Remarks: Test calcareous, trochospiral. This is a deep-water species that sometimes can occur in shelf environments and appears to respond positively to high surface productivity.

Fursenkoina fusiformis   (Williamson)

Plate II, Figs. 6a,b

Bulimina pupoides d'Orbigny var. *fusiformis*   Williamson, 1858, p. 64, pl. 5, figs. 129, 130.
Fursenkoina fusiformis (Williamson). Gregory, 1970, p. 232; Scott et al., 1980, p. 228, pl. 3, figs. 9, 10.

Remarks: Test calcareous, irregularly triserially coiled and usually with a thin, transparent test. This species has been shown by several workers, most notably Alve (1990, 1991), to be the last species that survives in low-oxygen, relatively high-salinity lower estuary conditions – i.e., it tolerates organic matter even better than some of the agglutinated species; this is puzzling considering that low oxygen often means low pH and dissolution of carbonate.

Globobulimina auriculata   (Bailey)

Plate II, Figs. 7a,b

Bulimina auriculata   Bailey, 1851, p. 12, figs. 25–27.
Globobulimina auriculata (Bailey). Schnitker, 1971, p. 202, pl. 5, fig. 6; Williamson et al., 1984, pl. 1, fig. 12.

PLATE II

Remarks: Test calcareous, thin and transparent, irregularly coiled. This species commonly inhabits low-oxygen shelf basins with relatively warm water; it can also live in low-oxygen slope waters; it has been found living infaunally to a depth of a few centimeters.

Haplophragmoides manilaensis Andersen

Plate II, Figs. 8a,b

Haplophragmoides manilaensis Andersen, 1953, p. 22, pl. 4, fig. 8; Scott et al., 1990, p. 730, pl. 1, figs. 9a, b; Scott et al., 1991, p. 385, pl. 1, figs. 18, 19; Scott et al., 1995d, p. 292, pl. 1, figs. 3, 4.

Haplophragmoides bonplandi Todd and Brönnimann, 1957, p. 23, pl. 2, fig. 2. Scott and Medioli, 1980b, p. 40, pl. 2, figs. 4, 5.

Remarks: Test agglutinated, planispirally coiled. This species is characteristic of low-salinity high marsh areas worldwide.

Haynesina depressula (Walker and Jacob)

Plate II, Figs. 9a,b

Nautilus depressulus Walker and Jacob, 1798, p. 641, fig. 33.

Nonionina depressula (Walker and Jacob). Brady, 1884, p. 725, pl. 109, figs. 6, 7.

Nonion depressulus (Walker and Jacob). Murray, 1965, p. 148, pl. 25, figs. 6, 7, pl. 26, figs. 7, 8; Haynes, 1973, p. 209, pl. 22, figs. 8–11, pl. 29, fig. 9, text-fig. 44, no. 1–3.

Protelphidium depressulum (Walker and Jacob). Levy et al., 1969, p. 98; Scott et al., 1979, p. 258, pl. 15, fig. 7.

Haynesina depressula (Walker and Jacob). Banner and Culver, 1978, p. 200, pl. 10, figs. 1–10.

Remarks: Test calcareous, planispirally coiled, moderately compressed, with tubercules developed on the umbilicus and parts of the sutures. This species characterizes intertidal and shallow subtidal environments in warmer subtropical and tropical areas, often occurring with the *Elphidium* species mentioned above. It is distinguished from *Elphidium* by the absence of sutural pores.

Haynesina orbiculare (Brady)

Plate II, Figs. 10a,b

Nonionina orbiculare Brady, 1881, p. 415, pl. 21, fig. 5.

Elphidium orbiculare (Brady). Hessland, 1943, p. 262; Gregory, 1970, p. 228, pl. 14, figs. 5, 6.

Protelphidium orbiculare (Brady). Todd and Low, 1961, p. 20, pl. 2, fig. 11; Scott et al., 1977, p. 1579, pl. 5, figs. 5, 6; Schafer and Cole, 1978, p. 28, pl. 10, fig. 5; Scott and Medioli, 1980b, p. 43, pl. 5, fig. 7.

Haynesina orbiculare (Brady). Scott et al., 1980, p. 226 (note).

Remarks: Morphology very similar to *H. depressula*, from which it differs by being more inflated. This species lives in waters colder than those prefers by *H. depressula*, of which it is possibly a cold-water, low-salinity ecophenotype. The two species are kept separated because there is not sufficient evidence to decide the exact status of *H. orbiculare*. When conditions prevent the secretion of a calcareous test, this species sometimes occurs with a protective arenaceous sheath (illustrated in Scott et al., 1977).

Hemisphaerammina bradyi Loeblich and Tappan

Plate II, Figs. 11a–c

Hemisphaerammina bradyi Loeblich and Tappan, in Loeblich and Collaborators, 1957, p. 224, pl. 72, fig. 2; Scott et al., 1977, p. 1579, pl. 3, figs. 7, 8; Schafer and Cole, 1978, p. 28, pl. 1, fig. 5; Scott and Medioli, 1980b, p. 40, pl. 1, figs. 4, 5.

Remarks: Test unilocular, agglutinated. This species appears to have a distribution similar to that of *A. cassis* but it is less widespread, except when it can live in shallower water. It is often attached, sometimes forming groups of specimens clumped together.

Islandiella teretis (Tappan)

Plate II, Figs. 12a,b

Cassidulina teretis Tappan, 1951, p. 7, pl. 1, figs. 30a–c.

Islandiella teretis (Tappan). Scott, 1987, p. 328, pl. 2, fig. 13.

Remarks: Test calcareous, irregularly coiled planispirally. This species is characteristic of cold (2–4° C), high-salinity water.

■ Genus LAGENA   Walker and Jacob (in Kanmacher)

Plate II, Figs.13a–c

Remarks: A small selection of these calcareous, unilocular species is shown in the plates because the variation within the genus has led to the erection of some highly questionable species. Since, even as a group, these species

---

Plate II. (1) *Elphidium gunteri* Cole: 1a, side view; 1b, opposite side view. (2) *Elphidium margaritaceum* Cushman: 2a, side view; 2b, apertural view. (3) *Elphidium poyeanum* (d'Orbigny): side view. (4) *Elphidium williamsoni* Haynes: side view. (5) *Epistominella exigua* (Brady): 5a, dorsal view; 5b, ventral view; 5c, edge view. (6) *Fursenkoina fusiformis* (Williamson): 6a, side view; 6b, apertural view. (7) *Globobulimina auriculata* (Bailey): 7a, apertural view; 7b, side view. (8) *Haplophragmoides manilensis* Andersen: 8a, apertural view; 8b, side view. (9) *Haynesina depressula* (Walker and Jacob): 9a, side view; 9b, apertural view. (10) *Haynesina orbiculare* (Brady): 10a, side view; 10b, apertural view. (11) *Hemisphaerammina bradyi* Loeblich and Tappan: 11a, dorsal view; 11b, lateral vie; 11c, detail of the attachment structure. (12) *Islandiella teretis* (Tappan): 12a, side view; 12b, apertural view. (13) *Lagena* spp. Walker and Jacob (in Kanmacher): 13a, 13b, 13c, different species of the genus. (14) *Miliammina fusca* (Brady): 14a, side view; 14b, apertural view; 14c, opposite side view. (15) *Nonion barleeanum* (Williamson): 15a, side view; 15b, apertural view. (16) *Nonionella atlantica* Cushman: 16a, side view; 16b, apertural view; 16c, opposite side view. (17) *Nonionellina labradorica* (Dawson): 17a, side view; 17b, apertural view. (18) *Oolina* sp. d'Orbigny: 18a, side view; 18b, apertural view.

often represent less than 1% of the foraminiferal association, it is usually sufficient to just note the presence of the genus. This genus usually occurs in deep water, but in small percentages. It can also occur in deep estuarine and shelf environments.

Miliammina fusca (Brady)

Plate II, Figs. 14a–c

Quinqueloculina fusca Brady, 1870, p. 286, pl. 11, figs. 2, 3.
Miliammina fusca (Brady). Phleger and Walton, 1950, p. 280, pl. 1, figs. 19a, b; Phleger, 1954, p. 642, pl. 2, figs. 22, 23; Scott et al., 1977, p. 1579, pl. 2, figs. 8, 9; Schafer and Cole, 1978, p. 28, pl. 12, fig. 2; Scott and Medioli, 1980b, p. 40, pl. 2, figs. 1–3. Scott et al., 1991, p. 386, pl. 1, fig. 14.

Remarks: Test agglutinated, coiled in a "quinqueloculine" pattern. This species occurs almost worldwide in low-salinity low-marsh and upper estuarine areas.

Nonion barleeanum (Williamson)

Plate II, Figs. 15a,b

Nonionina barleeanum Williamson, 1858, p. 32, pl. 4, figs. 68, 69.
Nonion barleeanum (Williamson). Scott, 1987, p. 328.

Remarks: Test calcareous with large perforations, planispiral throughout, laterally compressed and bilaterally symmetrical. This species is common in outer shelf and bathyal areas. It is reported under several specific names, although it is quite distinctive.

Nonionella atlantica Cushman

Plate II, Figs. 16a–c

Nonionella atlantica Cushman, 1947, p. 90, pl. 20, figs. 4, 5.

Remarks: Test calcareous, slightly compressed in a low trochospire, final chamber extending to cover the umbilicus. The genus differs from *Nonion* for being asymmetrical and trochospiral. This species is common to many polar and subpolar shelf environments in the North Atlantic.

Nonionellina labradorica (Dawson)

Plate II, Figs. 17a,b

Nonionina labradorica Dawson, 1860, p. 191, fig. 4.
Nonionellina labradorica (Dawson). Williamson et al., 1984, p. 224, pl. 1, fig. 11.

Remarks: Test calcareous, in early stages trochospiral, later stages almost planispiral with inflated basal lobes at the umbilical end of the chamber, with a flared last chamber; it differs from *Nonionella* in not having the umbilicus covered by the lobe of the last chamber. This species is an important indicator of warming conditions after the last glaciation in North Atlantic shelf areas.

■ Genus OOLINA d'Orbigny

Plate II, Figs. 18a,b

Remarks: As with *Lagena,* no species are discussed for this diverse, calcareous, unilocular genus because, even as a group, it usually represents extremely low percentages. Its presence, however, may be indicative of more open marine conditions in outer estuarine areas.

Polysaccammina hyperhalina Medioli, Scott, and Petrucci

Plate III, Figs, 1a,b

Reophax sp.   Phleger and Ewing, 1962, pl. 1, fig. 1.
Protoschista findens (Parker). Scott, 1976a, p. 170.
Polysaccammina hyperhalina Medioli, Scott and Petrucci, in Petrucci et al., 1983, p. 72, pls. 1, 2; Scott et al., 1990, p. 731.

Remarks: Test agglutinated, elongated uniserial, aperture simple on top of the last chamber. This species, although not as widely spread, appears to replace *M. fusca* in warmer, higher-salinity marsh–estuarine areas such as California, Mexico, and the Adriatic.

Pseudothurammina limnetis (Scott and Medioli)

Plate III, Fig. 2

Astrammina sphaerica (Heron-Allen and Earland). Zaninetti et al., 1977, pl. 1, fig. 9.
Thurammina (?) limnetis Scott and Medioli, 1980b, p. 43, pl. 1, figs. 1–3.
Pseudothurammina limnetis Scott and others, in Scott et al., 1981, p. 126; Scott et al., 1991, p. 386, pl. 2, fig. 4; Scott et al., 1995d, p. 292, fig. 6.2.

Remarks: Test agglutinated, unilocular with an organic inner lining which makes it comparatively flexible. This species is commonly found in middle marsh sediments, but it does not appear to fossilize well.

Miliolids

Miliolids belong to the suborder Miliolina and have characteristics that make them easily identifiable as members of the suborder. The Miliolina are extremely diverse morphologically, but the following description applies to all of them.

Test calcareous, porcelaneous (= opaque, and massively calcareous), commonly with pseudochitinous lining; may also include some adventitious material in wall (such as sand grains), imperforate in mature stages. The fact that the carbonate of the test is mixed with organics makes it less stable, in terms of dissolution, than the tests of other calcareous foraminifera. Carboniferous–Recent.

Only three species mentioned in this book are miliolids: *Pyrgo williamsoni* (Silvestri), *Quinqueloculina seminulum* (Linné), and *Triloculina oblonga* (Montagu).

Pyrgo williamsoni (Silvestri)

Plate III, Figs. 3a,b

Biloculina williamsoni Silvestri, 1923, p. 73.
Pyrgo williamsoni (Silvestri). Loeblich and Tappan, 1953, p. 48, pl. 6, figs. 1–4.

Remarks: Test imperforate, porcelanous, with chambers opposing each other, so that only two chambers are visible from the outside; aperture terminal with a biphid tooth. *Pyrgo* is generally a deep-sea genus, but it occurs in the Bay of Fundy in a high tidal energy environment.

Quinqueloculina rhodiensis Parker

Plate III, Figs. 5a,b

Quinqueloculina rhodiensis Parker, in Parker et al., 1953, p. 12, pl. 2, figs. 15–17; Seiglie, 1975, p. 484, pl. 3, figs. 4–10.

Remarks: This species is strongly ribbed as opposed to the smooth surface of *Q. seminulum* (below). Seiglie (1975) reported that it is often found deformed in polluted areas in Cuba's coastal zone.

Quinqueloculina seminulum (Linné)

Plate III, Figs. 4a–c

Serpula seminulum Linné, 1758, p. 786.
Quinqueloculina seminulum (Linné). d'Orbigny, 1826, p. 301; Scott et al., 1980, p. 231, pl. 3, figs. 3–5; Scott et al., 1991, p. 386, pl. 2, fig. 16.

Remarks: Test imperforate, porcelanous, with chambers coiled 72° apart, so that characteristically four chambers are visible from one side and three from the other. This very resilient species is found virtually everywhere from marshes to shelf environments.

Reophax arctica Brady

Plate III, Figs. 6a,b

Reophax arctica Brady, 1881, p. 405, pl. 21, fig. 2; Scott et al., 1980, p. 321, pl. 2, fig. 1; Miller et al., 1982a, p. 2362, pl. 1, fig. 6.

Remarks: Test agglutinated, uniserial, elongated and flexible because of an inner organic lining; chambers increasing in size gradually; aperture simple on the top of the last chamber. This species is common in deep estuarine areas, but does not appear to be very resistant to anthropogenic contamination.

Reophax nana Rhumbler

Plate III, Figs. 7a,b

Reophax nana Rhumbler, 1911, p. 182, pl. 8, figs. 6–12; Scott et al., 1977, p. 1579, pl. 3, figs. 1, 2; Schafer and Cole, 1978, p. 29, pl. 2, fig. 4; Scott and Medioli, 1980b, p. 43, pl. 2, fig. 6.

Remarks: Test agglutinated, uniserial, elongated; characteristically, chambers increase in size more rapidly than in *R. arctica;* aperture simple on top of the last chamber. This species occurs over a wide area but appears to be more common in places like southern California.

Reophax scottii Chaster

Plate III, Fig. 8

Reophax scottii Chaster, 1892, p. 57, pl. 1, fig. 1; Miller et al., 1982a, p. 2362, pl. 1., fig. 7.

Remarks: Test agglutinated, uniserial, elongated; usually very thin and with somewhat angular chambers; an inner organic lining makes the test particularly flexible. This species is a good indicator of high organic matter contamination.

Rosalina floridana (Cushman)

Plate III, Figs. 9a–c

Discorbis floridana Cushman, 1922a, p. 39, pl. 5, figs. 11, 12.
Rosalina floridana (Cushman). Schnitker, 1971, p. 210, pl. 5, fig. 19.

Remarks: Test calcareous, planoconvex, attached to the substrate with the ventral side; all chambers visible from the dorsal side, only those of the last whorl visible from the ventral side. This species lives attached in high-energy environments such as tide pools and rocky coasts.

Saccammina difflugiformis (Brady)

Plate III, Fig. 10

Reophax difflugiformis Brady, 1879, p. 51, pl. 4, figs. 3a, b.
Saccammina difflugiformis (Brady). Thomas et al., 1990, p. 234, pl. 2, figs. 10–12.

Remarks: Test agglutinated, unilocular, flask-shaped. This species is common in upper estuarine environments.

Spiroplectammina biformis (Parker and Jones)

Plate III, Figs. 11a,b

Textularia agglutinans (d'Orbigny) var. *biformis* Parker and Jones, 1865, p. 370, pl. 15, figs. 23, 24.
Spiroplectammina biformis (Parker and Jones). Cushman, 1927a, p. 23, pl. 5, fig. 1; Schafer and Cole, 1978, p. 19, pl. 3, fig. 2; Scott et al., 1980, p. 231, pl. 2, fig. 2.

Remarks: Test agglutinated, elongated, early chambers coiled planispirally, later chambers arranged biserially. This species is common in deep estuarine areas and has some tolerance to anthropogenic contamination.

Textularia earlandi Parker

Plate III, Figs. 12a,b

Textularia earlandi Parker, 1952, p. 458 (footnote).

Remarks: Test agglutinated, chambers biserially arranged, laterally compressed; aperture a simple arch at the base of the last chamber. This species is common in most coastal environments, but is usually not a dominant taxon.

Tiphotrocha comprimata (Cushman and Brönnimann)

Plate III, Figs. 13a–c

Trochammina comprimata Cushman and Brönnimann, 1948b, p. 41, pl. 8, figs. 1–3; Phleger, 1954, p. 646, pl. 3, figs. 20, 21.
Tiphotrocha comprimata (Cushman and Brönnimann). Saunders, 1957, p. 11, pl. 4, figs. 1–4; Scott et al., 1977, p. 1579, pl. 4, figs. 3, 4; Scott and Medioli, 1980b, p. 44, pl. 5, figs. 1–3; Scott et al., 1990, pl. 1, figs. 10a, b; Scott et al., 1991, p. 388, pl. 2, figs. 5, 6.

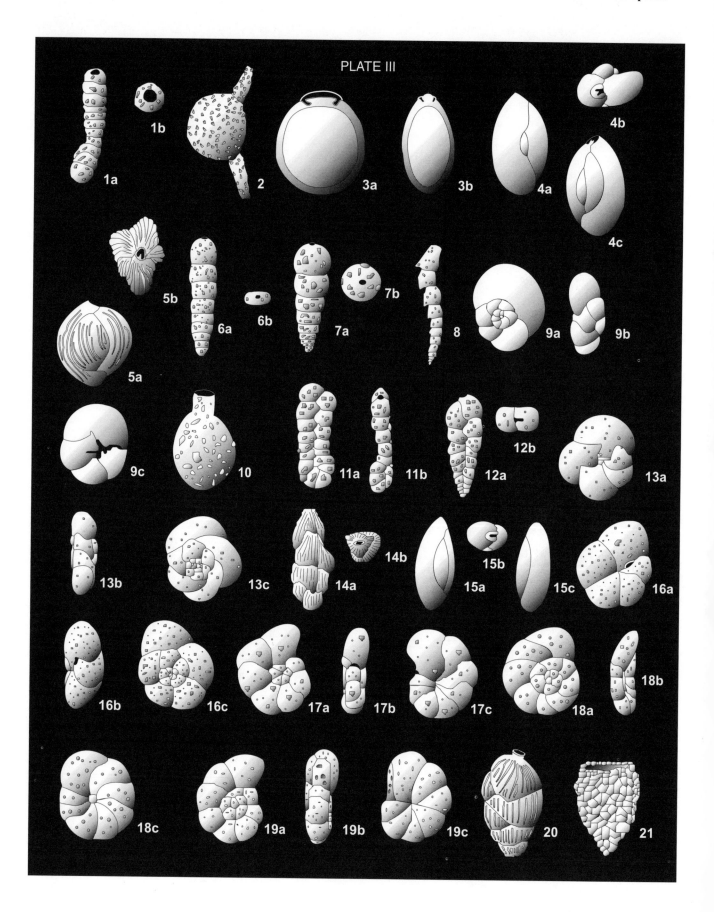

PLATE III

Remarks: Test agglutinated, trochospiral, ventral side somewhat concave. It is distinguished from *Trochammina* by a siphon-like extension to the aperture in the umbilical area. This species is common in middle and high-marsh environments and in brackish areas, except for the Pacific basin.

Trifarina fluens (Todd)

Plate III, Figs. 14a,b

Anglogerina fluens Todd, in Cushman and Todd, 1947, p. 67, pl. 16, figs. 6, 7.

Trifarina fluens (Todd). Scott et al., 1980, p. 231, pl. 4, figs. 12, 13; Scott, 1987, p. 329.

Trifarina angulosa (Williamson). Williamson et al., 1984, pl. 1, fig. 15.

Remarks: Test calcareous, finely perforate, triserial, triangular in cross section, with longitudinal ridges; aperture terminal on a short neck. This species is common in some shelf environments, but is best known for its preference for continental slope environments.

Triloculina oblonga Montagu

Plate III, Figs. 15a–c

Vermiculum oblongum Montagu, 1803, p. 522, pl. 14, fig. 9.

Triloculina oblonga (Montagu). Thomas et al., 1990, p. 240.

Remarks: Test imperforate, porcelanous, with chambers coiled 120° apart so that, characteristically, only three chambers are visible externally; aperture terminal with biphid tooth. This miliolid species is common worldwide in lagoon habitats.

Trochammina inflata (Montagu)

Plate III, Figs. 16a–c

Nautilus inflatus Montagu, 1808, p. 81, pl. 18, fig. 3.

Rotalina inflata Williamson, 1858, p. 50, pl. 4, figs. 93, 94.

Trochammina inflata (Montagu). Parker and Jones, 1859, p. 347. Phleger, 1954, p. 646, pl. 3, figs. 22, 23; Scott et al., 1977, p. 1579, pl. 4, figs. 6, 7; Scott and Medioli, 1980b, p. 44, pl. 3, figs. 12–14, pl. 4, figs. 1–3; Scott et al., 1990, p. 733, pl. 1, figs. 3a, b; Scott et al., 1991, p. 388, pl. 2, figs. 7, 8; Scott et al., 1995d, p. 294, figs. 6.10–6.17.

Remarks: Test agglutinated, trochospiral, chambers rather inflated, increasing in size gradually; aperture a low arch with a bordering lip. This is the type species of the genus *Trochammina*. This is perhaps the best known and most distinctive of all the endemic marsh species, as well as being one of the earliest species ever described. It characterizes high-marsh environments worldwide.

Trochammina macrescens Brady

(forma *macrescens*)

Plate III, Figs. 17a–c

(forma *polystoma*)

Plate III, Figs. 19a–19c

Trochammina inflata (Montagu) var. *macrescens* Brady, 1870, p. 290, pl. 11, fig. 5; Scott, 1976b, p. 320, pl. 1, figs. 4–7; Scott et al., 1977, pl. 4, figs. 6, 7.

Jadammina polystoma Bartenstein and Brand, 1938, p. 381, figs. 1, 2.

Trochammina macrescens Brady. Parker, 1952a, p. 460, pl. 3, fig. 3; Phleger, 1954, p. 646, pl. 3, fig. 24; Scott and Medioli, 1980b, p. 44, pl. 3, figs. 1–12; Scott et al., 1990, p. 733, pl. 1, figs. 1a, b, 2a–c; Scott et al., 1991, p. 388, pl. 2, figs. 10, 11; Scott et al., 1995d, p. 294, figs. 6.6–6.8.

Remarks: This species was first listed as a variety of *T. inflata* – from which it differs in being more compressed – but its distribution tends to be limited to somewhat lower salinity conditions. A high-salinity ecophenotype, *T. polystoma*, often occurs with *T. inflata*. This high-salinity form is sometimes called *Jadammina polystoma*. *T. macrescens* forms, when they occur by themselves in high numbers, generally indicate a very narrow zone near higher high water.

Trochammina ochracea (Williamson)

Plate III, Figs. 18a–c

Rotalina ochracea Williamson, 1858, p. 55, pl. 4, fig. 112, pl. 5, fig. 113.

Trochammina squamata Parker and Jones, 1865, p. 407, pl. 15, figs. 30, 31; Scott and Medioli, 1980b, p. 45, pl. 4, figs. 6, 7.

Trochammina squamata (Parker and Jones, and related species). Parker, 1952, p. 460, pl. 3, fig. 5.

Plate III. (1) *Polysaccammina hyperhalina* Medioli, Scott and Petrucci (In Petrucci et al.): 1a, side view; 1b, apertural view. (2) *Pseudothurammina limnetis* Scott, Medioli and Williamson (in Scott et al.): top view. (3) *Pyrgo Williamsoni* (Silvestri): 3a, 3b, apertural view of different morphotypes of the species. (4) *Quinqueloculina seminulum* (Linné): 4a, 3 chambers side view; 4b, apertural view; 4c, 4 chambers side view. (5) *Quinqueloculina rhodiensis* Parker (in Parker et al.): 5a, 4 chamber side, 5b, apertural view. (6) *Reophax arctica* Brady: 6a, side view; 6b, apertural view. (7) *Reophax nana* Rhumbler: 7a, side view; 7b, apertural view. (8) *Reophax scottii* Chaster: side view. (9) *Rosalina floridana* (Cushman): 9a, dorsal view; 9b, edge view; 9c, ventral view. (10) *Saccammina difflugiformis* (Brady): side view. (11) *Spiroplectammina biformis* (Parker and Jones): 11a, side view; 11b, edge view. (12) *Textularia earlandi* Parker: 12a, side view; 12b, apertural view. (13) *Tiphotrocha comprimata* (Cushman and Brönnimann): 13a, ventral view; 13b, edge view; 13c, dorsal view. (14) *Trifarina fluens* (Todd): 14a, side view; 14b, apertural view. (15) *Triloculina oblonga* Montagu: 15a, 3 chambers side view; 15b, apertural view; 15c, 2 chambers side view. (16) *Trochammina inflata* (Montagu): 16a, ventral view; 16b, edge view; 16c, dorsal view. (17) *Trochammina macrescens* Brady (forma *macrescens*): 17a, dorsal view; 17b, apertural edge view; 17c, ventral view. (18) *Trochammina ochracea* (Williamson): 18a, dorsal view; 18b, edge view; 18c, ventral view. (19) *Trochammina macrescens* Brady (forma *polystoma*): 19a, dorsal view; 19b, edge view; 19c, ventral view. (20) *Uvigerina peregrina* Cushman: side view. (21) *Tintinnopsis rioplatensis* Souto: side view.

Trochammina ochracea (Williamson). Cushman, 1920, p. 75, pl. 15, fig. 3; Scott and Medioli, 1980b, p. 45, pl. 4, figs. 4, 5.

Remarks: *T. ochracea* is distinguished from the previous two species of *Trochammina* by being very flat and concave ventrally. The distribution of this species is very hard to define because it shows up in some very strange places, such as high marsh areas in Tierra del Fuego and Alaska, as well as in upper estuarine areas in Nova Scotia and most oddly in the reefs of Bermuda (Javaux, 1999). This species is believed to be opportunistic.

Uvigerina peregrina   Cushman

Plate III, Fig. 20

Uvigerina peregrina   Cushman, 1923, p. 166, pl. 42, figs. 7–10.

Remarks: Test calcareous, elongate, triserial, rounded in cross section, with strong ribbing and a stalked aperture. This species occurs as a low-oxygen indicator in both shelf and slope areas.

Tintinnids

Although in some cases Tintinnids may occur together with foraminifera and thecamoebians, they are ciliate protozoans. Their exact taxonomic position is subphylum Ciliophora, class Ciliata, while thecamoebians and foraminifera belong to the phylum Sarcodaria, superclass Rhizopoda.

Tintinnids are the only ciliates with a long fossil record.

Tintinnopsis rioplatensis   Souto

Plate III, Fig. 21

Tintinnopsis rioplatensis   Souto, 1973, p. 251, figs. 5–8.
Difflugia bacillariarum   Perty. Medioli and Scott, 1983, p. 20, pl. 5, figs. 16–19, pl. 6, figs. 1–4.

Remarks: *Tintinnopsis* is characterized by a cup-shaped lorica (test) made of xenosomes and is more or less pointed at the bottom, aperture simple and large. This tintinnid taxon occurred with foraminifera in some samples and, being pelagic, proved to be an excellent indicator of high amounts of suspended particulate matter. Medioli and Scott (1983) misidentified specimens of this species – from the Hudson Bay Lowland – as a thecamoebian. Later, after finding it in marine environments, they recognized its correct taxonomic position.

Thecamoebians

■ Genus *Amphitrema*   Archer

Plate IV, Figs. 1a,b

(Pleistocene–Recent)

Type species: *Amphitrema wrightianum*   Archer, 1869.
Definition: Test organic, occasionally including foreign material, transparent, and, when empty, usually light brown, shaped like a hot-water bottle, more or less enlarged and laterally compressed. Apertures on a short collar at both ends of the test.

Approximate length: 50–100 microns.
Habitat: Freshwater.

Tests of *Amphitrema* can survive the HFl treatment used for the preparation of pollen samples.

■ Genus *Arcella*   Ehrenberg

Plate IV, Figs. 3a,b, 4a,b

(Pleistocene–Recent)

Type species: *Arcella vulgaris* Ehrenberg, 1832.
Definition: Test proteinaceous (= organic); in fundal and oral view roughly subcircular, in lateral view beret-shaped with many variations (from hemispherical to polygonal). Surface smooth or punctate. Aperture ventral and subcentral, subcircular and invaginated.
Approximate diameter: 20–200 microns.
Habitat: Fresh or slightly brackish water.

■ Genus *Archerella*   Loeblich and Tappan

Plate IV, Figs. 2a,b

(Pleistocene–Recent)

Type species: *Ditrema flavum*   Archer, 1877.
Definition: Test organic, thick-walled, does not incorporate foreign material; elongate ovoid. Apertures without a collar at both ends of the test.
Approximate length: 40–80 microns.
Habitat: Sphagnum bogs.

Tests of *Archerella* can survive the HFl treatment used for the preparation of pollen samples.

■ Genus *Bullinularia*   (Penard) in Grassé

Plate IV, Fig. 5

(Recent)

Type species: *Bullinella indica* Penard, 1907
Definition: Test formed by a proteinaceous (= organic) base, usually coated with fine xenosomes; from planoconvex to concavoconvex, elliptical in fundus view. The aperture consists of an elongate, eccentric slit; the upper lip is perforate and overlaps the smooth lower lip.
Approximate diameter: 150–200 microns.
Habitat: Wet moss. Relatively common in proximal sediment in arctic fjords, probably reworked from the original habitat.
Approximate length: 40–80 microns.
Habitat: Freshwater.

■ Genus *Centropyxis*   Stein

Plate IV, Figs. 6, 7

(Miocene–Recent)

Type species: *Arcella aculeata*   Ehrenberg, 1830.
Definition: Test from discoid (anterior angle of about 15°) to oval with flattened apertural side (anterior angle of about 60°) through a series of forms with increasingly higher anterior angle. The forms having a high anterior

angle develop a backward-leaning appearance somewhat similar to that of the terrestrial gastropod *Helix*. This characteristic at first sight differentiates these forms from *Difflugia* with which they have often been confused. Peripheral spine may or may not be present; their presence and number may vary even within the same clone. Aperture variable in outline, from irregularly rounded to polyradiate, invaginated, usually in an anterior ventral position.

Approximate diameter: 100–400 microns.
Habitat: Fresh or slightly brackish water.

Centropyxis aculeata (Ehrenberg)

Plate IV, Figs 6a,b

Arcella aculeata Ehrenberg, 1832 (ab Ehrenberg, 1830, p. 60, *nomen nudum*), p. 91.
Centropyxis excentricus (Cushman and Brönnimann). Scott, 1976b, p. 320, pl. 1, figs. 1, 2; Scott et al., 1977, p. 1578, pl. 1, figs. 1, 2; Scott et al., 1980, p. 224, pl. 1, figs. 1–3.
Centropyxis aculeata (Ehrenberg). Stein, 1859, p. 43; Medioli and Scott, 1983, p. 39, pl. 7, figs. 10–19; Scott and Medioli, 1983, p. 819, fig. 9I; Patterson et al., 1985, p. 134, pl. 4, figs. 1–7; Scott et al., 1991, p. 384, pl. 1, figs. 7–9.

Description: Test depressed; although quite variable it can be described as beret-shaped; in dorsal view, usually large and more or less circular; anterior sloping at 15° to 40°; posterior slope more pronounced; height: length ratio usually low (mostly 0.4 to 0.5). Aperture subcentral, usually slightly anterior, invaginated. Spines not always present; when present, mostly concentrated along the posterior margin. Test basically organic, mature specimens usually covered with somewhat loose, amorphous, siliceous particles, in most cases completely covering the membrane.

Approximate diameter: 100–300 microns.
Habitat: Fresh or slightly brackish water.

Centropyxis constricta (Ehrenberg)

Plate IV, Figs. 7a,b

Arcella constricta Ehrenberg, 1843, p. 410, pl. 4, fig. 35, pl. 5, fig. 1.
Difflugia constricta (Ehrenberg). Leidy, 1879, p. 120, pl. 18, figs. 8–55.
Urnulina compressa Cushman, 1930a, p. 15, pl. 1, fig. 2; Parker, 1952, p. 460, pl. 1, fig. 9; Scott et al., 1977, p. 1578, pl., figs. 7, 8; Scott et al., 1980, p. 224, pl. 1, figs. 13–15.
Centropyxis constricta (Ehrenberg). Deflandre, 1929, p. 340, text-figs. 6–67; Medioli and Scott, 1983, p. 41, pl. 7, figs. 1–9; Scott and Medioli, 1983, p. 819, fig. 9K; Patterson et al., 1985, p. 134, pl. 4, figs. 8–14; Scott et al., 1991, p. 384, pl. 1, fig. 4.

Description: Test much less depressed than in *C. aculeata* and usually elliptical in dorsal view, with a profile usually raised posteriorly. Anterior angle 40° to 65°. Fundus raised in uppermost position. Ventral side often relatively small, with invaginated aperture in anteromarginal position.

Height/length ratio is typically high (usually 0.5 to 1.1). The fundus often carries two or more spires, as is common in most forms of Centropyxis. Test largely organic, often completely covered with mineral particles of various nature.

Approximate length: 100–400 microns.
Habitat: Fresh or slightly brackish water.

■ Genus *Corythion* Taránek

Plate IV, Figs. 8a,b

(Pleistocene–Recent)

Type species: *Corythion dubium* Taránek, 1882.
Definition: Test formed by irregularly overlapping – or not overlapping at all – oval siliceous idiosomes; small, transparent; pear-shaped with apertural side flattened. Aperture rounded, slightly invaginated, in eccentric position at the periphery of the apertural side, and formed of strongly denticulate idiosomes.

Differs from *Trinema* in having oval, instead of round, idiosomes, in the irregular or absent overlapping of the plates, and for the more marked denticulation of the aperture.

Approximate length: 15–45 microns.
Habitat: Freshwater.

■ Genus *Cucurbitella* Penard

Plate IV, Figs. 9a–f

(Recent)

Type species: *Cucurbitella mespiliformis* Penard, 1902.
Definition: Test subspherical to ovate, either autogenous or largely xenogenous with organic or mineral xenosomes. Aperture from irregularly subcircular to regularly lobate and denticulate, often surrounded by a more or less complicated organic collar.

Cucurbitella tricuspis (Carter)

Plate IV, Figs. 9a–f

Difflugia tricuspis Carter, 1856, p. 221, pl. 7, fig. 80. Medioli and Scott, 1983, p. 28, pl. 4, figs. 5–19; Scott and Medioli, 1983, p. 818, fig. 9Q,R; Patterson et al., 1985, p. 134, pl. 2, figs. 15, 16; Haman, 1986, p. 47, pl. 1, figs. 1–14, pl. 2, figs. 1–12.
Cucurbitella tricuspis (Carter). Medioli et al., 1987, p. 42, pl. 1, figs. 1–10, pl. 2, figs. 1–10, pl. 3, figs. 1–7, pl. 4, figs. 1–9.

Description: Test subspherical to ovate, either autogenous with "cauliflower" or "root-like" microstructures, or largely xenogenous with organic or mineral xenosomes (depending on availability). Aperture from irregularly subcircular to regularly lobate with regular denticles, often surrounded by a more or less complicated organic collar.

The collar can become expanded and complicated to the point of forming a sort of second chamber with the aperture itself becoming invaginated to form a typical "*Cucurbitella*-structure."

Approximate diameter: 30–160 microns.

PLATE IV

Habitat: Freshwater. During the summer, it can live as a "pseudoplanktic" form in an apparently parasitic relationship with the filamentous alga *Spyrogyra* which forms floating mats in eutrophic lakes. Autogenous forms are usually produced during this period. During the other seasons, it falls to the bottom and lives as a normal benthic form. Xenogenous tests are usually produced during the benthic stage. For a detailed description of the life cycle of this genus, see Medioli et al. (1987). The xenogenous forms differ from *D. corona* because the latter normally has more than six indentations in the aperture. Not infrequently, however, forms can be found with intermediate numbers of lobes; in these cases identification becomes problematic. *C. tricuspis,* however, is usually considerably smaller than *D. corona.*

■ **Genus *Cyphoderia*   Schlumberger**

Plate IV, Figs. 10a–c

Type species: *Difflugia ampulla*   Ehrenberg, 1840.
Definition: Test elongate and usually with a characteristically bent neck (approx. 35°); test composed of very small rounded siliceous idiosomic plates; aperture simple.
Approximate length: 60–190 microns.
Habitat: Freshwater on sphagnum.

■ **Genus *Difflugia*   Leclerc in Lamarck**

Plate IV, Figs. 11–14; Plate V, Figs. 1–6

(Eocene–Recent)

Type species: *Difflugia protaeiformis*   Lamarck, 1816.
Definition: Test agglutinated; outline extremely variable, from subglobular to flask-shaped to bullet-shaped, and often complicated by the irregular presence of blunt to acuminate spines. This genus includes a number of species that are by far the commonest fossilized thecamoebians in lacustrine deposits.
Approximate length: 30–450 microns.
Habitat: Cosmopolitan in freshwater where it is probably the commonest genus.

Difflugia bidens   Penard

Plate IV, Figs. 12a,b

Difflugia bidens   Penard, 1902, p. 264, text-figs. 1–8.
Difflugia bidens   Penard, Medioli, and Scott, 1983, pl. 1, figs. 1–5.

Description: Test regularly ovoid, usually laterally compressed; transversal cross section ovoid. Fundus obtusely and evenly rounded, usually furnished with two to three short and blunt hollow spires. Usually the test appears to be composed of small, reasonably well-sorted quartz grains. Mouth wall thickened internally; no external neck; aperture round and well defined.

Approximate dimensions: Insufficient information.
Habitat: Freshwater.

This species differs from *D. corona* in (1) being laterally compressed, whereas the latter never is, (2) having a smooth apertural rim quite different from the strongly crenulated one of *D. corona,* and (3) being always somewhat elongated while most specimens of D. *corona* characteristically tend to be spheroidal. Rare specimens of *D. bidens* and *D. bacillariarum,* at the extremes of their limits of variability, could be confused. They can easily be separated because the former species is flattened and has a smaller aperture diameter/maximum diameter ratio (0.3 to 0.4, versus 0.4 to 0.6).

Difflugia corona   Wallich

Plate IV, Figs. 13a–c

Difflugia proteiformis (sic) (Ehrenberg) subspecies *D. globularis* (Dujardin) var. *D. corona* (Wallich). Wallich, 1864, p. 244, pl. 15, fig. 4b, pl. 16, figs. 19, 20.
Difflugia corona   Wallich. Archer, 1866, p. 186; Medioli and Scott, 1983, p. 22, pl. 1, figs. 6–14; Scott and Medioli, 1983, p. 818, fig. 9P; Patterson et al., 1985, p. 134, pl. 2, figs. 1–6.

Description: Test subspherical, ovoid to spheroid, circular in transversal cross section. Fundus furnished with a variable number of spines (one to ten or more); mouth central, roughly circular but crenulated by six to twenty regular indentations forming a thin collar. Test composed of fine, angular quartz grains of varied sizes; smaller pieces fill the gaps in between larger ones. Spines delicate and very easily broken, composed of the same material. Although highly variable in size and shape, *D. corona* is a distinctive and easily recognized species.
Approximate dimensions: Insufficient information.
Habitat: Freshwater.

D. corona is easily differentiated from xenosomic specimens of *D. tricuspis* because the former usually has a much higher number of apertural indentations (minimum of six) than the latter (maximum of six clear indentations, some-

Plate IV. **(1)** *Amphitrema* sp. Archer: 1a, edge view; 1b, side view. **(2)** *Archerella* Loeblich and Tappan: 2a, apertural view; 2b, side view. **(3)** *Arcella* sp. Ehrenberg: 3a; 3b: lateral views of hemispherical specimens. **(4)** *Arcella* sp. Ehrenberg: 4a; 4b: lateral views of flattened specimens. **(5)** *Bullinularia* sp. Penard: latero-apertural view. **(6)** *Centropyxis aculeata* Ehrenberg: 6a, edge view; 6b, apertural view. **(7)** *Centropyxis constricta* Ehrenberg: 7a, latero-apertural view; 7b, edge view. **(8)** *Corythion dubium* Taránek: 8a, latero-apertural view; 8b, enlargent of the aperture. **(9)** *Cucurbitella tricuspis* (Carter): 9a, lateral view showing the apertural collar; 9b and 9c, variability in the aperture; 9d, enlargment of xenogenous test; 9e, enlargement of mixed test; 9f, enlargement of autogenous test. **(10)** *Cyphoderia* sp. Schlumberger: 10a, edge view; 10b, enlargment of the arrangement of the round idiosomes; 10c, latero-apertural view. **(11)** *Difflugia bidens* Penard: 11a, side view; 11b, apertural view. **(12)** *Difflugia corona* Wallich: 12a, apertural view; 12b details of the aperture; 12c, side view. **(13)** *Difflugia urceolata* Carter: 13a and 13b morphological variabilityin side view; 13c, aperture; 13d, *Difflugia urceolata* "elongata" – Patterson et al. **(14)** *Difflugia globulus* (Ehrenberg): 14a, side view; 14b, apertural view.

times more but in that case the indentations are irregular and poorly defined). There are rare specimens that are intermediate between the two taxa and cannot be attributed with certainty to either one. *D. corona* is differentiated from *D. urceolata* by its apertural crenulation, and the lack of a collar.

Difflugia globulus (Ehrenberg)

Plate IV, Figs. 14a,b

Difflugia proteiformis Lamarck. Ehrenberg, 1848, p. 131 (part), pl. 9, figs. 1a, b.
Difflugia globulus (Ehrenberg). Cash and Hopkinson, 1909, p. 33, text-figs. 52–54, pl. 21, figs. 5–9.
Difflugia globulus (Ehrenberg). Medioli and Scott, 1983, pl. 5, figs. 1–15.

Description: Test spheroidal to ellipsoidal (up to 20% longer than wide) with the oral pole truncated by a circular, occasionally slightly invaginated aperture which is usually large but can decrease in diameter to as little as one-quarter maximum width. Overall shape resembling that of the sea urchin *Echinus*. At times the aperture is slightly protruding or slightly invaginated. Test composed of a chitinoid membrane covered by agglutinated quartz particles and/or diatom frustules.

The species differs from *D. corona* by the complete lack of apertural crenulation and spires, and from *D. urceolata* by the lack of a pronounced collar and by the relatively shorter main axis.

Approximate dimensions: Insufficient information.
Habitat: Freshwater.

Difflugia oblonga Ehrenberg

Plate V, Figs. 1a–c

Difflugia oblonga Ehrenberg, 1832, p. 90; Ehrenberg, 1838, p. 131, pl. 9, fig. 2; Medioli and Scott, 1983, p. 25, pl. 2, figs. 1–17, 24–26; Scott and Medioli, 1983, p. 818, figs. 9a–c; Patterson et al., 1985, p. 134, pl. 1, figs. 4–12.
Difflugia capreolata (Penard). Scott et al., 1977, p. 1578, pl. 1, figs. 3, 4; Scott et al., 1980, p. 224, pl. 1, figs. 4–7.

Description: Test extremely variable in shape and size, pyriform to compressed and flask-shaped. In cross section rounded to slightly compressed. Fundus rounded to subacute or expanded into one to three blunt, rounded conical processes. Neck subcylindrical, more or less long, gradually narrowed toward the oral end. Aperture terminal, circular to slightly oval. Test made of sand particles sometimes mixed with a variable amount of diatom frustules which, if large, can partly or completely obscure the overall shape of the specimen.

Approximate dimensions: Insufficient information. The test ranges from 60 to 580 microns in length, 40 to 240 microns in width, 16 to 120 microns in apertural diameter.
Habitat: Freshwater.

Differs from *D. proteiformis* by often being compressed

and by lacking the acute spinal process that is so characteristic of that species. The ratio apertural diameter/maximum diameter varies between 0.5 and 0.2, while in *D. protaeiformis* it varies from 0.5 to 0.7.

Difflugia proteiformis Lamarck

Plate V, Figs. 2–5

Difflugia proteiformis Lamarck, 1816, p. 95 (with reference to material in a manuscript by LeClerc).
Difflugia proteiformis Lamarck, Medioli and Scott, 1983, p. 17, text-fig. 4, pl. 1, figs. 15–20.

Description: Test shape extremely variable; amphora-like to elongate oval, cylindroconical, pyriform. Fundus more or less tapering, acute, either acuminate or prolonged into one or more blunt spine processes. The test blends into these processes with smooth curves. Neck long, short, or absent. Aperture large, terminal, subcircular. Test composed of quartz grains of variable size and abundance, at times mixed with variable amounts of diatom frustules that, when abundant, completely obscure the shape of the test.

Approximate dimensions: Ranges from 84 to 520 microns in length, 36 to 184 microns in width, 24 to 100 microns in apertural diameter.
Habitat: Freshwater.

Differs from *D. oblonga* in having smoother transition from test to spines and for its larger ratio of *aperture diameter/maximum diameter* which is about 0.7 to 0.5 for *D. proteiformis* and 0.5 to 0.2 for *D. oblonga*.

Difflugia urceolata Carter

Plate IV, Figs. 11a–c

Difflugia urceolata Carter, 1864, p. 27, pl. 1, fig. 7; Scott et al., 1977, p. 1578, pl. 1, figs. 3, 4; Scott et al., 1980, p. 224, pl. 1, figs. 10–12; Medioli and Scott, 1983, p. 31, pl. 3, figs. 1–23, pl. 4, figs. 1–4; Scott and Medioli, 1983, p. 818, figs. 9F, G; Patterson et al., 1985, p. 134, pl. 2, figs. 11, 12.
Lagunculina vadescens Cushman and Brönnimann, 1948a, p. 15, pl. 3, figs. 1, 2; Parker, 1952a, p. 451, fig. 8.

Description: Test spheroid to acutely ovate; general appearance amphora-like to cauldron-like. Fundus rounded to acuminate, at times provided with blunt protuberances. Neck short, terminating in an evaginated, sometimes recurved or straight, collar of variable shape and size. Mouth wide, circular, terminal. Test xenosomic, usually composed of sand grains of variable coarseness.

Approximate dimensions: Insufficient information.
Habitat: Freshwater.

Differs from *D. corona*, with which it could be confused in few, extreme cases, by the pronounced collar and the lack of apertural crenulation.

Difflugia urens R. T. Patterson, K. D. MacKinnon, D. B. Scott, and F. S. Medioli

Plate V, Figs. 6a,b

Difflugia urens R. T. Patterson, K. D. MacKinnon, D. B. Scott, and F. S. Medioli, 1985, p. 135, pl. 3, figs 5–14.

Description: Small difflugid characterized by a very small aperture and sometimes by a flange folded over to become almost part of the main test. Test spheroid, aperture is not always visible. This species has seldom been reported outside eastern Canada.

Approximate dimensions: Insufficient information.
Habitat: Freshwater.

■ Genus *Heleopera* Leidy

Plate V, Fig. 8

(Pleistocene–Recent)

Type species: *Heleopera picta* Leidy, 1879.

Definition: Test xenogenous, usually made of idiosomes of other thecamoebians with mineral grains at the fundus.
The shape is usually oval-pyriform, strongly laterally compressed.
Aperture terminal, either a narrow slit covered by two overlapping lips or a more or less elongate elliptical opening.

Approximate maximum width: 50–120 microns.
Habitat: Freshwater, common in sphagnum bogs.

Heleopera sphagni (Leidy)

Plate V, Figs. 8a,b

Difflugia (*Nebela*) *sphagni* Leidy, 1874, p. 15.
Heleopera sphagni (Leidy). Cash and Hopkinson, 1909, p. 143, pl. 30, figs. 4–9; Medioli and Scott, 1983, p. 37, pl. 6, figs. 15–18; Scott and Medioli, 1983, p. 819, fig. 9E.

Description: Test strongly compressed, ovoid; oral pole narrower in broadside view. In those tests that are made of foreign idiosomes and are apparently autogenous, the mouth forms an elongated, narrow ellipse with acute commissures. The tests made of mineral xenosomes usually have a wider, oval aperture that becomes almost subcircular in extreme cases. Commonly, coarse mineral xenosomes tend to concentrate at the fundus. In fossil material, strongly mineral forms appear to be selectively preserved while forms with abundant autogenous plates are almost completely absent.

Approximate maximum width: 50–120 microns.
Habitat: Freshwater, common in sphagnum bogs.

■ Genus *Euglypha* Dujardin

Plate V, Figs. 7a,b

(Eocene–Recent)

Type species: *Euglypha tuberculata* Dujardin, 1841.
Description: Test ovate to acuminate, rounded in cross section. Idiosomes from round to oval or variously shaped, apertural idiosome denticulate (in some forms, modified plates may form spines); aperture terminal and rounded.
Approximate diameter: 20–150 microns.
Habitat: Freshwater, on moss, sphagnum, and water plants.

■ Genus *Hyalosphenia* Stein

Plate V, Figs. 9a,b

(Pleistocene–Recent)

Type species: *Hyalosphenia cuneata* Stein, in Schulze, 1875.
Definition: Test autogenous, proteinaceous, hyaline, at times pitted, never agglutinated; ovate or pyriform, strongly laterally compressed. Aperture terminal, elliptical and supported by a more or less developed collar.
Approximate length: 30–150 microns.
Habitat: Freshwater.

■ Genus *Lagenodifflugia* Medioli and Scott

Plate V, Figs. 10a,b

(Pleistocene–Recent)

Type species: *Lagenodifflugia vas,* Medioli and Scott, 1983.
Test agglutinated, with mineral xenosomes; flask-shaped, radially symmetrical and never laterally compressed; always consisting of two distinct chambers separated by a diaphragm whose position is usually revealed from the outside by a marked constriction. Aperture simple at the upper end of the second chamber; a simple perforation in the diaphragm provides communication with the first chamber.
Approximate length: 90–300 microns.
Habitat: Freshwater.

■ Genus *Lesquereusia* Schlumberger

Plate V; Figs. 11,12

(Recent)

Type species: *Lesquereusia jurassica* Schlumberger, 1845.
Definition: Test from completely autogenous with siliceous vermicular idiosomes to completely xenogenous with mineral xenosomes; intermediate forms are very common.
The genus is characterized by a structure rather uncommon among thecamoebians: an asymmetrical flask-shaped second chamber separated from the main one by a diaphragm.
The overall shape of the test is that of an asymmetrical flask, ovoid to subglobose, moderately compressed laterally, simulating – due to the asymmetry of the second chamber – a sort of spiral coiling.
Approximate length: 120–160 microns.
Habitat: Freshwater, common in sphagnum bogs.

Lesquereusia spiralis (Ehrenberg)

Plate V, Figs. 11a,b

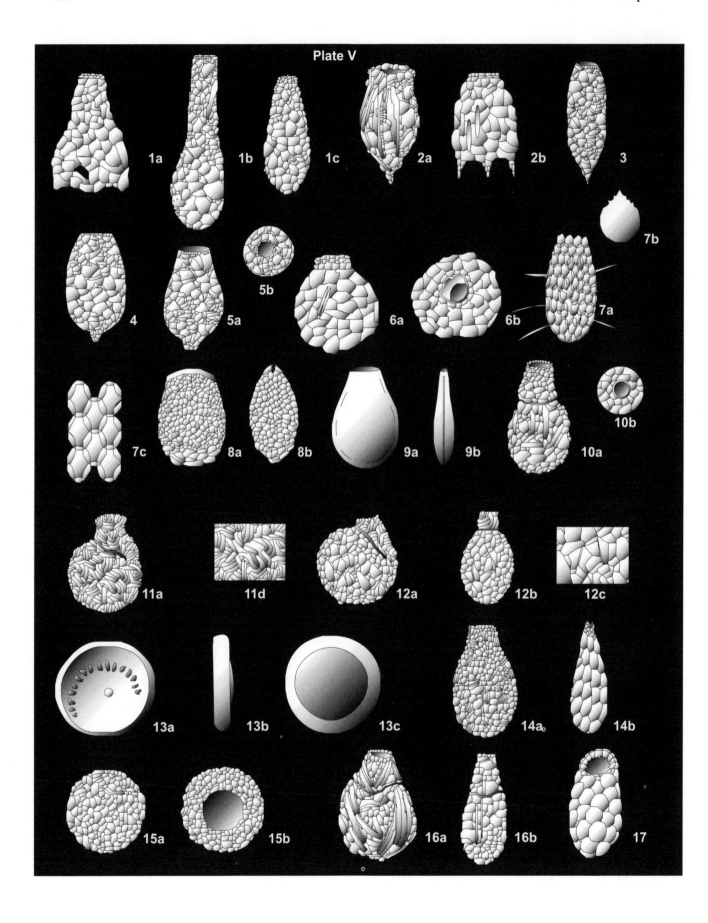

Plate V

Difflugia spiralis   Ehrenberg, 1840a, p. 199.
Lesquereusia spiralis (Ehrenberg). Penard, 1902, p. 36,
    text-figs. 1–10. Patterson et al., 1985, p. 135, pl. 2,
    figs. 9, 10; Scott et al. 1991, p. 386, pl. 1, fig. 10.

■ Genus *Mississippiella* Haman

Plate V, Figs. 13a,b

(Recent)

Type species: *Mississippiella multiapertura* Haman,
1982.

Definition: Test autogenous calcitic, circular or subcircular, discoidal to hemispherical in lateral view; ventral side
flat to concave, dorsal side convex. Aperture multiple,
formed by a series of ten to eighteen pores with irregular
outline.

Approximate diameter: 100 microns.

Habitat: Found so far only in the Mississippi Delta
deposits.

■ Genus *Nebela* Leidy

Plate V, Figs. 14a,b

(Carboniferous–Recent)

Type species: *Difflugia (Nebela) numata*   Leidy, 1875.

Test thin, transparent but xenogenous, often pseudoauto-
genous and built with the transparent plates of other thecamoebians upon which *Nebela* preys.

Outline usually sharply pyriform, strongly compressed
laterally and, at times, with large hollow spines that are the
continuation of the test's structure.

Approximate length: 100–180 microns.

Habitat: Cosmopolitan in freshwater.

■ Genus *Phryganella* Penard

Plate V, Figs. 15a,b

(Pleistocene–Recent)

Type species: *Phryganella nidulus*   Penard, 1902.

Definition: Test mainly autogenous, organic but covered
with xenosomes; shape hemispherical to ovate; aperture usually large but at times relatively small, rounded.

Approximate diameter: 150–250 microns.

Habitat: Wet moss.

Empty tests of *Phryganella* can be distinguished from
those of some *Difflugia* with great difficulty because the dif-
ferentiation between the two can only be based on the nature
of the pseudopods, which are broadly to narrowly lobate and
pointed in *Phryganella* and lobose in *Difflugia*.

■ Genus *Pontigulasia* Rhumbler

Plate V, Fig. 16

(Eocene?–Recent)

Type species: *Pontigulasia compressa*   Rhumbler, 1895.

Definition: Test composed only of agglutinated foreign
particles; flask-shaped, invariably laterally compressed;
always consisting of two distinct chambers separated by a
diaphragm whose position is usually revealed from the outside by two marked constriction forming a wide "V" at the
base of the second chamber. Aperture simple at the upper
end of the second chamber; two perforations in the diaphragm provide communication with the first chamber. The
double perforation, frequently reported in the literature,
seems to be destroyed by taphonomic processes and is seldom visible in fossilized material.

Pontigulasia compressa (Carter)

Plate V, Figs. 16a,b

Difflugia compressa   Carter, 1864, p. 22, pl. 1, figs. 5, 6.
Pontigulasia compressa   Rhumbler, 1895, p. 105, pl. 4,
    figs. 13a,b. Averintsev, 1906, p. 169; Scott et al., 1977,
    p. 1578, pl. 1, figs. 5, 6; Scott et al., 1980, p. 224, pl. 1,
    figs. 10–12. Medioli and Scott, 1983, p. 34, pl. 6,
    figs. 5–14; Scott and Medioli, 1983, p. 819, fig. 9M;
    Patterson et al., 1985, p. 135, pl. 2, figs. 7, 8.

Description: Test usually large, rounded to pyriform, laterally compressed. Neck well defined, tapering regularly
toward the narrow aperture. Mouth truncated, rounded or
broadly elliptical in cross section. The junction between the
neck and the test proper is marked usually by a clearly visible constriction (which may not be visible when diatoms are
agglutinated in the test). This constriction marks the position
of what is described in the literature as a doubly perforated
internal diaphragm, which is often missing in fossil forms.
The main part of the test appears to be composed of minute

Plate V. (1) *Difflugia oblonga* Ehrenberg: 1a, 1b and 1c, side views of different morphotypes of the species. **(2)** *Difflugia proteiformis* Lamarck: 2a and 2b, side views of different morphotypes of the species. **(3)** *Difflugia proteiformis* Lamarck "proteiformis"
Asioli, Medioli, and Patterson: side view. **(4)** *Difflugia proteiformis* Lamarck "crassa" Asioli, Medioli, and Patterson: side view. **(5)**
Difflugia proteiformis Lamarck " rapa" Asioli, Medioli, and Patterson: 5a, side view; 5b, apertural view. **(6)** *Difflugia urens* Patterson, MacKinnon, Scott, Medioli: 6a, side view; 6b, apertural view. **(7)** *Euglypha* sp. Dujardin: 7a, side view; 7b, details of apertural
plate; 7c, details of test plates. **(8)** *Heleopera sphagni* (Leidy): 8a, side view; 8b, edge view. **(9)** *Hyalosphenia* sp. Stein: 9a, side
view; 9b, edge view. **(10)** *Lagenodifflugia vas:* (Leidy): 10a, side view; 10b, apertural view. **(11)** *Lesquereusia spiralis* (Ehrenberg):
11a, side view of autogenous specimen; 11b, details of the secreted vermicular structure. **(12)** *Lesquereusia spiralis* (Ehrenberg):
12a, side view of partly agglutinated specimen; 12b, edge view of the same specimen; 12c, details of the agglutinated mineral xenosomes. **(13)** *Mississippiella* sp. Haman: 13a, ventral view with multiple apertures; 13b, edge view; 13c, dorsal view. **(14)** *Nebela* sp.
Leidy: 14a, side view; 14b, narrowside view of specimen agglutinating plates of other thecamoebians. **(15)** *Phryganella* sp. Penard:
15a, side view; 15b, apertural view. **(16)** *Pontigulasia compressa* Rhumbler: 16a, side view; 16b, edge view. Notice external mark of
internal diaphragm. **(17)** *Trinema* sp. Dujardin: latero-apertural view.

quartz grains arranged to confer a rough appearance; the neck is usually smoother.

Approximate length: 80–300 microns.

Habitat: Freshwater, common in sphagnum bogs.

■ **Genus *Trinema*   Dujardin**

Plate V, Fig. 17

(Recent)

Type species: *Trinema acinus*   Dujardin, 1841.

Definition: Test formed by overlapping rounded siliceous idiosomes; small, transparent; pear-shaped with apertural side flattened. Aperture rounded, slightly invaginated, in eccentric position at the periphery of the apertural side, and formed by a variable number (fifteen to thirty) of denticulate idiosomes.

Approximate length: 20–100 microns.

Habitat: Freshwater.

Bibliography

Alhonen, P., Eronen, M., Nunez, M., Salomaa, R., and Uusi-noka, R. 1978. A contribution to Holocene shore displacement and environmental development in Vantaa, South Finland: The stratigraphy of Lake Lammaslampi. *Bulletin of the Geological Society of Finland,* v. 50, pp. 69–79.

Alve, E. 1990. Variations in estuarine foraminiferal biofacies with diminishing oxygen conditions in Drammensfjord, SE Norway. In Hemleben, C., Kaminski, M. A., Kuhnt, W., and Scott, D. B. (eds.), *Paleoecology, Biostratigraphy, Paleoceanography and Taxonomy of Agglutinated Foraminifera,* NATO ASI Series C. Mathematical and Physical Sciences, v. 327, pp. 661–694.

——— 1991. Benthic foraminifera in sediment cores reflecting heavy metal pollution in Sørfjord, western Norway. *Journal of Foraminiferal Research,* v. 21, pp. 1–19.

——— 1995. Benthic foraminiferal responses to estuarine pollution: a review. *Journal of Foraminiferal Research,* v. 25(3), pp. 190–203.

——— 1999. Colonization of new habitats by benthic foraminifera: a review. *Earth-Science Reviews,* v. 46, pp. 167–185.

Alve, E., and Bernhard, J. M. 1995. Vertical migratory response of benthic foraminifera to controlled oxygen concentrations in an experimental mesocosm. *Marine Ecology Progress Series,* v. 116, pp. 137–51.

Alve, E., and Nagy, J. 1986. Estuarine foraminiferal distribution in Sandebukta, a branch of the Oslo Fjord. *Journal of Foraminiferal Research,* v. 16, pp. 261–84.

Alvisi, F., Appleby, A, Asioli, A., Frignani, M., Oldfield, F., Ravaioli, M., and Vigliotti, L. 1996. Recent environmental changes as recorded by the sediment of Lake Orta (Northern Italy). Atti IV Workshop del Progetto Strategico "Clima, ambiente e Territorio nel Mezzogiorno," Lecce (Italy), November 11–14, 1991, Tono I, pp. 243–56.

Amos, C. L., and Joice, J. H. 1977. The sediment budget of the Minas Basin, Bay of Fundy, Nova Scotia. Bedford Institute of Oceanography Data Report Series, no. BI-D-77-3, 411 p.

Amos, C. L., and Long, B. 1980. The sedimentary character of the Minas Basin, Bay of Fundy. Geological Survey of Canada, Special Publication 80–15, Ottawa, 57 p.

Andersen, H. v. 1951. Two new genera of foraminifera from recent deposits in Louisiana. *Journal of Paleontology,* v. 25, pp. 31–4.

1952. *Buccella,* a new genus of the rotalid foraminifera. *Journal of the Washington Academy of Science,* v. 42, pp. 143–51.

1953. Two new species of *Haplophragmoides* from the Louisiana coast. *Contributions from the Cushman Foundation for Foraminiferal Research,* v. 4, pp. 21–2.

Archer, W. 1866. Untitled. *Quarterly Journal of Microscopical Science,* new ser., v. 6, pp. 185–8.

1867. Untitled. (Remarks on freshwater rhizopoda). *Quarterly Journal of Microscopical Science,* new ser., v. 7, pp. 173–4.

1869. On some fresh-water Rhizopoda, new or little-known. *Quarterly Journal of Microscopical Science,* new ser., v. 9, pp. 386–97, pls. 16, 17, 20.

1877. Proceedings of the Dublin Microscopical Club, session July 13, 1876. *Quarterly Journal of Microscopical Science,* new ser., v. 17, pp. 102–4.

Asioli, A., and Medioli, F. S. 1992. Ricostruzione dei paleoambienti attraverso le Tecamebe in alcuni laghi sudalpini (Orta, Varese e Candia). *Atti X Congresso dell'Associazione Italiana di Oceanologia e Limnologia [A.I.O.L.],* pp. 487–501.

Asioli, A., Medioli, F. S., and Patterson, R. T. 1996. Thecamoebians as a tool for reconstruction of paleoenvironments in some Italian lakes in the foothills of the southern Alps (Orta, Varese and Candia). *Journal of Foraminiferal Research,* v. 26, no. 3, pp. 248–61.

Atkinson, K. 1969. The association of living foraminifera with algae from the littoral zone, south Cardigan Bay, Wales. *Journal of Natural History,* v. 3, pp. 517–42.

Atwater, B. T. 1987. Evidence for great Holocene earthquakes along the outer coast of Washington State. *Science,* v. 236, pp. 942–4.

1992. Geologic evidence for earthquakes during the past 2000 years along the Copalis River, southern coastal Washington. *Journal of Geophysical Research,* v. 97(B2), pp. 1901–19.

Auster, P. J., Malatesta, R. J., Langton, R. W., Watling, L., Valentine, P. C., Lee, C., Donaldson, S., Langton, E. W., Shepard, A. N., and Babb, I. G. 1996. The impacts of mobile fishing gear on seafloor habitats in the Gulf of Maine (Northwest Atlantic): implications for conservation of fish populations. *Reviews in Fisheries Science,* v. 4, pp. 185–202.

Averintsev, S. 1906. Rhizopoda prêsnykh vod. *Imperatorskoe Sankt-Peterburgskoe Obshchestvo Estestvoispytatelei Trudy,* v. 36, pp. 1–346.

Bailey, J. W. 1851. Microscopical examination of soundings made by the U.S. Coast Survey off the Atlantic coast of the U.S. *Smithsonian Contributions to Knowledge,* v. 2, pp. 1–15.

Bamber, R. N. 1995. The influence of rising background temperature on the effects of marine thermal effluents. *Journal of Thermal Biology,* v. 20, p.105–10.

Bandy, O. L. 1954. Distribution of some shallow water foraminifera in the Gulf of Mexico. *U.S. Geological Survey,* Professional Paper 254-F, pp. 125–41.

Bandy, O., Ingle, J. C. Jr., and Resig, J. M. 1964. Foraminifera, Los Angeles County outfall area, California. *Limnology and Oceanography,* v. 9, pp. 124–37.

Banner, F. T., and Culver, S. J. 1978. Quaternary *Haynesina* n. gen. and Paleogene *Protelphidium* Haynes; their morphology, affinities and distribution. *Journal of Foraminiferal Research,* v. 8, pp. 177–207.

Barker, R. W. 1960. Taxonomic notes on the species figured by H.B. Brady in his report on the foraminifera dredged by *H.M.S. Challenger* during the years 1873–76. *Society of Economic Paleontology and Mineralogy,* Special Publication 9, 238 p., 114 pls.

Barmawidjaja, D. M., Jorissen, F. J., Puskaric, S., and Van der Zwaan, G. J. 1994. Microhabitat selection by benthic foraminifera in the northern Adriatic Sea. *Journal of Foraminiferal Research,* v. 22, pp. 297–317.

Bartenstein, H., and Brand, E. 1938. Die foraminiferan-fauna des Jade-Gebietes. 1. *Jadammina polystoma* n. g., n. sp. aus dem Jade-Gebietes (for). *Senckenbergiana,* v. 20, pp. 381–5.

Bartlett, G. A. 1964. Benthic foraminiferal ecology in St. Margaret's Bay and Mahone Bay, southeast Nova Scotia. Bedford Institute of Oceanography, Report 64–8, Dartmouth, Nova Scotia, 159 p.

1966. Distribution and abundance of foraminifera and thecamoebina in Miramichi River and Bay. Bedford Institute of Oceanography, Report no. 66–2, 104 p.

Bartsch-Winkler, S., and Schmoll, H. R. 1987. Earthquake-caused sedimentary couplets in the upper Cook Inlet region. *U.S. Geological Survey,* Circular 998, pp. 92–5.

Bates, J. M., and Spencer, R. S. 1979. Modification of foraminiferal trends by the Chesapeake–Elizabeth sewage outfall, Virginia Beach, Virginia. *Journal of Foraminiferal Research,* v. 9, pp. 125–40.

Bé, A. W. H. 1960. Ecology of recent planktonic foraminifera: Part II – bathymetric and seasonal distribution in the Sargasso Sea off Bermuda. *Micropaleontolgy,* v. 6, pp. 373–92.

1977. 1: An ecological, zoogeographic and taxonomic review of recent planktonic foraminifera. In Ramsay, A.T.S. (ed.), *Oceanic Micropaleontology.* New York: Academic Press, pp. 1–100.

Berglund, B. E. 1971. Littorina transgressions in Blekinge, South Sweden. A preliminary survey. *Geologiska foreningens i Stockholm Forhandlingar,* v. 93, pp. 625–52.

Bernhard, J. M., and Alve, E. 1996. Survival, ATP pool, and ultrastructural characterization of benthic foraminifera from Drammensfjord (Norway): response to anoxia. *Marine Micropaleontology,* v. 28, pp. 5–17.

Bernhard, J. M., and Bowser, S. S. 1999. Benthic foraminifera of dyoxic sediments: chloroplast sequestration and functional morphology. *Earth Science Reviews,* v. 46, pp. 149–65.

Bernhard, J. M., Sen Gupta, B. K., and Borne, P. F. 1997. Benthic foraminiferal proxy to estimate dysoxic bottom-water oxygen concentrations: Santa Barbara Basin, U.S. Pacific continental margin. *Journal of Foraminiferal Research,* v. 27, pp. 301–10.

Bhupathiraju, V. K., Hernandez, M., Krauter, P., and Alvarez-Cohen, L. 1999. A new direct microscopy based method for evaluating in-situ bioremediation. *Journal of Hazardous Materials,* v. 67, pp. 299–312.

Boltovskoy, E. 1963. The littoral foraminiferal biocoenosis of Puerto Desado (Patagonia, Argentina). *Contributions to the Cushman Foundation for Foraminiferal Research,* v. 14, pp. 58–70.

——— 1965. Twilight of foraminiferology. *Journal of Paleontology,* v. 39, pp. 383–90.

Boltovskoy, E., and Lena, H. 1969. Seasonal occurrences, standing crop and production in benthic foraminifera of Puerto Desado. *Contributions from the Cushman Foundation for Foraminiferal Research,* v. 20, pp. 81–95.

Boltovskoy, E., Scott, D. B., and Medioli, F. S. 1991. Morphological variations of benthic foraminiferal tests in response to changes in ecological parameters: a review. *Journal of Paleontology,* v. 65, pp. 175–85.

Boltovskoy, E., and Wright, R. 1976. *Recent Foraminifera.* The Hague: Junk, 515 p.

Bonacina, C. 1990. Lo Zooplancton del Lago. *Documento dell'Istituto Italiano di Idrobiologia,* v. 28, pp. 101–8.

Bonomi, G. 1962. La dinamica produttiva delle principali popolazioni macrobentiche del Lago di Varese. *Memorie dell'Istituto Italiano di Idrobiologia,* v. 15, pp. 207–54.

Bradley, W. H. 1931. Origin and microfossils of the oil shale of the Green River formation of Colorado and Utah: U.S. Geological Survey, Professional Paper 168, 58 p.

Bradshaw, J. S. 1957. Laboratory studies on the rate of growth of the foraminifer *Streblus beccarii* (Linne) var. *tepida* (Cushman). *Journal of Paleontology,* v. 31(6), pp. 1138–47.

——— 1961. Laboratory experiments on the ecology of foraminifera. *Contributions to the Cushman Foundation for Foraminiferal Research,* v. 12(3), pp. 87–106.

Brady, H. B. 1870. Analysis and descriptions of foraminifera, Part II. *Annals and Magazine of Natural History,* ser. 4, v. 6, pp. 273–309.

——— 1878. On the reticularian and radiolarian rhizopoda (foraminifera and polycystina) of the North-Polar Expedition of 1875–76. *Annals and Magazine of Natural History,* ser. 5, v. 1, pp. 425–40.

——— 1879. Notes on some of the reticularian rhizopoda of the *Challenger* Expedition, Part I, on new or little known arenaceous types. *Quarterly Journal of Microscopic Sciences,* London, new ser., v. 19, pp. 20–63.

——— 1881. On some arctic foraminifera from soundings obtained on the Austro-Hungarian North Polar Expedition of 1872–76. *Annals and Magazine of Natural History,* v. 8, pp. 393–418.

——— 1884. Report on the foraminifera dredged by *H.M.S. Challenger* during the years 1873–76. In *Reports of the Scientific Results of the Voyage of the* H.M.S. Challenger. *Zoology,* v. 9, London, pp. 1–814.

Brasier, M. D. 1980. *Microfossils.* London: George Allen and Unwin, 193 p.

Bresler, V., and Yanko, V. 1995a. Acute toxicity of heavy metals for benthic epiphytic foraminifera *Pararotalia spinigera* (LeCalvez) and influence of seaweed-derived DOC. *Environmental Toxicology and Chemistry,* v. 14, pp. 1687–95.

——— 1995b. Chemical ecology: a new approach to the study of living benthic epiphytic foraminifera. *Journal of Foraminiferal Research,* v. 25, no. 3, pp. 267–79.

Brink, B. J. E., Hosper, S. H., and Colijn, F. 1991. A quantita-

tive method for description and assessment of ecosystems: the AMOEBA approach. *Marine Pollution Bulletin,* v. 23, pp. 265–70.

Brünnich, M. T. 1772. *M. T. Brünnich Zoologiae Fundamentals: Grunde i Dyreloeren* (Hafniae at Lipsiae) 253 p.

Bryant, J. D., Jones, D. S., and Mueller, P. A. 1995. Influence of freshwater flux on $^{87}Sr/^{86}Sr$ chronostratigraphy in marginal marine environments and dating of vertebrate and invertebrate faunae. *Journal of Paleontology,* v. 69, pp. 1–6.

Buckley, D. E., Owens, E. H., Schafer, C. T., Vilks, G., Cranston, R. E., Rashid, M. A., Wagner, F.J.E., and Walker, D. A. 1974. Canso Strait and Chedabucto Bay: a multidisciplinary study of the impact of man on the marine environment. In *Offshore Geology of Eastern Canada,* Geological Survey of Canada, Paper 74–30(1), pp. 133–60.

Burbidge, S. M., and Schröder, C. J. 1998. Thecamoebians in Lake Winnipeg: a tool for Holocene paleolimnology. *Journal of Paleolimnology,* v. 19, pp. 309–28.

Buzas, M. A. 1965. The distribution and abundance of foraminifera in Long Island Sound. *Smithsonian Institution Miscellaneous Collection,* no. 149, 94 p.

——— 1968. On the spatial distribution of foraminifera. *Contributions from the Cushman Foundation for Foraminiferal Research,* v. 19, pp. 1–11.

——— 1970. On the quantification of biofacies. *Proceedings of the North American Paleontological Convention,* Part B, pp. 101–16.

——— 1982. Regulation of foraminiferal densities by predation in the Indian River, Florida. *Journal of Foraminiferal Research,* v. 36, pp. 617–25.

Calderoni, A., and Mosello, R. 1990. Evoluzione delle caratteristiche chimiche del Lago d'Orta nel quadriennio febbraio 1984 – febbraio 1988. *Documenti dell'Istituto Italiano d'Idrobiologia,* v. 28, pp. 71–87.

Carter, H. J. 1856. Notes on the freshwater infusoria of the island of Bombay, no. 1. *Organization: Annals and Magazine of Natural History,* ser. 2, v. 18, no. 104, pp. 115–32; no. 105, pp. 221–49.

——— 1864. On freshwater rhizopoda of England and India. *Annals and Magazine of Natural History,* ser. 3, v. 13, pp. 18–39.

Cash, J., and Hopkinson, J. 1909. The British freshwater rhizopoda and heliozoa, v. II: *Rhizopoda,* Part II. Ray Society (London), publication no. 89, pp. i–xviii, 1–166, pls. 17–32.

Cattaneo, G. 1878. Intorno all'ontogenesi dell'*Arcella vulgaris* Ehr. *Societá Italiana di Scienze Naturali,* v. 21, pp. 331–43.

Chagnon, J.-Y. 1968. Les coulées d'argile dans la province de Quebec. *Le Naturalist Canadien,* v. 95, pp. 1327–43.

Chapman, V. J. 1960. *Salt Marshes and Salt Deserts of the World.* Leonard Hill Limited, London, 392 p.

Chaster, G. W. 1892. Foraminifera. *First Report of the Southport Society of Natural Science, 1890–91,* pp. 54–72.

Choi, S.-C., and Bartha, R. 1994. Environmental factors affecting mercury methylation in estuarine sediments. *Bulletin of Environmental Contamination and Toxicology,* v. 53, pp. 805–12.

Clague, J. J., and Bobrowsky, P. T. 1994a. Tsunami deposits beneath tidal marshes on Vancouver Island, British Columbia. Geological Society of America, *Bulletin,* v. 106, pp. 1293–303.

1994b. Evidence for a large earthquake and tsunami 100–400 years ago on western Vancouver Island, British Columbia. *Quaternary Research,* v. 41, pp. 176–84.

Cockey, E., Hallock, P., and Lidz, B. H. 1996. Decadal-scale changes in benthic foraminiferal assemblages off Key Largo, Florida. *Coral Reefs,* v. 15, pp. 237–48.

Cole, W. S. 1931. The Pliocene and Pleistocene foraminifera of Florida: Florida State Geological Survey, *Bulletin 6,* 79 p.

Collins, E. S. 1996. Marsh-estuarine benthic foraminiferal distributions and Holocene sea-level reconstructions along the South Carolina coastline. Ph.D. diss., Dalhousie University, Halifax, Canada (unpublished manuscript), 240 p.

Collins, E. S., McCarthy, F. M., Medioli, F. S., Scott, D. B. and Honig, C. A. 1990. Biogeographic distribution of modern thecamoebians in a transect along the Eastern North American Coast. In Hemleben, C., Kaminski, M. A., Kuhnt, W. and Scott, D. B. (eds.), *Paleoecology, Biostratigraphy, Paleoceanography and Taxonomy of Agglutinated Foraminifera,* NATO ASI Series C. Mathematical and Physical Sciences, v. 327, pp. 783–91.

Collins, E. S., Scott, D. B., and Gayes, P. T. 1999. Hurricane records on the South Carolina coast: can they be detected in the sediment record? *Quaternary International,* v. 56, pp. 15–26.

Collins, E. S., Scott, D. B., Gayes, P. T., and Medioli, F. S. 1995. Foraminifera in Winyah Bay and North Inlet marshes, South Carolina: relationship to local pollution sources. *Journal of Foraminiferal Research,* v. 25, pp. 212–23.

Combellick, R. A. 1991. Paleoseismicity of the Cook Inlet region, Alaska: Evidence from peat stratigraphy in Turnagain and Knik Arms. Alaska Division of Geological & Geophysical Surveys, Professional Report, Fairbanks, 52 p.

1994. Investigation of peat stratigraphy in tidal marshes along Cook Inlet, Alaska, to determine the frequency of 1964-style great earthquakes in the Anchorage region. Alaska Division of Geological & Geophysical Surveys Report of Investigations 94–97, Fairbanks, 24 p.

1997. Evidence of prehistoric great earthquakes in the Cook Inlet Region, Alaska. In Hamilton, T. D. (ed.), IGCP Project 367, *Late Quaternary Coastal Records of Rapid Change: Application to Present and Future Donditions.* 4th annual meeting, Girdwood, Alaska, May 11–18, Field Trip Guide Book, p. 114.

Conservation Law Foundation. 1998. *Effects of Fishing Gear on the Sea Floor of New England* (Dorsey, E.M., and Pederson, J., eds.). Boston: Conservation Law Foundation, 202 p.

Cooper, J. D., Miller, R. H., and Patterson, J. 1990. *A Trip through Time,* 2nd edition. Toronto: Merrill Publishing Co., 544 p.

Coulbourn, W. T., and Resig, J. M. 1975. On the use of benthic foraminifera as sediment tracers in a Hawaiian Bay. *Pacific Science,* v. 29, pp. 99–115.

Culver, S. J. 1993. Foraminifera. In Lipps, J. H., (ed.), *Fossil Prokaryotes and Protists.* Boston: Blackwell Scientific Publications, 342 p.

Culver, S. J., and Buzas, M. A. 1995. The effects of anthro-pogenic habitat disturbance, habitat destruction, and global warming on shallow marine benthic foraminifera. *Journal of Foraminiferal Research,* v. 25, pp. 204–11.

Cushman, J. A. 1918. Some Pliocene and Miocene foraminifera of the coastal plain of the United States. *U.S. Geological Survey Bulletin 676,* pp. 1–100.

1920. The foraminifera of the Atlantic Ocean. Part 2, Lituoidae *United States National Museum Bulletin,* v. 104, pp. 1–111.

1922a. The foraminifera of the Atlantic Ocean. Part 3, Textulariidae. *United States Natural History Museum Bulletin,* v. 104, no. 3, pp. 1–149.

1922b. Results of the Hudson Bay expedition, 1920. I – the foraminifera. Canada, Biological Board, *Contributions to Canadian Biology* (1921), 1922, no. 9, pp. 135–47.

1923. The foraminifera of the Atlantic Ocean. Part 4, Lagenidae. *United States National Museum Bulletin,* v. 104, pp. 1–228.

1927a. An outline of a re-classification of the foraminifera. *Contributions from the Cushman Laboratory for Foraminiferal Research,* v. 3, pp. 1–105.

1927b. Some characteristic Mexican fossil foraminifera. *Journal of Paleontology,* v. 1, pp. 147–72.

1930a. The foraminifera of the Chaoctawhatchee Formation of Florida. *Florida State Geological Survey Bulletin 4,* pp. 1–63.

1930b. The foraminifera of the Atlantic Ocean. Part 7, Nonionidae, Camerinidae, Peneroplidae and Alveolinellidae. *United States National Museum Bulletin,* v. 104, pp. 1–79.

1933. New arctic foraminifera collected by Capt. R. A. Bartlett from Fox Basin and off the northeast coast of Greenland. *Smithsonian Miscellaneous Collections,* v. 89, no. 9, pp. 1–8.

1935. Upper Eocene foraminifera of the southeastern United States. *U.S. Geological Survey,* Professional Paper 181, 88 p.

1937. A monograph of the foraminiferal family Valvulinidae. Cushman Laboratory for Foraminiferal Research, Special Publication no. 8, 210 p.

1941. Some fossil foraminifera from Alaska. Cushman Laboratory for Foraminiferal Research, *Contributions,* v. 17, pp. 33–8.

1947. New species and varieties of foraminifera from off the southeastern coast of the United States. *Contributions from the Cushman Laboratory for Foraminiferal Research,* v. 23, pp. 86–92.

1955. Foraminifera, Their Classification and Economic Use. Boston: Harvard University Press, 4th edition. 604 p.

Cushman, J. A., and Brönnimann, P. 1948a. Some new genera and species of foraminifera from brackish water of Trinidad. Cushman Laboratory for Foraminiferal Research, v. 24, pp. 15–21.

1948b. Additional new species of arenaceous foraminifera from shallow waters of Trinidad. Cushman Laboratory for Foraminiferal Research, v. 24, pp. 37–42.

Cushman, J. A., and Cole, W. S. 1930. Pleistocene foraminiferida from Maryland. *Contributions to the Cushman Laboratory for Foraminiferal Research,* v. 6, pp. 94–100.

Cushman, J. A., and McCulloch, I. 1939. A report on some arenaceous foraminifera. *Allan Hancock Pacific Expedition,* v. 6, pp. 1–113.

Cushman, J. A., and Todd, R. 1947. A foraminiferal fauna from Amchitka Island, Alaska. *Contributions from the Cushman Laboratory for Foraminiferal Research,* v. 23, pp. 60–72.

Dallimore, A, Schröder-Adams, C. J., and Dallimore, S. 2000. Holocene environmental history of thermokarst lakes on Richards Island, Northwest Territories, Canada: thecamoebians as paleolimnological indicators. *Journal of Paleolimnology,* vo. 23, pp. 261–83.

Danovaro, R., Fabiano, M., and Vinci, M. 1995. Meiofauna response to the Agip Abruzzo oil spill in subtidal sediments of the Ligurian Sea. *Marine Pollution Bulletin,* v. 30, pp. 133–45.

Davis, C. A. 1916. On the fossil algae of the petroleum-yielding shales of the Green River Formation of Colorado and Utah. National Academy of Science, *Proceedings,* v. 2, pp. 114–19.

Dawson, G. M. 1870. On foraminifera from the Gulf and River St. Lawrence. *Canadian Natural and Quaternary Journal of Science,* v. 5, new se., pp. 172–80.

Dawson, J. W. 1860. Notice of tertiary fossils from Labrador, Maine, etc., and remarks on the climate of Canada in the newer Pliocene or Pleistocene period. *Canadian Naturalist,* v. 5, pp. 188–200.

Dawson, W. 1917. Tides at the head of the Bay of Fundy. Ottawa: Department of Naval Sciences, p. 34.

Debenay, J.-P., Eichler, B. B., Duleba, W., Bonetti, C., and Eichler-Coelho, P. 1998. Water stratification in coastal lagoons: its influence on foraminiferal assemblages in two Brazilian lagoons. *Marine Micropaleontology,* v. 35, pp. 67–89.

Decloître, L. 1953. Recherches sur les Rhizopodes thécamoebiens d'A.O.F. Bulletin de l'Institut Français de l'Afrique Noire, *Mémoires,* no. 31, 249 p.

Deflandre, G. 1929. Le genre *Centropyxis* Stein. *Archiv für Protistenkunde,* v. 67, pp. 322–75.

  1953. Ordres des testaceolobosa (De Saedeleer, 1934), testaceofilosa (De Saedeleer, 1934), thalamia (Haeckel, 1862) ou thécamoebiens (Auct.) (Rhizopoda, Testacea). In Grassé, P. P. (ed.), *Traité de Zoologie,* v. 1. Paris: Masson, pp. 97–148.

DeLaca, T. E., Lipps, J. H., and Hessler, R. R. 1980. The morphology and ecology of a new large agglutinated antarctic foraminifer (*Textularina notodendroidae,* sp.n.). *Linnean Society Zoological Journal,* v. 69, pp. 205–24.

Den Dulk, M., Zachariasse, W. J., and Van der Zwaan, G. J. 1998. Benthic foraminifera as proxies of organic flux and oxygen in the Arabian Sea oxygen minimum zone. *Forams '98,* Conference, Monterrey, Mexico (Abstract), p. 28.

Doig, R. 1998. 3000-year paleoseismological record from the region of the 1988 Saguenay, Quebec, earthquake. *Bulletin of the Seismological Society of America,* v. 88, pp. 1198–203.

Dujardin, F. 1840. Mémoires sur une classification des infusoires en rapport avec leur organisation. *Comptes Rendus Hebdomadaires des Séances de l'Académie des Sciences de Paris,* v. 11, no. 7, pp. 281–6.

  1841. Histoire naturelle des zoophytes. Infusoires, comprenant la physiologie et la classification de ces animaux, et la manière de les étudier à l'aide du microscope. De Roret, collection *Nouvelle Suites a Buffon, Formant, avec les Oeuvres de Cet Auteur, un Cours Complet d'Histoire Naturelle* (Paris).

Ehrenberg, C. G. 1830. Organisation, systematik und geographisches Verhältnis der Infusionsthierchen (Berlin). Printed by Druckerei der Königlichen Akademie der Wissenschaften, pp. 1–108.

  1832. Über die Entwicklung und Lebensdauer der Infusionsthiere, nebst ferneren Beiträgen zu einer Vergleichung ihrer organischen Systeme. Königliche Akademie der Wissenschaften zu Berlin, Abhandlungen, 1831, *Physikalische Abhandlungen,* pp. 1–154.

  1838. Die Infusionsthierchen als vollkommene Organismen. *Ein Blick in das Tiefere Organische Leben der Natur,* 2 vols. Leipzig: L. Voss, pp. i–xviii, 1–547, pls. 1–64.

  1840. Untitled. *Bericht über die zur Bekanntmachung Geeigneten Verhandlungen der Königliche Preussischen Akademie der Wissenschaften zu Berlin,* v. 5, pp. 197–219. [Loeblich and Tappan (1964) reported the title as *"Das grössere Infusorienwerke."*]

  1843. Verbreitung und Einfluss des mikroskopischen Lebens in Süd- und Nord-Amerika: Königliche Akademie der Wissenschaften zu Berlin, Abhandlungen, 1841, *Physikalische Abhandlungen,* pp. 291–446.

  1848. Fortgesetzte Beobachtungen über jetzt herrschende atmosphärische mikroskopische Verhältnisse. *Bericht über die zur Bekanntmachung Geeigneten Verhandlungen der Königliche Preussischen Akademie der Wissenschaften zu Berlin,* v. 13, pp. 370–81.

  1872. Übersicht der seit 1847 fortgesetzten Untersuchungen über das von der Atmosphäre unsichtbar getragene reiche organische Leben. *Königliche Akademie der Wissenshaften zu Berlin, Physikalische Abhandlungen,* 1871, pp. 1–150.

Ellison, R. L. 1972. *Ammobaculites,* foraminiferal proprietor of Chesapeake Bay estuaries. *Geological Society of America Mem.,* no. 133, pp. 247–62.

  1995. Paleolimnological analysis of Ullswater using testate amoebae. *Journal of Paleolimnology,* v. 13, pp. 51–63,

Ellison, R. L., and Nichols, M. M. 1976. Modern and Holocene foraminifera in the Chesapeake Bay region. First International Symposium on Benthonic Foraminifera of the Continental Margins. Part A, Ecology and Biology, *Maritime Sediments,* Special Publication no. I, pp. 131–51.

Elverhoi, A., Liestol, O., and Nagy, J. 1980. Glacial erosion, sedimentation and microfauna in the inner part of Kongsfjordon, Spitsbergen. *Saertrykk av Norsk Blarinstitutt,* skrifter no. 172, 62 p.

Emery, K. O., and Garrison, L. E. 1967. Sea levels 7,000 to 20,000 years ago. *Science,* v. 157, pp. 684–87.

Fairweather, P. G. 1999. Determining the "health" of estuaries: priorities for ecological research. *Australian Journal of Ecology,* v. 24, pp. 441–51.

Ferraro, S. P., and Cole, F. A. 1995. Taxonomic level sufficient for assessing pollution impacts on the Southern California Bight macrobenthos – revisited. *Environmental Toxicology and Chemistry,* v. 14, pp. 1031–5.

Ferraro, S. P., Swartz, R. C., Cole, F. A., and Schultz, D. W. 1991. Temporal changes in the benthos along a pollution gradient: discriminating the effects of natural phenomena from sewage-industrial wastewater effects. *Estuarine, Coastal and Shelf Science,* v. 33, pp. 383–407.

Fichtel, L., and Moll, J.P.C. 1798. Testacea microscopica, aliaque minuta ex generibus *Argonauta* et *Nautilus,* ad naturam picta et descripta (microscopishe und andere klein Schalthiere aus den geschlechtern Argonaute und Schiffer). Vienna: Camesina, 124 p.

Flessa, K.W., and Kowalewski, M. 1994. Shell survival and time-averaging in nearshore and shelf environments – estimates from the radiocarbon literature. *Lethaia,* v. 27, pp. 153–65.

Frenguelli, G. 1933. Tecamebiani e diatomee nel Miocene del neuquén (Patagonia Settentrionale). *Bollettino della Societá Geologica Italiana,* v. 52, pp. 33–43.

Gayes, P. T., Scott, D. B., Collins, E. S., Nelson, D. D. 1992. A late Holocene sea-level irregularity in South Carolina. Society of Economic Paleontologist and Mineralists, Special Publication no. 48, pp. 154–60.

Gehrels, W. R. 1994. Deforming relative sea-level change from salt marsh foraminifera and plant zones on the coast of Maine, USA. *Journal of Coastal Research,* v. 10, pp. 990–1009.

Gibson, T. G., and Walker, W. 1967. Floatation methods for obtaining foraminifera from sediment samples. *Journal of Paleontology,* v. 41, pp. 1294–7.

Ginsburg, R., and Glynn, P. 1994. Summary of the Colloquium and Forum on Global Aspects of Coral Reefs: health, hazards and history. In Ginsburg, R. N. (Compiler), 1993. *Proceedings, Colloquium and Forum on Global Aspects of Coral Reefs: Health, Hazards and History,* Rosenstiel School of Marine and Atmospheric Science, University of Miami, Florida, pp. i–viii.

Giussani, G., and Galanti G. 1992. Experience in eutrophication recovery by biomanipulation. *Memorie dell'Istituto Italiano di Idrobiologia,* v. 50, pp. 397–416.

Gonzales-Oreja, J. A., and Saiz-Salinas, J. I. 1998. Exploring the relationships between abiotic variables and benthic community structure in a polluted estuarine system. *Water Research,* v. 32, pp. 3799–3807.

Goldberg, E. D. 1998. Marine pollution – an alternative view. *Marine Pollution Bulletin,* v. 36, pp. 112–13.

Gooday, A. J., and Rathburn, A. E. 1999. Temporal variability in living deep-sea benthonic foraminifera: a review. *Earth Sciences Reviews,* v. 46, pp. 187–212.

Grabert, B. 1971. Zur eignung von foraminiferen als indikatoren für sandwanderung. *Deutsche Hydrographische Zeitschrift,* v. 24, pp. 1–14.

Grant, J., Hatcher, A., Scott, D. B., Pocklington, P., Schafer, C. T., and Winters, G. A. 1995. A multidisciplinary approach to evaluating benthic impacts of shellfish aquaculture. *Estuaries,* v. 18, pp. 124–44.

Grassé, P.-P. 1953. *Traité de Zoologie: Protozoaires,* v. 1, pt. 2, 1,160 pp., 833 text figs.

Green, K. E. 1960. Ecology of some arctic foraminifera. *Micropaleontolgy,* v. 6, pp. 57–78.

Green, M. A., Aller, R. C., and Aller, J. Y. 1993. Carbonate dissolution and temporal abundances of foraminifera in Long Island Sound sediments. *Limnology and Oceanography,* v. 38, pp. 331–45.

Greenstein, B. J., Harris, L. A., and Curran, H. A. 1998. Comparison of recent coral life and death assemblages to Pleistocene reef communities: implications for rapid faunal replacement on recent reefs. *Carbonates and Evaporites,* v. 13, pp. 23–31.

Gregory, M. R. 1970. Distribution of benthic foraminifera in Halifax Harbour, Nova Scotia, Canada: Ph.D. diss., Dept. of Geology, Dalhousie University, Halifax, Nova Scotia (unpublished manuscript).

Greiner, G.O.G. 1970. Environmental factors causing distributions of recent foraminifera. Ph.D. diss., Case Western Reserve, reproduced by University Microfilms, Ann Arbor, Michigan, 194 p. + charts (unpublished manuscript).

Grell, K. G. 1957. Untersuchungen über die Fortpflazung uns Sexualität der Foraminiferen. I – *Rotaliella roscoffensis. Archiv für Protistenkunde,* v. 102; pp. 147–64.

1958a. Untersuchungen über die Fortpflazung uns Sexualität der Foraminiferen. II – *Rubratella intermedia. Archiv für Protistenkunde,* v. 102; pp. 291–308.

1958b. Untersuchungen über die Fortpflazung uns Sexualität der Foraminiferen. III – *Glabratella sulcata. Archiv für Protistenkunde,* v. 102; pp. 449–72.

Guilizzoni, P., and Lami, A. 1988. Sub-fossil pigments as a guide to the phytoplankton history of the acidified Lake Orta (N. Italy). *Verhandlungen International Vereinigung Limnologie,* v. 23, pp. 874–9.

Guilizzoni, P., Lami, A., and Manca, M. 1989. Sull'uso di alcuni carotenoidi in ricerche sul plancton e in paleolimnologia. *Atti Societá Italiana di Ecologia,* v. 7, pp. 303–8.

Guilizzoni, P., Lami, A., Ruggiu, D., and Bonomi, G. 1986. Stratigraphy of specific algal and bacterial carotenoids in the sediments of Lake Varese (N. Italy). *Hydrobiologia,* v. 143, pp. 321–25.

Guinasso, N. L., and Schink, D. R. 1975. Quantitative estimates of biological mixing rates in abyssal sediments. *Journal of Geophysical Research,* v. 80, pp. 3032–43.

Gustafsson, M., and Nordberg, K. 1999. Benthic foraminifera and their response to hydrography, periodic hypoxic conditions and primary production in the Koljo fjord on the Swedish west coast. *Journal of Sea Research,* v. 41, pp. 163–78.

Haake, W. H. 1962. Untersuchungen an der Foraminiferenfauna in Wattgebiet zwischen Langeog und dem Zestland. *Meyniana,* v. 12, pp. 25–64.

Hallock, P. 1981. Light dependence in Amphistegina. *Journal of Foraminiferal Research,* v. 11, pp. 40–6.

Hallock, P., Rottger, R., and Wetmore, K. 1991. Hypotheses on form and function in Foraminifera. In Lee, J. J., and Anderson, O. R. (eds.), *Biology of Foraminifera.* New York: Academic Press, pp. 41–72.

Hallock, P., Talge, H. K., Cockey, E. M., and Müller, R. G. 1995. A new disease in reef-dwelling foraminifera: implications for coastal sedimentation. *Journal of Foraminiferal Research,* v. 25, no. 3, pp. 280–6.

Haman, D. 1982. Modern thecamoebinids (Arcellinida) from the Balize Delta, Louisiana: Gulf Coast Association of Geological Societies, *Transactions,* v. 32, pp. 353–76, pls. 1–4.

1986. Testacealobosa from Big Bear Lake, California, with comments on *Difflugia tricuspis* Carter, 1856. *Revista Española de Micropaleontlogia,* v. 18, pp. 47–54.

1990. Living thecamoebid distribution, biotopes and biofacies, in an upper deltaic plain lacustrine subenvironment, Lac des Allemands, Louisiana. *Revista Española de Micropaleontologica,* v. 22, pp. 47–60.

Hansen, H. J., and Lykke-Andersen, A.-L. 1976. Wall structure and classification of fossil and recent Elphidiid and Nonionid foraminifera. *Fossils and Strata,* Universitetsforlaget Oslo, no. 10, 37 p.

Haq, B. U., and Boersma, A. 1978. Introduction to Marine Micropaleontology. New York: Elsevier, 376 p.

Hayes, M. O. 1980. General morphology and sediment patterns in tidal inlets. *Sedimentary Geology,* v. 26, pp. 139–56.

Haynes, J. 1973. Cardigan Bay recent foraminifera (Cruises of the *R.V. Antur,* 1962–1964). British Museum (Natural History) Bulletin, *Zoology,* Supplement 4, London, pp. 1–245.

Haynes, J. R. 1981. *Foraminifera.* New York: John Wiley and Sons, 433 p.

Hayward, B. W., and Hollis, C. J. 1994. Brackish foraminifera in New Zealand: a taxonomic and ecological review. *Micropaleontology,* v. 40(3), pp. 185–222.

Hayward, B. W., Grenfell, H. R., and Scott, D. B. 1999. Tidal range of marsh foraminifera for determining former sea-level heights in New Zealand. *New Zealand Journal of Geology and Geophysics,* v. 42, pp. 395–413.

Hemphill-Haley, E. 1995. Diatom evidence for earthquake-induced subsidence and tsunami 300 years ago in southern Washington. Geological Society of America, *Bulletin,* v. 107, pp. 367–78.

Hessland, I. 1943. Marine Schalenablager-ungen Nord-Borduslans. Geological Institute of Uppsala, *Bulletin,* 31 p.

Hewitt, J. E, Thrush, S. F., Cummings, V. J., and Turner, S. J. 1998. The effect of changing sampling scale on our ability to detect effects of large-scale processes on communities. *Journal of Experimental Marine Biology and Ecology,* v. 227, pp. 251–64.

Hillaire-Marcel, C. 1981. Paleo-oceanographie isotopique des mers post-glaciares du Quebec. *Palaeogeography, Paleoclimatology, Paleoecology,* v. 37, pp. 63–119.

Hjülstrom, F. 1939. Transport of detritus by moving water. In Trask, P. D. (ed.), *Recent Marine Sediments.* Tulsa, Oklahoma: American Association of Petroleum Geologists, p. 5.

Höglund, H. 1947. Foraminifera in the Gullmar Fjord and the Skagerak Ph.D. diss., University of Uppsala, Sweden, 328 p., 32 pls.

Holmden, C., Creaser, R. A., and Muehlenbachs, K. 1997b. Paleosalinities in ancient brackish water systems determined by 87Sr/86Sr ratios in carbonate fossils: a case study from the Western Canada Sedimentary Basin. *Geochimica et Cosmochimica Acta,* v. 61, pp. 2105–18.

Holmden, C., Muehlenbachs, K., and Creaser, R. A. 1997a. Depositional environment of the early Cretaceous ostracode zone: Paleohydrologic constraints from O, C and Sr isotopes. In Pemberton, S. G., and James, D. P. (eds.), *Petroleum Geology of the Cretaceous Mannville Group,* *Western Canada.* Canadian Society of Petroleum Geologists, *Memoir* 18, pp. 77–92.

Honig, C. A., and Scott, D. B. 1987. Post-glacial stratigraphy and sea-level change in southwestern New Brunswick. *Canadian Journal of Earth Sciences,* v. 24, pp. 354–64.

Horton, B. P., Edwards, R. J., and Lloyd, J. M. 1999a. A foraminiferal-based transfer function: implications for sea-level studies. *Journal of Foraminiferal Research,* v. 29, no. 2, pp. 117–29.

Horton, B. P., Edwards, R. J., and Lloyd, J. M. 1999b. UK intertidal foraminiferal distributions: implications for sea-level studies. *Marine Micropaleontology,* v. 36, pp. 205–23.

Houghton, J. T., Jenkins, G. J., and Ephraums, J. J. (eds.). 1990. *Climate Change, The IPCC Scientific Assessment.* Cambridge: Cambridge University Press, 365 p.

Howe, H. V. 1959. Fifty years of micropaleontology. *Journal of Paleontology,* v. 33, pp. 511–17.

Ingram, B. L., and DePaolo, D. J. 1993. A 4300 year strontium isotope record of estuarine paleosalinity in San Francisco Bay, California. *Earth and Planetary Science Letters,* v. 119, pp. 103–19.

Ingram, B. L., and Sloan, D. 1992. Strontium isotopic composition of estuarine sediments as paleosalinity-paleoclimate indicator. *Science,* v. 255, pp. 68–72.

Ives, A. R. 1995. Predicting the response of populations to environmental change. *Ecology,* v. 76, pp. 926–41.

Jahnke, R. A., Craven, D. B., and Gaillard, J-F. 1994. The influence of organic matter diagenesis on $CaCO_3$ dissolution at the deep-sea floor. *Geochimica et Cosmochimica Acta,* v. 58, pp. 2799–2809.

Javaux, E.J.J.M. 1999. Benthic foraminifera from the modern sediments of the Bermuda: implications for Holocene sea-level studies. Ph.D. diss., Dalhousie University, Halifax, Canada, 621 p. (unpublished manuscript).

Jennings, A. E., and Nelson, A. R. 1992. Foraminiferal assemblage zones in Oregon tidal marshes – relation to marsh floral zones and sea-level. *Journal of Foraminiferal Research,* v. 22, pp. 13–29.

Jennings, A. E., Nelson, A. R., Scott, D. B., and Aravena, J. C. 1995. Marsh foraminiferal assemblages in the Valdivia Estuary, south-central Chile, relative to vascular plants and sea-level. *Journal of Coastal Research,* v. 11, pp. 107–23.

Jennings, H. S. 1916. Heredity, variation and the results of selection in the uniparental reproduction of *Difflugia corona. Genetics,* v. 1, pp. 407–534.

1929. Genetics of the protozoa. *Bibliographia Genetica,* v. 5, pp. 105–330.

1937. Formation, inheritance and variation of the teeth in *Difflugia corona:* A study of the morphogenic activities of rhizopod protoplasm. *Journal of Experimental Zoology,* v. 77, pp. 287–336.

Jorissen, F. J. 1998. Towards a quantification of benthic foraminiferal paleoproductivity record. Forams '98 Conference, Monterrey, Mexico (abstract), pp. 55.

Jorissen, F. J., and Wittling, I. 1999. Ecological evidence from live–dead comparisons of benthic foraminiferal faunas off Cape Blanc (Northwest Africa). *Palaeogeography, Palaeoclimatology, Palaeoecology,* v. 149, pp. 151–70.

Josefson, A. B., and Widbom, B. 1988. Differential response of benthic macrofauna and meiofauna to hypoxia in the Gullmar Fjord basin. *Marine Biology,* v. 100, pp. 31–40.

Kemp, A. L. W., Thomas, R. L., Dell, C. I., and Jacquet, J. M. 1976. Cultural impact on the geochemistry of sediments in Lake Erie. *Journal of the Fisheries Research Board of Canada,* v. 33, pp. 440, 462.

Kanmacher, F. (ed.). 1798. *Adam's Essays on the Microscope: The Second Edition, with Considerable Additions and Improvements.* London: Dillon and Keating, 712 p.

Kautsky, L. 1998. Monitoring eutrophication and pollution in estuarine environments – focusing on the use of benthic communities. *Pure and Applied Chemistry,* v. 70, pp. 2313–8.

Kerr, H. A. 1984. Arcellaceans in Eastern Canada: selected biostratigraphic and biological studies. Honours thesis, Dalhousie University, Halifax, Nova Scotia (unpublished manuscript), 49 p.

Kitazato, H., Yamaoka, A., Ohga, T., and Kusano, H. 1998. Seasonal changes in the population ecology of bathyal benthic foraminifera in Sagami Bay, Japan: What do eight years of record tell us? Forams '98. Conference, Monterrey, Mexico (abstract), p. 56.

Kliza, D. A. 1994. Distribution of Arcellacea in freshwater lakes of Pond Inlet and Bylot Island, Northwest Territories. Honours thesis, Carleton University, Ottawa, Ontario (unpublished manuscript), 52 p.

Kornfeld, M. M. 1931. Recent littoral foraminifera from Texas and Louisiana. *Contributions from the Department of Geology, Stanford University,* v. 1, pp. 77–107.

Kota, S., Borden, R. C., and Barlaz, M. A. 1999. Influence of protozoan grazing on contaminant biodegradation. *FEMS Microbiology Ecology,* v. 29, pp. 179–89.

Kövary, J. 1956. Thékamöbák (Testaceák) a magyarorszagy alsópannóniai korú üled ékekböl. *Földtani Közlöny,* v. 86, pp. 266–73.

Laidler, R. B., and Scott, D. B. 1996. Foraminifera and arcellacea from Porters Lake, Nova Scotia: modern distribution and paleodistribution. *Canadian Journal of Earth Sciences,* v. 33, pp. 1410–27.

Lamarck, J. B. 1816. Histoire naturella des animaux sans vertèbres. *Tone* 2, pp. 1–568, Verdière (Paris).

Lambert, J., and Chardez, D. 1978. Intérêt criminalistique de la microfaune terrestre. *Revue Internationale de Police Criminelle,* no. 319, pp. 158–70.

Lami, A. 1986. Paleolimnology of the eutrophic Lake Varese (Northern Italy). 3. Stratigraphy and organic matter, carbonates and nutrients in several sediment cores. *Memorie dell'Istituto Italiano di Idrobiologia,* v. 44, pp. 27–46.

Latimer, J., Boothman, W., Tobin, R., Keith, D., Kiddon, J., Scott, D. B., Jayaraman, S., McKinney, R., Cobb, D., and Chmura, G. 1997. Historical reconstruction of contamination levels and ecological effects in a highly contaminated estuary. Abstract to Estuarine Research Federation Annual Meeting, Providence, RI (October).

Lee, J. J., and Anderson, O. R. 1991. *Biology of Foraminifera.* London: Academic Press, 368 p.

LeFurgey, A., and St. Jean, J. 1976. Foraminifera in brackishwater ponds designed for waste control and aquaculture studies in North Carolina. *Journal of Foraminiferal Research,* v. 6, pp. 274–94.

Leggett, R. F. 1945. Pleistocene deposits of the Shipshaw area, Quebec. *Transactions of the Royal Society of Canada,* sec. 4, ser. 3, v. 39, pp. 27–39.

Leidy, J. 1875. Notice of some rhizopods. *Proceedings of the Academy of Natural Sciences of Philadelphia,* ser. 3, v. 26, pp. 155–7.

1879. Freshwater rhizopods of North America. U.S. Geological Survey of the Territories, *Report,* v. 12, 324 p.

Lévy, A., Mathieu, R., Momeni, I., Poignant, A., Rosset-Moulinier, M., Rouvillois, A., and Ubaldo, M. 1969. Les représentants de la famille de elphidiidae (foraminifères) dans les sables des plages des environs de Dunkerque: remarques sur les espèces de *Polystomella* signalées par O. Terquem. *Revue de Micropaleontologie,* v. 12, no. 2, pp. 92–98, pls. 1, 2.

Li, C., Jones, B., and Blanchon, P. 1997. Lagoon-shelf sediment exchange by storms – evidence from foraminiferal assemblages, east coast of Grand Cayman, British West Indies. *Journal of Sedimentary Research,* v. 67, pp. 17–25.

Liddell, W. D., and Martin, R. E. 1989. Taphofacies in modern carbonate environments: implications for formation of foraminiferal sediment assemblages. 28th International Geological Congress, Washington, D.C., Abstracts, v. 2, p. 299.

Linné, C., 1758. Systema naturae per regna tria naturae, secundum classes, ordines, genera, species, cum characteribus, differentiis, synonymis, locis. *G. Engelmann (Lipsiae),* ed. 10, v. 1, pp. 1–824.

Lipps, J. H. 1983. Biotic interactions in benthic foraminifera. In Trevesz and McCall (eds.):, *Biotic Interactions in Recent and Fossil Benthic Communities.* New York: Plenum Press, pp. 331–76.

Lipps, J. H. 1993. *Fossil prokaryotes and protists.* Boston: Blackwell Scientific Publications, 342 p.

Lister, A. 1895. Contributions to the life history of the foraminifera: Royal Society of London, *Philosophical Transactions,* ser. B, v. 186, pp. 401–53.

Liu, K.-B., and Fearn, M. L. 1993. Lake sediment record of Late Holocene hurricane activities from coastal Alabama. *Geology,* v. 21, pp. 793–6.

Livingstone, D. A. 1968. Some interstadial and postglacial pollen diagrams from eastern Canada. *Ecological Monographs,* v. 38, pp. 87–125.

Loeblich, A. R. Jr., and Collaborators (Tappan, H., Beckman, J. P., Bolli, H. M., Gallitelli, E. M., Troeslsen, J. C.). 1957. Studies in foraminifera. United States National Museum, *Bulletin* 215, 321 p.

Loeblich, A. R., Jr., and Tappan, H. 1953. Studies of arctic foraminifera. *Smithsonian Miscellaneous Collection,* v. 121, pp. 1–150.

1964. Sarcodina, chiefly "thecamoebians" and foraminiferida. In Moore, R. C. (ed.), *Treatise on Invertebrate Paleontology. Part C, Protista 2.* Geological Society of America and University of Kansas Press, v. 1, pp. i–xiii+ cl, c510a.

Loeblich, A. R., Jr., and Tappan, H. 1988. *Foraminiferal Genera and Their Classification.* New York: Van Nostrand Reinhold, 2 v., pp. 1–970, pls. 1–847.

Loose, T. L. 1970. Turbulent transport of benthonic foraminifera. *Contributions from the Cushman Foundation for Foraminiferal Research,* v. 21, pt. 4, pp. 164–6.

Loubere, P. 1989. Bioturbation and sedimentation rate control of benthyic microfossil taxon abundances in surface sediments: a theorethical approach to the analusis of species microhabitats. *Marine Micropaleontology,* v. 14, pp. 317–25.

Loubere, P., Gary, A., and Lagoe, M. 1993. Generation of the benthic foraminiferal assemblage: theory and preliminary data. *Marine Micropaleontology,* v. 20, pp. 165–81.

Lynts, G. W. 1966. Variation of foraminiferal standing crop over short lateral distances in Buttonwood Sound, Florida Bay. *Limnology and Oceanography,* v. 11, pp. 562–6.

Margalef, R. 1968. *Perspectives in Ecological Theory.* Chicago: University of Chicago Press, 111 p.

Martin, R. E., and Liddell, W. D. 1989. Relation of counting methods to taphonomic gradients and information content of foraminiferal sediment assemblages. *Marine Micropaleontology,* v. 15, pp. 67–89.

Martin, R. E., and Steinker, D. C. 1973. Evaluation of techniques for recognition of living foraminifera. *Compass,* v. 50, pp. 26–30.

Martin, R. E., and Wright, R. C. 1988. Information loss in the transition from life to death assemblages of foraminifera in back reef environments, Key Largo, Florida. *Journal of Paleontology,* v. 62, pp. 399–410.

Maxwell, W. G. H. 1968. *Atlas of the Great Barrier Reef.* Amsterdam: Elsevier.

McCarthy, F. M. G., Collins, E. S., McAndrews, J. H., Kerr, H. A., Scott, D. B., and Medioli, F. S. 1995. A comparison of postglacial arcellacean (thecamoebians) and pollen succession in Atlantic Canada, illustrating the potential of arcellaceans for paleoclimatic reconstruction. *Journal of Paleontology,* v. 69, no. 5, pp. 980–93.

McCrone, A. W., and Schafer, C. T. 1966. Geochemical and sedimentary environments of foraminifera in the Hudson River estuary, New York. *Micropaleontology,* v. 12, pp. 505–5.

McCulloch, D. S., and Bonilla, M. G. 1970. Effects of the earthquake of March 27, 1964 on the Alaska Railroad. U.S. Geological Survey Professional Paper, 545-D, 161 p.

McGee, B. L., Schlekat, C. E., Boward, D. M, and Wade, T. L. 1995. Sediment contamination and biological effects in a Chesapeake Bay marina. *Ecotoxicology,* v. 4, pp. 39–59.

McLean, J. R., and Wall, J. H. 1981. The Early Cretaceous Moosebar Sea in Alberta. *Bulletin of Canadian Petroleum Geology,* v. 29, pp. 334–77.

Medioli, B. E. 1995a. Marginal marine foraminifera and thecamoebians in the Upper Cretaceous to Eocene deposits of the south-central Pyrenees, Spain. Honors BSc. thesis, Dalhousie University (unpublished manuscript).

1995b. Marginal marine foraminifera and thecamoebians in the Upper Cretaceous to Eocene deposits of the south-central Pyrenees, Spain. Abstract, Atlantic Universities Geological Conference 1995, *Atlantic Geology,* v. 31, no. 3, p. 211.

Medioli, F. S., and Scott, D. B, 1983. Holocene arcellacea (thecamoebians) from Eastern Canada. Cushman Foundation for Foraminiferal Research, Special Publication no. 21, 63 p.

1988. Lacrustrine thecamoebians (mainly arcellaceans) as potential tools for paleolimnological interpretations. *Palaeogeography, Paleoclimatology, Paleoecology,* v. 62, pp. 361–86.

1988. Lucrustrine thecamoebians (mainly Arcellaceans) as potential tools for paleolimnological interpretation. *Palaeogeography, Palaeoclimatology, Palaeoecology,* v. 62, pp. 361–86.

Medioli, F. S., Asioli, A., and Parenti, G. 1994. Manuale per l'identificazione delle tacamebe con informazioni sul loro significato paleoecologico e stratigrafico. *Palaeopelagos,* v. 4, pp. 317–64.

Medioli, F. S., Scott, D. B., and Abbott, B. H. 1987. A case study of protozoan intraclonal variability: taxonomic implications. *Journal of Foraminiferal Research,* v. 17, pp. 28–47.

Medioli, F. S., Scott, D. B, Wall, J. T., and Collins, E. S. 1990a. Thecamoebians from Early Cretaceous deposits of Ruby Creek, Alberta (Canada) In Hemleben, C., Kaminski, M. A., Kuhnt, W., and Scott, D. B. (eds.), *Paleoecology, Biostratigraphy, Paleoceanography and Taxonomy of Agglutinated Foraminifera,* NATO ASI Series C. Mathematical and Physical Sciences, v. 327, pp. 793–812.

Medioli, F. S., Scott, D. B., Collins, E. S., and McCarthy, F. M. G. 1990b. Fossil thecamoebians: present status and prospects for the future. In Hemleben, C., Kaminski, M. A., Kuhnt, W., and Scott, D. B. (eds.), *Paleoecology, Biostratigraphy, Paleoceanography and Taxonomy of Agglutinated Foraminifera,* NATO ASI Series C. Mathematical and Physical Sciences, v. 327, pp. 813–39.

Medioli, F. S., Scott, D. B, and Wall, J. T. 1986. Early Cretaceous arcellacea from Ruby Creek, Alberta. *Abstract,* Annual Geological Society of America Meeting, San Antonio, 1986.

Menon, M. G., Gibbs, R. J., and Phillips, A. 1998. Accumulation of muds and metals in the Hudson River Estuary turbidity maximum. *Environmental Geology,* v. 34, pp. 214–19.

Miller, A.A.L., Mudie, P. J., and Scott, D. B. 1982a. Holocene history of Bedford Basin, Nova Scotia: foraminifera, dinoflagellate and pollen records. *Canadian Journal of Earth Sciences,* v. 19, pp. 2342–67.

Miller, A.A.L., Scott, D. B., and Medioli, F. S. 1982b. *Elphidium excavatum* (Terquem): ecophenotypic versus subspecific variation. *Journal of Foraminiferal Research,* v. 12, pp. 116–44.

Miner, E. L. 1935. Paleobotanical examinations of Cretaceous and Tertiary coals. *The American Midland Naturalist,* v. 16, pp. 585–625.

Montagu, G. 1803. *Testacea Britannica, or Natural History of British Shells, Marine, Land, and Fresh-water, including the Most Minute.* Romsey, England: J. S. Hollis, 606 p.

1808. *Testacea Britannica.* Supplement Exeter, England: S. Woolmer, 183 p.

Montfort de, P. D. 1808. Conchyliologie systématique et classification méthodique des coquilles 1. Paris: F. de Schoell, 409 p.

Monti, R. 1930. La graduale estinzione della vita nel Lago d'Orta. *Rendiconti del Regio Istituto Lombardo di Scienze e Lettere,* v. 63, pp. 22–32.

Moodley, L., and Hess, C. 1992. Tolerance of infaunal benthic foraminifera for low and high oxygen concentrations. *Biology Bulletin*, v. 183, pp. 94–8.

Mott, R. J. 1975. Palynological studies of lake sediment profiles from southwestern New Brunswick. *Canadian Journal of Earth Sciences*, v. 12, no. 1, pp. 273–88.

Murray, J. W. 1965. Two species of British recent foraminiferida. *Contributions from the Cushman Foundation for Foraminiferal Research*, v. 16, pp. 148–50.

1973. *Distribution and Ecology and Living Benthic Foraminiferids*. London: Heineman, 274 p.

1980. The foraminifera of the Axe Estuary. The Devonshire Association for the Advancement of Science, Literature and Art, Special Volume no. 2, pp. 89–115.

1991. *Ecology and Paleoecology of Benthic Foraminifera*. London: Longman Scientific and Technical, 397 p.

Murray, J. W., Sturrock, S., and Weston, J. 1982. Suspended load transport of foraminiferal tests in a tide- and wave-swept sea. *Journal of Foraminiferal Research*, v. 12, pp. 51–65.

Mutti, E., Seguret, M., and Sgavetti, M. 1988. Sedimentation and deformation in the Tertiary Sequences of the Pyrenees. American Association of Petroleum Geologists, Mediterranean Basin Conference. Special Publication of the University of Parma, Field Trip 7, 153 p.

Myers, E. H. 1935. Morphogenesis of the test and the biological significance of dimorphism in the foraminifer *Patellina corrugata* Williamson. *Bulletin of the Scripps Institute of Oceanography*, Technical Series, v. 3, pp. 393–404.

1942. A qualitative study of the productivity of the Foraminifera in the sea. American Philosophical Society, *Proceedings*, v. 85, pp. 325–42.

Nelson, A. R. 1992. Discordant ^{14}C ages from buried tidal-marsh soils in the Cascadia subduction zone, southern Oregon coast. *Quaternary Research*, v. 38, pp. 74–90.

Nelson, A. R., Jennings, A. E., and Kashima, K. 1996. An earthquake history derived from stratigraphic and micro-fossil evidence of relative sea-level change at Coos Bay, southern coastal Oregon. Geological Society of America, *Bulletin*, v. 108, pp. 141–54.

Nichols, M. M. 1974. Foraminifera in estuarine classification. In Odum, H. T., Copeland, B. J., and McMahan, E. A., (eds), *Coastal Ecosystems of the United States*, v. 1, pp. 85–103.

Nørvang, A. 1945. The zoology of Iceland. *Foraminifera*, v. 2, pt. 2. Copenhagen and Reykjavik: Ejnar Munksgaard, pp. 1–79.

Ogden, C. G., and Hedley, R. H. 1980. *An Atlas of Freshwater Testate Amoebae*. British Museum (Natural History). Oxford University Press, pp. 1–222.

Ogden, J. G. III. 1987. Vegetational and climatic history of Nova Scotia. I. Radiocarbon-dated pollen profiles from Halifax, Nova Scotia. *Canadian Journal of Botany*, v. 65, pp. 1482–7.

Orbigny, A. D. d'. 1826. Tableau méthodique de la classe des Cephalopodes. *Annales des Sciences Naturelles*, v. 7, pp. 245–314.

Orbigny, A. D. d'. 1839a. Foraminifères. In Sagra, R. de la, *Histoire Physique, Politique et Naturelle de l'Île de Cuba*, Paris: A. Bertrand, 224 p.

1839b. *Voyage dans l'Améque Méridionale – Foraminifères*, v. 5, pt. 5, 86 p., 9 pls. Paris: Pitois-Levrault et Co. Strasbourg: V. Levrault.

Palmer, M. R., and Edmund, J. M. 1989. The Strontium isotopic budget of the modern ocean. *Earth and Planetary Science Letters*, v. 92, pp. 11–26.

Parenti, G. 1992. Le Tecamebe nei sedimenti nel Lago Maggiore di Mantova. Master's thesis, Universitá degli Studi di Parma (unpublished manuscript), 110 p.

Parker, F. L. 1952. Foraminiferal distribution in the Long Island Sound–Buzzards Bay area. *Bulletin of the Harvard Museum of Comparative Zoology*, v. 106, pp. 438–73.

1954. Distribution of the foraminifera in the northeastern Gulf of Mexico. *Bulletin of the Harvard Museum of Comparative Zoology*, v. 111, pp. 453–588.

Parker, F. L., and Athearn, W. D. 1959. Ecology of marsh foraminifera in Poponesset Bay, Massachusetts. *Journal of Paleontology*, v. 33, pp. 333–43.

Parker, W. K., and Jones, T. R. 1859. On the nomenclature of the foraminifera. II. On the species enumerated by Walker and Montagu. *Annals and Magazine of Natural History*, ser. 3, v. 4, pp. 333–51.

Parker, W. K., and Jones, T. R. 1865. On some foraminifera from the North Atlantic and Arctic Oceans, including Davis Strait and Baffin's Bay. *Philosophical Transactions of the Royal Society*, v. 155, pp. 325–441.

Parker, F. L., Phleger, F. B., and Peirson, J. F. 1953. Ecology of foraminifera from San Antonio Bay and environs, southwest Texas. Cushman Foundation for Foraminiferal Research, Special Publication, no. 2, 75 p.

Patterson, R. T. 1990. Intertidal benthic foraminiferal biofacies on the Fraser River Delta, British Columbia – modern distribution and paleoecological importance. *Micropaleontology*, v. 36, pp. 229–45.

Patterson, R. T., Barker, T., and Burbridge, S. M. 1996. Arcellaceans (thecamoebians) as proxies of arsenic and mercury contamination in Northeastern Ontario lakes. *Journal of Foraminiferal Research*, v. 26, no. 2, pp. 172–83.

Patterson, R. T., and Kumar, A. 2000. Use of Arcellacea (thecamoebian) to gage levels of contamination and remediation in industrially polluted lakes. In Martin, R. E. (ed.), *Environmental Micropaleontology*, v. 15 of Topics in Geobiology. New York: Kluwer Academic Press, pp. 257–78.

Patterson, R. T., MacKinnon, K. D., Scott, D. B., and Medioli, F. S. 1985. Arcellaceans (thecamoebians) in small lakes of New Brunswick and Nova Scotia: Modern distribution and Holocene stratigraphic changes. *Journal of Foraminiferal Research*, v. 15, no. 2, pp. 114–37.

Pemberton, G. S., Risk, M. J., and Buckley, D. E. 1975. Supershrimp: deep bioturbation in the Strait of Canso, Nova Scotia. *Science*, v. 192, pp. 790–1.

Penard, E. 1902. *Faune Rhizopodique du Bassin du Léman*. Geneva: Henry Kündig, 714 p.

1905. *Les Sarcodinés des Grands Lacs*. Geneva: Henry Kündig, pp. 1–134.

1907. On some rhizopods from the Sikkim Himalaya. *Journal of the Royal Microscopical Society*, pp. 274–8, pl. 14.

Petrucci, F., Medioli, F. S., Scott, D. B., Pianetti, F. A., and Cavazzini, R. 1983. Evaluation of the usefulness of foraminifera as sea-level indicators in the Venice Lagoon (N. Italy). *Acta Naturalia de l'Ateneo Parmense,* v. 19, pp. 63–77.

Phleger, F. B. 1951. Ecology of foraminifera, Northwest Gulf of Mexico. Part 1, foraminiferal distribution. Geological Society of America, *Memoir* 46, 86 p.

——— 1954. Ecology of foraminifera and associated microorganisms from Mississippi Sound and environs. *Bulletin of the American Association of Petroleum Geologists,* v. 38, pp. 584–647.

——— 1960. *Ecology and Distribution of Recent Foraminifera.* Balitmore, Md: Johns Hopkins Press, 297 p.

——— 1965a. Living foraminifera from a coastal marsh, southwestern Florida. *Bolletin de la Sociedad Geologica Mexicana,* v. 28, pp. 45–59.

——— 1965b. Patterns of marsh foraminifera, Galveston Bay, Texas. *Limnology and Oceanography,* v. 10 (supplement), pp. R169–R184.

——— 1965c. Patterns of living marsh foraminifera in south Texas coastal lagoons. *Bolletin de la Sociedad Geologica Mexicana,* v. 28, pp. 1–44.

——— 1967. Marsh foraminiferal patterns, Pacific coast of North America. *Annales Instituto de Biologia,* Universidad Nacional Autonoma de Mexico, v. 38, serie del Mar y Limnologia (1), pp. 11–38.

Phleger, F. B, and Bradshaw, J. S. 1966. Sedimentary environments in a marine marsh. *Science,* v. 154, pp. 151–3.

Phleger, F. B, and Ewing, G. C. 1962. Sedimentology and oceanography of coastal lagoons in Baja California, Mexico. Geological Society of America, *Bulletin,* v. 73, pp. 145–81.

Phleger, F. B., and Walton, W. R. 1950. Ecology of marsh and bay foraminifera, Barnstable Mass. *American Journal of Science,* v. 248, pp. 274–94.

Plafker, G. 1969. Tectonics of the March 27, 1964, Alaska earthquake. U.S. Geological Survey, Professional Paper 543-I, 74 p.

Pocklington, P., Scott, D. B., and Schafer, C. T. 1994. Polychaete response to different aquaculture activities. In Dauvin, L., Laubier, L., and Reish, D.J. (eds.), *Actes de la 4eme Conference Internationale des Polychaetes.* Memoires du Museum National d'Histoire Naturelle, v. 162, pp. 511–20.

Porter, S. M., and Knoll, A. H. 2000. Testate amoebae in the Neoproterozoic Era: Evidence from vase-shaped microfossils in the Chuar Group, Grand Canyon. *Journal of Paleobiology,* v. 26, n. 3, p. 360.

Reinhardt, E. G., Patterson, R. T., Blenkinsop, J., and Raban, A. 1998a. Paleoenvironmental evolution of the inner basin of the ancient harbor at Caesarea Maritima, Israel; foraminiferal and Sr isotopic evidence. *Revue de Paléobiologie,* v. 17, pp. 1–21.

Reinhardt, E. G., Stanley, D., and Patterson, R. T. 1998b. Strontium isotopic-paleontological method as a high-resolution paleosalinity tool for lagoonal environments. *Geology,* v. 26, no. 11, pp. 1003–6.

Rhumbler, L. 1895. Beiträge zur Kenntnis der Rhizopoden (Beiträg III, IV und V). *Zeitschrift für Wissenschaftliche Zoologie,* v. 61, pp. 38–110.

——— 1911. Die foraminiferen (thalamophoren) der Plankton-Expedition; Teil 1. Die allegemeinen Organisationsverhaltnisse der foraminiferen. *Plankton-Expedition der Humboldt-Stiftung,* Ergenbn, v., 3 L.C., 331 p.

Ricci, N. 1991. Protozoa as tools in pollution assessment. *Marine Pollution Bulletin,* v. 22, pp. 265–8.

Riedel, H. P. 1985. General report on Sub-Theme C (b) – fundamentals of sediment movement in coastal areas and estuaries. *Proceedings of the 21st IAHR Congress,* Melbourne, Australia, pp. 19–23.

Rijk (de), S. 1995. Salinity control on the distribution of salt marsh foraminifera (Great Marshes, Massachusetts). *Journal of Foraminiferal Research,* v. 25, pp. 156–66.

Risk, M. J., Venter, R. D., Pemberton, S. G., and Buckley, D. E. 1978. Computer simulation and sedimentological implications of burrowing by Axius serratus. *Canadian Journal of Earth Sciences,* v. 15, pp. 1370–4.

Ros, J. D., and Cardell, M. J. 1991. Effect on benthic communities of a major input of organic matter and other pollutants (coast off Barcelona, western Mediterranean). *Toxicological and Environmental Chemistry,* v. 31–2, pp. 441–50.

Ruggiu, D., Saraceni, C., and Mosello, R. 1981. Fitoplancton, produzione primaria e caratteristiche chimiche di un lago fortemente eutrifizzato: il Lago di Varese. *Memorie dell'Istituto Italiano di Idrobiologia,* v. 39, pp. 47–64.

Rygg, B. 1985. Distribution of species along pollution-induced diversity gradients in benthic communities in Norwegian fjords. *Marine Pollution Bulletin,* v. 16, no. 12, pp. 469–74.

——— 1986. Heavy metal pollution and log-normal distribution of individuals among species in benthic communities. *Marine Pollution Bulletin,* v. 17, pp. 31–6.

Sanders, H. L. 1968. Marine benthic diversity: a comparative study. *American Naturalist,* v. 102, pp. 243–82.

——— 1969. Benthic marine diversity and the stability-time hypothesis. In *Diversity and Stability in Ecological Systems,* Brookhaven Symposia in Biology, v. 22, pp. 71–81.

Saunders, J. B. 1957. Trochamminidae and certain lituolidae (foraminifera) from the recent brackish-water sediments of Trinidad, British West Indies. *Smithsonian Miscellaneous Collections,* v. 134, pp. 1–16.

Sayles, F. L. 1985. CaCO$_3$ solubility in marine sediments: evidence for equilibrium and non-equilibrium behavior. *Geochimica et Cosmochimica Acta,* v. 49, pp. 877–88.

Schafer, C. T. 1968. Lateral and temporal variation of foraminifera populations living in nearshore water areas. *Atlantic Oceanographic Laboratory Report,* no. 68–4, 27 p.

Schafer, C. T. 1971. Sampling and spatial distribution of benthic foraminifera. *Limnology and Oceanography,* v. 16, pp. 944–51.

——— 1973. Distribution of foraminifera near pollution sources in Chaleur Bay. *Water, Air and Soil Pollution,* v. 2, pp. 219–33.

——— 1976. In situ environmental responses of benthonic foraminifera. *Geological Survey of Canada,* Paper 76–1C, pp. 27–32.

Schafer, C. T., and Cole, F. E. 1976. Depth distribution patterns in the Restigouche Estuary: proceedings of the First International Symposium on benthic foraminifera of the continental margins (Benthonics '75). *Maritime Sediments,* Special Publication no. 1, pp. 1–24.

1978. Distribution of foraminifera in Chaleur Bay, Gulf of St. Lawrence. *Geological Survey of Canada,* Paper 77–30, 55 p.

1986. Reconnaissance survey of benthonic foraminifera from Baffin Island fjord environments. *Arctic,* v. 39, pp. 232–9.

1995. Marine habitat recovery in the Saguenay Fjord, Canada: the legacy of environmental contamination. *Proceedings of the Oceans 95 Conference,* San Diego (October 9–12), pp. 925–40.

Schafer, C. T., Cole, F. E., Frobel, D., Rice, N., and Buzas, M. A. 1996. An in situ experiment on temperature sensitivity of nearshore temperate benthonic foraminifera. *Journal of Foraminiferal Research,* v. 26, pp. 53–63.

Schafer, C. T., Collins, E. S., and Smith, J. N. 1991. Relationship of Foraminifera and thecamoebian distributions to sediments contaminated by pulp mill effluent: Saguenay Fjord, Quebec, Canada. *Marine Micropaleontology,* v. 17 pp. 255–83.

Schafer, C. T., and Frape, F. E. 1974. Distribution of benthic foraminifera: their use in delimiting local nearshore environments. *Geological Survey of Canada,* Paper no. 74-30-1, pp. 103–8.

Schafer, C. T., and Mudie, P. J. 1980. Spatial variability of foraminifera and pollen in nearshore sediment sites, St. Georges Bay, Nova Scotia. *Canadian Journal of Earth Sciences,* v. 17, pp. 313–24.

Schafer, C. T., and Smith, J. N. 1983. River discharge, sedimentation, and benthic environmental variations in Miramichi Inner Bay, New Brunswick. *Canadian Journal of Earth Sciences,* v. 20, pp. 388–98.

1987a. Evidence of the occurrence and magnitude of terrestrial landslides in recent Saguenay Fjord sediments. *Proceedings of the International Symposium on Natural and Man-Made Hazzards,* Rimouski, Quebec, pp. 137–45.

1987b. Marine sedimentary evidence for a 17th century earthquake-triggered landslide in Quebec. *Geo-Marine Letters,* v. 7, pp. 31–7.

Schafer, C. T., Smith, J. N., and Coté, R. 1990. The Saguenay Fjord: a major tributary to the St. Lawrence Estuary. In Elsabh, M. I., and Silverberg, N. (eds.), *Oceanography of a Large-Scale Estuary: The St. Lawrence.* New York: Springer Verlag, pp. 421–8.

Schafer, C. T., Smith, J. N., and Loring, D. H, 1979. Recent sedimentation events at the head of the Saguenay Fjord. *Environmental Geology,* v. 3, pp. 139–50.

Schafer, C. T., Smith, J. N., and Seibert, G. 1983. Significance of natural and anthropogenic sediment inputs to the Saguenay Fjord, Quebec. *Sedimentary Geology,* v. 36, pp. 177–94.

Schafer, C. T., Wagner, F. J. E., and Ferguson, C. 1975. Occurrence of foraminifera, molluscs and ostracods adjacent to the industrialized shoreline of Canso Strait, Nova Scotia. *Water, Air and Soil Pollution,* v. 5, pp. 79–96.

Schafer, C. T., Winters, G. V., Scott, D. B., Pocklington, P., Cole, F. E., and Honig, C. 1995. Survey of living foraminifera and polychaete populations at some Canadian aquaculture sites: potential for impact mapping and monitoring. *Journal of Foraminiferal Research,* v. 25, pp. 236–59.

Schafer, C. T., You, K., Cole, F., and Zhu, X. 1992. Foraminifera distribution patterns as markers of tidal circulation modes in Sanya Harbour, China. In *Island Environment and Coast Development.* Nanjing, China Nanjing University Press, pp. 221–41.

Schafer, C. T., and Young, J. A. 1977. Experiments on mobility and transportability of some nearshore benthonic foraminifera species. Geological Survey of Canada, Paper 77–1C, pp. 27–31.

Schaudinn, E. 1895. Über den dimorphismus bei foraminiferen. *Sitzungsberichte der Gesellschaft Naturforschender Freunde zu Berlin,* no. 5. pp. 87–97.

Schlumberger, P. 1845. Observations sur quelques nouvelles espéces d'infusoires de la famille des rhizopodes. *Annales des Sciences Naturelles, Zoologie,* ser. 3, v. 3, pp. 254–6.

Schmitz, B., Åberg, G., Werdelin, L., Forey, P., and Bendix-Almgreen, S. E. 1991. $^{87}Sr/^{86}Sr$, Na, F, Sr and La in skeletal fish debris as a measure of the paleosalinity of fossil-fish habitats. Geological Society of America, *Bulletin,* v. 103, pp. 786–94.

Schmitz, B., Ingram, S. L., Dockey, D. T. III, and Åberg, G. 1997. Testing $^{87}Sr/^{86}Sr$ as a paleosalinity indicator on mixed marine, brackish-water and terrestrial vertebrate skeletal apatite in the late Paleocene–early Eocene near coastal sediments, Mississippi. *Chemical Geology,* v. 140, pp. 275–87.

Schnitker, D. 1971. Distribution of foraminifera on the North Carolina continental shelf. *Tulane Studies in Geology and Paleontology,* v. 8, pp. 169–215.

1974. Ecotypic variation in *Ammonia beccarii* (Linné). *Journal of Foraminiferal Research,* v. 4, no. 4, pp. 216–23.

Schönborn, W. 1962. Uber planktismus und zyklomorphose bei *Difflugia limnetica* (Levander) Penard. *Limnologica,* v. 1, pp. 21–34.

1984. Studies on remains of Testacea in cores of the Great Woryty Lake (NE-Poland). *Limnologica* (Berlin), v. 16, pp. 185–90.

Schröder, C. J., Scott, D. B., and Medioli, F. S. 1987. Can smaller benthic foraminifera be ignored in paleoenvironmental analysis? *Journal of Foraminiferal Research,* v. 17, pp. 101–5.

Schulze, F. E. 1875. Rhizopoden. In *Zoologische Ergebnisse der Nord-Seefahrt vom 21 Luli bius 9 September 1872* (series of articles), Jahresbericht der Kommission zur wissenschaftlichen Untersuchung der deutschen Meere in Kiel, v. 1, no. 2–3, pp. 97–114, pl. 2.

Scott, D. B. 1976a. Quantitative studies of marsh foraminiferal patterns in southern California and their application to Holocene stratigraphic problems. *First International Symposium on Benthonic Foraminifera of Continental Margins.* Part A, *Ecology and Biology.* Maritime Sediments Special Publication no. 1, pp. 153–70.

1976b. Brackish-water foraminifera from southern California and description of *Polysaccammina ipohalina* n. gen., n. sp. *Journal of Foraminiferal Research,* v. 6, pp. 312–21.

1987. Quaternary benthic foraminifers from Deep Sea Drilling Project Sites 612 and 613, Leg 95, New Jersey transect. In Poag, C. W., Watts, A. B., et al., *Initial Reports of the Deep Sea Drilling Project,* v. 95. Washington, D.C.: U.S. Government Printing Office, pp. 313–37.

1996. The earliest salt marsh foraminifera: foraminifera from an organic horizon in Cambrian rocks from Nova Scotia. *Abstract to Annual Meeting,* Geological Society of America, Denver, Colorado, October, p. A-486.

Scott, D. B., Baki, V., and Younger, C. D. 1989b. Late Pleistocene–Holocene paleoceanographic changes on the eastern Canadian margin: stable isotopic evidence. *Paleoecology, Paleogeography, Paleooceanography,* v. 74, pp. 279–95.

Scott, D. B., Boyd, R., and Medioli, F. S. 1987b. Relative sea-level changes in Atlantic Canada: observed level and sedimentological changes vs. theoretical models. In Nummendal, D., Pilkey, O. H., and Howard, J. D. (eds.), *Sea-level Fluctuations and Coastal Evolution.* Society of Economic Paleontologists and Mineralogists, Special Publication no. 41, pp. 87–96.

Scott, D. B., Boyd, R., Douma, M., Medioli, F. S., Yuill, S., Leavitt, E., and Lewis, C.F.M. 1989a. Holocene relative sea-level changes and Quaternary glacial events on a continental shelf edge: Sable Island Bank. In Scott, D. B., Pirazzoli, P. A., and Honig, C. A. (eds.), *Late Quaternary Sea-level Correlation and Applications,* NATO ASI Series C, Math and Physical Sciences, v. 256. Dordrecht, The Netherlands: Kluwer Academic Publisher, pp. 105–20.

Scott, D. B., Brown, K., Collins, E. S., and Medioli, F. S. 1995c. A new sea-level curve from Nova Scotia: evidence for a rapid acceleration of sea-level rise in the late mid-Holocene. *Canadian Journal of Earth Sciences,* v. 32, pp. 2071–80.

Scott, D. B., and Collins, E. S. 1996. Late mid-Holocene sea-level oscillation: a possible cause. *Quaternary Science Reviews,* v. 15, pp. 851–6.

Scott, D. B., Collins, E. S., Duggan, J., Asioli, A., Saito, T., and Hasegawa, S. 1996. Pacific Rim marsh foraminiferal distributions: implications for sea-level studies: *Journal of Coastal Research,* v. 12, pp. 850–61.

Scott, D. B., Collins, E. S., and Tobin, R. 1997. Historical reconstruction of impact histories from several sites on the east coast of North America using benthic foraminifera as indicators. Abstract to Estuarine Research Federation (ERF) Annual Meeting, Providence, R.I. (October).

Scott, D. B., Gayes, P. T., and Collins, E. S. 1995b. Mid-Holocene precedent for a future rise in sea-level along the Atlantic coast of North America. *Journal of Coastal Research,* v. 11, pp. 615–22.

Scott, D. B., Hasegawa, S., Saito, T., Ito,. K., and Collins, E. 1995d. Marsh foraminiferal and vegetation distributions in Nemuro Bay wetland areas, eastern Hokkaido. *Transactions and Proceedings of the Paleontological Society of Japan,* no. 180, pp. 282–95.

Scott, D. B., and Hermelin, J. O. R. 1993. A device for precision splitting of micropaleontological samples in liquid suspension. *Journal of Paleontology,* v. 67, pp. 151–4.

Scott, D. B., and Medioli, F. S. 1978. Vertical zonations of marsh foraminifera as accurate indicators of former sea-levels. *Nature,* v. 272, pp. 528–31.

1980a. Living vs. total foraminiferal populations: their relative usefulness in paleoecology. *Journal of Paleontology,* v. 54, pp. 814–34.

1980b. Quantitative studies of marsh foraminiferal distributions in Nova Scotia: their implications for the study of sea-level changes. Cushman Foundation for Foraminiferal Research, Special Publication 17, 58 p.

1980c. Post-glacial emergence curves in the Maritimes determined from marine sediments in raised basins. *Proceedings of Coastlines '80,* published by National Science and Engineering Research Council, pp. 428–46.

1983. Agglutinated rhizopods in Lake Erie: modern distribution and stratigraphic implications. *Journal of Paleontology,* v. 54, pp. 809–20.

1986. Foraminifera as sea-level indicators. In van de Plassche, P. (ed), *Sea-level Research: A Manual for the Collection and Evaluation of Data,* Norwich, England: GEO Books, pp. 435–56.

1988. Tertiary–Cretaceous reworked microfossils in Pleistocene glacial-marine sediments: an index to glacial activity. *Marine Geology,* v. 84, pp. 31–41.

1998. Earliest multichambered foraminifera from the Cambrian of Nova Scotia: Abstract to International Symposium on Foraminifera, Monterrey, Mexico, July 1998, p. 97.

Scott, D. B., Medioli, F. S., and Miller, A.A.L, 1987a. Holocene sea-levels, paleoceanography, and the Late Glacial ice configurations near the Northumberland Strait, Maritime Provinces. *Canadian Journal of Earth Sciences,* v. 24, pp. 668–75.

Scott, D. B., Medioli, F. S., and Schafer, C. T. 1977. Temporal changes in foraminiferal distribution in Miramichi River Estuary, New Brunswick. *Canadian Journal of Earth Sciences,* v. 14, pp. 1566–87.

Scott, D. B., Mudie, P. J, Vilks, G., and Younger, C. D. 1984. Latest Pleistocene–Holocene paleoceanographic trends on the continental margin of eastern Canada: foraminiferal, dinoflagellate and pollen evidence. *Marine Micropaleontolology,* v. 9, pp. 181–218.

Scott, D. B., Piper, D.J.W., and Panagos, A. G. 1979. Recent salt marsh and intertidal mudflat foraminifera from the western coast of Greece. *Rivista Italiana de Paleontologia,* v. 85, no. 1, pp. 243–66, pls. 15, 16.

Scott, D. B., Schafer, C. T., Honig, C., and Younger, D. C. 1995a. Temporal variations of benthic foraminiferal assemblages under or near aquaculture operations: documentation and impact history. *Journal of Foraminiferal Research,* v. 25, pp. 224–35.

Scott, D. B., Schafer, C. T., and Medioli, F. S. 1980. Eastern Canadian estuarine foraminifera: a framework for comparison. *Journal of Foraminiferal Research,* v. 10, pp. 205–34.

Scott, D. B., Schnack, E. S., Ferrero, L., Espinosa, M., and Barbosa, C. F. 1990. Recent marsh foraminifera from the east coast of South America: comparison to the northern hemisphere. In Hemleben, C., Kaminski, M. A., Kuhnt, W., and Scott, D. B. (eds.), *Paleoecology, Biostratigraphy, Paleoceanography and Taxonomy of Agglutinated Foraminifera,* NATO ASI Series C, 327, Math and Physical Sciences, pp. 717–38.

Scott, D. B., Shennan, I. A., and Combellick, R. A. 1998. Evidence for pre-cursor events prior to the 1964 great Alaska earthquake from buried forest deposits in Girdwood,

Alaska. Abstract to Annual Geological Society of America Meeting, Toronto (October), pp. A253.

Scott, D. B., Suter, J. R., and Kosters, E. C. 1991. Marsh foraminifera and arcellaceans of the lower Mississippi Delta: controls on spatial distribution. *Micropaleontology,* v. 37, no. 4, pp. 373–92.

Scott, D. B., Williamson, M. A., and Duffett, T. E. 1981. Marsh foraminifera of Prince Edward Island: their recent distribution and application for former sea-level studies. *Maritime Sediments and Atlantic Geology,* v. 17, pp. 98–124.

Scott, D. K., and Leckie, R. M. 1990. Foraminiferal zonation of Great Sippewissett salt marsh. *Journal of Foraminiferal Research,* v. 20, pp. 248–66.

Seiglie, G. A. 1971. A preliminary note on the relationship between foraminifers and pollution in two Puerto Rican bays. *Caribbean Journal of Science,* v. 11, pp. 93–8.

——— 1975. Foraminifers of Guayamilla Bay and their use as environmental indices. *Revista Española de Micropaleontologia,* v. 7, pp. 453–87.

Sen Gupta, B. K. 1999. Modern foraminifera. Dordrecht, The Netherlands, Kluwer Academic Publishers, 384 p.

Sen Gupta, B. K, Platon, E., Bernhard, J. M., and Aharon, P. 1997. Foraminiferal colonization of hydrocarbon-seep bacterial mats and underlying sediment, Gulf of Mexico slope. *Journal of Foraminiferal Research,* v. 27, pp. 292–300.

Sen Gupta, B. K., and Schafer, C. T. 1973. Holocene benthonic foraminifera in leeward bays of St. Lucia, West Indies. *Micropaleontology,* v. 19, pp. 341–65.

Sen Gupta, B. K., Shin, I. C., and Wendler-Scott, T. 1987. Relevance of specimen size in distribution studies of deep-sea benthic foraminifera. *Palaios,* v. 2, pp. 332–8.

Sen Gupta, B. K., Turner, R. E., and Rabalais, N. N. 1996. Seasonal oxygen depletion in continental shelf waters of Louisiana: historical record of benthic foraminifers. *Geology,* v. 24, pp. 227–30.

Shannon, C. E., and Weaver, W. 1963. *The Mathematical Theory of Communications.* Urbana: University of Illinois Press, 313 p.

Shaw, K. M., Lambshead, P.J.D., and Platt, H. M. 1983. Detection of pollution-induced disturbance in marine benthic assemblages with special reference to nematodes. *Marine Ecology Progress Series,* v. 11, pp. 195–202.

Shennan, I., Long, A. J., Rutherford, M. M., Green, F. M., Innes, J. B., Lloyd, J. M., Zong, Y., and Walker, K. J. 1996. Tidal marsh stratigraphy, sea-level change and large earthquakes. I: a 5000 year record in Washington, U.S.A. *Quaternary Science Reviews,* v. 15, pp. 1023–59.

Shennan, I., Long, A. J., Rutherford, M. M., Innes, J. B., Green, F. M., and Walker, K. J. 1998. Tidal marsh stratigraphy, sea-level change and large earthquakes. II: Submergence events during the last 3500 years at Netarts Bay, Oregon, USA. *Quaternary Science Reviews,* v. 17, pp. 365–93.

Shennan, I. A., Scott D. B., Rutherford M., and Zong Y. 1999. Microfossil analysis of sediments representing the 1964 earthquake, exposed at Girdwood Flats, Alaska, USA. *Quaternary International,* v. 60, pp. 55–74.

Shepard, F. P. 1963. *Submarine Geology.* New York: Harper and Row, pp. 128.

Shu, G., and Collins, M. 1995. Net sand transport direction in a tidal inlet using foraminifera tests as natural tracers. *Estuarine, Coastal and Shelf Science,* v. 40, pp. 681–97.

Silvestri, A. 1923. Microfauna pliocenia a rizopodi reticolari di Copocolle presso Forlí. *Memorie della Pontifica Accademia delle Scienze,* Nuovi Lincei, Roma, v. 76, pp. 70–7.

Simon, A., Poulicek, M., Velimirov, B., and MacKenzie, F. T. 1994. Comparison of anaerobic and aerobic biodegradation of mineralized skeletal structures in marine and estuarine conditions. *Biogeochemistry,* v. 25, pp. 167–95.

Smart, C. W., King, S. C., Gooday, A. J., Murray, J. W., and Thomas, E. 1994. A benthic foraminiferal proxy of pulsed organic matter paleofluxes. *Marine Micropaleontology,* v. 23, pp. 89–99.

Smith, J. N., and Schafer, C. T. 1984. Bioturbation processes in continental slope and rise sediments delineated by Pb^{-210}, microfossil and textural indicators. *Journal of Marine Research,* v. 42, pp. 1117–45.

——— 1987. A 20th century record of climatologically modulated sediment accumulation rates in a Canadian fjord. *Quaternary Research,* v. 27, pp. 232–47.

——— 1999. Sedimentation, bioturbation and Hg uptake in the sediments of the estuary and Gulf of St. Lawrence. *Limnology and Oceanography,* v. 44(1), pp. 207–19.

Smith, R. K. 1987. Fossilization potential in modern shallow-water benthic foraminiferal assemblages. *Journal of Foraminiferal Research,* v. 17, pp. 117–22.

Snyder, S. W., Hale, W. R., and Kontrovitz, M. 1990. Assessment of postmortem transportation of modern benthic foraminifera of the Washington continental shelf. *Micropaleontology,* v. 36, pp. 259–82.

Sokal, R. R., and Sneath, P. H. A. 1963. *Principles of Numerical Taxonomy.* London: W. H. Freeman & Co., 359 p.

Solomons, W., and Mook, W. G. 1987. Natural tracers for sediment transport studies. *Continental Shelf Research,* v. 7, pp. 1333–43.

Souto, S. 1973. Contribucion al conocimiento de los tintinnidos de agua dulce de la Republica Argentina. *I Rio de la Plata y Delta del Parana: Physis,* Seccion B, v. 32, no. 85, pp. 249–54.

Stein, S.F.N., von. 1859. Über die ihm aus eigener Untersuchung bekannt gewordenen Süswasser-Rhizopoden. *Königliche Böhmishce Gesellschaft der Wissenschaften Abhandlungen,* ser. 5, v. 10, Berichte der Sectionen, pp. 41–3.

Sternberg, R. W., and Marsden, M. A. 1979. Dynamics, sediment transport, and morphology in a tide-dominated embayment. *Earth Surface Processes,* v. 4, pp. 117–39.

Stott, L. D., Hayden, T. P., and Griffith, J. 1996. Benthic foraminifera at the Los Angeles County Whites Point outfall revisited. *Journal of Foraminiferal Research,* v. 26, no. 4. pp. 357–68.

Stubbles, S. J. 1997. Post-impact assessment of Restronguet Creek, southwest Cornwall and investigation into the absence of agglutinated foraminifera. Abstract to 5th International Workshop on Agglutinated Foraminifera, Plymouth, U.K. (October).

Syvitski, J. P. M., and Schafer, C. T. 1996. Evidence for an earthquake-triggered basin collapse in Saguenay Fjord, Canada. *Sedimentary Geology,* v. 104, pp. 127–53.

Tappan, H. 1951. Northern Alaska index foraminifera. *Cushman Foundation for Foraminiferal Research,* v. 2, pp. 1–8.

Tarànek, K. J. 1882. Monographie der Böhmen's: Ein Beitrag zur Kenntniss der Süsswasser-Monothalamien. *Abhandlungen der Königlichen Böhmischen Gesellschaft der Wissenschaften,* ser. 6, v. ll, Mathematischnaturwissenschaftliche Classe, no. 8, p. i–iv, 1–56, pls. 1–5.

Terquem, O. 1876. Essai sur le classement des animaux qui vivant sur la plage et dans les environs de Denkerque. Pt. 1: Mémoires de la Sociéte Dunkerquoise pour l'Encouragement des Sciences des Lettres et des Arts (1874–1875), v. 19, pp. 405–57.

Thibaudeau, S. A. 1993. Agglutinated brackish water foraminifera and arcellaceans from the upper Carboniferous, coal-bearing strata of the Sydney Basin, Nova Scotia: Taxonomic descriptions, assemblages, and environments of deposition. M.Sc. thesis, Dalhousie University (unpublished manuscript), 142 p.

Thibaudeau, S. A., and Medioli, F. S. 1986. Carboniferous thecamoebians and marsh foraminifera: new stratigraphic tools for ancient paralic deposits. Abstract to the Geological Society of America, Annual Meeting, San Antonio, pp. 771.

Thibaudeau, S. A., Medioli, F. S., and Scott, D. B. 1987. Carboniferous marginal-marine rhizopods: a morphological comparison with recent correspondents. Abstract to the Geological Society of America, Annual Meeting, Phoenix, pp. 866.

Thomas, E., and Varekamp, J. C. 1991. Paleo-environmental analyses of marsh sequences (Clinton, Connecticut): evidence for punctuated rise in relative sea-level during the last Holocene. *Journal of Coastal Research,* Special Issue no. 11, pp. 125–58.

Thomas, F. C. 1977. Foraminifera of the Minas Basin and their distributions. BSc. diss., Dalhousie University, Halifax, Nova Scotia (unpublished manuscript), 107 p.

Thomas, F. C., Medioli, F. S., and Scott, D. B. 1990. Holocene and latest Wisconsinan benthic foraminiferal assemblages and paleocirculation history, Lower Scotian Slope and Rise. *Journal of Foraminiferal Research,* v. 20, pp. 212–45.

Thomas, F. C., and Murney, M. E. 1981. Techniques for extraction of foraminifera and ostracods from sediment samples. Canadian Technical Report, *Hydrographic and Ocean Science,* no. 54, 24 p.

Thomas, F. C., and Schafer, C. T. 1982. Distribution and transport of some common foraminiferal species in the Minas Basin, Eastern Canada. *Journal of Foraminiferal Research,* v. 12, pp. 24–38.

Thompson, T. L, 1983. Late Cretaceous marine foraminifers from Pleistocene fluviolacustrine deposits in eastern Missouri. *Journal of Paleontology,* v. 57, no. 6, pp. 1304–10.

Thorn, M. F. C. 1987. Modelling and predicting channel sedimentation. In *Maintenance Dredging.* London: TTL, pp. 41–68.

Tibert, N. E. 1996. A paleoecological interpretation for the ostracoda and agglutinated foraminifera from the earliest carboniferous marginal marine Horton Bluff formation (Blue Beach member, Nova Scotia, Canada): M.Sc. thesis, Dalhousie University (unpublished manuscript).

Todd, R., and Brönnimann, P. 1957. Recent foraminifera and thecamoebina from the eastern Gulf of Paria. Cushman Foundation for Foraminiferal Research, Special Publication 3, 43 p.

Todd, R., and Low, D. 1961. Near-shore foraminifera of Martha's Vineyard Island, Massachusetts. *Cushman Foundation for Foraminiferal Research,* v. 12, pp. 5–21.

Torigai, K. 1996. Distribution of recent thecamoebians in Lake Winnipeg. Honours thesis, Carleton University, Ottawa, Ontario (unpublished manuscript), 57 pp.

Torigai, K., Schröder-Adams, C. J., and Burbridge, S. M. 2000. A variable lacustrine environment in Lake Winnipeg, Manitoba: Evidence from modern thecamoebian distribution. *Journal of Paleolimnology,* v. 23, pp. 305–18.

Valkanov, A. 1962a. Über die kopulation der testaceen (rhizopoda-testacea). *[Doklady Bolgarskoi Akademii Nauk] Report of the Bulgarian Academy of Science,* v. 15, pp. 305–8.

1962b. *Paraquadrula madarica* n. sp. (rhizopoda-testacea) und ihre kopulation. *[Doklady Bolgarskoi Akademii Nauk] Report of the Bulgarian Academy of Science,* v. 15, pp. 423–6.

1962c. *Euglyphella delicatula* n. g., n. sp. (rhizopoda-testacea) und ihre kopulation. *[Doklady Bolgarskoi Akademii Nauk] Report of the Bulgarian Academy of Science,* v. 15, no. 2, pp. 207–9.

1966. Über die fortpflanzung der testaceen (rhizopoda-testacea). [Bolgarska Akademiya na naukite, *Izvestiya na Zoologischeskiya Institut s Muzei*] Bulgarian Academy of Science, *Bulletin of the Institut and the Museum of Zoology* (Sofia), v. 22, pp. 5–49.

Vance, R. E. 1996. Paleobotany of Lake Winnipeg sediments. In Todd, B. J., Lewis, C. F., Thorleifson, L. H., and Nielsen, E. (eds.), *Lake Winnipeg Project: Cruise Report and Scientific Results:* GSC Open File, pp. 3113–311.

Van der Zwaan, G. J., Duijnstee, I. A. P., den Dulk, M., Ernst, S. R., Jannink, N. T., and Kouwenhoven, T. J. 1999. Benthic foraminifers: proxies or problems? A review of paleoecological concepts. *Earth-Science Reviews,* v. 46, pp. 213–36.

Vašíček, M., and Růžička, B. 1957. Namurian techamoebina from the Ostrava-Karvina coal district: Sbornik Naradniho Musea v Praze, Rada B., Prirodni Vedy-Acta Musei Nationalis Pragae, ser. B, *Historia Naturalis,* v. 13, 333–40.

Van Voorthuysen, J. H. 1957. Foraminiferen aus dem Eemien (Riss-Würm Interglazial) in der Bohrung Amersfoort I (Locus typicus). *Mededelingen van de Geologische Stichting,* new series, no. 11, pp. 27–39, pls. 23–26.

Vilks, G., Schafer, C. T., and Walker, D. A. 1975. Influence of a causeway on oceanography and foraminifera in the Strait of Canso, Nova Scotia. *Canadian Journal of Earth Sciences,* v. 12, pp. 2086–2102.

Wagner, F. J., and Schafer, C. T. 1982. Upper Holocene paleoceanography of Inner Miramichi Bay. *Maritime Sediments and Atlantic Geology,* v. 16, pp. 5–10.

Walker, D. A., Linton, A. E., and Schafer, C. T. 1974. Sudan Black B: a superior stain to Rose Bengal for distinguishing living from non-living foraminifera. *Journal of Foraminiferal Research,* v. 4, pp. 205–15.

Wall, J. H. 1976. Marginal marine foraminifera from the late Cretaceous Bearpaw-Horseshoe Canyon transition, Southern Alberta, Canada. *Journal of Foraminiferal Research,* v. 6, pp. 193–201.

Wallich, G. C. 1864. On the extent, and some of the principal causes, of structural variation among the difflugian rhizopods. *Annals and Magazine of Natural History,* ser. 3, v. 13, pp. 215–245.

Walton, W. R. 1952. Techniques for recognition of living foraminifera. *Contributions of the Cushman Foundation for Foraminiferal Research,* v. 3, pp. 56–60.

Wang, Y., Schafer, C. T., and Smith, J. N. 1986. Characteristics of tidal embayments designated for deep-water harbour development, Hainan Island, China. Second International Dredging Conference, Beijing, pp. 46.

Wefer, G. 1976. Unwelt, produktion, und sedimentation benthischer foraminiferen in der Westlichen Ostee. Reports Sonderforschungsbereich 95, Universitat Kiel, no. 14, pp. 103 p.

Wightman, W. G., Scott, D. B., Medioli, F. S., and Gibling, M. R. 1992a. Upper Pennsylvanian agglutinated foraminifers from the Cape Breton coalfield, Nova Scotia: their use in the determination of brackish-marine depositional environments: Geological Association of Canada, *Abstract* 17, p. A117.

——— 1992b. Agglutinated foraminifera from the Sydney coalfield, Nova Scotia: their use as indicators of sea-level changes in carboniferous coal-bearing strata: Geological Society of America, *Abstract* 24, p. A226.

——— 1993. Carboniferous marsh foraminifera from coal bearing strata at the Sydney basin, Nova Scotia: a new tool for identifying paralic coal, forming environments. *Geology,* v. 21, pp. 631–4.

——— 1994. Agglutinated foraminifera and thecamoebians from the Late Carboniferous Sydney coalfield, Nova Scotia. paleoecology, paleoenvironments and paleogeographical impli-

cations. *Paleogeography, Paleoclimatology, Paleoecology,* v. 106, pp. 187–202.

Williamson, M. A. 1983. Benthic foraminiferal assemblages in the continental margin off Nova Scotia: a multivariate approach. Ph.D. diss., Dalhousie University, Halifax, Canada (unpublished manuscript), 269 p.

Williamson, M. A., Keen, C. E., and Mudie, P. J. 1984. Foraminiferal distribution on the continental margin off Nova Scotia. *Marine Micropaleontology,* v. 9, pp. 219–39.

Williamson, M. L. 1999. Reconstruction of pollution history at Mill Cove, Bedford Basin, using benthic foraminifera. B.Sc. Honours thesis, Dalhousie University, Halifax, Canada, 77 p.

Williamson, W. C. 1858. *On Recent Foraminifera of Great Britain.* London: Ray Society, 107 p.

Wilson, J. G. 1988. *Biology of Estuarine Management.* London: Croom Helm, 197 p.

Yanko, V., Ahmad, M., and Kaminski, M. 1998. Morphological deformities of benthic foraminiferal tests in response to pollution by heavy metals: implications for pollution monitoring. *Journal of Foraminiferal Research,* v. 28, pp. 177–200.

Yassini, I., and Jones, B. G. 1995. Foraminiferida and ostracoda from estuarine and shelf environments on the southeastern coast of Australia. University of Wollongong Press, Australia, 484 p.

Yodzis, P. 1989. *Introduction to Theoretical Ecology.* New York: Harper and Row, 384 p.

Yong, C., Williams, D. D., and Williams, N. E. 1998. How important are rare species in aquatic community ecology and bioassessment? *Limnology and Oceanography,* v. 43, pp. 1403–9.

Zaninetti, L., Brönnimann, P., Beurlen, G., and Moura, J. A. 1977. La mangrove de Guaratiba et la Baie de Sepetiba, état de Rio de Janeiro, Brésil: foraminifères et écologie. *Archives des Sciences* (Genève), v. 30, pp. 161–78.

Name Index

Subject Index